## DATE DUE

| | | |
|---|---|---|
| 12/28/07 | | |
| | | |
| | | |
| | | |
| | | |
| | | |
| | | |
| | | |
| | | |
| | | |
| | | |
| | | |
| | | |
| | | |
| | | |
| | | |

| Brodart Co. | Cat. # 55 137 001 | Printed in USA |
|---|---|---|

## Controversies in the Sciences

# Homosexuality and Science

## A Guide to the Debates

*Vernon A. Rosario*

*Foreword by Richard Pillard*

**ABC-CLIO**

Santa Barbara, California
Denver, Colorado
Oxford, England

Library of Congress Cataloging-in-Publication Data
Rosario, Vernon A.
    Homosexuality and science : a guide to the debates / Vernon A. Rosario
II ; foreword by Richard Pillard.
        p.    cm. — (Controversies in science)
    Includes bibliographical references and index.
    ISBN 1-57607-281-9
    1. Homosexuality—Research—History.    I. Title.    II. Series.
QP81.6.R656    2002
616.85'83—dc21

                                                                            2002000201


08    07    06    05    04    03    02        10    9    8    7    6    5    4    3    2    1

ABC-CLIO, Inc.
130 Cremona Drive, P.O. Box 1911
Santa Barbara, California 93116-1911

This book is printed on acid-free paper ∞.

*For Andrea*

# Contents

# *Foreword*

Attraction between the sexes is so much the rule in human nature that same-sex desire cries for an explanation. Sexologists for 150 years have argued about whether homosexuality is a form of mental disorder-a perversion-or a normal variant of desire, and whether this desire is inborn, the product of culture, or by some alchemy as yet unknown, something of both.

More recently the study of sexual orientation has moved from the back chapters of psychopathology texts to become an influential topic in the scientific disciplines from molecular biology to bioethics. The sentinel event in this evolution was the publication of the two "Kinsey reports" in 1948 and 1953. Kinsey's sex histories taken from some 18,000 Americans showed that we were busily at work with sexual endeavors of every sort: before, during, and after marriage; from infancy to senility; alone; with each other; and now and then with other species. Kinsey's work did not in fact differ radically from prior sexuality surveys save in the monumental scope and obsessive detail that were Kinsey's academic style. But coming as they did to a postwar, pleasure-starved America, the "Kinsey Reports" were greeted with delight and a place on the best-seller list.

The censure of the erotophobes was of course expected. Particularly troubling to them was the incidence Kinsey reported for same-sex behavior. It appeared that homosexuality was not limited to an effete coterie in Greenwich Village or Paris but was reported by a substantial minority of Americans and they were of every demographic stripe that the Kinsey team could measure. Gays, it turned out, were everywhere-teaching children, hearing confession, running for office, standing under the next shower head at the gym.

The recognition of a critical mass of potential members encouraged the first lesbian and gay organizations, the Daughters of Bilitis and the Mattachine Society, who in turn worked to expand research on sexual orientation beyond the prisons and mental hospitals. But two decades passed before the social revolution of the 1960s stimulated lesbians and gays to declare their sexual orientation openly-come out-as a matter of survival politics.

Another two decades went by during which the study of sexual orientation developed as an academic discipline in the social and medical sciences. This happened at first because of the research effort required to deal with the crisis as AIDS evolved from a "gay disease" to a worldwide epidemic. Also important was research indicating that a gay orientation may be innate: its precursors appear in early childhood, and a strong familial trend suggests possible hereditary components. This raises a fundamental question: how can a trait that must surely confer a reproductive penalty have survived in substantial numbers in human populations everywhere?

Your guide to the history of scientific thought about these matters is Dr. Vernon Rosario, a friend and discussion colleague of many years. Trained as a physician and historian of science, Dr. Rosario describes the mutual influence of sexual science and the social context that surrounds it. His scholarship will impress those among you who already know something about this subject; his balanced and lucid exposition will appeal to most of you and annoy a few. I have watched Dr. Rosario's prodigious intellect over the years and am delighted to recommend this book. You will be entertained, informed, and piqued to read it.

*Richard C. Pillard, M.D.*

# Acknowledgments

The work of this book really began my first year in graduate school, so its publication affords me the enormous pleasure of thanking a great many people who have been dear friends, colleagues, and supporters for many years. My colleagues and mentors at Harvard University, the University of Pennsylvania, the University of California at Los Angeles (UCLA), and the cyberacademy have had a direct hand in shaping how I think about the history of science and psychiatry: Garland Allen, Allan Brandt, Anne Fausto-Sterling, David Halperin, Anne Harrington, Karla Jay, Maggie Magee, Diana Miller, Everett Mendelsohn, Robert Nye, Dorothy Porter, James Steakley, Jennifer Terry, and Shirah Vollmer. I particularly thank Jonathan Ned Katz for his pioneering work, which first inspired my research in the field.

Many friends, in more or less formal ways, have been equally intrigued by the historical, clinical, and political issues I deal with in this book. They have engaged me in ongoing conversation and debate over the years, and I am grateful for their enduring wisdom, encouragement, and affection: Paula Bennett, Joel Braslow and Christine Schneider, Alice Dreger, Sandra Harding, Martha Kirkpatrick and Nadia Doubins, Harlan Lane and Frank Philip, Andrew London, Richard Pillard, Susan Rosenfeld, Margaret Schabas, William Summers, and Sharon Traweek. Luisa, Giovanni, and Ann Koll have been my warmest supporters and my New York family on numerous research trips to the Big Apple. I have undoubtedly stolen many a good idea from dinner conversations with my closest friends: Kent Brintnall, Lawrence Cohen, Kaila Compton, Lawrence Eaton, Robert Grimm, Severino Lozano, Micheline and Edward Rice-Maximin, Thomas Spear, Chris Thorman, and Marshall Wong.

I have rehearsed many of the ideas and narratives here with my students at Harvard University and UCLA over the years, and I appreciate their curiosity and challenges. I am especially grateful to Margaret Gibson and Matthew Macintosh, who volunteered as research assistants. My editors at ABC-CLIO, Kevin Downing and Melanie Stafford, have been good-humored and patient throughout the publication process. Finally, I am thankful for the love and support of my family and my partner, Andrea Medici, despite the inevitable neglect caused by my preoccupation with dusty books and my computer.

My research and writing on this project were sustained by multiple sources: a National Science Foundation Graduate Research Fellowship; the UCLA Center for Cultural Studies of Science, Technology, and Medicine; the UCLA Center for the Study of Women; and the Mellon Fellowship in the Humanities at the University of Pennsylvania. I greatly appreciate their support.

*Vernon A. Rosario*

# Introduction

S cientist Says Study Shows Gay Change Is Possible," blared the headline of a *New York Times* article reporting on the 2001 annual meeting of the American Psychiatric Association (APA). The APA is the leading professional association of psychiatrists in the United States and one of the most influential in the world. It publishes the *Diagnostic and Statistical Manual of Mental Disorders* (DSM), which is written by multiple committees of experts in every area of mental health. The DSM has become the international bible of psychiatric classification and diagnosis. The APA annual meeting gathers thousands of psychiatrists from around the world for a frenzy of papers, workshops, seminars, and poster talks on the latest in psychiatric science. Yet of all this wealth of information, only two items made it to the *New York Times* (the other was on the increasing use of antidepressants for youths). The exceptional media attention paid to the treatment of gays betrays the enduring scientific controversy and social preoccupation with the causes and "cure" of homosexuality.

The great irony of this news story is that the scientist in question was Dr. Robert Spitzer, a senior Columbia University psychiatrist who had been instrumental in getting the diagnosis of homosexuality out of the DSM in the early 1970s. Spitzer had originally wanted to substitute "sexual orientation disturbance." Instead, because of pressure from psychiatrists and gay activists, homosexuality ultimately disappeared as an official mental disorder. That did not stop people from trying to engage in "reparative therapy" of homosexuals. Fundamentalist Christian groups in the United States drew particular attention to "ex-gay" ministries with a media blitz in 1998. Most of Spitzer's subjects were recruited through these groups, and his research was soundly criticized for this bias at the APA meeting.

Clearly, the scientific battle over defining, explaining, and treating homosexuality remains intense. Since the mid-nineteenth century, scientists have asked a variety of questions about the nature of homosexuality: Is it a biologically determined erotic drive or a willful act? Is it the result of experiences: parental influences, chance infantile associations, or homosexual seduction? Is it associated with particular temperamental, anatomical, or physiological traits? Is it a neuropsychiatric disorder in itself; is it associated with other disorders; or is it a normal variant of human behavior? Can sexual orientation be altered, and is there any justification for doing so? Over the past two centuries, doctors and scientists have deployed the whole gamut of biomedical methods to answering these questions. They have relied on the biological and psychological approaches of the time: humoral theory, neuroanatomy, evolutionary biology, endocrinology, genetics, embryology, psychology, psychoanalysis, and molecular biology. Doctors have applied all varieties of therapeutic modalities to curing homosexuality and other "disorders" of gender identity and sexual orientation. This book offers a largely chronological history of the biomedical struggle with the "question of homosexuality."

Over the past two centuries, as the biological and medical sciences evolved, so too did research on homosexuality. As with other areas of biomedicine, existing theories were modified, amplified, and sometimes even discredited as new scientific methods emerged. However, the science of homosexuality is exceptional because of the degree to which the subjects implicated—from Victorian "sexual inverts" to contemporary gay men and lesbians—have been involved in the process of shaping theories of homosexuality. They have not just been the passive guinea pigs of biomedical research—subjecting themselves to physical examinations, laboratory testing, questionnaires, and sometimes even surgery. They have also actively challenged the ethics and aims of this research. Because of this pressure they have induced vast transformations in how biomedicine attempts to explain homosexuality and sexuality in general (Terry 1999).

Contemporary historians and philosophers of science and sexuality have rightly criticized biomedical models of homosexuality, noting that lesbians and gay men have been subjected to useless and often life-threatening treatments, including hormone therapy, psychoanalysis, aversion therapy, and even neurosurgery, to name a few (Stein 1999). However, the medical record is quite complex. Biomedical scientists have offered a variety of often conflicting opinions on the nature and causes of homosexuality. Whether they believe that homosexuality is the result of biological or developmental forces, some physicians do not believe it is a condition that can or *should* be altered. Furthermore, we must keep in mind that nineteenth-century inverts or twentieth-century homosexuals often willingly sought treatment, undoubtedly because they were overburdened by the familial, societal, and legal condemnation of homosexuality.

We should also note that since the nineteenth century, many homosexuals who were *comfortable* with their sexuality were, nevertheless, vocal supporters of biological theories of homosexuality, and they volunteered for biomedical research on sexual orientation. A hereditary explanation, in particular, fit with the experience of some lesbians and gays that their sexual orientation was sensed from earliest childhood and was not chosen (Rosario 2000). This congenital argument or "argument from immutability" (Halley 1994) has long been used within families and in courts to argue that homosexuals should not be persecuted because, like race or sex, sexual orientation is biologically determined. However, as ethicists have noted, a biological explanation is inadequate, indeed superfluous, to a fundamental question of equal human rights (Murphy 1997). For example, societies choose to protect religious freedom regardless of the fact that religion is elective and not biologically determined. However, the political and legal reality is that the biological question does play a significant role in U.S. debates about gay rights; therefore, sexual orientation researchers must take into account the serious ethical, legal, and cultural repercussions of their work.

Current academic debates about scientific research on homosexuality have often revolved around fundamental theories of *social constructionism* versus *biological essentialism* (Stein 1999). There are many variants of both of these, but to put it simply, constructionists argue that homosexuality is a historical and social phenomenon specific to modern Euro-American cultures. Essentialists believe that, while there may be superficial historical and cultural variations, homosexual orientation is a basic aspect of human nature that is the same around the world and throughout time; furthermore, it is primarily determined by biological forces. Although these two positions are usually portrayed as diametrically opposed, I would argue that we need to rely on both historico-cultural and biological analysis to help us understand human sexuality in all its great complexity and variability.

I believe questions about the nature of sexual orientation are genuinely fascinating and valid for scientific research. However, this research is fraught with many technical and theoretical difficulties. From my perspective as both a social historian of science and a clinical psychiatrist, I recognize that biomedicine does not operate in a void. Therefore, I present the ongoing scientific debates on homosexuality in the historical context of the social politics that fueled them—just as Spitzer's "scientific evidence" on converting homosexuals is entangled in a web of U.S. religious, professional, and cultural politics. One must also remember that the scientists of sexuality are not dealing with rocks or insects, but human beings. Therefore, I pay close attention to the voices of these "patients," for they, and we, are profoundly affected by and can influence the workings of science. My hope is that this book will help readers better understand the complex social history of research on homosexuality. By being more informed about this research, you can be more critical of future scientific findings that impact our daily lives in countless ways.

## References

Halley, Janet E. 1994. "Sexual Orientation and the Politics of Biology: A Critique of the Argument from Immutability." *Stanford Law Review* 46: 503–568.

Murphy, Timothy F. 1997. *Gay Science: The Ethics of Sexual Orientation Research.* New York: Columbia University Press.

Rosario, Vernon. 2000. "Gay Genes: Analyzing the Evidence of Experience." *Gender and Psychoanalysis* 5: 209–219.

"Scientist Says Study Shows Gay Change Is Possible." 2001. *New York Times,* May 9.

Stein, Edward. 1999. *The Mismeasure of Desire: The Science, Theory, and Ethics of Sexual Orientation.* New York: Oxford University Press.

Terry, Jennifer. 1999. *An American Obsession: Science, Medicine, and Homosexuality in Modern Society.* Chicago: University of Chicago Press.

## Further Reading

Several books have explored the history and current research on the causes and treatment of homosexuality. They each have their particular perspective and intended audience. Jennifer Terry's *An American Obsession: Science, Medicine, and Homosexuality in Modern Society* (Chicago: University of Chicago Press, 1999) is an excellent scholarly and theoretically dense analysis, highly critical of science. In contrast, two historical works by contemporary scientists working on the biology of sexual orientation are, not surprisingly, very supportive of this enterprise. Simon LeVay (1991) published a preliminary article on hypothalamic differences between gay and straight men. His subsequent books, *The Sexual Brain* (Cambridge: MIT Press, 1993) and *Queer Science* (Cambridge: MIT Press, 1996), provide readable surveys of twentieth-century scientific research, particularly that which bolsters his own hypothesis that homosexuals have cross-gendered brains. Dean Hamer and Peter Copeland's *The Science of Desire: The Search for the Gay Gene and the Biology of Behavior* (New York: Simon and Schuster, 1994) focuses on his own molecular genetics research. John De Cecco and David Parker's anthology, *Sex, Cells, and Same-Sex Desire: The Biology of Sexual Preference* (Binghamton, NY: Harrington Park, 1995), is an eclectic collection including a few historical reviews, current scientific articles, and critiques of the diverse biological approaches. It is geared to specialists and scientists in the field. In *The Mismeasure of Desire: The Science, Theory, and Ethics of Sexual Orientation* (New York: Oxford University Press, 1999), Edward Stein provides a detailed and incisive philosophical critique of research on sexual orientation. His position is that homosexuality is a sociological phenomenon and not a natural one; therefore, he is skeptical of the possibility of any biological research in the area. Finally, my own anthology, *Science and Homosexualities* (New York: Routledge, 1997b), focuses on particular issues in this complex history rather than providing a survey. These and other historical works cited throughout this book will be useful to readers interested in exploring specific topics in this field in greater depth.

# 1

## Victorian Doctors Tackle Onanism
## and the Sexual Perversions

Homosexuality thoroughly shocked Victorian doctors. Undoubtedly, every educated person was familiar with the "unspeakable vice" of the ancient Greeks, and there is a long history of Christian teaching and criminal laws condemning "sodomy": any sexual acts, between people of any sex, not involving penile penetration of a vagina. The criminal status of sodomy changed radically in Europe after the French Revolution. As part of its agenda to secularize the legal system, the French Constituent Assembly (1789–1791) deleted antisodomy laws from the new penal code of 1791 and did not restore them in the Napoleonic penal code of 1810 (Sibalis 1996). This was also the case in other countries that adopted French legal principles by force or by choice. Austria, Tuscany, Russia, Prussia, and Brazil all decriminalized consensual homosexual acts. The same would later be true throughout much of Europe and in many Latin American countries (Greenberg 1988, 352). Britain, Germany, and the United States, however, continued to treat nonconjugal, penetrative sex acts as crimes—in some settings, as capital crimes punished by burning at the stake. This position was largely based on moral and religious tradition. The Massachusetts Bay Commonwealth, for example, established sodomy among its fifteen capital crimes simply by quoting Leviticus 20:13 (Katz 1983, 76). Massachusetts, like half of the United States, still retain these antisodomy laws.

Despite the more liberal legal stance in nineteenth-century France, sodomy could still be persecuted if it involved "crimes against decency" (sex in public spaces) or sex with minors (pederasty). Therefore, medico-legal experts were sometimes called on to evaluate suspected perpetrators and victims. Dr. Ambroise Tardieu (1857), for example, was one of the first to publish on the issue of detecting

*Two illustrations from the New Orleans* Mascot *(Oct. 21, 1893) demonstrate a new concern with same-sex relationships in the Victorian era (Tulane University Library).*

**GOOD GOD!**

The Crimes of Sodom and Gomorrah Discounted.

true sodomites entrapped by police or caught in blackmail scams. Tardieu proposed that sodomites or pederasts betrayed their deviant sexual penchants by deformities of the penis and anus, as well as effeminate character traits and dress. He offered the following portrait of the flamboyant "auntie":

> Curled hair, made-up skin, open collar, waist tucked in to accentuate the figure; fingers, ears, chest loaded with jewelry, the whole body exuding an odor of the most penetrating perfumes, and, in the hand, a handkerchief, flowers, or some needlework: such is the strange, revolting, and rightfully suspect physiognomy that betrays the pederast. . . . Hairstyles and dress constitute one of the most continual preoccupations of pederasts. (Tardieu 1857, 216–217)

Tardieu also suggested that in certain cases pederasty might be the result of insanity or "monomania" that led to a specific type of personality. It was especially the case, he argued, with educated, upper-class men who pursued sex with laborers. These otherwise refined pederasts exhibited "the saddest and most shameful insanity" because they consorted with individuals of "profound degradation and revolting filthiness" (213).

No doubt homosexual acts have always been practiced throughout history and in all societies—although usually with great secrecy. However, as more doctors were called upon to testify in court cases of sodomy, public sex, transvestitism, and sex determination, they began to declare that they were discovering something new—and revolting. The very term *homosexuality,* in fact, was only coined in the 1860s and was used primarily in the medical literature. Until then, medical discussions of same-sex acts were quite limited and typically employed the terms *sodomy* and *pederasty* interchangeably. In the eighteenth and nineteenth centuries, however, a growing sodomitical urban culture and heightened public concern about sex in public spaces stimulated European medical interest in same-sex eroticism (Haggerty 1999; Maccubbin 1987; Trumbach 1998; Weeks 1981; D'Emilio and Freedman 1988).

Confronting this growing "problem," physicians drew upon existing medical science concerning sexuality, which was not much. Natural scientists had studied and speculated on reproduction and heredity for millennia, but it was only in the early nineteenth century that new experimental methods and tools (like the microscope) began to yield more scientific information in these areas. Physicians had also long been concerned with venereal (sexually transmitted) diseases, yet

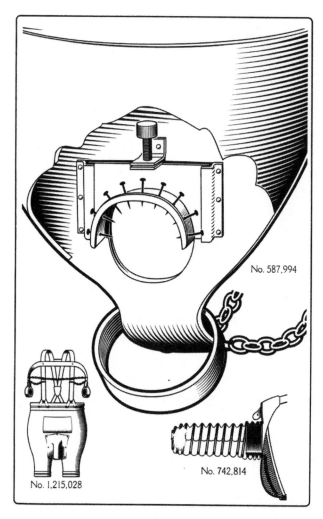

No. 587,994

No. 742,814

No. 1,215,028

*Patented devices designed to prevent masturbation: the device with pins (top) was intended to control lascivious "waking thoughts" (1897). The anti-masturbation overalls (bottom left) were made of iron, rubber, canvas, and chains, and available in male and female versions (1917). The harness (bottom right) was electrified to prevent erection (1903) (U.S. Patent Office).*

again it was only in the nineteenth century that discoveries in microbiology led to new models of infectious diseases. However, the most important body of knowledge that was brought to bear on the mysterious new illness of homosexuality was research about the "disease" of masturbation. Although today we may joke about going blind from too much masturbation, in the eighteenth and nineteenth centuries, it was no laughing matter. Doctors and the general public believed it was a deadly disease of epidemic proportions. The prevention and treatment of masturbation was the medical profession's major new foray into the realm of sexuality. The "disease" of masturbation was central to biomedical explanations of homosexuality and closely tied to new theories about the psychosexual pathology, hereditary degeneration, and gender perversion of homosexuals (Bullough and Voght 1976).

## Does Masturbation Cause Homosexuality?

In a one-paragraph letter dated October 17, 1899, Sigmund Freud, the founder of psychoanalysis, wrote to Dr. Wilhelm Fliess (his dearest colleague at the time): "What would you say if masturbation was to reduce itself to homosexuality, and the latter, that is male homosexuality (in both sexes) were the primitive form of sexual longing? (The first sexual aim, analogous to the infantile one—a wish that does not extend beyond the inner world.)" (Freud 1985, 380). A link between masturbation and a variety of psychosexual "disorders" (neurasthenia [nervous weakness], hysteria, melancholia, and neuroses, as well as homosexuality) appears scattered throughout Freud's correspondence and publications. He called masturbation the "primary addiction" at the root of all other addictive behavior

(Freud 1985, 287). Freud's hypothesis, however, was not original. It was based on nearly two centuries of medical thinking concerning the pathology of masturbation. In fact, it was quite widely believed in Victorian Europe and the United States that masturbation in childhood was a significant cause of "sexual inversion" (the most common nineteenth-century term for same-sex attraction and sexual activity).

How did such a seemingly fanciful notion take root in the medical tradition? By what physiological and psychological mechanisms did physicians explain the link between sexual inversion and masturbation? Why did these concerns become so acute in the nineteenth century that doctors sometimes undertook extreme and cruel measures to curtail masturbation? To begin to understand the seriousness of nineteenth-century masturbation fears, we need to go back to one of the most central and long-lived theories of physiology: the four humors.

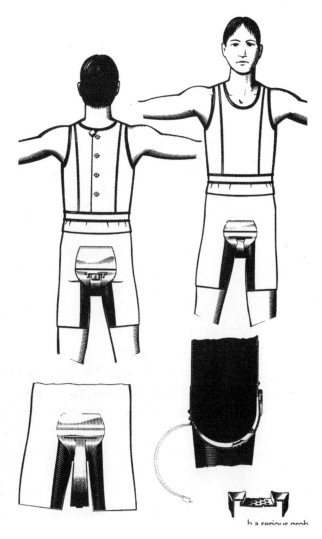

*This metal anti-masturbation "sexual armor" specifically targeted the "solitary vice" among asylum inmates (1908) (U.S. Patent Office).*

## Humoral Theory: Impotence and the Squandering of Seminal Liquor

From ancient Greek times to the eighteenth century, most European doctors believed that good health depended on the proper balance of the four humors. These were blood, phlegm, yellow bile, and black bile (*melancholia*). These, in turn, arose from combinations of the four elemental properties (heat, cold, dryness, and humidity). Doctors believed that all the fluids and tissues of the body were made of various combinations and distillations of the four humors. One of the most refined of bodily fluids was the "precious seminal liquor." The word *semen* was used not in its modern sense but in its Latin meaning of "seed." Therefore, all warnings concerning "seminal loss" theoretically applied equally to females and males, but effectively, varying emphasis was placed on male versus female masturbation.

In the Middle Ages, the dangers of "self-defilement by the hand" (*manustupratione,* hence *masturbation*) were discussed by theologians evaluating God's condemnation of Onan in the Old Testament. The book of Genesis (38:7–10) relates how Onan "spilt his seed" rather than impregnate his brother's widow to grant his brother an heir, as Jewish law demanded. God was angered by Onan's violation and killed him (Stengers and van Neck 1984). From this biblical story emerged the Christian condemnation of any seminal waste, both willful or "involuntary" (i.e., through nocturnal emissions or "wet dreams"). The celibate clergy's own spilling of seed was of particular concern. Medieval medical writers, however, were not so quick to condemn the practice of masturbation. Some believed it could in fact be *therapeutic* for celibate women (such as nuns and maidens) to expel unused seed, which, they believed, would otherwise rot in the body and cause pain or even hysteria (Thomasset and Jacquart 1985, 236). Doctors would even prescribe that nurse-midwives rub the patient's genitals with warm oils to expel the corrupt seed. But this practice had to be administered by professional hands (*manus medicans*), as opposed to self-defiling hands (*manus poluens*) (241). This notion even persisted into the nineteenth century: Dr. William Acton worried about the ill effects of chronic sexual abstinence in males (particularly when imposed by frigid or "asexual" wives). He believed it could result in serious nervous disorders (Acton 1875, 59–60).

Doctors did worry that truly excessive seminal emissions could produce widespread illness. The celebrated eighteenth-century Dutch physician and philosopher Hermann Boerhaave (1668–1738) noted: "The *Semen* discharged too lavishly, occasions a Weariness, Weakness, Indisposition to Motion, Convulsions, Leanness, Driness [*sic*], Heats and Pains in the Membranes of the Brain, with a Dulness [*sic*] of the Senses; more especially of the Sight, a *Tabes Dorsalis,* Foolishness, and Disorders of the like kind" (Boerhaave 1708, 456). The reason for these terrible disorders was that seed, being a highly refined and precious humor, was equal to many times its volume in lesser humors, so that the "loss of a few drops of semen weakens more than the Loss of a large Quantity of Blood" (92, 93n). Medical books usually declared that it took 40 ounces of blood to make 1 ounce of semen. Despite this frightening exchange rate, Boerhaave, like other pre-Enlightenment physicians, held that illness from masturbation was an extremely rare disease (456, 1n).

This situation changed radically beginning in 1715 with the anonymous publication in England of a little pamphlet entitled *Ona-*

*nia, or the Heinous Sin of Self-pollution, and Its Frightful Consequences in Both Sexes Considered, with Spiritual and Physical Advice to Those Who Have Already Injured Themselves by This Abominable Practice.* The quack author depicted the effects of "self-pollution" in the most terrifying terms:

> [Onanism] manifestly hinders the growth, both in girls and boys, and few of either sex, that in their youth commit this sin to excess for any considerable time, come ever to that robustness or strength which they would have arrived to without it. . . . The frequent use of this pollution likewise causes Stranguries, Priapisms, and other disorders of the Penis and Testis, but especially Gonorrhoeas, more difficult to be cured, than those contracted from women actually labouring under foul diseases. . . . [As adults] their faces are pale, their buttocks weak, legs feeble, their generative faculties diminished, if not destroyed in the bloom of youth: they are an object of derision for all others, and of torment to themselves. . . . Many young men, who were strong and lusty before they gave themselves to this vice, have been worn out by it, and by its robbing the body of its balmy and vital moisture, without cough or spitting, dry and emaciated, sent to their graves. (*Onania* [1715] 1986, 12–13)

He blamed the epidemic on the innocent ignorance of youths and the prudish silence of doctors and the general public. In addition to prevention, he recommended his own patent medicines for the treatment of those already worn out by the "solitary vice."

However sensationalist *Onania* was, it was given full medical validity with the publication in 1760 of *Onanism: A Medical Dissertation on the Ills Produced by Masturbation* written by the respected Swiss physician Samuel-Auguste Tissot (1728–1781). Following the humoral model, Tissot warned that excessive stimulation of the nerves led to their eventual weakening. Neurological problems and insanity were the eventual outcome:

> All the intellectual faculties are enfeebled, memory fails, ideas are dimmed, the sick sometimes fall into a light insanity; they suffer a type of incessant interior uneasiness, a continual anguish, a reproach of their conscience, so powerful that they often weep. They are subject to vertigo; all the senses, but especially sight and hearing, are weakened; their sleep, if indeed they can sleep, is troubled by disturbing dreams. (Tissot 1760, 41)

He approvingly quoted another doctor's observation that young masturbators "become pale, effeminate, numb, lazy, cowardly, stupid, and even imbecile" (28). He depicted horrific deathbed scenes of youth masturbating even until their last breath, their thin, blood-tinged semen flowing with minimal "manufriction."

Antimasturbation pamphlets and books proliferated in nineteenth-century Europe and the United States. Doctors and the general public alike were convinced that masturbation weakened the body and particularly the nerves—a condition called "neurasthenia." The term was actually coined by an American physician, George M. Beard (1839–1883), in 1869. Doctors also believed that masturbation weakened the "seed," leading to the generation of enfeebled offspring. A British doctor, Samuel Solomon (1780–1818), dramatically laid out this theory in his *Guide to Health; or Advice to Both Sexes,* which by 1800 was supposedly in its fifty-second edition! Like many doctors before him, Solomon condemned the "immoderate evacuation of semen," but he especially emphasized the neurological damage of orgasm or "the too frequent repetition of the convulsive motion by which [semen] is discharged; for the highest pleasure is followed by an universal resolution of the natural powers, which cannot frequently take place without enervation. . . . The brain being weakened by this two-fold cause [humoral and nervous] is successively deprived of all its faculties, and the miserable victims fall into a state of imbecility without any other than frantic intervals" (1800, 191–192). (Ever since the classical Greek Hippocratic medical writings, doctors had likened orgasm to an epileptic fit.)

Solomon also warned that seed, as well as sensation, had to be spent wisely for the greatest return in pleasure and offspring. He advised that "the best semen, and from which we may expect good healthy offspring, if not rendered poor by previous pollutions, is that which is at *least* twenty four hours in collecting in a *sound* man, who has not abused his constitution by debaucheries of any kind; and which must be ejected with fervency, love and pleasure" (192). In addition to discouraging overexcitement and stimulating foods, such as tea, coffee, and "ardent spirits," Solomon hawked his patent medicine for masturbation and all venereal and genital diseases: the most marvelous "Cordial Balm of Gilead."

Similar dietary recommendations came from American cleric and social reformer Sylvester Graham (1794–1851). In *A Lecture to Young Men* (1833), he cautioned parents against animal products and other heat-stimulating foods that would hasten puberty and heighten the risk of self-pollution (39). He developed a special whole-wheat flour (the Graham flour used in graham crackers), in part as a healthful means of preventing precocious puberty and solitary vice. Masturbation, he feared, would also lead to an aversion to the opposite sex. Graham warned that self-defilers "feel none of the manly confidence, gallant spirit, and chaste delight, in the presence of virtuous females, which stimulate young men to pursue the course of ennobling refinement, and mature them for the social relations and enjoyments of life" (46).

One of Graham's followers, Mary S. Gove (later Nichols) (1810–1884), focused attention on female masturbation (Blake 1984). This self-described "Lecturer in Anatomy and Physiology" went crusading around the country to condemn the evils of self-pollution. She was no Victorian "Just Say No" celibacy promoter though. Gove founded a free-love utopian commune called Memnonia in Yellow Springs, Ohio, with her husband in the 1850s (D'Emilio and Freedman 1988, 115). Nevertheless, she considered masturbation a terrible social ill. In her pamphlet, *Solitary Vice. An Address to Parents and Those Who Have the Care of Children* (1839), she especially warned *mothers* to beware of the terrible prevalence of the vice. She reported on girls who began as early as age four. To support her medical arguments, she cited Dr. Samuel B. Woodward, superintendent of the Worcester State Lunatic Asylum, who declared that masturbation was the third leading cause of insanity among his patients and that it "stamps its victims with every abhorrent and loathsome stigmata of degradation" (Gove 1839, 5). She went on to blame the epidemic on the "increased and increasing luxury and effeminacy of the people . . . for the present unhealthy and stimulating method of living is in great measure the root of this awful evil" (17).

Although there were a few medical writers in the nineteenth century who began to question these sorts of antimasturbation claims, for the most part both doctors and the general public were convinced that the "solitary vice" was a serious and widespread cause of illness. In addition to the physical deterioration wrought by "self-pollution," doctors also associated a distinctive psychopathology with masturbation, particularly in a subclass of introverted, delicate youths. Doctors imagined the inevitable feelings of guilt and fear that would engulf the onanist, eventually leading to isolation, antisocial behavior, and paranoid dementia. Dr. Woodward gave a classic description of the terrifying decline of the sensitive onanist: "In the progress of the disease, the victim of it becomes apprehensive that friends dislike and avoid him, that he is the subject of ridicule and censure and is an object of inspection. . . . Hence he retires from society and chooses to be alone—while alone he sometimes talks to himself, and often laughs much and frequently, and sometimes aloud" (Woodward 1838, 18).

The same was true in women. In fact, they were even more vulnerable. As one Dr. Rozier explained in a popular book on female onanism, "women are very similar, in their constitution, to children" and thus they are weak, hypersensitive, and particularly vulnerable to nervous disorders. The female onanist risked losing "all the feminine charms of the beautiful sex" (1830, 26, 129). Through self-pleasuring, women could become sexually independent of men and eventually even lose their maternal calling.

Everyone was concerned with the neural and genital enfeeblement and the psychological shame and solitude of masturbators. These problems all weakened normal sexual attraction and opened the door to deviations or "perversions" of the sexual instinct. Woodward put it in the most explicit terms: "[Masturbation] is equally opposed to moral purity and mental vigor. It gives the passions ascendancy in the character—fills the mind with lewd and corrupt images, and transforms its victim into a filthy and disgusting reptile" (1838, Note).

### The Shocking Discovery of the Sexual Perversions

The first professional concerns about the "sexual perversions" began in the 1860s. German doctors were soon followed by their Italian, French, and British colleagues in reporting cases. What exactly did doctors mean by "sexual perversion"? One doctor put it most succinctly: sexual perversion is all sexual activity and feeling that is "not of such a character to lead to the preservation and increase of the species" (Spitzka 1881, 359). Although this was a pretty broad definition, doctors nevertheless believed that sexual perversion was in fact rare. In 1882, Dr. Alder Blumer, an alienist (psychiatrist) at the New York State Lunatic Asylum, could still write with an enormous sense of discovery: "The attention of physicians was first directed to the existence of perverted sexual instincts by Professor Westphal, of Berlin, in 1869. . . . Subsequent observers have, from time to time, added, from their personal knowledge, to the literature of the subject, till the record of cases in which the anomaly has been recognized and described now numbers seventeen" (1882, 22). From that small group of seventeen, the number of "sexual perverts" described in the medical literature exploded in the last two decades of the nineteenth century.

Doctors of the time believed that this "repulsive form of alienation" (insanity) was completely novel and they found it quite baffling. For example, the editor of the U.S. journal *Alienist and Neu-*

*rologist,* Dr. Charles H. Hughes, surmised the situation in 1893 as follows:

> Within the past few years the neurologist and the alienist have become familiar with so many strange morbid perversions and reversions of the erotic sentiments and sexual passion, that they must be considered and classified in their relation to society, to morals and to law, and Science must severally category these perversions of proper and natural human passion, as they may be found to be purely psychological moral perversities or to belong among the neuroses or the neuro-psychoses. . . . [A] difficult task, yet one now imperatively demanded of psychiatry. (Hughes 1893a, 531)

Hughes saw the duties of the neuro-psychiatric profession as three-fold: (1) to devise a system of classification for these sexual perversions, (2) to uncover the psychological or biological basis for this group of "diseases," and (3) to determine the degree of legal and moral responsibility of the "sexually perverse."

Many systems of classification (or nosologies) of sexual disorders were proposed and continue to be debated today. But the largest group of sexual perverts discussed in the medical literature was the "sexual inverts." This term was first applied to those "in whom dwelt a soul of the opposite sex" or those of "contrary sexual appetite" as first described by the German doctor Karl Westphal in 1869. In the same period, a homosexual German lawyer, Karl Heinrich Ulrichs, was writing a series of pamphlets in defense of same-sex love (1864–1879). He labeled himself and others like him "Urnings," and he argued that they possessed a "female soul confined in a male body" (see Sidebar 1.1). Although not a scientist, Ulrichs relied on biological explanations of Urnings since he believed that only science could correct social, religious, and legal prejudice. As one

### Sidebar 1.1 Karl Heinrich Ulrichs: Urning Pioneer

German doctors were the first to describe "contrary sexual sensation" or "sexual inversion." This interest was instigated partly by Karl Heinrich Ulrichs, a Hanoverian legal official who argued in a series of pamphlets published from 1864 to 1879 that Uranism (as he called it) was congenital, natural and, therefore, did not warrant legal persecution. He described himself and others of his kind as possessing a "female soul confined in a male body" (Ulrichs 1868, 289). Ulrichs's writings influenced the eminent psychiatrist Karl Westphal, who in 1869 described the case of a woman with "contrary sexual feeling": masculine behavior and dress during childhood, and sexual attraction toward women as an adult. Westphal asserted that the condition was congenital and betrayed no other signs of insanity. This model of "sexual inversion" or "psychosexual hermaphroditism" would be stamped on subsequent theories of homosexuality well into the twentieth century. Hubert Kennedy (1988) has written the most extensively on Ulrichs and the importance of his diverse political engagements.

*Richard von Krafft-Ebing (Culver Pictures)*

doctor exclaimed, also in reference to the perversions, "Science, like fire, purifies everything it touches."

The third task that Hughes described—determining the legal responsibility of "sexual perverts"—became increasingly critical in the last third of the nineteenth century. Medical experts were increasingly called upon to evaluate the mental state and moral responsibility of individuals charged with engaging in "unnatural acts" or being blackmailed for these acts. Were these sexual perverts simply vice-ridden criminals, as the police and lawyers argued, or were they mentally deranged people who had no control over their sexual preference and therefore should be treated with lenience, or even sympathy (Hamilton 1895)? And how could medical science explain these supposedly "unnatural" propensities?

Not only were physicians dismayed by what they believed were the "unnatural acts" of perverse clients, but also doctors were equally disturbed by the fact that so many of these patients were otherwise apparently intelligent, well-bred middle- and upper-class ladies and gentlemen. The French alienist Paul Moreau de Tours (1804–1884) addressed this dilemma in his 1880 treatise, *On the Aberrations of the Genesic Sense:* "How shall we explain these infamous habits, with instructed, well educated and high ranking persons, if not by an anomaly of the genital sense, determining sympathetically a true moral perversion?" (1884, 378).

### Masturbation, Hereditary Degeneration, and Inversion

For Victorian physicians, the most probable cause of "anomalies of the genital sense" was childhood masturbation. It was already widely accepted as a cause of multiple ills and genital dysfunction. And if theory was not enough, physicians' suspicion that masturbation was at the root of sexual perversion was confirmed when they interrogated their sexually inverted patients. These almost invariably admitted to youthful indulgence in the "solitary vice," or else they admitted to "mutual onanism" with partners of the same sex. This was the case, for example, in a patient of Dr. Richard von Krafft-Ebing. This German neurologist ignited a widespread discourse on the medico-legal considerations of sexual perversion with his controversial book *Psychopathia Sexualis* (1886) (see Sidebar 1.2). Krafft-Ebing provided a typical early example of a sexual invert:

> Herr von H., age 30. Family history good. From childhood indisposed to engage in boy's pursuits—effeminate in all his tastes. In his 17th year, began to suffer from nocturnal and diurnal pollutions [seminal emissions], and as a consequence developed various symptoms of disturbances of the nervous system. . . . His feelings towards men are those of the opposite sex, whilst towards women he feels entire indifference. Denies sexual intercourse with men, though it is known to be a fact that he has attempted it. . . . His whole appearance is decidedly effeminate, thorax and pelvis like those of a woman. Voice high-pitched and without masculine tone. His time he spends chiefly in his boudoir, his conversation is of fashion, household employments, cooking, etc.; *symptoms of Neurasthenia, induced by his effeminate mode of life. . . . Masturbation must be held to have been the original cause of the affection,* and the existence of a spermatorrhoea [involuntary seminal loss] may constitute an element of the case. (Krafft-Ebing 1882, 674; my emphasis)

His clinical description shows that stereotypes of the "effeminate male" were already well established in nineteenth-century medicine and were central to the conceptualization of "sexual inversion." Inverted men had a female psyche at least and were thoroughly examined for signs of effeminate anatomy. Yet how did doctors reason that masturbation caused homosexuality?

# PSYCHOPATHIA SEXUALIS

## A Medico-Forensic Study

### By DR. RICHARD von KRAFFT-EBING

WITH AN INTRODUCTION BY
Dr. Ernest van den Haag

TRANSLATION FROM THE LATIN BY
Dr. Harry E. Wedeck

*First Unexpurgated Edition in English*

**G. P. Putnam's Sons New York**

*Title page of Psychopathia Sexualis, with Especial Reference to the Antipathic Sexual Instinct (Library of Congress)*

Richard von Krafft-Ebing's *Psychopathia Sexualis* (1886) was the most translated and widely published Victorian sexological work. Although inserts sometimes warned that its sale was limited to medical professionals, it found its way into many other hands. One American reviewer warned: "Surely, it would be an extraordinary appetite for nastiness that would not be satiated by the records which it contains of the inconceivable depths of degradation into which human beings . . . may be plunged by the vagaries and perversions of the sexual passion" (Review of *Psychopathia Sexualis* 1893, 91).

*Psychopathia Sexualis* was an encyclopedia of sexual perversions that coined many of the terms we currently use for sexual disorders or paraphilias. From a modest pamphlet in its first 1886 edition, it swelled in each of the subsequent eleven editions with the first-person testimonials of "perverts." The largest group were homosexuals, who were delighted to find that they were not unique in the world. They took advantage of the legitimate platform Krafft-Ebing provided to defend and sometimes celebrate their same-sex love. Krafft-Ebing even reprinted letters that outright condemned his scientific hypotheses even while recognizing their political value:

> Your opinion that the phenomenon under consideration is primarily due to an inborn "pathological" disposition will, perhaps, make it soon possible to overcome existing prejudices and awaken pity for us poor, "abnormal" men, instead of the present repugnance and contempt. Much as I believe that the viewpoint expressed by you is possibly beneficial to us, I am still not willing, in the interest of science, to accept unconditionally the word "pathological." (reprinted in Oosterhuis 2000, 166)

Harry Oosterhuis's *Stepchildren of Nature: Krafft-Ebing and the Making of Sexual Identity* (2000) provides the best cultural history of Krafft-Ebing and his work.

As we have already seen, it was widely believed that masturbation softened the body and particularly the nerves, a condition called "neurasthenia." Doctors also believed that masturbation weakened the "seed," leading to the conception of enfeebled offspring. If this process continued, each subsequent generation would be weaker and weaker. This notion of progressive hereditary decay, or degeneration, became a dominant biological concept in the nineteenth century after the work of French physician Bénédict Morel (Pick 1989).

Bénédict A. Morel (1809–1873) was an abandoned child raised by priests, who struggled to put himself through medical studies. He qualified as a doctor in 1839 and became increasingly interested in mental disorders, particularly "cretinism." It was an all too common form of congenital mental retardation accompanied by characteristically coarse facial features. Although it is now considered the result of prenatal iodine deficiency, in the early nineteenth century cretinism was associated with living in lowland and inland areas with their toxic fumes, or "miasma." Morel studied cretins and became convinced that the condition was incurable. In his influential *Treatise on the Physical, Intellectual and Moral Degeneration of the Human Species* (1857), Morel proposed that cretinism was just one manifestation of a broader class of hereditary disorders that were the result of environmental toxins, poor climate, and alcohol or other substance abuse. He was writing well before genes and chromosomes had been identified, and the notion of inheritance was quite vague by today's standards. According to the theory of degeneration, any type of bodily damage could weaken the individual and his or her seed, thereby being manifested as any other type of congenital physical or mental malady in the offspring. Degeneration was thus the negative version of "Lamarckian evolution": the acquisition and hereditary transmission of positive traits. Furthermore, subsequent generations might exhibit different ailments, but the overall process was one of progressive deterioration culminating in infertility and the termination of family lines. Thus, the outlines of hereditary degeneration resembled the decline of the individual masturbator, and masturbation was blamed as a potent cause of inheritable degeneration.

Hereditary degeneration became an especially popular model for explaining neurological diseases. Hysteria, in particular, was one of the mental disorders that had perplexed doctors for millennia. It had long been viewed as a disorder exclusively of women because doctors since antiquity had associated it with a diseased uterus (*hystera* in Greek). By the nineteenth century, most physicians believed it to be a neurological illness; however, the possibility of male hysteria remained controversial (Micale 1990). Popular representations of hysteria still portray it as a caricature of femininity: excessive emotionality, anxiousness, and unexplainable pain complaints or sensory loss. In the mid–nineteenth century, doctors increasingly argued that *men* could suffer from these symptoms too. Most commonly, it was congenitally effeminate men (usually with nervous or hysterical mothers) who were diagnosed with hysteria. In addition to degenerate heredity, "frenetic masturbation" was often a contributing factor, so doctors

scrutinized these men for inherited and acquired traits of emasculation (Rosario 1996). Doctors reasoned that through excessive masturbation, a man could lose "his virile attributes to bear those of a
woman, and thereby becoming vulnerable to the diseases of the
weaker sex, could end up with hysteria" (Bonnemaison 1875, 675).

Thus the various pieces of the puzzle of "sexual inversion" were
falling into place. Degenerate heredity could produce young men and
women with frail nervous systems and cross-gendered bodies and
brains. Childhood masturbation only further weakened their feeble
nervous system and induced them to pursue sexual encounters that
were appropriate for their degenerate, gender-inverted nervous system—but not their external genitals. In other words, doctors believed
the inverted woman had a masculine brain and nervous system. Sometimes they even had an enlarged phallic-like clitoris from excessive
solitary vice or "tribadism" (rubbing against other women) (Gibson
1997). Doctors suspected inverted men to have feminine nervous systems, which would explain their effeminacy and attraction to other
men. We can thus begin to understand the medical reasoning behind
Krafft-Ebing's description of Herr von H. Indeed, Krafft-Ebing was a
strong proponent of the neurodegeneration model of homosexuality.
But the model could explain even more, since it also incorporated the
emerging concept of evolution. We can identify three interrelated
mechanisms whereby Victorian doctors placed the blame for homosexuality on nervous weakening: it was devirilizing or demasculiniz-
ing, it was also de-eroticizing, and it led to evolutionary regression.

*Neural Sex Changes*

At the 1882 American Neurological Association conference, Dr.
William A. Hammond (1828–1900) graphically documented what he
believed to be examples of neural devirilization among Native Americans. Hammond had been surgeon general of the Union Army during
the Civil War and later professor of diseases of the mind and nervous
system at the New York Post-Graduate Medical School. He was a
prominent New York neurologist, had published over a dozen books
on psychiatry and sexual disorders, and had served as president of the
American Neurological Association. So Hammond was no quack. Yet
his presentation is startling. He described the *bote,* or *mujerados,*
among certain western American Indian tribes. The *mujerados* are men
who dress as women, take on women's occupations, and serve
shamanistic roles in their tribe. They can also have male sexual partners. According to Hammond's investigations:

A *mujerado* is an essential person in the saturnalia or orgies, in which these Indians, like the ancient Greeks, Egyptians and other nations indulge. He is the chief passive agent in the pederastic ceremonies, which form so important a part in the performances. . . . For the making of a *mujerado,* one of the most virile men is selected and the act of masturbation is performed upon him many times every day. At the same time he is made to ride almost continuously on horseback. [This practice occasions involuntary seminal emissions to the point of impotence.] In the meantime the penis and testicles begin to shrink, and in time reach their lowest plane of degradation. . . . His courage disappears, and he becomes timid to such an extent that if he is a man occupying a prominent place in the councils he is at once relieved of all power and responsibility, and his influence is at an end. . . . Indeed, his endeavor seems to be to assimilate himself as much as possible to the female sex, and to get rid as far as may be of all the attributes, mental and physical, of manhood. (Hammond 1882, 347–348)

*American Indian "third sex" people often cross-dressed and took on the roles of the opposite sex. This 1879 photograph shows We-Wa, a Zuni man, engaged in weaving, traditionally a woman's activity (National Archives).*

More recent anthropological work has shown that Hammond's observations on the *bote* are seriously flawed (Blackwood 1984; Roscoe 1994). Nevertheless, we can understand that Hammond's reasoning is consistent with the physiological principles of the time that associated masturbation with nervous weakening, impotence, and eventual sexual inversion.

The equivalent female case, the virilized women, was described quite emotionally by Dr. William L. Howard: "The female possessed of masculine ideas of independence; the viragint [masculine female] who would sit in the public highways and lift up her pseudovirile voice, proclaiming her sole right to decide questions of war or religion, or the value of celibacy and the curse of woman's impurity, and that disgusting antisocial being, the female sexual pervert, are simply different degrees of the same class—degenerates" (1900, 687). It is clear from both Hammond's and Howard's articles that the sexual activities of the two sexes were tightly bound to rigid notions of gender roles and the stratification of authority. Aggressiveness, courage, power, leadership, and independence were all the exclusive attributes of those with a normal male sexual organ. Any degeneration of the male genitalia necessarily produced the *psychological,* as well as physical, emasculation characteristic of the "sexual invert." Conversely, any woman exhibiting any of these masculine traits was under suspicion of being a cross-gendered female or hermaphrodite.

The second mechanism for the creation of sexual inversion involved the weakening of the "nerves of sexual sensibility" and was clearly described in 1884 by Dr. James Kiernan (1852–1923), the medical superintendent of the Chicago County Asylum for the Insane, the editor of the "Sexology" column of the *Urological and Cutaneous Review,* and a prolific writer on questions of sexuality. He reminded his readers that "repeated stimulation tends to exhaust the power of the nerves to respond to the normal stimulation, for this reason the sated voluptuary seeks to arouse his flagging sexual system by unwonted stimuli" (1884b, 121). Doctors firmly believed that these forms of sexual dysfunction were the result of organic disorder, not just psychological peculiarities. As Dr. Charles H. Hughes pointed out, "excessive masturbation" led to neurasthenic degeneration of the "genito-spinal centers" as demonstrated by the loss of the "virile reflex" or "penile percussion reflex" (a supposedly diagnostic sign of the "loss or abeyance of the sexual powers in man" that is elicited by tapping the penis and watching for a reflexive penile retraction). Hughes believed he was the first to describe this neurological reflex and gave a detailed description of how to elicit it, warning: "Some skill in palpation—a sort of *tactus eruditus* [learned touch] is necessary in examining for this sign" (1891a, 44–45). It was fundamentally the sexual impotence of the masturbator that emasculated men, exhausting their normal attraction to women and turning them instead into "women-in-men's-bodies" who were the *passive* sexual partners of immoral but otherwise physiologically normal sexually *active* men.

In women, masturbation destroyed all the "charms of femininity," turning ladies into aggressive "viragints" who pursued weak, passive women (Hamilton 1895, 505). In addition to sexual inversion, doctors believed onanism could also lead to a whole spectrum of "sexual perversions"—from zoophilia to sadomasochism—as masturbators sought increasingly exotic and "unnatural" means of exciting their debilitated sexual nerves. Although these other "sexual perversions" were not directly related to sexual inversion, they were often portrayed as part of a continuum of degenerate sexual states representing varying degrees of developmental and evolutionary psychosexual regression (Rosario 1997a).

## Phylogenetic Mechanisms: Genetic Degeneration, Sexual Atavism, and Psychosexual Arrest

The third important trend in explanations of sexual inversion involved various forms of phylogenetic arrest or regression. *Phylogeny* is the evolutionary or racial history of a species or organism and is usually distinguished from *ontogeny,* or the embryological development of an individual. The eighteenth-century fascination with taxonomies and the classification of plants, animals, and cultures into hierarchies of relative perfection spurred evolutionary thinking in the nineteenth century. This influence was keenly felt in medical theorizing, in which Lamarckian notions of evolution remained popular throughout the nineteenth century (Buican 1984). French naturalist Jean-Baptiste de Lamarck (1744–1829) hypothesized that species were transformed over the millennia through a process of hereditary transmission of acquired traits. For example, the giraffe gradually evolved its long neck as generations of giraffes stretched to graze from treetops. This model of *Lamarckian evolution* is often contrasted with *Darwinian evolution,* Charles Darwin's theory of the natural selection of advantageous traits from the great pool of natural variation (Bowler 1989). However, Darwin also believed acquired traits could be inherited.

Evolutionary theories tried to explain the improvement and growing complexity of species, whereas theories of degeneration explained the opposite process. We have already seen how Bénédict Morel's theory of degeneration presented evolution in reverse: external harm, such as masturbation, could lead to worsening varieties of mental defects from one generation to the next. These inferior mental states were also inheritable (Morel 1857). In this model, the progress of the intellectual and moral faculties ran parallel to the evolution of sexual behavior: the most *advanced,* civilized people engaged in the fittest and most acceptable sex, namely, reproductive coitus. All forms of "sexual perversion" could therefore be explained as hereditary *regressions* to varieties of "primitive" sexuality or as *fixations* of the sexual appetite at immature stages in sexual evolution (Bleys 1995).

Shobal Clevenger (1843–1920) was a special pathologist and institutional reformer at the Cook County Lunatic Asylum in Chicago, who later published *The Evolution of Man and His Mind* (1903). He relied upon this sort of phylogenetic scale of sexual behavior to trace the development of human "sexual appetite" back to the ancient "protoplasmic hunger" of amoebas and other protista (single-celled organisms). These, he believed, engaged in cannibalism prior to reproductive fission

*Biologist Ernst Haeckel (left) and a friend (Hulton-Duetsch Collection / Corbis)*

(1881). Clevenger's evolutionary framework is indebted to the embryological work of Ernst Haeckel (1834–1919) who formulated the "fundamental biogenetic law": "ontogeny is the short and rapid recapitulation of phylogeny" (Haeckel 1866, 2:300; Sulloway 1983, 199). This powerful and persistent model suggested that the embryological development of a human, for example, from one-celled egg to fully formed person repeated, as if in fast forward, the entire evolutionary history of the species from unicellular bacteria to reptiles to primitive mammals

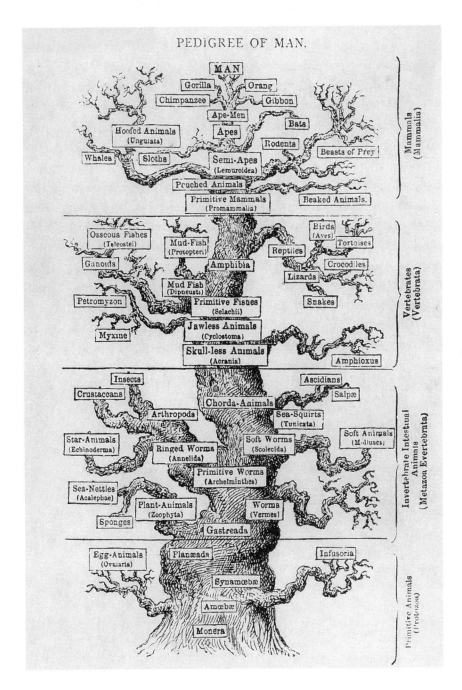

The evolutionary tree culminating with "man," as conceived by Ernst Haeckel. Other hierarchies of evolution would explicitly place European (or even more specifically, German) males at the top, with women and "primitive races" closer down to the animals (Ernst Haeckel, Generelle Morphologie der Organismen [Berlin: Reimer, 1866]).

and finally *homo sapiens*. Furthermore, Haeckel believed that the basic drive behind sexual selection and phylogenetic differentiation remained the primal "erotic chemotropism" (chemical attraction) drawing the male and female cells to fuse, or consume each other (1874, 2:793).

Embryologists also noted that embryos at an early stage possessed the cellular rudiments of both sexes before differentiating in either a male or female direction. Applying these observations to the psychology of sex, doctors speculated that humans also passed through "primitive" anatomical and even psychological stages both in utero and during infancy that were "bisexual" or hermaphroditic. The sexual drive itself was represented as an animalistic appetite that was anatomically localized to the "lower" nervous system: the spinal cord, midbrain, or the cerebellum (Magnan 1885). Psychologists proposed that human infants passed through stages of sexual attraction and morality from base animal instincts to more civilized sexual behavior, as the supposedly higher, more evolved areas of the central nervous system matured. Furthermore, psychologists of sex also depicted this individual maturation of the sexual behavior as paralleling the historical evolution of human sexuality from that of "primitive" races to the supposed promiscuity of lower-class Europeans to the sexual reserve of the middle class. It was therefore easy to liken the genital and sensual uninhibitedness of children to that of supposed primitives (Sulloway 1983, 199). We can schematize these parallel hierarchies of evolution from inferior/primitive forms to superior/evolved forms in Table 1.1.

Clevenger's superior at the Cook County Lunatic Asylum, James G. Kiernan, relied on these phylogenetic-ontogenetic parallelisms in explaining the development of "sexual perversion" (1884b). He considered this disease to be an "atavistic reversion to primitive conditions" (1892, 197). In Kiernan's ladder of sexual evolution, it was the "sexual appetite" (in Clevenger's sense) that had been slowly refined

**Table 1.1**

| *Inferior* | *Superior* |
|---|---|
| Unicellular organisms | Multicellular organisms |
| Asexual/hermaphroditic | Sexually dimorphic (male *v.* female) |
| Ovum or spermatid | Embryo |
| Lower animals | Humans |
| "Primitive" humans | Civilized (European) people |
| Infant | Adult |
| Females | Males |
| Working class | Middle class |
| Sexual perversion | Marital heterosexuality |

over the millennia. Therefore, sexual inverts who practiced oral-genital sex, for example, were reverting to the primitive, cannibal sexual eating behaviors of unicellular organisms. According to Kiernan, the possibility for same-sex relationships was a part of all human beings' primitive background since "man, like vermes [worms], was originally hermaphroditic" (1892, 189). Indeed, "the original bisexuality of the ancestors of the race, shown in the rudimentary female organs of the male, could not fail to show occasional functional if not organic reversions when mental or physical manifestations were interfered with by disease or congenital defect" (1891, 195). Masturbation was particularly dangerous in this sense, and Kiernan agreed with his colleague G. Frank Lydston that "sexual perversion from overstimulation of the nerves of sexual sensibility and the receptive sexual centres, incidental to sexual excesses and masturbation" was the only definite, willful cause of "acquired sexual perversion" (Kiernan 1892, 197).

Although Kiernan and Lydston agreed on the masturbatory causation of sexual inversion, they differed in their theory of the pathophysiology of perversion. Rather than relying on the notion of *atavism* (primitive reversion), Lydston (1857–1923) conceived of sexual perversions in terms of "arrested development": "That mal-development, or arrested development, of the sexual organs should be associated with sexual perversion is not at all surprising; and the more nearly the individual approximates the type of fetal development which exists prior to the commencement of sexual differentiation, the more marked is the aberrance of sexuality" (1889, 255). Because of their immature, primitive-like brains, children were particularly at risk of acquiring permanent and perhaps genetically transmissible sexual perversion. Lydston warned careless parents: "Boys who are allowed to associate intimately, are apt to turn their inventive genius to account by inventing novel means of sexual stimulation, with the result of ever after diminishing the natural sexual appetite" (255).

These phylogenic mechanisms of sexual development were singularly original contributions by American physicians to a new field that was otherwise dominated by continental doctors. Even European psychiatrists, such as Krafft-Ebing and Freud, acknowledged the importance of these American theorists. To summarize the phylogenetic perspective, doctors believed that a morbid addiction to masturbation by the infant or growing child could drain nervous energies essential to the child's sexual development. Youthful masturbators could thus stunt both their neurological and sexual development, fixating themselves at or reverting to one of the many phylogenetically primitive forms of sexuality, such as "contrary sexual appetite."

## Social Trouble and Sexual Trouble

*Sexologist Havelock Ellis in 1893, around the time he began working on* Sexual Inversion, *the first volume of his seven-volume* Studies in the Psychology of Sex *(1897–1927) (Brown Brothers). Havelock's wife, Edith Lees Ellis (right) was a lesbian writer and feminist activist, whom he included (under the name Miss X.) in an article on female sexual inversion (1895) (Brown Brothers).*

Having tried to illuminate the scientific reasoning behind the masturbation theories and their connection to homosexuality, we are left wondering: Why did this double concern with seminal squandering and "sexual inversion" became so grave in the nineteenth century? Medical journals from a surprising variety of specialties (from neurology to urology and gynecology) abounded with articles concerning masturbation. Numerous monographs warned both physicians and the general public about the devastating effects of "self-abuse." The late nineteenth century was also a time particularly rich in medical discussions of "sexual perversion" and "sexual inversion": What were they? What should the different varieties be called? What caused them? Could "sexual perverts" be recognized? How could they be cured? Numerous physicians achieved fame and notoriety as "sexologists" at the end of the century and into the early twentieth century: Richard von Krafft-Ebing, Albert Moll, Havelock Ellis, Magnus Hirschfeld, and, best known of all, Sigmund Freud.

We enter into a more speculative domain when we try to understand why these concerns about deviant sexuality became so acute in the nineteenth century and why *physicians* became the arbiters of sexual norms. I can only begin to suggest some answers. Most probably,

the Industrial Revolution and resulting demographic upheavals played a major role. In the United States, the population grew at an enormous rate, particularly at mid-century, with a large influx of poor immigrants who were stigmatized as inferior, degenerate, and criminal (Rosen 1985). The filth of the city slums was viewed as a reflection of the moral turpitude of their indigent and working-class inhabitants. To physicians and moral reformers, the urban miasma and overcrowding seemed conducive to the epidemic spread of moral infection (Mort 1987, 40). Medical articles frequently accused immoral, lower-class nursemaids of initiating middle-class infants into masturbation (Shrady 1884; Acton 1875; Howe 1883, 209). Luther V. Bell warned in his monograph on onanism that "the voluntary indulgence of an unnatural, depraved, degrading animal propensity," which was common among the "scum of Europe," was spreading like a "foul plague in our midst, cutting off among the youth, the beautiful and the promising of our land" (1840, 16, 17, vi).

Although such "importationist" or "contagionist" theories of disease were common (Rosenberg 1962, 135–138; Pernick 1985), there were many real, *local* problems that arose as the urban, industrial centers swelled and family units changed drastically. Young people left home to find work in the city. Women and children were drawn into the workplace. With higher concentrations of independent men and women in the cities—without familial supervision—there were greater opportunities for people attracted to those of their own sex to congregate (D'Emilio and Freedman 1988, 122–123). A growing public concern (perhaps fascination) with homosexual meeting places is chronicled in police records, as well as in medical journals (Hughes 1891b, 1892, 1893a, 1893b; Dohousset 1892; Weeks 1981, 100). Sounding uncannily like contemporary gay conspiracy theorists, Dr. Frank Lydston warned in 1889:

> There is in every community of any size a colony of male sexual perverts; they are usually known to each other, and are likely to congregate together. At times they operate in accordance with some definite and concerted plan in quest of subjects wherein to satisfy their abnormal sexual impulses. . . . There exists in every great city so large a number of sexual perverts, that seemingly their depraved tastes have been commercially appreciated by the *demi-monde*. This has resulted in the formation of establishments whose principal business it is to cater to the perverted sexual tastes of a numerous class of patrons. Were the names and social positions of these patrons made public in the case of our city, society would be regaled with something fully as disgusting, and

## Sidebar 1.3 An Italian Invert Confesses

*Monsieur Emile Zola, Paris*

It is to you, Monsieur, who are the greatest novelist of our time and who, with the eye of the savant and the artist, capture and paint so powerfully *all* the failings, all the shame, all the ills that afflict humanity that I send these *human documents* so cherished by the cultivated people of our age. This confession, which no spiritual advisor has ever learned from my lips, will reveal to you a frightful illness of the soul, a rare case—if not, unfortunately, unique—that has been studied by learned psychologists, but which till now no novelist has dared to stage in a literary work.

So opens a unique confession of the late 1880s: a series of letters written to novelist Emile Zola by a twenty-three-year-old Italian aristocrat in the hope that Zola would turn him into a novelistic hero. He describes in explicit detail his childhood cross-dressing and masturbatory addiction, his infatuation with stable boys, and his love affair with a fellow military officer. He refused to label himself a "pederast" but had no other name for his condition.

The Italian, however, had no reservations about explicitly detailing his sexual activities. In blue prose he describes his seduction by an older cavalry captain:

He lay on top of me, panting and groaning loudly, and he clasped me so tightly in his arms that I almost suffocated; he began stroking himself on top of my body. He had a huge member which, when rubbed over me, gave me an extraordinarily pleasurable sensation. Meanwhile, he sucked my ears, inserted his tongue in my mouth, and caressed my entire body with his hands. He kept saying the sweetest nothings to me in a broken voice. When he emitted his semen, he inundated me and didn't cease thrusting, but roared like a bull. Meanwhile I had ejaculated copiously, and for a long time we clung to one another as if unconscious and indeed glued together; in fact, we struggled to unstick ourselves.

Instead of fictionalizing the confession, Zola submitted it to a medical friend who published it in the *Archives of Criminal Anthropology* as part of a series of articles on sexual inversion. As with other sexological publications of the time, the erotic passages were translated into Latin in the hope that only educated professionals could read them.

Years later, the Italian invert discovered himself in the pages of the medical literature rather than a novel. He was nevertheless happy to be publicized there. He even submitted further information directly to the physician and admitted that, "like every sick person who sees in a doctor a friend, . . . I am filled with friendship and gratitude for those who occupy themselves with the odious illness that haunts me, and . . . I seek to render them service by exhibiting that which they painfully seek, and which I, on the contrary, know so well: *by innate science*" (quoted in Rosario 1997a, 89, 96). Although the Italian did not wish to change his sexuality, his interaction with the medical profession is characteristic of upper-class men of the time, who saw medical science as a vehicle for publicizing and even defending same-sex eroticism. Book reviewers, however, complained that sexological texts were just pornography disguised as medicine.

coming much nearer home, than the *Pall Mall Gazette* exposures [of juvenile prostitution in London]. (Lydston 1889, 254, 256)

As the medical profession and society in general grew to better define sexual inverts in the nineteenth century, sexual inverts naturally became more evident. Some sexual inverts began to recognize that their sexuality was branded as deviant, and in a secular age, they sought the attention of the medical profession that had *scientifically* created their diagnosis and promised a cure—rather than religious or legal condemnation (see Sidebar 1.3). As already mentioned, physicians were increasingly consulted in legal cases involving sexual inverts, and physicians claimed exclusive jurisdiction in the matter. As the editor of the *New York Medical Record* declared: "We believe it to be demonstrated that conditions once considered criminal are really pathological, and come within the province of the physician" (Shrady 1884, 71).

The medical profession's claim to authority in the legal domain was based on positivist ideals that the scientific foundations of medicine gave it the power to truly understand and ameliorate human life. This stance was confidently expounded by Dr. Henry Landor: "[Medicine's] principles cannot be reversed by bending them to the retrograde action of the law, for that would be a stoppage of all progress. The profession must be firmly on the only ground it can occupy— that law must yield to medicine, and bring its rules into agreement with the state of modern science" (1871, 71).

The positivist optimism of certain members of the medical profession was repeatedly called into question by the living conditions in the industrialized urban centers. Cities were crowded and squalid; they were perceived as places of crime, poverty, and sickness. In the first half of the century, militant moral reformers launched crusades to alert all God-fearing Christians to the extent of sexual sins brought on by modern, urban lifestyles, even among the upper classes (Smith-Rosenberg 1985, 109–128). Many feared that the nervous system might not be capable of dealing with the sensory overload and frantic pace of modern civilization. Dr. George Beard warned that Americans were most at risk since they were "the most nervous people of all history" because of their "nerve-exhausting climate" (1886, 64).

In the second half of the nineteenth century, many began to worry that instead of evolving, the human species was degenerating under the pressures of modernity. Degenerationist theories of *racial* atavism proliferated, and as I have already pointed out, "sexual inversion" was construed as a threatening form of *sexual* atavism. The sexual invert was dangerous because he or she was theorized as *cross-sexed*—

Ps-s-s-t
Nix
Lady
Nix!
You're not
my kind
of a
Valentine

*Caricatures of the New Woman in popular media suggest the widespread concern about female sexual inversion (Gibson Art Company).*

thus blurring any sense of *natural* order, which should correspond to the *social* order.

The "masculine-female" was easily equated with the so-called New Woman, who was increasingly entering the workforce and the political arena in the late nineteenth century (Chauncey 1982–1983; Smith-Rosenberg 1985). These New Women not only threatened male-dominated institutions but also were accused of abandoning their sacred role as mothers and by this negligence were contributing to the formation of the equally dangerous "monster," the "effeminate male." The gender ideal of the virile, aggressive male must have been particularly valued during the period of aggressive U.S. territorial and industrial expansion (Rotundo 1987). On the other side of the Atlantic, among the European imperial powers at the turn of the century, the loss of virility was equated with national decline (Weeks 1981; Nye 1989; Mosse 1968). As historian George Mosse argues: "Manliness was invoked to safeguard the existing order against the perils of modernity, which threatened the clear distinction between what was considered normal and abnormality . . . [and] symbolized the nation's spiritual and material vitality" (Mosse 1985, 23).

The masturbation diagnosis in its various pathophysiological schemes was particularly versatile in accounting for conflicting views of homosexuality: that sexual inversion was a *disease* on the one hand, that it was a *perversion* on the other; that it was a result of *impotence* and also a product of *insatiable* sexual appetite. In whatever shape it was molded, the masturbation hypothesis gave a supposedly scientific basis to judge sexual inversion as a pathological state. But it appears that the pathological condition did not lie so much in the sexually inverted patients but in society itself. The sexual invert in the late nineteenth century became the seed around which crystallized a variety of social fears: fears that were warranted given the economic and political upheavals of the time but that could not be effectively treated by the medical regimentation of sexual activity.

## References

Acton, William. [1875] 1987. "The Functions and Disorders of the Reproductive Organs, in Childhood, Youth, Adultage, and Advanced Life, Considered in Their Physiological, Social and Moral Relations." Extract, pp. 57–73 in *The Sexuality Debates*. Edited by Sheila Jeffreys. New York: Routledge and Kegan Paul.

Beard, George. 1886. *Sexual Neurasthenia*. New York: E. B. Tweat.

Bell, Luther Vose. 1840. *An Hour's Conference with Fathers and Sons in Relation to a Common and Fatal Indulgence of Youth*. Boston: Whipple and Damrell.

Blackwood, Evelyn. 1984. "Sexuality and Gender in Certain Native American Tribes." *Signs* 10: 27.

Blake, John B. 1984. "Mary Gove Nichols, Prophetess of Health." Pp. 359–375 in *Women and Health in America*. Edited by J. W. Leavitt. Madison: University of Wisconsin Press.

Bleys, Rudi C. 1995. *The Geography of Perversion: Male-to-Male Sexual Behavior Outside the West and the Ethnographic Imagination, 1750–1918*. New York: New York University Press.

Blumer, Alder. 1882. "A Case of Perverted Sexual Instinct (*Contrære Sexualempfindung*)." *American Journal of Insanity* 39: 22–35.

Boerhaave, Hermann. [1708] 1742. *Academic Lectures on the Theory of Physic*. 5 vols. London: W. Innys.

Bonnemaison, Julien. 1875. "Sur un cas d'hystérie chez l'homme." *Archives générales de médecine*, 6th ser., 25: 664–679.

Bowler, Peter. 1989. *Evolution: The History of an Idea*. Berkeley: University of California Press.

Buican, Denis. 1984. *Histoire de la génétique et de l'évolutionisme en France*. Paris: Presses Universitaires de France.

Bullough, Vern L., and Martha Voght. 1976. "Homosexuality and Its Confusion with the 'Secret Sin' in pre-Freudian America." Pp. 112–124 in *Sex, Society and History*. Edited by Vern L. Bullough. New York: Science History Publications.

Chauncey, George. 1982–1983. "From Sexual Inversion to Homosexuality: Medicine and the Changing Conceptualization of Female Deviance." *Salmagundi* 58: 114–146.

Clevenger, Shobal. 1881. "Hunger and Primative Desire." *Science* 2: 14.

———. 1903. *The Evolution of Man and His Mind. A History and Discussion of the Evolution and Relations of the Mind and Body of Man and Animals*. Chicago: Evolution Publishing.

D'Emilio, John, and Estelle Freedman. 1988. *Intimate Matters: A History of Sexuality in America*. New York: Harper and Row.

Dohousset. 1892. "Impregnation of One Sexual Pervert Female by Another." *Alienist and Neurologist* 13: 545–546.

Freud, Sigmund. [1935] 1951. "A Letter from Freud." *American Journal of Psychiatry* 107: 786–787.

———. 1985. *The Complete Letters of Sigmund Freud to Wilhelm Fliess, 1887–1904*. Edited by Jeffrey Masson. Cambridge, MA: Harvard University Press.

Gibson, Margaret. 1997. "Clitoral Corruption: Body Metaphors and American Doctors' Constructions of Female Homosexuality, 1870–1900." Pp. 108–132 in *Science and Homosexualities*. Edited by V. Rosario. New York: Routledge.

Gove, Mary S. (Nichols). 1839. *Solitary Vice: An Address to Parents and Those Who Have the Care of Children*. Portland, ME: Journal Office.

Graham, Sylvester. [1833] 1975. *A Lecture to Young Men*. New York: Arno Press.

Greenberg, David F. 1988. *The Construction of Homosexuality*. Chicago: University of Chicago Press.

Haeckel, Ernst. 1866. *Generelle Morphologie der Organismen*. 2 vols. Berlin: George Reimer.

———. [1874] 1891. *Anthropogenie, oder Entwickelungsgeschichte des Menschen*. Leipzig: W. Englemann.

Haggerty, George. 1999. *Men in Love: Masculinity and Sexuality in the Eighteenth Century*. New York: Columbia University Press.

Hamilton, Allan. 1895. "The Civil Responsibilities of Sexual Perverts." *American Journal of Insanity* 50: 501–511.

Hammond, William. 1882. "The Disease of the Scythians (*morbus feminarum*)." *American Journal of Neurology* 1: 339–355.

Howard, William Lee. 1900. "Effeminate Men and Masculine Women." *N. Y. Medical Journal* 21: 686–687.

Howe, Joseph W. 1883. *Excessive Venery, Masturbation, and Continence. The Etiology, Pathogenesis, Treatment*. New York: Bermingham and Co.

Hughes, Charles H. 1891a. "Note on the Virile Reflex." *Alienist and Neurologist* 12: 44–46.

———. 1891b. "Perversions of the Sexual Feeling." [Editorial.] *Alienist and Neurologist* 12: 423–425.

———. 1892. "The Alice Michel Case." [Editorial.] *Alienist and Neurologist* 13: 554–557.

———. 1893a. "Erotopathia—Morbid Eroticism." *Alienist and Neurologist* 14: 531–578.

———. 1893b. "Postscript to Paper on 'Erotopathia'—An Organization of Colored Erotopaths." *Alienist and Neurologist* 14: 731–732.

Katz, Jonathan Ned. 1983. *Gay/Lesbian Almanac*. New York: Harper and Row.

Kennedy, Hubert. 1988. *Ulrichs: The Life and Work of Karl Heinrich Ulrichs, Pioneer of the Modern Gay Movement*. Boston: Alyson Publications.

Kiernan, James. 1884b. Letter to the Editor. *Detroit Lancet* 8: 121.

———. 1891. "Psychological Aspects of the Sexual Appetite." *Alienist and Neurologist* 12: 188–219.

————. 1892. "Responsibility in Sexual Perversion." *Chicago Medical Recorder* 3: 185–210.

Krafft-Ebing, Richard von. 1882. "Perverted Sexual Feeling." Translated by E. W. Saunders. *Alienist and Neurologist* 3: 373–376.

————. 1886. *Psychopathia Sexualis: Eine klinische-forensische Studie.* 1st ed. Stuttgart: Ferdinand Enke.

Landor, Henry. 1871. "Insanity in Relation to the Law." *American Journal of Insanity* 28: 56–77.

Lydston, George Frank. 1889. "Sexual Perversion, Satyriasis, and Nymphomania." *Medical and Surgical Reporter* 61: 253–258; 281–285.

Maccubbin, Robert P., ed. 1987. *Tis Nature's Fault: Unauthorized Sexuality during the Enlightenment.* Cambridge: Cambridge University Press.

Magnan, Valentin. 1885. "Des anomalies, des aberrations et des perversions sexuelles." *Progrès médicale,* 2nd ser., 13:49–50, 65–68, 84–86.

Micale, Mark S. 1990. "Charcot and the Idea of Hysteria in the Male: Gender and Mental Science, and Medical Diagnosis in Late Nineteenth-Century France." *Medical History* 34: 363–411.

————. 1995. *Approaching Hysteria: Disease and Its Interpretations.* Princeton, NJ: Princeton University Press.

Moreau (de Tours), Paul. 1884. "On the Aberration of the Genesic Sense." *Alienist and Neurologist* 5: 367–385.

Morel, Bénédict A. 1857. *Traité des dégénérescences physiques, intellectuelles et morales de l'espèce humaine et des causes qui produisent ces variétés maladives.* Paris: Baillière.

Mort, Frank. 1987. *Dangerous Sexualities. Medico-Moral Politics in England since 1830.* London: Routledge and Kegan Paul.

Mosse, George L. 1968. "Max Nordau and His Degeneration." Introduction to *Degeneration* by Max Nordau. New York: Howard Fertig.

————. 1985. *Nationalism and Sexuality: Respectability and Abnormal Sexuality in Modern Europe.* New York: Howard Fertig.

Nye, Robert A. 1989. "Sex Difference and Male Homosexuality in French Medical Discourse, 1800–1930." *Bulletin of the History of Medicine* 63: 32–51.

*Onania.* [1715] 1986. New York: Garland Press.

Oosterhuis, Harry. 2000. *Stepchildren of Nature: Krafft-Ebing and the Making of Sexual Identity.* Chicago: University of Chicago Press.

Pernick, Martin. 1985. "Politics, Parties and Pestilence: Epidemic Yellow Fever in Philadelphia and the Rise of the First Party System." Pp. 356–371 in *Sickness and Health in America.* Edited by J. W. Leavitt and R. L. Numbers. Madison: University of Wisconsin Press.

Pick, Daniel. 1989. *Faces of Degeneration, A European Disorder, c. 1848–c. 1918.* Cambridge, UK: Cambridge University Press.

Review of *Psychopathia Sexualis with Special Reference to Contrary Sexual Instinct* by Richard von Krafft-Ebing. 1893. *American Journal of Insanity* 50: 91–95.

Rosario, Vernon. 1996. "Pointy Penises, Fashion Crimes, and Hysterical Mollies: The Pederasts' Inversions." Pp. 146–176 in *Homosexuality in Modern France.* Edited by J. W. Merrick and B. Ragan. New York: Oxford University Press.

————. 1997a. *The Erotic Imagination: French Histories of Perversity.* New York: Oxford University Press.

Roscoe, Will. 1994. "How to Become a Berdache: Toward a Unified Analysis of Gender Diversity." Pp. 329–372 in *Third Sex, Third Gender: Beyond Sexual Dimorphism in Culture and History.* Edited by Gilbert Herdt. New York: Zone.

Rosen, George. 1985. "The First Neighborhood Health Center Movement: Its Rise and Fall." Pp. 475–489 in *Sickness and Health in America.* Edited by J. W. Leavitt and R. L. Numbers. Madison: University of Wisconsin Press.

Rosenberg, Charles. 1962. *The Cholera Years.* Chicago: University of Chicago Press.

Rotundo, Anthony. 1987. "Learning about Manhood: Gender Ideals and the Middle Class Family in Nineteenth-century America." Pp. 35–51 in *Manliness and Morality.* Edited by J. A. Mangan and James Walvin. New York: St. Martin's Press.

Dr. Rozier. 1830. *Des habitudes secrètes ou des maladies produites par l'onanisme chez les femmes.* 3rd ed. Paris: Audin.

Shrady, George F. 1884. "Perverted Sexual Instinct." *The Medical Record* (NY) 26: 70–71.

Sibalis, Michael. 1996. "The Regulation of Male Homosexuality in Revolutionary and Napoleonic France, 1789–1815." Pp. 80–101 in *Homosexuality in Modern France.* Edited by J. Merrick and B. T. Ragan, Jr. New York: Oxford University Press.

Smith-Rosenberg, Carol. 1985. *Disorderly Conduct: Visions of Gender in Victorian America.* New York: Knopf.

Solomon, Samuel. 1800. *A Guide to Health; or Advice to Both Sexes.* 52nd ed. Stockport, England: J. Clarke.

Spitzka, Edward. 1881. "Gynomania." *The Medical Record* (NY) 19: 359.

Stengers, Jean, and Anne van Neck. 1984. *Histoire d'une grande peur: La masturbation.* Brussels: Editions de l'Université de Bruxelles.

Sulloway, Frank. 1983. *Freud, Biologist of the Mind.* New York: Basic Books.

Tardieu, Ambroise Auguste. [1857] 1878. *Etude médico-légale sur les attentats aux mœurs.* 7th ed. Paris: J.-B. Baillière.

Thomasset, Claude, and Danielle Jacquart. 1985. *Sexualité et savoir médicale au Moyen Age.* Paris: Presses Universitaires de France.

Tissot, Samuel-Auguste-André-David. [1760] 1991. *L'Onanisme, ou Dissertation physique sur les maladies produites par la masturbation.* 7th ed. Reprint ed., Paris: Editions de la Différence. Translated as *Onanism.* New York: Garland Press, 1985.

Trumbach, Randolph. 1998. *Sex and the Gender Revolution: Heterosexuality and the Third Gender in Enlightenment London.* Chicago: University of Chicago Press.

Ulrichs, Karl Heinrich. [1864–1879] 1994. *The Riddle of "Man-Manly" Love: The Pioneering Work on Male Homosexuality.* Translated by Michael A. Lombardi-Nash. 2 vols. Buffalo, NY: Prometheus.

Weeks, Jeffrey. 1981. *Sex, Politics, and Society: The Regulation of Sexuality since 1800.* London: Longman.

Westphal, Karl Ernest. 1869. "Die Conträre Sexualempfindung: Symptom eines neuropathischen (psychopathischen) Zustandes." *Archiv für Psychiatrie* 2: 73–108.

Woodward, Samuel B. [1838] 1856. "Hints for the Young in Relation to the Health of Body and Mind." Boston: G. W. Light.

## Further Reading

This chapter covers a wide sweep of time as well as vast transformations in the history of medicine. Readers interested in learning more about classical and medieval medicine in relation to sex and sexuality can refer to Joan Cadden's *Meanings of Sex Difference in the Middle Ages: Medicine, Science, and Culture* (Cambridge: Cambridge University Press, 1993). It will help make better sense of humoral theory and its centrality to medical physiology for millennia. For more on the early history of masturbation, see Jean Stenger and Anne Van Neck's *Masturbation: The History of a Great Terror* (New York: St. Martin's Press, 2001). For a broader cultural study of autoeroticism, see *Solitary Pleasures: The Historical, Literary, and Artistic Discourses of Autoeroticism* (New York: Routledge, 1995), a collection of essays edited by Paula Bennett and Vernon Rosario. Randolph Trumbach's *Sex and the Gender Revolution*, vol. 1: *Heterosexuality and the Third Gender in Enlightenment London* (Chicago: University of Chicago Press, 1998) provides a dense social history of sexuality in eighteenth-century England, exploring the many manifestations of gender transgressive behaviors and identities, such as "sodomy." Michel Foucault's *The History of Sexuality: An Introduction* (New York: Vintage, 1990) is one of the most influential books on nineteenth-century European sexology and provides the theoretical foundation for much contemporary work in the history of sexuality.

Paul Starr's *The Social Transformation of American Medicine: The Rise of a Sovereign Profession and the Making of a Vast Industry* (New York: Basic Books, 1982) is the classic history of the evolution of the American medical profession from surprisingly chaotic and humble origins to its current managed care crisis. Similarly, Gerald Grob's *Mental Illness and American Society, 1875–1940* (Princeton, NJ: Princeton University Press, 1983) is the best history of the American psychiatric profession and its institutional move from insane asylums to more lucrative outpatient psychiatry. *The Care of Strangers: The Rise of America's Hospital System* (New York: Basic Books, 1987) by Charles E. Rosenberg is a more accessible account of American medicine. The theory of degeneration is critical to the medical perspective on homosexuality in the nineteenth century and is carefully examined by Daniel Pick in *Faces of Degeneration, A European Disorder, c.1848–c.1918* (Cambridge: Cambridge University Press, 1989).

Peter Gay's entertaining yet scholarly *Education of the Senses,* the first volume of his series on *The Bourgeois Experience: Victoria to Freud* (New York: Oxford University Press, 1984), relies on a psychoanalytic perspective to explore the surprisingly un-Victorian psychology of sexuality in nineteenth-century England and the United States. Victorian sexual behaviors and attitudes are also well covered in John D'Emilio and Estelle Freedman's *Intimate Matters: A History of Sexuality in America* (New York: Harper and Row, 1988), which is one of the most approachable surveys on the subject. They especially pay attention to same-sex relations in U.S. history. For a grand survey of homosexuality globally and from prehistory to the present, David F. Greenberg's sociological study, *The Construction of Homosexuality* (Chicago: University of Chicago Press, 1988), is exceedingly readable and richly documented.

# 2

# *Turn-of-the-Century Sexual Inverts*

In the New York *Medical Record* of 1881, a mysterious Dr. H— described what he believed to be a new disorder, which he named "gynomania." He outlined the case of a man who had become addicted to masturbation and cross-dressing at an early age. After forswearing these habits until he had married and had children, the patient returned with new fury to his transvestite predilections—even attending church in drag! Dr. H— begged his medical brethren for assistance in treating this strange disorder. In the meanwhile, he prescribed abstinence from masturbation and a strict regimen of nonstimulating foods. As we have seen in the previous chapter, these had long been advocated by American health reformers such as Sylvester Graham and John Harvey Kellogg (of cracker and cereal fame, respectively) as means of treating and preventing the much-dreaded disease of masturbation. These sorts of dietary and environmental therapies were part of the venerable tradition of humoral medicine. However, medicine had been moving forward, thanks particularly to European scientific advances.

Edward Spitzka (1852–1914), a prominent New York neurologist, promptly responded to Dr. H—'s appeal by informing him that this was not a new condition but an example of "contrary sexual feeling" that Europeans had already extensively described and declared incurable. Dr. H—'s gynomaniac thus became the first officially diagnosed contrary sexual in the United States. The European-trained Spitzka (who was notably disdainful of American medicine) nevertheless misdiagnosed the case. Dr. H— gave no indication that his patient was attracted to men—he merely enjoyed cross-dressing. The case demonstrates how a variety of "symptoms" were conflated in the diagnosis of "contrary sexuality" or "sexual perversion." Any gender atypicality in behavior, anatomy, or dress, as well as same-sex attraction, could be the basis for diagnosing someone as a sexual invert or "psychosexual hermaphrodite."

*Sanitarium electric bathroom, Kalamazoo, Michigan, c. 1900. "Hydrotherapies," electrical or Faradic treatment, and dietary therapies were popular, old-fashioned treatments in Victorian America for a variety of ailments, including the supposedly neurodegenerative condition of sexual inversion (Archive Photos).*

Doctors desperately searched for or simply assumed a variety of anatomical, psychological, neurological, and hormonal hermaphroditic traits in the invert. The sexual attraction of a woman for a woman, for example, could not be simply seen as an independent psychological phenomenon; doctors felt that it had to result from the persistence of a masculine factor of some sort. In the case of men, doctors believed that "true" or congenital inverts had to possess some degree of effeminacy and, like "normal" women, were attracted to virile men. Doctors did not believe that these virile male lovers of the "fairy" or "pansy" were inverts themselves but simply immoral or sexually indiscriminate men. The idea that two inverts could be attracted to each other was inconceivable—gender complementarity was assumed to be an inescapable law of nature.

## The Discovery of American "Erotopaths"

Dr. H—'s patient may have been the first officially (mis)diagnosed invert in the United States, but after him, a torrent of cases poured forth. American medical literature of the turn of the century, like its European counterpart earlier, seems to have become obsessed with inversion or perversion, especially among marginalized groups: American Indians, blacks, poor immigrants, and women. Several physicians, especially U.S. surgeon general William Hammond (discussed in Chapter 1), showed an interest in Native American *bote, berdache,* or *mujerados:* men who took on female social roles as well as male sexual partners. Other doctors disputed Hammond's hypothesis of the creation and function of *mujerados* and described other tribes in which *bote* specialized in fellatio (oral sex) rather than sodomy (anal sex). Rural physicians later described the female counterparts to the *berdache.* These people were all used as examples of the "primitive" morality of American Indians (Seligman 1902; Trexler 1995).

The medical press published brief, tabloidlike news bulletins about "negro sexual perverts" and police raids of "colored erotopath" drag balls. Dr. Charles H. Hughes, editor of the prestigious *Alienist and Neurologist,* painstakingly described in his journal one such "orgie [*sic*] of lascivious debauchery beyond pen power of description" (1893b). At this annual "drag dance" in Washington, D.C., black men—or "colored erotopaths," as he called them—were "lasciviously dressed in womanly attire, short sleeves, low-cut dresses and the usual ball-room decorations and ornaments of women, feathered and ribboned head-dresses, garters, frills, flowers, ruffles, etc. and deported themselves as women." They danced around the "naked queen (a male)," who stood on a pedestal offering his beribboned "phallic member" for all to palpate. Hughes was shocked that members of this "lecherous gang of sexual perverts and phallic fornicators" were domestics to high-class Washington families or were "subordinates in the Government departments" (1893b). Even more worrisome were "homosexualist" balls where men of different races mixed promiscuously (1907).

Other sensational articles reported on passing women, wives who eloped with their sapphic lovers, and lesbian love crimes. Probably the most widely publicized lesbian crime of passion was the Alice Mitchell

NORMA TRIST

A STORY OF THE
INVERSION OF THE SEXES.
Price, 50 Cents.

Cover illustration from Dr. John Wesley Carhart's Norma Trist: A Story of the Inversion of the Sexes (1895), a lesbian love story perhaps inspired by the notorious Alice Mitchell-Freda Ward murder case of 1895 (Library of Congress).

case in 1892 (Duggan 1993). In reporting on it, Dr. Griswold Comstock enthused: "The facts about Alice Mitchell will long be treasured in medical works on insanity, and mental and moral perversion" (1892). Alice developed an "unnatural passion" for Freda Ward, a young woman of a good Memphis family. Alice proposed marriage to Freda, and the latter accepted. They planned to elope, and Alice would take on a male identity and role so they could marry. However, their plans were foiled by Freda's family. Threatened with permanent separation from Freda, Alice murdered Freda by slashing her throat. At Alice's trial, medical experts argued she was insane. Comstock, who had treated Alice's mother thirty years previously, declared: "Physically, Alice Mitchell was a woman, but psychically her cerebral functions were those of a male, and still her preferences, like other Urnings—were for her own sex" (172). Relying on Richard von Krafft-Ebing's theory of hereditary degeneration, Comstock blamed Alice's condition on her mother's own history of insanity.

The case led to suspicious reevaluation of adolescent girls' crushes and women's same-sex intimacy as hotbeds for lesbian love (see Sidebar 2.1). The growing women's movement and its trailblazers, the "New Women," also provoked doctors' concerns. In Chapter 1, we encountered Dr. William L. Howard's searing condemnation of "the female possessed of masculine ideas of independence" (1900). Not only did he equate feminists with lesbians, but he blamed them all for being unnatural mothers: "The weak, plastic, developing cells of the brain are twisted, distorted, and a perverted psychic growth promoted by the false teachings of a discontented mother. These are

# The Mannish Maid

You frown upon your gentle sex,
And mannish traits assume;
With Nature's perfect harmony
You're sadly out of tune.
Just be content to be yourself
And here, for thought is food,
The greatest gift of God to Man
Is gentle Womanhood.

*Bishop*

the conditions which have been prolific in producing the antisocial 'new woman' and the disgusting effeminate male, both typical examples of the physiological degenerate." Howard was not alone in his opinion of New Women. Medical writers into the 1910s still claimed that "it is only the male element in emancipated women that craves for emancipation. Women really interested in intellectual matters are sexually intermediate forms" (Weininger 1918).

Doctors could attribute these types of sexual perversity to the "natural" mental and moral debility of American Indians, blacks, and women. However, as Dr. Howard indicates, physicians and the general public feared that middle-class, male perversion was also on the rise. Both the medical and popular press increasingly reported cases of blackmail, homosexual crimes of passion, and police raids on underground homosexual clubs. Medical social critics blamed these ills on the effects of modernity, particularly urbanization and leisure culture. The disruption of nuclear families, the women's emancipation movement, the commingling of classes and races, foreign influences, irreligion, political liberalism, excess wealth and leisure, and titillating popular entertainment—all sorts of social ills seemed to conspire in the generation of perverts. Male perversity especially seemed to threaten the hereditary vigor of the nation and thus provoked far more careful professional consideration than lesbianism.

*The New Women of the turn of the century sought higher education, a professional career, and equal rights for women. This caricature lampoons them as "mannish maids," urging them to return to traditional Victorian domestic roles (Gibson Art Company).*

## Sidebar 2.1 The "Forbidden Fruit": Interracial Crushes

Psychologist Margaret Otis reported in the *Journal of Abnormal Psychology* (1913–1914) that "a form of perversion that is well known among workers in reform schools and institutions for delinquent girls, is that of love-making between white and colored girls." Until the late nineteenth century, passionate same-sex friendships had been common and even socially approved since socializing between the sexes, particularly before marriage, was frowned upon. Historians have documented same-sex declarations of love in medieval Europe (Boswell 1994). In Victorian United States, upper-class spinster couples sharing a household were called "Boston marriages." Although some of them were well-hidden sexual relationships, these intimate friendships were generally not socially suspect or condemned (Faderman 1981). In the late nineteenth century, however, this tolerance grew thin. Growing professional and public awareness of homosexuality had begun to make same-sex schools and intimate friendships highly suspicious. The previously benign schoolgirl "crush" was now a potential lesbian affair.

In the case of Otis's reform school, the element of racial intercourse heightened the anxieties about sexual perversity. The interracial love affairs had become such a problem at the institution that segregation was enforced, which only added the element of "the forbidden fruit." The affairs were largely conducted through clandestine notes passed between the race-segregated buildings. Although Otis admits that some of these notes "show the feeling of true love," she quickly adds that they also betray "the expression of a passionate love of a low order, many coarse expressions are used and the animal instinct is seen to be paramount." At times, however, their passion "seems almost ennobling":

> On one occasion a girl, hearing that danger threatened her love in another cottage, was inconsolable, quite lost her head and called out: "Oh my baby! my baby! What will become of my baby!" . . . The intense emotion dispelled all fear and anxiety, for her love alone occupied the field of consciousness. Later, after suffering punishment for her fault, she wrote to a friend: "You can see by this that I am always thinking of you. Oh, sister dear, now this is between you and I. Lucy Jones asks me to give Baby up, for she tries to tell me that Baby does not love me. Don't you see what she is trying to do? To get my love back Ah! sister darling, I might say I will give my Baby up, but ah, in my heart I love her and always shall." (Otis 1913–1914, 115)

Otis dismissed the idea that the "nigger lovers" were mental defectives, since some of the most intelligent girls indulged in this kind of passion. She did note that gender roles seemed to correspond with race: the colored girls were accused of being the more inverted masculine aggressive partner in the couple. One white girl "admitted that the colored girl she loved seemed the man, and thought it was so in the case of the others." One concern was that, upon leaving the institution, a white girl might fall in love with and marry a black man—as did one girl. However, Otis reassured readers that the white girls rarely mixed with coloreds after leaving the school. Furthermore, the "high-class" girls had better moral standards and "despised and detested" the nigger lovers. "That water seeks its own level is true among the delinquent girls themselves," Otis concluded. "Certain sets and cliques appear, and those who are 'high up' scorn the 'common kind'" (116).

As in Europe, American medico-legal and psychiatric experts argued that willful vice had to be distinguished from irrepressible psychopathology. Only the latter mitigated responsibility and deserved a modicum of legal, if not public, sympathy. However, unlike some of the leaders in fin-de-siècle German sexology, American doctors did not go so far as to advocate the decriminalization of sodomy. Even those such as Frank Lydston, who argued that "the sexual pervert is generally a physical aberration," felt uneasy about suggesting that medicine should blur the "line of demarcation between physical and moral perversion" (1889, 253). Like many of his colleagues, Lydston was quite contradictory in proposing both *congenitalist* and *environmentalist* explanations of perversion. The congenitalist argument adopted the hereditary degeneracy model that perversion was inborn and incurable (as Spitzka informed Dr. H——). The environmentalist model suggested that perversion was acquired, like masturbation, by example or through seduction by immoral people. It was the fear of acquired perversion that prompted calls for persistent legal prosecution of inverts—or worse.

The hereditary degeneracy model, although it might offer the reassurance that inversion was not contagious, did invite eugenic interventions. Following the lead of the Italian degeneracy criminologist Cesare Lombroso, Dr. F. E. Daniel had argued that criminality and perversion were hereditary and particularly common among the poor and "negroes." *Alienist and Neurologist* (Review of *Castration*, 1895), in reviewing Daniel's article, agreed on the necessity of radical treatment: "Science and law owe it to the world and posterity, to see that crime and moral depravity are not propagated through their neglect of plain remedies. It is better that certain neuropaths should go through life maimed by castration and spaying than that their defects should be bred into unborn generations to pervert their lives and breed the misery and crime of their wrongly organized progenitors." Clearly, an understanding of inversion as hereditary and not chosen did not automatically imply tolerance.

The issue of whether homosexuality was chosen or congenital continued to play a major role in medical, legal, and social examinations of homosexuality in the twentieth century. As Dr. Howard's vitriolic indictment of effeminate men and masculine women suggests, biomedical theories could easily hypothesize that environment distorted the brain and the mind. Thus, there was no sharp distinction between nature and nurture. Physicians and biomedical scientists thereby felt they legitimately should take individual and public health measures to protect society against the spread of sexual perversion.

## A Case of "Sexual Contrariety"

The *St. Louis Courier of Medicine* (1903) reprinted a lecture by Dr. William Barker to a local medical society. Dr. Barker alerted his medical colleagues to the problem of sexual perversity masquerading as common neurological ailments. "Charlatans" may have exaggerated the morbidity of certain sexual ailments (probably referring to masturbation); nevertheless, "the medical man of today," Barker warned, should not underestimate the impact of perverted sexual feelings. They should be suspected in otherwise inexplicable cases, including instances of "shocking suicide and homicide." He presented two such mysterious cases. One was that of W——, a thirty-two-year-old married man, and B——, "the younger and passive member of the improper association." When the young man married and did "all he could to avoid this unnatural and disgusting associate," W—— murdered B—— and then committed suicide.

The second example was of L——, a twenty-year-old woman, "of a decidedly neurotic temperament." Typical for its time, Barker's case description relied on neuro-hereditary degeneracy theory. He was surprised that her family history was "fairly exempt" from nervous disorders. Nevertheless, at eighteen the patient had suffered a mysterious fit: "a kind of trance, or hystero-cataleptic state." Two years after this hystero-epileptic episode, the patient suffered a two-week attack of paralysis, aphasia (speech loss), and anorexia (loss of appetite). An unsuspecting doctor had attributed these symptoms to a cerebral hemorrhage or stroke. But Dr. Barker was more astute.

> I had previously learned about the association of another woman in this case; that the relations between the two were rather suspicious; that the hystero-cataleptic attack, occurring previously, and this peculiar condition, in which aphasia was the dominant expression, were dependent on some violent nerve storm. Direct accusation, in a confidential and kindly way, was the next step. There was some venture in the card that was played, but my knowledge of the peculiar temperament of the patient led me to expect what followed—a free confession, which made everything much clearer. She was really an honest, well-disposed person, and, convinced of only kind intentions, and shown the evil of perversion and the way to better health, her cooperation was at once gained and her "aphasia" at once disappeared, to the surprise of the rest of the household. Her improvement was rapid, a change of scene and systematic calisthenics [physical exercises] helping along. (Barker 1903, 270)

Although Barker suspected that a hereditary taint and "neurotic temperament" caused L——'s lesbianism, like other Victorian doctors, he also believed the patient's willpower—assisted by lifestyle changes and exercise—could cure her conscious perversity and her neurological ailments. Just two years later, Freud would instead suggest that homosexuality was the product of subconscious, infantile psychological dynamics—not hereditary and neurological disease. Lengthy psychoanalysis, not calisthenics, would have been the recommended treatment. Barker, however, was quite convinced of his therapeutic victory: "She married soon afterwards and has now an apparently healthy child, the *vita sexualis* [sexual life] in her case being quite normal as far as can be discovered" (271). As in other reports of homosexual conversion therapy, marriage and reproduction were the litmus test of a successful outcome.

## The Biology and Politics of Sexual Intermediates

Not all physicians were intent on pathologizing and curing homosexuality. Magnus Hirschfeld (1868–1935) was the first known homosexual sexologist and a persistent advocate for homosexual civil rights. He was born in the coastal city of Kolberg, Germany. His family was Jewish, and his father was a physician specializing in balneotherapy: seaside cures like other Victorian hydrotherapies and rest cures. His family was politically progressive, and Hirschfeld would remain a dedicated Social Democrat his whole life (Steakley 1997). He received his medical degree in Berlin in 1893. Early in his medical career he founded the Scientific Humanitarian Com-

*Sexologist Magnus Hirschfeld and his longtime partner Karl Giese, in exile from the Nazis in Nice, France, ca. 1934 (Magnus Hirschfeld Society, Berlin)*

mittee (1897), which campaigned for the decriminalization of homosexual acts. It grew to twenty-five local chapters throughout Germany, Austria, and the Netherlands by 1922. The group recruited the support of important figures such as Albert Einstein, Richard von Krafft-Ebing, and Thomas Mann. The committee also sponsored the *Yearbook of Intermediate Sexual Stages* (1899–1922), which published scientific research on homosexuality. In 1991, Hirschfeld founded the Institute for Sexual Science in Berlin, which became one of the largest interdisciplinary centers for sexology. The institute, however, was shut down with the rise of the Nazis in 1933, and the institute's extensive library and archives were burned. Hirschfeld (who was in Paris at the time with his longtime companion Karl Giese) remained in exile in France until his death in 1935. He had his life's motto engraved on his tombstone: *Per scientiam ad justiciam* (Through science to justice).

Like other homosexuals then and now, Hirschfeld trusted that the scientific understanding of sexuality would dispel religious superstition and traditional prejudice. He was profoundly influenced by Darwinism, particularly the work of Ernst Haeckel on natural variation and sexual selection. Hirschfeld was convinced that homosexuality was primarily biologically determined and he was adamantly opposed to the psychoanalytic theories of homosexuality that suggested it was the result of disordered child rearing. Instead, he believed homosexuality was a congenital form of psychosexual hermaphroditism or an intermediary sex between the ideal full male and full female. He described sexual intermediacy as a congenital "impediment of evolution" and likened it to color blindness. Homosexuality, he proposed, was one of many natural variations of sexual behavior and structure among plants and animals. Relying on Haeckel's "universal biogenetic law" (that ontogeny recapitulates phylogeny), Hirschfeld highlighted the embryological bisexuality of *all* mammals. Some degree of bisexuality should thus be expected in adult humans as well. In 1912, he hypothesized that both male and female hormones (which he speculatively named "andrin" and "gynecin") would be discovered in every individual. It was actually not until the 1920s that sex steroids were isolated, and indeed males and females were found to have both estrogens and androgens (Kenen 1997).

Hirschfeld was convinced homosexuality was the result of endocrinological factors. He was impressed by Eugen Steinach's experiments in altering the sexual behavior of rats with testicular implants or by castration. These interventions supposedly could make female rats exhibit male sexual behavior and vice versa. Although Hirschfeld did not believe that homosexuality was a disease, he nonetheless referred

## Sidebar 2.2 A Letter from an Invert (1919)

William J. Robinson (1867–1936), chief of the Department of Genito-Urinary Diseases and Dermatology at Bronx Hospital and a friend of homosexual rights advocate Dr. Magnus Hirschfeld, edited the *American Journal of Urology and Sexology*. The journal frequently published items on homosexuality, including the following poignant letter from an anonymous invert in 1919:

> I know you will disagree with me, but it is my belief that two men who love each other have as much right to live together as a man and a woman have. Also that it is as beautiful when looked at in the right light and far more equal!
>
> There are many men who believe as I do. One might say they are abnormal. Does that have anything to do with the right or wrong of the question? To sleep all day, to work all night, is an abnormal condition. It isn't natural. Does that go to prove that the one who does it is right or wrong? There is that abnormal condition; to bring in a moral question would be foolishness. "Wrong" and "abnormal" seem to mean the same thing to many people. Or shall I put it—"wrong" and "unnatural"? From the way people look at me who know my belief, you would think me a leper or a negro!
>
> May I not have as high an ideal in my love towards men, as a man towards a woman? Higher no doubt, than most men have toward women!
>
> The idea people hold is making me bitter. All that I might be is being killed. I can understand the thoughts of Jean Valjean [the hero of Victor Hugo's novel *Les Miserables*], who held to his high ideals and asked only to be left alone—yet had to lose his whole life fleeing, ever fleeing, from people.
>
> I wish the question might be discussed in your magazine. I have never known of any other magazine which gave its readers the liberty of expressing their own opinions, as gladly as your magazine does.
>
> There are reasons (positions, etc.) why it would be better to withhold my name. You need not doubt the good faith in which this letter is written.
>
> [Signed] A Man

The author indicates that literate inverts of the time turned to sexological works as one of the few sites for somewhat enlightened thinking on homosexuality. Robinson even footnoted the mention of Negroes with an observation that the correspondent himself was "no more broadminded on the racial question than most people are on the subject of sexual abnormalities and perversions" ("Letter" 1919, 455). Robinson, along with Hirschfeld, held some of the most liberal views at the time on the "homosexual question." He was not, however, unreservedly supportive. In 1914, he concluded an essay in his *Journal of Urology and Sexology* with a qualified defense: "Let us demand the abolition of all stupid laws against the homosexuals, laws which do no good but only breed disgrace and foster blackmail. Let us work for a humane, intelligent attitude towards them, but let us not minimize their faults, let us not exaggerate their virtues, in short let us not falsely idealize them" (Robinson 1914, 552).

some unhappy homosexual patients to Steinach for experimental castration and transplantation with "heterosexual" testes. Hirschfeld's usual therapeutic approach was instead to help homosexual individuals accept their sexual variation and find appropriate loving relationships.

He developed an extensive "Psychobiological Questionnaire" with which he studied over 10,000 people. His work and that of his institute were hugely influential throughout Europe and the United States. Newspapers even dubbed him the "Einstein of Sex"!

### The Psychoanalysis of Inversion

Most turn-of-the-century sexologists believed homosexuality was a product of neurohereditary degeneration, according to the model proposed by Krafft-Ebing. A few European psychologists, however, began developing models of the childhood *acquisition* of sexual predilections and of psychosexual development in general. The most influential of these were the ideas of Sigmund Freud (1856–1939) presented in *Three Essays on the Theory of Sexuality* (1905). Although, at the time, Freud had not treated any homosexuals, the first essay focused on "sexual inversion," indicating its centrality to late-Victorian sexology. He summarized and criticized the work of colleagues and advanced several original conjectures about infantile sexuality. He later bolstered and altered these theories as he gained experience working with homosexual patients.

*Sigmund Freud in 1932 (Bettmann/ Corbis)*

Freud began the *Three Essays* by differentiating *sexual object choice* (whether male, female, animal, or inanimate fetishes) from *sexual aim* (the preferred erotic acts). Sexual inversion represented an aberration of object choice: attraction to the same sex. He distinguished three varieties of inverts: (1) *absolute* inverts were exclusively attracted to the same sex; (2) *amphigenic* inverts were attracted to both sexes (what today we would call "bisexuals"); and (3) *contingent* inverts engaged in homosexual behavior because of lack of opposite-sex partners (1905, 2–3). Freud dismissed the degeneracy theories of Krafft-Ebing as well as Karl Heinrich Ulrichs's hermaphroditism model of homosexuality since there were too many otherwise healthy and masculine male inverts. He was, however, inclined to believe that all lesbians exhibited some degree of masculinity and were erotically attracted to traditionally feminine women. Freud *was* impressed by the models of universal bisexuality or "psychical hermaphroditism" advanced by American doctors George Frank Lydston and James G. Kiernan (see Chapter 1). At the time, "bisexual" did not refer to erotic attraction to both men and women, but to the possession of both male and female physical or psychological sex traits. Freud took these models of bisexuality a step further to suggest not only a universal, infantile bisexuality but a capacity for all varieties of sexual object choice and aim: "The disposition to perversions is itself of no great rarity but must form a part of what passes as the normal constitution. . . . The conclusion now presents itself to us that there is indeed something innate lying behind the perversions but it is something innate in *everyone*" (1905, 171).

The second essay developed his controversial theory of infantile sexuality, wherein lay the "germs of all the perversions" (172). Although not the first to suggest children had a sexual instinct, he elaborated a coherent and influential theory of it. He proposed that the baby's entire body was a source of autoerotic pleasure, but it became focused during early development on three zones: oral, anal, and then genital. The last occurred around age four and was accompanied by the Oedipal conflict: the boy's love for his mother is thwarted by his father through the threat of the boy's castration. Girls at this stage, according to Freud, recognize their genital inferiority and are seized with "penis envy." After this Oedipal stage, children's sexuality went into a period of *latency*. During this time, children prefer same-sex companions.

The third essay explored the erotic developments of puberty, when the individual progresses from autoerotic sexuality to attraction to other sexual objects. At this stage, the cultural demand to mate and reproduce was normally incorporated into the psyche. Most boys become interested in sex with girls. Freud expected that adolescent girls would normally shift the focus of sensual pleasure from their phallic-like clitoris to the vagina in order to mature erotically and be prepared for marital, reproductive heterosexuality. Although Freud's model was bound by conventional social values, there was also a radical aspect of his theory (Davidson 1987). Freud argued that "the exclusive sexual interest felt by men for women is also a problem that needs elucidating and is not a self-evident fact based upon an attraction that is ultimately of a chemical nature" (1905, 146n). Psychoanalytic theory suggested that we were all born "polymorphously perverse," with a capacity for sexual pleasure throughout all parts of the body and with any variety of "sexual objects" (males or females). Thus homosexual attraction was a universal and normal possibility in childhood. It was only social forces—acting through the parents—that directed most children to conventional heterosexuality once they reached puberty.

Ultimately, Freud sided with conventional values, and the third essay concludes with child-rearing suggestions for preventing inversion. He noted that the first erotic inclinations of puberty could go in many directions, usually with no long-term problems. So, even if it was common for adolescent boys and girls to develop sentimental friendships with same-sex peers, children usually still became heterosexual adults. He suggested that inversion was probably determined earlier in life, around the oedipal stage in childhood. Otherwise he hypothesized that child rearing by servants of the same sex might lead to inversion, particularly among the aristocracy. The death or absence of the opposite-sex parent might also determine a child's sexual object choice. However, even on the topic of the "prevention of inversion," Freud showed an unusual open-mindedness. He concluded that the main deterrent to homosexual orientation was the "authoritative prohibition by society." "Where inversion is not regarded as a crime," Freud wrote, "it will be found that it answers fully to the sexual inclinations of no small number of people" (229).

On the cause of homosexuality, Freud steered a course between congenitalist and environmental models—neither of which he felt explained all cases fully. Originally, he seemed confident that psychoanalysis would elucidate the psychological origins of homosexuality. Later in his career, as new biological research was published in the first decades of the twentieth century, he came to believe that there was an unalterable organic foundation to the "problem of homosexuality" (147 n.). Freud's position on homosexuality was surprisingly tolerant for his time. He stated firmly in the *Three Essays* that "psychoanalytic research is most decidedly opposed to any attempt at separating off homosexuals from the rest of mankind as a group of a special character" (145, n. 1). He also argued against the exclusion of homosexuals from analytic training—something the institutes nevertheless did until the 1990s. In a letter written in 1935 and posthumously published in 1951, he reassured the mother of a homosexual man that the condition was nothing shameful, degraded, or sick (Freud 1935). Nevertheless, he still believed it was abnormal and the result of arrested psychosexual development. Over the years, Freud explained this contradiction though a variety of psychoanalytic scenarios, mainly concentrating on male homosexuality.

Initially, in the *Three Essays,* he suggested that the homosexual man had overidentified with his mother and, as an adult, sought young men who reminded him of himself so he could love them as his mother had loved him. Freud also proposed that it was the boy's horror upon discovering his mother's castration at the Oedipal stage that led him to turn to effeminate young men who represented a "woman with a penis." After Freud had fully developed the notion of the Oedipal conflict with the father, he explained that homosexuality was the result of a negative or inverted Oedipus complex: a boy subconsciously chose his father as a sexual object and sought to be a woman his father could love. Finally, Freud hypothesized that homosexuality might paradoxically result from sibling rivalry through "reaction formation": a boy's fratricidal wishes were subconsciously transformed into love of men (Lewes 1988).

Freud's ideas initially met with great resistance in Europe but found strong adherents in the United States. Not particularly fond of Americans, Freud was anxious that the easily won popularity of psychoanalysis in the United States was a result of Americans' misunderstanding of his theories. In the case of sexual inversion, American psychoanalysts, particularly after Freud's death in 1939, distorted or discarded Freudian explanations and tolerance for homosexuality (see Chapter 4).

Abraham A. Brill (1874–1948) was one of the first advocates of psychoanalysis in the United States. He was the first to translate Freud's early psychoanalytic works into English, including the *Three Essays* in 1910. Brill's views at that time represent some of the most liberal in the United States. He firmly dismissed the old associations between masturbation, homosexuality, and degeneracy. He believed that homosexual experiences and masturbation were often intermediary stages in the evolution of normal heterosexuality and did no harm in themselves. "Most of the inverts I know," he bravely stated, "belong to our highest types both mentally and physically and show absolutely no hereditary taint" (Brill 1913, 336). He argued that everyone has a homosexual component "which allows us to get along and form friendships with people of our own sex " (1935, 251). Most homosexuals, he claimed, did not want to be "cured," nor could they be. The class of homosexuals who *did* seek therapy were of the "compulsion neurotic type," and these, he and many of his colleagues believed, could be cured (Brill 1935, 250).

Other psychoanalysts were less optimistic. Hungarian analyst Sándor Ferenczi (1873–1933) completely rejected the notion of congenital homosexuality. He believed the "homosexual component" was a universal element in childhood sexuality. He distinguished between two types of homosexuals: (1) passive homosexuals, or "subject-homoerotics," who experienced inversion of psychic gender; and

(2) active homosexuals, or "object-homo-erotics," who were not gender inverted. The former he believed to be completely incurable, although analysis might help relieve their anxiety symptoms. Nor could he report having great success in curing the object-homo-erotics. The number of *obsessional* homo-erotics, he believed, was on the rise in modern society because of the "exaggeration of hetero-eroticism for the purpose of repressing love towards the same sex," which increasingly failed (1911, 267). Ferenczi's social diagnosis suggests that the public awareness of and anxiety about homosexuality had become so widespread that it was causing a homophobic reaction. The mechanisms of this harmful defense against homoeroticism were later formulated in the concept of "homosexual panic" (see Chapter 3).

### The Debate over Homosexual Analysts

On December 1, 1921, psychoanalyst Ernest Jones wrote to Sigmund Freud in Vienna about a query from the Dutch psychoanalytic society concerning the application of a homosexual man to training there. Jones had advised the Dutch against it; however, he still sought Freud's opinion: "Do you think this would be a safe general maxim to act on?" Freud replied in a terse letter circulated among the institutes and cosigned by Otto Rank:

> Your query, dear Ernest, concerning prospective membership of homosexuals has been considered by us and we disagree with you. In effect we cannot exclude such persons without other sufficient reasons, as we cannot agree with their legal prosecution. We feel that a decision in such cases should depend upon a thorough examination of the other qualities of the candidate. (December 11, 1921)

Jones retorted: "It is hard to see how [homosexuals] could perform a thorough [psychoanalysis] with understanding. Further, our condemnation of the punishment of homosexuality does not alter the fact that to the world it is an abhorrent crime, the committal of which by one of our members would certainly discredit us seriously" (December 21, 1921). From Berlin, analysts Karl Abraham, Hanns Sachs, and Max Eitington circulated a letter in which they generally agreed with Freud and Rank, but they expressed serious reservations: "We have had the experience that homosexuals with an overt behavior pattern can travel only part of the way with us" (January 11, 1922).

Freud and Rank replied: "We recognize the arguments against the analytic participation of homosexuals as somewhat of a guideline.

But we have to warn against making it into a law considering the various types of homosexuality and the different mechanisms of their cause" (January 22, 1922). Although the analytic institutes did not establish a formal rule excluding homosexual trainees, they effectively did so fairly openly until the 1990s. Only in 1992 did the American Psychoanalytic Association adopt a formal resolution that opposed discrimination against homosexuality in the selection of analytic trainees and supervisors (Magee and Miller 1997, 234). Meanwhile, many homosexuals did gain analytic training by not confessing their orientation and suffered greatly as they struggled to change sexual orientation or remain in the closet (Isay 1996).[1]

## Inversion: Genetic or Psychogenic?

In the early decades of the twentieth century, doctors continued to debate whether homosexuality might be congenital or not. A purely psychodynamic theory of causation certainly suggested the possibility that all homosexuals were potential candidates for psychoanalytic conversion therapy. Yet even those who minimized congenital explanations continued to believe a subclass of inverts had some degree of gender-atypical behavior or physiognomy. Thus many medical articles focused on cross-dressing "fairies" and virile women. Throughout the interwar period, congenitalist and environmental theories and organic and psychological models of homosexuality competed or were hybridized as physicians developed new approaches to restoring "normal" heterosexuality.

## Notes

1.  This correspondence was discovered in the 1970s in the Otto Rank Collection (IIa / 238–254) in the Rare Book and Manuscript Library of the Columbia University Libraries. It was translated by historian James Steakley and excerpted by Spiers and Lynch (1977). I am grateful to Professor Steakley for corrections and additional material not previously published.

## References

Barker, William S. 1903. "Two Cases of Sexual Contrariety." *St. Louis Courier of Medicine* 28: 269–271.

Boswell, John. 1994. *Same-Sex Unions in Premodern Europe.* New York: Villard.

Brill, Abraham Arden. 1913. "The Conception of Homosexuality." *Journal of the American Medical Association* 61: 335–340.

————. 1935. "The Psychiatric Approach to the Problem of Homosexuality." *The Journal-Lancet* 55: 249–252.

Comstock, T. Griswold. 1892. "Alice Mitchell of Memphis. A Case of Sexual Perversion or 'Urning' (a Paranoiac)." *N. Y. Medical Times,* September 20, 170–173.

Davidson, Arnold I. 1987. "How to Do the History of Psychoanalysis: A Reading of Freud's *Three Essays on the Theory of Sexuality.*" *Critical Inquiry* 13: 215–409.

Duggan, Lisa. 1993. "The Trials of Alice Mitchell: Sensationalism, Sexology, and the Lesbian Subject in Turn-of-the-Century America." *Signs* 18: 791–814.

Faderman, Lillian. 1981. *Surpassing the Love of Men: Romantic Friendship and Love between Women from the Renaissance to the Present.* New York: William Morrow.

Ferenczi, Sándor. [1911] 1916. "The Nosology of Male Homosexuality." Pp. 250–268 in *Contributions to Psychoanalysis.* Translated by Ernest Jones. Boston: Richard G. Badger.

Freud, Sigmund. [1905] 1955. *Three Essays on the Theory of Sexuality.* In *Standard Edition* 7: 136–137.

————. [1935] 1951. "A Letter from Freud." *American Journal of Psychiatry* 107: 786–787.

Howard, William L. 1900. "Effeminate Men and Masculine Women." *N. Y. Medical Journal* 21: 504–505.

Hughes, Charles H. 1893b. "Postscript to Paper on 'Erotopathia'—An Organization of Colored Erotopaths." *Alienist and Neurologist* 14: 731–732.

————. 1907. "Homo Sexual Complexion Perverts in St. Louis." *Alienist and Neurologist* 28: 487–488.

Isay, Richard. 1996. *Becoming Gay: The Journey to Self-Acceptance.* New York: Pantheon.

Kenen, Stephanie H. 1997. "Who Counts When You're Counting Homosexuals? Hormones and Homosexuality in Mid-twentieth-century America." Pp. 197–218 in *Science and Homosexualities.* Edited by V. Rosario. New York: Routledge.

"Letter from an Invert, A." 1919. *American Journal of Urology and Sexology* 15: 454–455.

Lewes, Kenneth. 1988. *The Psychoanalytic Theory of Male Homosexuality.* New York: Simon and Schuster.

Lydston, George Frank. 1889. "Sexual Perversion, Satyriasis, and Nymphomania." *Medical and Surgical Reporter* 61: 253–258, 281–285.

Magee, Maggie, and Diana Miller. 1997. *Lesbian Lives: Psychoanalytic Narratives Old and New.* Hillsdale, NJ: Analytic Press.

Otis, Margaret. 1913–1914. "A Perversion Not Commonly Noted." *Journal of Abnormal Psychology* 8: 113–116.

Review of *Castration of Sexuals Perverts* by F. E. Daniel. 1895. *Alienist and Neurologist* 16: 109.

Robinson, William Josephus. 1914. "My Views on Homosexuality." *American Journal of Urology and Sexology* 10: 550–552.

Seligman, C. G. 1902. "Sexual Inversion among Primitive Races." *Alienist and Neurologist* 23: 11–15.

Spiers, Herb, and Michael Lynch. 1977. "The Gay Rights Freud." *Body Politic* (Toronto) 33: 8–10.

Steakley, James D. 1997. "*Per scientiam ad justitiam:* Magnus Hirschfeld and the Sexual Politics of Innate Homosexuality." Pp. 133–154 in *Science and Homosexualities.* Edited by V. Rosario. New York: Routledge.

Trexler, Richard. 1995. *Sex and Conquest: Gendered Violence, Political Order, and the European Conquest of the Americas.* Ithaca, NY: Cornell University Press.

Weininger, Otto. 1918. "The Masculine Element in Emancipated Women." *American Journal of Urology and Sexology* 14: 240.

## Further Reading

Lillian Faderman's two volumes on the history of women's same-sex relationships in Europe and the United States are moving and well documented: *Surpassing the Love of Men: Romantic Friendship and Love between Women from the Renaissance to the Present* (New York: William Morrow, 1981) and *Odd Girls and Twilight Lovers: A History of Lesbian Life in Twentieth-Century America* (New York: Columbia University Press, 1991). They examine women's romantic friendships, schoolgirl crushes, and early feminism at the turn of the century.

Ethnographies of so-called primitives from Africa and the New World were important in shaping Enlightenment ideas of natural history and Victorian sexology, lending an anthropological and historical model for the evolution of "civilized" sexuality. Rudi Bleys's *The Geography of Perversion: Male-to-Male Sexual Behavior Outside the West and the Ethnographic Imagination, 1750–1918* (New York: New York University Press, 1995) is the most extensive analysis of the connections between anthropology and the medical construction of homosexuality. For contemporary, anthropological perspectives on same-sex behaviors beyond contemporary Europe and the United States, see the fascinating essays in Gilbert Herdt's anthology, *Third Sex, Third Gender: Beyond Sexual Dimorphism in Culture and History* (New York: Zone Books, 1994). *Changing Ones: Third and Fourth Genders in Native North America* (New York: St. Martin's Press, 1998) by anthropologist Will Roscoe sensitively examines the complex nature of the *bote,* or "third-sex" people in different North American Indian cultures.

There is a huge, multifaceted industry of Freudian scholarship, both clinical and academic. The classic biographical study of Sigmund Freud, written by his disciple Ernest Jones, is *The Life and Work of Sigmund Freud* (New York: Basic Books, 1953). Frank Sulloway's exhaustive intellectual history of Freud places psychoanalysis in the context of Victorian science: *Freud, Biologist of the Mind* (New York: Basic Books, 1983). Sulloway is particularly critical of the mythology erected around Freud by his psychoanalytic followers. The most comprehensive history of Freud's reception in the United States and the evolution of U.S psychoanalysis is Nathan Hale, Jr.'s two-volume *Freud in America* (New York: Oxford University Press, 1971 and 1995).

# 3

## From the Gay Twenties to Homosexual Panic

In 1929, neurologist John Meagher (1880–1931) noted in the pages of the *Urologic and Cutaneous Review* (a journal specially dedicated to venereal diseases and sexuality): "There has been a particularly great increase of morbid homosexuality since the war, especially in Europe. This, in part, was due to the changed social conditions and altered ways of living" (505). To many physicians, the postwar period was literally the "gay twenties." In the United States—as much as in Europe—the social impact of World War I, continued urbanization and immigration, and economic prosperity had all contributed to promoting gay communities in the big cities. Urban doctors were fully aware of this fact, and the ever-increasing medical publications on homosexuality ensured that physicians could no longer be surprised by the phenomenon.

The two major models of the nature of homosexuality tended to generalize homosexuality. The dominant *psychoanalytic model* argued that homosexuality was a universal, normal stepping-stone in infantile psychosexual development. The *somatic model* (most notably promoted by Magnus Hirschfeld [1901]) proposed that some degree of intersexuality, particularly hormonal, was the cause of homosexuality. In either case, the implication that everyone was potentially homosexual could lead to two opposing conclusions. Some physicians, particularly in the Roaring Twenties, argued that homosexuality was a widespread psychosexual variation that did not necessarily imply mental disorder; therefore, it did not require any medical interventions. However, many social hygienists perceived that homosexuality was on the rise. They feared that untold numbers of young people, whose developing sexuality was teetering between normality and perversity, might be tipped over toward homosexuality because of incorrect gender education, bad example, or seduction. These social hygienists became anxious and vigilant about preventing a potential epidemic of "sexual perversion" and its associated ills.

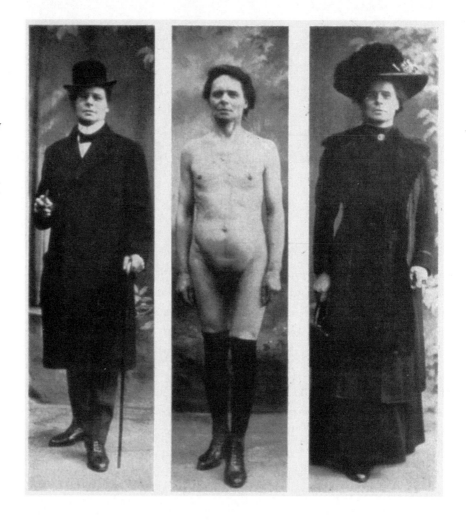

*Magnus Hirschfeld published these photos of Frederike Schmidt "as a man, naked, and as a woman in customary garb" (Magnus Hirschfeld Gesellschaft, Berlin).*

### "Does the 'Fairy' or 'Fag' Really Exist?"

Dr. Perry M. Lichtenstein, author of *A Handbook of Psychiatry* (1943), posed the question of whether fairies really exist. He regretted to have to answer: "There is no doubt but that this type of degenerate is a reality" (1921, 369). As a physician to inmates of New York prisons and houses of detention, he claimed to have encountered several hundred of them. His experience was quite skewed since most of these would have been individuals arrested for prostitution or public sex or simply because they were flamboyant enough to provoke police suspicion and harassment. Not surprisingly, Lichtenstein asserted that the fairy is a "freak of nature who in every way attempts to imitate women" (369).

As historian George Chauncey has amply documented in *Gay New York* (1994), by the 1920s New York City was teaming with homosexuals who had developed a rich and surprisingly visible subculture. There were distinct types of homosexuals, with their characteristic sartorial styles, jargon, and affectations. The term *queer* could be applied to all homosexually active men, but more specifically it referred to masculine-appearing homosexuals. The terms *fairy*, *fag*, or *queen* were reserved for effeminate homosexuals. Lichtenstein reported that fags "take feminine names, use perfume and dainty stationery which frequently is scented, and in many instances they wear women's apparel" (1921, 370). He described one twenty-year-old fairy with an effeminate walk and voice. He also lisped, and "when interviewed his answers were usually prefixed by 'my dear.'" Some fairies were young runaways who worked as prostitutes to survive. Others sought sexual gratification with "trade": "normal"-appearing heterosexually identified men who nonetheless enjoyed sex with men. Lichtenstein noted that these men who patronized "fags" sometimes set them up in handsome apartments. He reserved his most vehement condemnation for the john, or trade, "for such as he are worse than the pervert and deserve no sympathy" (374). As with female prostitutes, one of the great anxieties concerning fairies was that they transmitted venereal diseases. Lichtenstein related the story of a recently discharged soldier, fresh from France, supposedly being lured unsuspecting into a fairy's bed. The soldier awoke in the middle of the night while being sodomized by the "fag," who turned out to be syphilitic.

*Magnus Hirschfeld's 1903 illustration of the spectrum of sex from the "full male," to the "Uranian" or homosexual, to the "full female" (Magnus Hirschfeld Gesellschaft, Berlin).*

Lichtenstein did not neglect lesbians, or "lady lovers," as he called them. He claimed they were most commonly found among prisoners, chorus girls, and nurses. Although many had a virile habitus and sported masculine clothes, Lichtenstein noted that it was not the rule. He echoed the frequently made claim that lesbians had an enlarged clitoris (Gibson 1997). Lichtenstein guessed that the size was due to the practice of "bull diking" or "friction of the clitoris." Apparently, lady lovers were less of a public nuisance than fairies. To the contrary, he observed that "because of their dislike for men, they are, as a rule, looked upon by the community as virtuous" (373). They only came to public attention when a postmortem revealed that a deceased "husband" was really a crossdressed "lady lover."

*A double invert couple (1930): "the woman is a feminine man, the man a virile woman with a glued-on moustache" (Magnus Hirschfeld Gesellschaft, Berlin).*

The social role of the fairy and the lady lover, as well as Lichtenstein's medical explanation of them, fit the Victorian model of gender inversion. Accordingly, these perverts supposedly were only attracted to conventionally gendered individuals, not others like themselves. For doctors of the time, such profound gender inversion strongly implied a hereditary and somatic taint. Like many of his contemporaries, Lichtenstein approvingly cited Richard von Krafft-Ebing's theory of the hereditary degeneration of homosexuals (1886). Nevertheless, Lichtenstein also insisted that most of the perverts he had examined had no hereditary taints. He also claimed that fairies could be the result of defective childrearing, such as allowing boys to crochet, sew, and play with dolls. Whatever the cause of inversion, if the pervert committed "sex crimes," Lichtenstein recommended confinement in "intermediary institutions" where therapy might be implemented. He suggested that even hormonal treatment be attempted. His simultaneous and seemingly contradictory reliance on both psychological and biological explanations for homosexuality was, nevertheless, typical for the time. Even psychoanalysts who claimed that homosexuality was the product of infant-parent interactions would later recommend hormonal and shock therapies in addition to psychotherapy. Such punitive approaches to homosexuality were not universal, however. The homosexual advocacy of physicians such as Havelock Ellis and Magnus Hirschfeld, both of whom promoted the biological model, was taken to heart by many prominent physicians—including Sigmund Freud.

## Nature's Sex Stepchildren

In a brief article in 1919, Dr. G. Frank Lydston outlined his theory of the "biochemical basis of sex aberrations." Lydston was a professor of genito-urinary surgery and syphilology (the diagnosis and treatment of syphilis) in the State University of Illinois medical school. He had been writing on sexual inversion since the 1880s. His article summed up his decades of experience and proposed a hypothesis of the biology of homosexuality that is uncannily similar to current neurodevelopmental theories. "Sexual perversion and inversion—with or without physical aberrations—are purely biochemic in origin," he insisted. They were the result of defective hormonal effects on sperm, egg, and uterine environment. He prefigured research published by Günther Dörner in the 1980s that maternal psychic "accidents" could lead to in utero hormonal imbalances that, in turn, produced homosexual offspring (Dörner et al. 1980).

Although Lydston did not cite them by name, he was probably inspired by the work of Hirschfeld and the Viennese physiologist, Eugen Steinach (1861–1944). The latter had transplanted testes and ovaries in rodents to demonstrate the impact of glandular secretions on sexual development and behavior. Prompted in part by Hirschfeld's theories of homosexual intersexuality, Steinach attempted to cure effeminate homosexuals by castrating them and providing them with transplanted testicles of "normal" heterosexuals. In keeping with this hormonal logic, Lydston advocated the early detection and treatment of sexual perverts through sex gland implants. Even Hirschfeld—one of the most vocal defenders of homosexual civil rights—referred a few homosexuals who were unhappy with their sexuality to Steinach for testicular treatment. These operations were largely ineffective, or worse, severely debilitating.

Supporters of the biological model did not inevitably advocate the treatment of homosexuality. William Robinson, as we have seen in Chapter 2, advocated a sympathetic approach to "nature's sex stepchildren" (Krafft-Ebing's term). In an article in the *American Journal of Urology* (a journal Robinson edited), he condemned "our ignorant attitude towards any sexual abnormality, our brutal treatment of any man found guilty of homosexuality or of any other sexual perversion" (1914, 550). He admitted that his own attitude toward homosexuals had become "broader, more tolerant" over the years, thanks to meeting many homosexuals, "among them lovable, sympathetic types, some men and women of high intelligence" (1925, 475). Nevertheless, he still could not help "regarding the homosexual as abnormal, even if not inferior" (476). Despite his lingering queasiness, he was opposed to laws against homosexuality—that is, "true homosexuality." He firmly believed that true homosexuality was the congenital type. "As to the essence of homosexuality," he declared, "I stand on the biological basis and have no faith in incidental causes, such as seduction, infantile trauma, etc." (476). He vehemently dismissed psychoanalysts' claims of having ever cured a case of true homosexuality.

Other advocates of the biological model were even more liberal in their teachings on homosexuality. In 1931, Dr. Abraham Wolbarst lectured the New York Physicians Association on "Sexual Perversions: Their Medical and Social Implications." He urged his colleagues to abandon the moralistic approach to the subject and instead see it scientifically as a widespread variation of the sex life. Although he presented homosexuality as an abnormality, he also argued that coitus interruptus and celibacy were logically also perversions of natural intercourse. He called for abolition of outdated and ineffective laws criminalizing homosexuality (other than public or nonconsensual sex). As far as therapy was concerned, he urged colleagues to become better informed and to consider cases individually and sympathetically. In congenital cases in particular, he proposed: "We may possibly find ourselves on the correct road if we act on the theory that any sexual deviation which has always given satisfaction without injury to any particular individual must be considered normal for that individual. Moreover, it would be both unfair ethically and unsound scientifically to attempt to impose a conventionalized, arbitrary sex life on an individual which was not in complete harmony with his natural sex endowment" (64). Those who suffer because of their sexuality might find psychotherapy helpful, he concluded, but in no instance should it be imposed against the subject's will. Wolbarst's tolerance for homosexuality was in complete harmony with that of Freud—although not necessarily of other American psychoanalysts.

The biological, intermediate-sex model could even support enthusiastic paeans to homosexuals. Dr. Florence Beery (1924) explained Havelock Ellis's congenital bisexuality theory and firmly rejected the rigid psychoanalytic explanations of Wilhelm Stekel (discussed below). She went on to praise the psychology of the intermediate sex: "Homo-sexuals are keen, quick, intuitive, sensitive, exceptionally tactful and have a great deal of understanding. . . . Contrary to the general impression, homosexuals are not necessarily morbid; they are generally fine, healthy specimens, well developed bodily, intellectual[ly], and generally with a very high standard of conduct" (5). She gave the degeneration model a romantic interpretation by explaining that the homosexual "biologically stands nearer the less civilized types of mankind than the normal person," which led to a "precocious development of instinct" (5). Beery rejected claims that all homosexuals were betrayed by cross-sexed anatomical traits and could thereby be easily recognized. The "homo-genic woman," for example, generally had a thoroughly feminine body, Beery declared. It was her temperament that was "active, brave, originative, decisive. Such a woman is fitted for remarkable work in professional life or as a manageress of institutions, even as a ruler of a country" (7).

Although Robinson was not as enthusiastic as Beery about homosexuals, he did allow his journals to be a platform for their advocates, including one particularly flamboyant and outspoken "fairie boy," Earl Lind, who wrote under another alias, Ralph Werther, and his drag name, Jennie June. Werther published the first installment of his "Autobiographical Sketch" in Robinson's *American Journal of Urology and Sexology* in 1918 and completed it in 1934. He detailed his childhood as a "Nancy boy" and his discovery of the working-class fairy world of New York when he was a college student. Two years later, Werther continued his saga with personal wisdom about the "biological sport of fairie-ism" (referring to natural "sports" or mutations). Like Robinson, Werther argued that fairie-ism was constitutional: "I have probably made a more thorough study of male inversion than any sexologist—being myself an extreme androgyne," he proudly claimed. "I am emphatically of the opinion that the condition is practically always congenital" (1920, 242). He was therefore vehemently anti-Freudian. He dismissed claims of a cure, whether psychological or hormonal—having tried them all in vain himself.

## Psychoanalytic Readjustment

Even some psychoanalysts expressed skepticism about the possibility of "curing" homosexuality. In 1934, Dr. Ernst Bien posed the perplexing question: "Why Do Homosexuals Undergo Treatment?" Many doctors believed that fear of legal punishment impelled homosexuals to seek "readjustment." After all, the Victorian scientific literature on "sexual inversion" had emerged from a medico-legal context. Physicians versed in giving expert testimony or performing forensic evaluations had first described cases of "perverts" caught in the legal system because of public sex charges or because their relatives, distressed by their sexual inversion, had sought to have homosexual family members declared mentally unfit to dispose of their estate. However, from Bien's experience with twenty-two homosexual cases in his private practice, he concluded that none of the self-consciously homosexual subjects "had an instinctive longing for a change in his sexual attitude because of a dissatisfaction with the homosexual activity *per se*" (17). Most consulted psychiatrists because of other neurotic (anxiety) complaints, family coercion, or unhappiness over their inability to find an adequate same-sex partner. However, not a single homosexual case desired to change his or her sexuality because of legal or familial threats. Only four out of five bisexual patients desired and achieved a cure of their homosexuality.

Bien's study highlights the critical importance of considering from where research patients are recruited. Early researchers often overlooked this important bias in their clinical experience. A group of homosexuals (or indeed any category of subjects) recruited from a private practice can be dramatically different than a group collected from a prison hospital or a psychiatric asylum. All of these clusters of *patients* can differ significantly in terms of demographics (gender, race, socioeconomic status, education, etc.) and psychopathology from *non-patients:* people in the general population recruited randomly at home or from other non-clinical settings.

Psychoanalyst Abraham A. Brill was even more firm in coming to similar conclusions based on his experience with homosexuals in his private practice. "Only very few [homosexuals] seek treatment with the idea of becoming sexually normal; they are always neurotics who are either not satisfied with their homosexuality or have deep conflicts about it. Only the latter can be cured" (1935, 250). Families often forced homosexuals to undergo analysis. "You cannot do anything for such people," Brill concluded; "they do not wish to be cured, so it is simply a waste of time and money; they always remain the same" (250). The best thing to do in such situations was to induce the family to be more "broad-minded." Despite the vocal opposition of biologically oriented psychiatrists to the psychoanalytic model of homosexuality and despite many psychoanalysts' reservations about the value of analytic conversion therapy, the psychoanalytic approach continued to gain popularity among psychiatrists. But even then, there were many variations and a spectrum of professional attitudes toward homosexuality.

### The Psychoanalysis of Lesbianism

Freud wrote very little on lesbianism, and similarly, American analysts and psychiatrists generally devoted relatively scant attention to female homosexuality. Male homosexuality, sexual passivity, and effeminacy preoccupied the male-dominated profession, as well as legal authorities (Magee and Miller 1997). Freud's main statement on lesbianism appeared in an article entitled "The Psychogenesis of a Case of Homosexuality in a Woman." Here he described the case of an eighteen-year-old girl brought to him by her parents because of her devotion to a twenty-eight-year-old "society lady." Freud concluded that it was a case of congenital homosexuality, and he held out little hope of converting her to heterosexuality. The analysis, nevertheless, led him to the conclusion that the patient's homosexuality resulted from a revived Oedipal conflict at puberty. Her desire to have her father's baby was frustrated by her unconscious

At uptown New York clubs in the 1920s, not only could gays and straights mix but also different races. African American singer Gladys Bently was a cross-dressing lesbian who was open about her sexuality (Library of Congress).

rival—her mother. Resentful of her parents, "she turned away from her father and from men altogether. After this first great reverse she forswore her womanhood and sought another goal for her libido" (1920, 157).

Freud added that the young woman had retained a strong "masculinity complex" from childhood. She had been a tomboy and refused to be second to her older brother. Around age five, she had inspected his genitals and developed, according to Freud, "a pronounced envy for the penis," which continued to account for her politics. "She was in fact a feminist," Freud continued, "she felt it to be unjust that girls should not enjoy the same freedom as boys, and rebelled against the lot of women in general" (169). Freud felt that the patient transferred to him her "sweeping repudiation of men"—particularly her father. Sensing that he would fail to establish a positive transference (or therapeutic bond), Freud terminated treatment and recommended to the parents that she see a woman doctor.

Female psychoanalysts were not necessarily any more sympathetic to lesbianism. Helene Deutsch (1884–1982), one of Freud's leading disciples, was also an ardent feminist. She had been the founding president of the Vienna Psychoanalytic Training Institute, and she moved permanently to Boston in 1935, where she founded the Boston Psychoanalytic Society. Deutsch and Karen Horney (1926, 1933) were pioneers in addressing the matters of femininity, motherhood, and female libido—all seriously neglected in Freud's phallocentric theories.

Three years before her move to the United States, Deutsch published "On Female Homosexuality" (1932). Here she summarized her experience treating eleven lesbians. Female homosexuals, Deutsch argued, are unable to deal with the discovery of their castration and the consequent "thrust into passivity." Their libido instead turns from the father to the mother in a sadistic fashion since they blame her for their castration and the denial of their father's child. Mannish lesbians refused to accept their castration; instead, they sought confirmation of their masculinity through phallic masturbation with a woman. Lesbian relationships thus reenacted a variety of sadistic and masochistic mother-daughter conflicts and affections, either at the oral or phallic phases.

## Universal Homoeroticism

In his *Three Essays on the Theory of Sexuality* (1905), Freud had proposed that all infants began life "polymorphously perverse": every part of the body was a source of erotic pleasure. As psychosexual development proceeded, distinct body parts (mouth, anus, genitals) would become the focus of pleasure, and even sexual object choice (whether hetero- or homosexual) was ingrained through training and accident. In other words, from an unrestricted bisexuality, all individuals could theoretically develop in a hetero- or homosexual direction. In a famous 1915 addition to the *Three Essays,* Freud went even further in universalizing homoeroticism: "By studying sexual excitations other than those that are manifestly displayed, [psychoanalysis] has found that all human beings are capable of making a homosexual object-choice and have in fact made one in their unconscious. Indeed, libidinal attachments to persons of the same sex play no less a part as factors in normal mental life, and a greater part as a motive force for illness, than do similar attachments to the opposite sex" (145 fn.).

Some American doctors took to heart the radical implications of Freud's ideas. Clarence P. Oberndorf (1929) noted that American attitudes toward sex had become far less Victorian in the past few years. Homosexuality had become a topic for polite dinner conversation, at least in educated circles. Yet this familiarity did not necessarily lead to enlightened views. He politely ridiculed one physician who wrote that "lesbianism flows from idleness, boredom, and loneliness" (519). He even noted that the "distressed and fatalistic wail" of the lesbian heroine in Radclyffe Hall's *The Well of Loneliness* (1928) was hardly an accurate representation of current understandings of homosexuality. Hall's novel had fired a scandal in England when it was first published and then had promptly been banned as an "offense against public decency." Its heroine is an unhappy, masculine lesbian who makes frequent allusions to medical theories in order to explain her inversion. Oberndorf rejected these hereditary degenerationist models of sexual inversion. "As a matter of fact," he continued, "all people are homosexual to a limited degree, if we use the term in its very broadest application, and very few people pass through life without participating in some sexual experience, transiently or for a period of some time, of slight or greater intensity, with a person of the same sex" (1929, 519).

Nevertheless, he still believed that "homosexuality is a diseased process" and proposed a somewhat less rigid distinction than Wilhelm Stekel between biological and psychological homosexuality. Stekel (1868–1940), an Austrian analyst and early Freudian, had proposed a sharp dichotomy between effeminate, "passive" male homosexuality (which he claimed was congenital) and masculine, "active" homosexuality (which was a neurosis). Stekel (1930) made the same distinction between the masculine, aggressive lesbian and the feminine, passive lesbian. Oberndorf suggested that only a few cases were associated with biological deviations and that *most* homosexuality was a compulsive neurosis.

The inverse theory—that homosexuality *produced* compulsive neurosis—was one logical implication of the psychoanalytic generalization of homoeroticism. As Freud's comment cited above suggests, psychoanalysts lent a great deal of importance to *repressed, unconscious* homosexuality in the genesis of psychopathology. If, as Oberndorf claimed, everyone could be assumed to be homosexual to a certain degree, then perhaps any neurotic manifestation might be a symptom of repressed homosexuality. Doctor Robert Riggall proposed that alcoholism might serve the function of allowing repressed homosexuality to the surface. Artistic genius, he suggested, might be a form of neurotic defense mechanism against homosexuality. Even excessive displays of heterosexuality might fit the bill: "Don Juanism, . . . so far from proving a man's heterosexuality, may even be proof of his homosexuality" (1923, 159). Doctor John Meagher (1929) went even further when he suggested that physicians hostile to discussions of homosexuality should be suspected themselves of being latent homosexuals. The psychoanalytic theory of repressed or subconscious homosexuality introduced a form of homoparanoia: female frigidity, male impotence, premature ejaculation, and unhappy marriages were all suspected of having homosexual roots. One of the strongest corollaries of this theory was that paranoia and even schizophrenia were deeply rooted in homosexuality.

### Schizophrenia and Homosexuality

Psychoanalyst and historian Kenneth Lewes estimates that at least a third of *all* psychoanalytic articles until 1930 were about the "discovery" that schizophrenia, especially of the paranoid type, was a product of homosexuality (1988, 59). This theory was widely accepted as indubitable in the early twentieth century but today is thoroughly discredited since schizophrenia is believed to be primarily an organic brain disorder. Nevertheless, one of the theory's byproducts, the notion of "homosexual panic," remains in popular and even legal usage. It was developed by Dr. Edward Kempf (1885–1971) in his textbook *Psychopathology* (1921), and was often referred to as "Kempf's disease" (Karpman 1943; James 1947). It continues to be raised as a legal defense, as in the case of Matthew Shepard, a college student brutally slain by two young men in 1998. They claimed that Shepard had made sexual advances on them and that his behavior had triggered a "homosexual panic" during which they assaulted him. The court disallowed this use of the homosexual panic insanity defense. Indeed, it is a gross distortion of the concept of homosexual panic as originally described in the early twentieth century.

Freud had suggested in 1911 that repressed passive homosexual desires had contributed to the paranoid psychoses of judge Daniel Paul Schreber (1842–1911). Freud had not actually interviewed Schreber but had analyzed the judge's *Memoirs of My Mental Illness* (1903). Among many psychotic symptoms during his several bouts of mental illness, Schreber had suffered delusions that he was being persecuted by his doctor, who was feminizing Schreber's body. Divine rays would then impregnate him, and he would spawn a new race of men to save the world. Freud interpreted these troubling symptoms as psychotic fantasies expressing Schreber's desires to be sodomized by his doctor. These homosexual yearnings, however, could not be admitted into consciousness because of Schreber's strong moral sense. Instead, they were transformed by the defense mechanisms of *reaction formation* and *projection:* the forbidden feeling "I love him" became reversed as "I hate him" and was projected onto the doctor as "he hates me."

The Hungarian analyst, Sándor Ferenczi later generalized this principle. He surmised that "in the pathogenesis of paranoia, homosexuality plays not a chance part, but the most important one, and that paranoia is perhaps nothing else at all than disguised homosexuality" (1912, 133). His primary example was quite personal. His housekeeper's husband (initially a faithful servant "most desirous of giving me satisfaction") developed the delusion that his wife was having an affair with the doctor and threatened to kill his master (133–139).

The diagnosis of "homosexual panic," however, sprang from less domestic settings. The difficult living conditions and carnage of World War I directly contributed to a new medical condition termed "shell shock"—a form of male hysteria (Showalter 1985, 167). The crowded, all-male living conditions of military life also seem to have elicited panic reactions inflected with paranoia. These were the sorts of cases that caught Edward Kempf's attention, particularly since he was based at the Government Hospital for the Insane in Washington, D.C. (later renamed St. Elizabeth's Hospital). He defined homosexual panic as "panic due to the pressure of uncontrollable perverse sexual cravings" (1921, 477). The typical case involved a young man in his twenties who developed delusions that his friends, comrades, or even strangers believed that he was a homosexual: they stared at him strangely, whispered insults like "cock sucker," "woman," "fairy," and tried to induce him to engage in fellatio or sodomy. In many cases, the patient believed he was being poisoned with "dope," "cocaine," "cream," or, straightforwardly, semen. Some hallucinated that they heard voices accusing them of homosexual desires. Some suffered visual and sensory hallucinations of engaging in homosexual activities. The cases that Kempf presented also suffered panic attacks: sudden, brief episodes of fear with profuse sweating and a racing heart. Sometimes alcohol was a precipitant, as in Dr. Robert Riggall's cases (1923).

Kempf observed that in the worst instances, the homosexual paranoia could become chronic, and thus the patient progressed to a diagnosis of dementia praecox, or schizophrenia. (*Démence précoce* was a syndrome of premature intellectual decline and psychosis described by Bénédict Morel in 1852. Emil Krepelin renamed it dementia praecox in 1896 and it became synonymous with our current diagnosis of schizophrenia in the early twentieth century.) Since, according to some psychoanalytic theorists, homoeroticism—if only of the unconscious variety—was universal, then it might be possible that all cases of dementia praecox had a homosexual cause. Indeed, this hypothesis become so commonplace that one doctor called schizophrenia the "twin brother" of homosexuality. Dr. John Ernst stated as an established fact that paranoid dementia praecox "is always on a homosexual basis" (1928, 385). It is evident from his case studies that even in patients with no apparent indications of homosexuality, Ernst coaxed them, perhaps even badgered them, into confessing to some degree of homoeroticism. Take, for example, the case of F. C., a twenty-year-old man with delusions that people were making derogatory remarks about him, supposedly because of the bad odor of his perspiration. Doctors told him that his symptoms were a result of the fact that he was subconsciously homosexual and was projecting his own sense of guilt and uncleanness. After he refused to acknowledge this "fact," Ernst continued to press F. C. "to admit frankly to himself that he was biologically or congenitally homosexual" in order to make his "adjustment" less difficult. Ernst reassured F. C. that many inverts could successfully sublimate their sexuality into artistic or creative work. "This takes away the feeling of isolation and that they are social outcasts despised by all men," Ernst added patronizingly (1928, 384). After this attempt at being goaded to confess his repressed homosexuality, F. C. never returned for further psychotherapy.

Not only did many psychoanalysts believe that all paranoid schizophrenics were latent homosexuals, but some analysts also inverted the association. They proposed that overt homosexuals were at a particularly high risk of paranoia and schizophrenia. One Arkansas analyst, L. N. Bollmeier, described such a case in 1938. The twenty-four-year-old patient had what was, by then, the typical family background of homosexuals: a domineering, overattached mother and an aloof father. From the age of four he had developed a penile inferiority complex after he watched an older boy masturbate but then was unable to imitate him. Bollmeier explained that the patient's overt homosexual activity was a defense against his sense of masculine inferiority and his castration anxiety. Bollmeier reasoned that when these anxieties became too great and if the patient refused to turn to the homosexual defense mechanism, he would suffer from paranoid delusions that he was being trailed by detectives.

In this and F. C.'s case, as in most of the other published examples of homosexual schizophrenia, the patients do genuinely seem to be suffering from paranoia and psychoses. In many, the latent homosexual content of their delusions appears quite prominent. In some cases, such as Bollmeier's, patients consciously recognized their homosexual desires and acted on them. Psychiatrists erred, however, in identifying homosexuality as the *cause* of psychosis. Many of Kempf's and other doctors' patients had *heterosexual* erotic leanings or delusions, yet doctors did not claim that heterosexuality caused paranoia. The ill effects of the *repression* of homosexual desire should not be dismissed, however. For example, one married man (who had been seduced by a clergyman) reported that his paranoid feelings were regularly relieved by indulging in homosexual acts (Bollmeier 1938). Psychiatrists generally did not recommend the obvious, simple solution of indulging the homosexual desires to relieve the anguish and anxiety of repressed erotic yearnings. Some did suggest that recognition and acceptance of repressed homosexuality was the best relief for the psychiatric disorder; nevertheless, the analysts then proceeded to encourage the patient to consciously resist homosexual urges.

Although it appears that many homosexual men, burdened with guilt, did seek psychoanalytic "cures" (Duberman 1991; Isay 1996), others fought the analytic models. Henry Gerber (1892–1972) was one of the most astute critics of psychoanalysis. Gerber was born in Germany and emigrated to the United States in 1914. In 1924, he and six friends formed the first homosexual rights organization in the United States, the Society for Human Rights, which was legally chartered in Illinois (Katz 1976, 385–388). Writing under the pseudonym "Parisex," he published "In Defense of Homosexuality" (1932) as a rebuttal to Dr. W. Beran Wolfe's essay "The Riddle of Homosexuality," which had appeared in the April issue of *The Modern Thinker.* Wolfe had argued for the psychotherapeutic readjustment of homosexuality rather than its legal persecution. Although Gerber appreciated Wolfe's legal stance, he accused psychoanalysis of nonetheless creating a new form of persecution. Echoing some of Krafft-Ebing's homosexual correspondents fifty years earlier, Gerber insisted that homosexuality was not a neurosis in itself—it was societal pressure that led to homosexuals' mental disturbance. He was familiar with the German medical literature, particularly the work of Magnus Hirschfeld, which he endorsed and which he translated for *ONE Institute Quarterly* (an early homosexual journal, described in Chapter 5). However, Gerber still believed that homosexuality was probably the product of *both* hereditary and social factors (Katz 1976, 393). He was quite dedicated in sending similarly vigorous rebuttals to national magazines. In a 1944 letter to *Time,* he pointedly declared: "The subsidized psychiatrist—yes-man—always wears a policeman's badge under his white frock. . . . Those who refuse to believe the political, religious, and moral fairytales current in our conventions, are styled psychopaths, degenerates, perverts, radicals, infidels, etc." (quoted in Katz 1983, 561). Gerber was bravely writing at a time when there was an escalation in the media's preoccupation with "sexual perverts."

### Sex Fiends

During the early twentieth century, there was a continuing influx of immigrants into the crowded and increasingly squalid cities. The foreign poor were regularly accused of lacking moral restraint and blamed for the "social vice" of prostitution. Public hygienists especially worried about the spread of venereal diseases associated with prostitution. In 1910, John D. Rockefeller, Jr., chaired a grand jury charged with investigating "white slavery" and prostitution in New York City. As a continuation of this work, he established the Bureau of Social Hygiene in 1911. On its advisory board was Katharine Bement Davis (1860–1935), who conducted the first extensive sociological study of American women's sexuality, including lesbianism (1929) (see Sidebar 3.1). The bureau and other agencies funded by the Rockefellers supported much research into sexology and "problems of sex."

After the war, social anxieties escalated over "sex offenses"—not just prostitution but also voyeurism, indecent exposure, homosexuality, molestation of minors, and rape. One of the more liberal voices on

## Sidebar 3.1 The Sex Life of 2,200 Women

Katharine Bement Davis (1860–1935) joined the advisory board of the Bureau of Social Hygiene in 1911 at the behest of John D. Rockefeller, Jr. As warden of the Reformatory for Women at Bedford Hills, New York, she had gained much experience working with prostitutes—the main concern of the bureau. She had been successful in rehabilitating prostitutes through education and skills training. In 1912, Rockefeller funded her new Laboratory for Social Hygiene, which collected data on prostitution. In 1914 she was appointed commissioner for corrections of New York City prisons.

Through the 1920s, with the bureau's support, Davis conducted the first extensive sociological survey of female sexuality. Unlike many previous, smaller studies that examined institutionalized women, Davis studied "normal" women—college-educated females. The extensive questionnaire collected information on demographics, sex, sexuality, and satisfaction in relationships, marriage, and career. She also included questions on homosexuality. In her summary of the data, *Factors in the Sex Life of Twenty-two Hundred Women* (1929), she noted that nonanecdotal information on lesbianism was severely lacking. Her data filled a gaping scientific vacuum with some surprising information.

The study of 1,200 unmarried, college women (conducted with Maria E. Kopp), showed that 51.2 percent of these experienced "intense emotional relationships with other women" (Davis 1929, chap. 10). Over one-quarter of this population reported overt homosexual activity, and, of these, 80 percent continued to engage in overt homosexuality. Of those involved in some level of homosexual attachment, half felt it was helpful and stimulating. However, half also felt shame and disapproval, which the authors attributed to the pressure of public opinion. The survey confirmed the popular notion that women's colleges stimulated close female intimacies more than coeducational schools. However, half of those women who engaged only in female attachments (without sex) reported that these attractions had begun before college. The study uncovered one interesting career finding: that overt homosexuals entered social work at a significantly higher rate than women who experienced no same-sex attachment (16.2 versus 5.9 percent, respectively). Both groups reported equivalent levels of professional satisfaction and general happiness.

Even more shocking for the time were the findings from the married college-educated women (chap. 11). Thirty-two percent of them reported having had some homosexual attachment during their life. But only eighteen of the 1,000 women in this group admitted that they continued overt homosexual activity after marriage. Homosexual relations before marriage seemed to have no adverse effect on happiness in married life. Interestingly, a greater proportion of the women who had had homosexual relationships continued to have professional careers after marriage than those who had never felt intense attachments to other women.

Similarly rich data on married and unmarried women's sexuality would not appear again until Alfred Kinsey and his colleagues published *Sexual Behavior in the Human Female* in 1953.

---

sexuality, endocrinologist Harry Benjamin, urged for a more rational approach to issues of "vice." Benjamin would later become a pioneer in the treatment of transsexualism and founder of the Harry Benjamin International Gender Dysphoria Association. In a brief, polemical essay, Benjamin argued that prostitution could not be suppressed and that instead it should be legalized, as in more enlightened European countries. The criminalization of prostitution only led to disease, blackmail, and corruption. He also suggested that a scarcity of healthy, inexpensive female prostitutes had inadvertently prompted an increase in male homosexuality—a view apparently seconded by a prominent judge. Those especially at risk were youngsters whose psychosexual development was not complete: "These boys, mostly sensitive and very emotional, are longing for more than physical gratification only. They long for love and sympathy. When at this stage a homosexual man enters their lives, their own receding or latent homosexual component is brought temporarily or even permanently to the surface again" (Benjamin 1931a, 382). In a subsequent addendum to his essay, Benjamin noted that he believed most homosexuals were born that way. He was referring only to a small number of adolescents or bisexuals who were ambiguous or psychologically plastic in their sexuality. He was quick to add that he did not intend to disparage congenital homosexuals: "A homosexual love can be as strong, as fine, as altruistic as any other love. A physical gratification of the homosexual urge is just as essential for the well-being and happiness of the individual as that of the so-called 'normal' urge, and both are equally purely private affairs with which no law has any logical right to interfere" (1931b, 119).

Although Benjamin's sympathetic view, as we have seen, was shared by some of his colleagues at the time, other figures of authority were far more alarmist—including one especially powerful suspected homosexual: J. Edgar Hoover, the director of the Federal Bureau of Investigation. In the *N.Y. Herald Tribune* of September 26, 1937, Hoover declared "War on the Sex Criminal!" He warned that "the sex fiend, most loathsome of all the vast army of crime, has become a sinister threat to the safety of American childhood and womanhood" (2). Two reports on *Sex Crimes in N. Y. C.* (in 1937 and 1938), prepared by the Staff of the Citizens Committee on the Control of Crime in New York, seemed to confirm his view. They reported a 51 percent increase in sex crimes from 1936 to 1937 and a 110 percent increase above the average for 1929 through 1935 (Shaskan 1939). The panic about sex crimes came on the heels of the Great Depression and the repeal of Prohibition in 1933, when there was a broad backlash against the perceived laxity and promiscuity of the "Roaring Twenties." New York mayor Fiorello La Guardia promised to clean up the city and in the late 1930s launched a police crackdown on venues where homosexuals regularly congregated. Although homosexuals were not a majority of sex offenders (9 percent in one study from New York County for 1932–1938), they were arrested and prosecuted with particular zeal. In 1937, La Guardia

*The New York police began to regularly raid gay bars in the 1930s, part of a general crackdown on immorality and perversion. This drag queen, "The Gay Deceiver," nevertheless seems undaunted as "she" poses in the police wagon for photo journalist Weegee in 1940 (Weegee/ Magnum Photos).*

formed a Committee for the Study of Sex Crimes that enlisted psychiatrists in the battle against perverts (Freedman 1989; Terry 1999, 275). The medical literature of the time similarly reflects an inordinate preoccupation with homosexual sex offenders.

Drs. J. Frosch and W. Bromberg (court psychiatrists in New York) reported a higher rate of "maladjusted sex life," psychopathic personality, and neurosis among homosexuals compared to other sex offenders (1939). But as we have already seen, these symptoms had practically become synonymous with homosexuality in the medical literature. Frosch and Bromberg concluded their report with a qualified recommendation for the castration of sex criminals. Earlier European and U.S. reports had touted this "surgical treatment" as an effective approach to "habitual sex offenders"—including homosexuals. For example, Marie Kopp (a collaborator with Katharine Bement Davis on lesbianism) advocated the surgical treatment of sex criminals. Drawing on the Europeans' experience, she concluded that castration and sterilization not only served in the treatment and prophylaxis of sex delinquency but also had beneficial eugenic effects (Kopp 1937–1938). She recommended that offenders be allowed to freely choose between lifelong segregation or surgical treatment.

Increasingly, homosexuals were being portrayed in the popular press and the medical literature as an insidious menace to the health and morality of society. As such, they warranted even the most severe "therapies." Dr. A. W. Hackfield of Seattle, Washington, described a group of forty "habitual sex-offenders" subjected to "therapeutic castration." He reported that the "male homosexual psychopathic personalities" in the group "after castration were cured of the desire to commit abnormal sex offenses" (sex with minors) (1935, 27). These men had volunteered for or been coerced by their families into castration. He also described a group of women who had been castrated (i.e., had their ovaries removed) because of menstrual psychosis or sexual promiscuity, but with little benefit. Hackfield hypothesized that the therapeutic action of castration consisted in reducing "sex tension" to a level at which subjects with normal intellect could control their abnormal impulses. "In properly selected and otherwise incurable male sex offenders," Hackfield optimistically concluded, "castration (aside from permanent commitment) may be regarded as the only dependable measure for the social rehabilitation of such unfortunate individuals" (180).

*The Committee for the Study of Sex Variants*

In the late 1930s, a diverse group of doctors engaged in an extensive research project on homosexuality unrivaled even today for its depth and intrusiveness. The Committee for the Study of Sex Variants was formed in 1935 at the prompting of Robert Latou Dickinson, a distinguished gynecologist dedicated to the study of "sex adjustment" and sex education (Dickinson and Beam 1931 and 1934). He had been inspired by the work of a lesbian journalist, Jan Gay. Historian Jennifer Terry (1999), who has extensively researched the committee, shows how Gay (née Goldberg) was deeply influenced by the work of Magnus Hirschfeld and his notion that homosexuals were "sexual intermediates," or a third sex between male and female (Hirschfeld 1901; Steakley 1997). Adopting Hirschfeld's 1898 sexual questionnaire, Gay interviewed hundreds of lesbians. She and a young homosexual man, Thomas Painter, were the essential members of the committee who recruited the homosexual male and female subjects. These underwent extensive psychosexual interviews by the head of the committee, psychiatrist George Henry. They were also subjected to extensive physical exams, X-ray studies, nude photography, and tracings of their genitals and nipples—relaxed and erect.

## Sidebar 3.2 Chaotic Sexuality

Aaron J. Rosanoff (1878–1943) was a Los Angeles psychiatrist and the author of a popular book, *Manual of Psychiatry and Mental Hygiene* (1938). Although psychiatrists since the 1870s had conceived of a degenerative-hereditary form of "sexual inversion," Rosanoff was the first to hypothesize a detailed genetic model of the diverse manifestations of sexuality. He published a highly conjectural article on his "theory of chaotic sexuality" (1935). He was prompted by recent advances in genetics, particularly the discovery of sex chromosomes. Biologists had observed that women have two X chromosomes and men only one. Thomas H. Morgan, the Nobel Prize–winning geneticist, had proposed that X chromosomes carry more "female-producing" genes, whereas the autosomes (non-sex chromosomes) were responsible for maleness (1934, 205).

Extrapolating from this information, Rosanoff hypothesized that psychosexual gender was similarly determined and that masculinity and femininity came in strong and weak genotypes. These he denoted by upper- versus lowercase M's and F's. He thereby proposed that there were six types of psychosexual males corresponding to the genotypes MMF, MMf, MmF, Mmf, mmF, and mmf. There were nine genetic strains of females: MMFF, MMFf, MMff, MmFF, MmFf, Mmff, mmFF, mmFf, and mmff. Each of these, he suggested, corresponded to a variation in the balance of masculinity and femininity in individuals. He then drew up a table of the fifty-four possible matings between these sexual types. For example:

No. 31. Mmf X MmFF = MMF + 2MmF + mmF + MMFf + 2MmFf + mmFf

The startling conclusion of this fantastical mental exercise was that "extremely homosexual individuals [i.e., mmF men and MMff women] may be the offspring of approximately normal parents, and vice versa" (1935, 41). Rosanoff thus broke away from the degeneration model of chronic genetic deterioration. Instead, his theory suggested that homosexuality and other "abnormal" sexualities might be the product of widely distributed, recessive genotypes that were not eliminated through evolutionary pressures. Although he admitted having no idea what behavioral manifestations (phenotypes) corresponded to most of his various genotypic permutations, they undermined the notion of a simple dichotomy of sexualities: homo- and heterosexual. His theory was, however, purely speculative. Not until the development of molecular biology in the 1990s did researchers concretely attempt to locate genes for homosexuality (see Chapter 9 of this book).

---

Henry had already demonstrated an interest in the causes of homosexuality and its relation to personality disorders (1934). The committee's work allowed a more exhaustive approach to exploring the constitutional and familial roots of homosexuality. The choice of the term *sex variants* betrays both a cautious approach to the incendiary topic, as well as the profound influence of Hirschfeld. Henry reported their findings in brief articles (1937; Henry and Gross 1938), as well as a large two-volume publication that included verbatim interviews and photographs of the subjects (1941). Henry's conclusions from this massive undertaking were eclectic, supporting both constitutional/hereditary factors and psychological/familial factors. Following the lead of Krafft-Ebing and Hirschfeld, the committee desperately searched for and found anatomically intersexed stigmata in homosexuals: the women tended to have firm muscles, little fat, small or "infantile" genitalia and uterus, facial hair, and small breasts; the men tended to have effeminate bodies, small genitals, and feminine distribution of soft fat. These were the characteristic findings of degeneration and inversion. At the same time, Henry pointed to typically psychoanalytic factors such as family dynamics and "obstacles to heterosexual adjustment" (1937, 905).

Henry also adopted the model of hermaphroditic embryogenesis and bisexual infantile development. Although he argued that homosexual experiences and desires were universal, he nevertheless concluded that homosexuality was a disorder. It could be prevented, in most cases, through proper child rearing and eugenics: namely, preventing "sex variants" from breeding. This eclecticism in attitude and models is not atypical for the time (Carlston 1997). Perhaps more startling is that the homosexual subjects willingly submitted to these invasive examinations. As Terry (1999, chap. 7) suggests, the subjects shared the hope of many homosexuals before and after them that scientific findings would support their feeling that homosexuality was natural and innate, thereby stimulating social tolerance. Their free confessions and Henry's forays into gay New York do indeed provide one of the richest accounts of vibrant, joyful, unrepentant homosexuals and their culture in the 1930s. However, the participants hope of being socially redeemed was misplaced since their lives and bodies were exploited as evidence of homosexual maladjustment and perversity.

### From Permissiveness to Punishment

Throughout the 1920s and 1930s, congenitalist and psychological theories of homosexuality clashed or were combined empirically in psychiatrists' varied attempts to deal with the "problem of homosexuality" (see Sidebar 3.2). The increasingly complex theorization of homosexuality as a genetic, hormonal, neurological, or mental "abnormality" implied that it could and should be treated. Nevertheless, in the 1920s in particular there were significant professional objections to this approach. Some doctors, both from the somatic and psychological camps, argued that homosexuality was just a variant of human sexuality that implied no further psychiatric or bodily defects. One psychoanalyst from Portland, Oregon, for example, concluded his case study of a "passing" lesbian client with a poignant appeal: "If soci-

## Sidebar 3.3 Freud's Letter to an American Mother
April 9, 1935

Dear Mrs. . . .

I gather from your letter that your son is a homosexual. I am most impressed by the fact that you do not mention this term yourself in your information about him. May I question you, why you avoid it? Homosexuality is assuredly no advantage, but it is nothing to be ashamed of, no vice, no degradation, it cannot be classified as an illness; we consider it to be a variation of the sexual function produced by a certain arrest of development. Many highly respectable individuals of ancient and modern times have been homosexuals, several of the greatest men among them (Plato, Michelangelo, Leonardo da Vinci etc.). It is a great injustice to persecute homosexuality as a crime, and a cruelty too. If you do not believe me, read the books of Havelock Ellis.

By asking me if I can help, you mean, I suppose, if I can abolish homosexuality and make normal heterosexuality take its place. The answer is, in a general way, we cannot promise to achieve it. In a certain number of cases we succeed in developing the blighted germs of heterosexual tendencies that are present in every homosexual; in the majority of cases it is no more possible. It is a question of the quality and the age of the individual. The result of treatment cannot be predicted.

What analysis can do for your son runs in a different line. If he is unhappy, neurotic, torn by conflicts, inhibited in his social life, analysis may bring him harmony, peace of mind, full efficiency whether he remains a homosexual or gets changed. If you make up your mind he should have analysis with me—I don't expect you will—he has to come over to Vienna. I have no intention of leaving here. However don't neglect to give me your answer.

Sincerely yours with kind wishes,
Freud

This letter was first reproduced in 1951 thanks to Alfred Kinsey. He had recently received it from the mother herself, who praised Freud as a "Great and Good man."

ety will but let her alone, she will fill her niche in the world and leave it better for her bravery. . . . Instead of criticism and hounding, she needs and deserves the respect and sympathy of society, which is responsible for her existence as she is" (Gilbert 1920, 322).

Psychiatric and medico-legal journals even made room for the apologetic or sometimes enthusiastically proud voices of inverts themselves. Unfortunately, as the nation survived the devastation of World War I and weathered the Great Depression, and as ideological conflicts within the psychiatric profession grew, these lay and professional voices of tolerance were muted. In 1938, Dr. John Kerchner sketched a hyperbolic, caricatural, yet revealing history of sex in the early-twentieth-century United States. Before World War I, we "lived in an era of happy tranquillity—every boy was ambitious to find the girl—to establish a home and raise a family." With the death of hundreds of thousands of men to the war and the shortage of manpower, "we found women in men's trousers. . . . They were free; making men's wages. No wonder they got drunk with the victory of independence." He moaned that these hysterical, free-thinking women pushed for Prohibition and the suppression of prostitution. Furthermore, "negroes who used to work in the cotton fields in the South, now invaded the best residential district on the south side [of Chicago]." Then came the Great Depression and further male unemployment. Given all these blows to men's labor and sexual fulfillment, Kerchner concluded (1938, 171–172), was it any surprise that mental disorders and sex crimes were on the rise?

Many doctors, like Kerchner, became the mouthpieces for social anxiety and the desperate agents of change. The development of ever more drastic psychiatric interventions—from hormone treatment to shock therapy and neurosurgery—stimulated more punitive approaches to homosexuality. American psychoanalysts also became more strident in their dealings with homosexuals. Turning away from Freud's relatively sympathetic view, they made the homosexual "neurosis" increasingly central to the psychoanalytic interpretation of mental diseases. Accordingly, the readjustment of homosexuals became ever more essential to psychotherapists. As the United States entered World War II in 1941, psychiatrists made their profession and the screening of homosexuals essential to the territorial and mental defense of the nation.

## References

Beery, Florence. 1924. "The Psyche of the Intermediate Sex." *The Medico-Legal Journal* (New York) 41: 4–9.

Benjamin, Harry. 1931a. "For the Sake of Morality." *Medical Journal and Record* 133: 380–382.

———. 1931b. "An Echo of and an Addendum to 'For the Sake of Morality.'" *Medical Journal and Record* 134: 118–120.

Bien, Ernst. 1934. "Why Do Homosexuals Undergo Treatment?" *Medical Review of Reviews* 40: 5–18.

Bollmeier, L. N. 1938. "A Paranoid Mechanism in Male Overt Homosexuality." *Psychoanalytic Quarterly* 7: 357–367.

Brill, Abraham Arden. 1935. "The Psychiatric Approach to the Problem of Homosexuality." *The Journal-Lancet* 55: 249–252.

Carlston, Erin. 1997. "'A Finer Differentiation': Female Homosexuality and the American Medical Community, 1926–1940." Pp. 177–196 in *Science and Homosexualities*. Edited by Vernon Rosario. New York: Routledge.

Chauncey, George. 1994. *Gay New York: Gender, Urban Culture, and the Making of the Gay Male World, 1890–1940*. New York: Basic Books.

Davis, Katharine Bement. 1929. *Factors in the Sex Life of Twenty-two Hundred Women.* New York: Harper and Bros. Publishers.

Deutsch, Helene. 1932. "On Female Homosexuality." *Psychoanalytic Quarterly* 1: 484–510.

Dickinson, Robert Latou, and Lura Beam. 1931. *A Thousand Marriages: A Medical Study of Sex Adjustment.* Baltimore: William and Wilkins.

———. 1934. *The Single Woman: A Medical Study in Sex Education.* Baltimore: William and Wilkins.

Dörner, Günther, T. Geier, S. L. Ahren, L. Krell, G. Munx, H. Sieler, E. Kittner, and H. Muller. 1980. "Prenatal Stress as a Possible Aetiogenetic Factor of Homosexuality in Human Males." *Endokrinologie* 75: 365–368.

Duberman, Martin. 1991. *Cures: A Gay Man's Odyssey.* New York: Dutton.

Ernst, John R. 1928. "Dementia Praecox Complexes." *Medical Journal and Record.* 128: 381–386.

Ferenczi, Sándor. [1912] 1916. "On the Part Played by Homosexuality in the Pathogenesis of Paranoia." Pp. 131–156 in *Contributions to Psychoanalysis.* Translated by Ernest Jones. Boston: Richard G. Badger.

Freedman, Estelle. 1989. "'Uncontrolled Desires': The Response to the Sexual Psychopath, 1920–1960." Pp. 199–225 in *Passion and Power: Sexuality in History.* Edited by Kathy Peiss and Christina Simmons with R. Padgug. Philadelphia: Temple University Press.

Freud, Sigmund. [1905] 1955. *Three Essays on the Theory of Sexuality.* In *Standard Edition of the Complete Psychological Works of Sigmund Freud.* 24 vols. Edited by James Strachey. London: Hogarth Press.

———. [1920] 1955. "The Psychogenesis of a Case of Homosexuality in a Woman." In *Standard Edition* 18: 146–172.

Frosch, Jack, and Walter Bromberg. 1939. "The Sex Offender: A Psychiatric Study." *American Journal of Orthopsychiatry* 9: 761–776.

Gerber, Henry [Parisex, pseudonym]. [1932] 1975. "In Defense of Homosexuality." *The Modern Thinker* (June): 286–297. Reproduced in *A Homosexual Emancipation Miscellany, c. 1835–1952.* New York: Arno Press.

Gibson, Margaret. 1997. "Clitoral Corruption: Body Metaphors and American Doctors' Constructions of Female Homosexuality, 1870–1900." Pp. 108–132 in *Science and Homosexualities.* Edited by V. Rosario. New York: Routledge.

Gilbert, J. Allen. 1920. "Homo-sexuality and Its Treatment." *Journal of Nervous and Mental Disease* 52: 297–322.

Hackfield, A. W. 1935. "The Ameliorative Effects of Therapeutic Castration in Habitual Sex Offenders." *Journal of Nervous and Mental Disease* 82: 15–29, 169–181.

Hall, Radclyffe. [1928] 1980. *The Well of Loneliness.* New York: Avon.

Henry, George W. 1934. "Psychogenic and Constitutional Factors in Homosexuality: Their Relation to Personality Disorders." [Read to the New York Psychiatric Society, May 3, 1933.] *Psychiatric Quarterly* 8: 243–264.

———. 1937. "Psychogenic Factors in Overt Homosexuality." *American Journal of Psychiatry* 93: 889–908.

———. 1941. *Sex Variants. A Study of Homosexual Patterns.* New York: Hoeber.

Henry, George W., and Alfred Gross. 1938. "Social Factors in the Case Histories of One Hundred Underprivileged Homosexuals." *Mental Hygiene* 22: 591–611.

Hirschfeld, Magnus. [1901] 1915. *The Social Problem of Sexual Inversion.* London: C. W. Beaumont. Reprinted in *A Homosexual Emancipation Miscellany, c. 1835–1952.* New York: Arno, 1975. Revised and abridged translation of *Was soll das Volk vom dritten Geschlecht wissen? Eine Aufklärungsschrift über gleichgeschlechtlich (homosexuelle) empfindende Menschen.* Leipzig: Max Spohr, 1901.

Hoover, J. Edgar. 1937. "War on the Sex Criminal!" *New York Herald Tribune,* September 26.

Horney, Karen. 1926. "The Flight from Womanhood: The Masculinity Complex in Women, as Viewed by Men and Women." *International Journal of Psychoanalysis* 7: 324–339.

———. 1933. "The Denial of the Vagina, a Contribution to the Problem of Genital Anxieties Specific to Women." *International Journal of Psychoanalysis* 14: 57–70.

Isay, Richard. 1996. *Becoming Gay: The Journey to Self-Acceptance.* New York: Pantheon.

James, Robert E. 1947. "Precipitating Factors in Acute Homosexual Panic (Kempf's Disease) with a Case Presentation." *Quarterly Review of Psychiatry and Neurology* 2: 530–533.

Karpman, Benjamin. 1943. "Mediate Psychotherapy and the Acute Homosexual Panic (Kempf's Disease)." *Journal of Nervous and Mental Disease* 98: 493–506.

Katz, Jonathan Ned. 1976. *Gay American History: Lesbians and Gay Men in the U.S.A.* New York: Thomas Y. Crowell.

———. 1983. *Gay/Lesbian Almanac.* New York: Harper and Row.

Kempf, Edward John. 1921. *Psychopathology.* St. Louis, MO: C. V. Mosby.

Kerchner, John. 1938. "Sex Crimes." *Illinois Medical Journal* 73: 171–172.

Kopp, Marie E. 1937–1938. "Surgical Treatment as Sex Crime Prevention Measure." *Journal Criminal Law and Criminology* 28: 692–706.

Krafft-Ebing, Richard von. 1886. *Psychopathia Sexualis: Eine klinische-forensische Studie.* 1st ed. Stuttgart: Ferdinand Enke.

Lewes, Kenneth. 1988. *The Psychoanalytic Theory of Male Homosexuality.* New York: Simon and Schuster.

Lichtenstein, Perry Maurice. 1921. "The 'Fairy' and the Lady Lover." *Medical Review of Reviews* 27: 369–374.

Lydston, George Frank. 1889. "Sexual Perversion, Satyriasis, and Nymphomania." *Medical and Surgical Reporter* 61: 253–258, 281–285.

———. 1919. "The Biochemical Basis of Sex Aberrations." *Urologic and Cutaneous Review* 23: 384–385.

Magee, Maggie, and Diana Miller. 1997. *Lesbian Lives: Psychoanalytic Narratives Old and New.* Hillsdale, NJ: Analytic Press.

Meagher, John Francis Wallace. 1929. "Homosexuality: Its Psychobiological and Psychopathological Significance." *Urologic and Cutaneous Review* 33: 505–518.

Morgan, Thomas Hunt. 1934. *Embryology and Genetics.* New York: Columbia University Press.

Oberndorf, Clarence Paul. 1929. "Diverse Forms of Homosexuality." *Urologic and Cutaneous Review* 33: 518–523.

Riggall, Robert M. 1923. "Homosexuality and Alcoholism." *Psychoanalytic Review* 10: 157–169.

Robinson, William Josephus. 1914. "My Views on Homosexuality." *American Journal of Urology and Sexology* 10: 550–552.

———. 1925. "Nature's Sex Stepchildren." *Medical Critic and Guide* 25C: 475–477.

Rosanoff, Aaron Joshua. 1935. "A Theory of Chaotic Sexuality." *American Journal of Psychiatry* 92: 35–41.

———. 1938. *Manual of Psychiatry and Mental Hygiene.* 7th ed. New York: J. Wiley; London: Chapman and Hall.

Schreber, Daniel Paul. [1903] 1955. *Memoirs of My Mental Illness.* Translated and edited by Ida Macalpine and Richard A. Hunter. London: William Dawson and Sons.

Shaskan, Donald. 1939. "One Hundred Sex Offenders." *American Journal of Orthopsychiatry* 9: 565–569.

Showalter, Elaine. 1985. *The Female Malady: Women, Madness, and English Culture, 1830–1980.* New York: Pantheon.

Steakley, James D. 1997. "*Per scientiam ad justitiam:* Magnus Hirschfeld and the Sexual Politics of Innate Homosexuality." Pp. 133–154 in *Science and Homosexualities.* Edited by V. Rosario. New York: Routledge.

Stekel, Wilhelm. 1930. "Is Homosexuality Curable?" *Psychoanalytic Review* 17: 443–451.

Terry, Jennifer. 1999. *An American Obsession: Science, Medicine, and Homosexuality in Modern Society.* Chicago: University of Chicago Press.

Werther, Ralph (alias) [also Earl Lind and Jennie June]. 1918. "The Fairie Boy. An Autobiographical Sketch." *American Journal of Urology and Sexology* 14: 433–437.

———. 1920. "Studies in Androgynism." *Medical Life* (New York) 27: 235–246.

Wolbarst, Abraham L. 1931. "Sexual Perversions: Their Medical and Social Implications." *Medical Journal and Record* 134: 5–9, 62–65.

## Further Reading

Since 1985, a growing number of historical works have excavated the often secretive life of gays and lesbians in the United States in the early twentieth century. The anthology *Passion and Power: Sexuality in History* (Philadelphia: Temple University Press, 1989), edited by Kathy Peiss and Christina Simmons, provides a fascinating overview, with articles covering a variety of communities in the nineteenth and twentieth centuries. George Chauncey, *Gay New York: Gender, Urban Culture, and the Making of the Gay Male World, 1890–1940* (New York: Basic Books, 1994) is enormously entertaining and well documented and argues that there were vibrant, often highly visible, gay communities in New York City before World War II. *Odd Girls and Twilight Lovers: A History of Lesbian Life in Twentieth-Century America* (New York: Columbia University Press, 1991) by Lillian Faderman examines the breadth of lesbian experience in the twentieth century. Elizabeth L. Kennedy and Madeline Davis's *Boots of Leather, Slippers of Gold: The History of a Lesbian Community* (New York: Routledge, 1993) focuses instead on working-class lesbians in Buffalo, New York, for a richly textured account of their experience.

Maggie Magee and Diana Miller's *Lesbian Lives: Psychoanalytic Narratives Old and New* (Hillsdale, NJ: Analytic Press, 1997) provides the most extensive review of psychoanalytic writings on lesbianism. They provide a new perspective on psychotherapy with lesbians, based on their own personal and clinical experiences as lesbian analysts.

*The Double Helix: A Personal Account of the Discovery of the Structure of DNA* (New York: Norton, 1980) is a classic in the history of science, written by the James

Watson who discovered the molecular structure of DNA. Lily E. Kay's *Who Wrote the Book of Life? A History of the Genetic Code* (Stanford, CA: Stanford University Press, 2000) is a more critical analysis of genetic science. Nelly Oudshoorn has written one of the most recent and critical histories of the scientific discovery of sex hormones, *Beyond the Natural Body: An Archaeology of Sex Hormones* (New York: Routledge, 1994).

# 4

## Screening Out Homosexuals

Anyone curious about medical information concerning homosexuality in the 1940s who consulted the *Index Medicus* (the preeminent bibliography of medical literature) would have been referred to the generic rubric of "Sexual Perversions," where all varieties of nonreproductive sexual behaviors were grouped. The persistence of this half-century-old association betrays the continuity into the 1940s of the medical theorization of homosexuality as a behavioral and physiological pathology and helps explain the facile associations made between homosexuality and a variety of social and political concerns in the troubled decade of the U.S. entry into World War II and its engagement in the Cold War with the Soviet Union.

As pointed out in the previous chapters, gays, queens, and fairies had become visible, often flamboyantly so, in urban centers. In New York City, as historian George Chauncey (1994) has shown, a variety of homosexual subcultures had thrived in the 1920s and 1930s and even enjoyed a certain bohemian chic. Although many medical writers of that time had displayed remarkable tolerance, even sympathy, for homosexuals, the "problem of homosexuality" still baffled psychiatrists—the advocates of Freudian psychoanalysis and of somatic psychiatry alike. Therefore, Dr. Benjamin Karpman was exaggerating only slightly when he declared, "The problems of psychiatry will not be solved until we solve the problem of homosexuality" (quoted in Henry 1937, 906).

### Morals and Morale in Wartime

The problem of homosexuality would become particularly central to both the nation and the psychiatric profession as U.S. engagement in the war in Europe seemed increasingly inevitable. Beginning in 1938, psychiatric organizations such as the William Alanson White

Foundation, the Southern Psychiatric Association, and the American Psychiatric Association (APA) had suggested that psychiatrists become active in the impending war effort. Gerald Grob has pointed out the important role that psychiatrists played for the first time in the Selective Service System by helping to screen out individuals who might prove mentally unfit for military service (Grob 1991, 10). Mental illness had proven a heavy burden to the military during and after World War I. Acute and chronic psychiatric disorders were a significant cause of lost manpower. They also led to costly medical care for veterans who suffered from "shell shock" and other "war neuroses" (Babington 1997). One estimate from 1941 found that "one-half of those receiving treatment from federal facilities throughout the country were psychoneurotics" (Berlien and Waggoner 1966, 162). The military deemed it imperative to detect in advance those who might buckle under the stress of war and thus imperil their lives as well as company morale.

To address this issue, the Selective Service released Medical Circular No. 1 on November 7, 1940, to physicians who inspected draftees (Bérubé 1990, 11–12). It was a brief guide to identifying "incapacitating mental and personality factors" in registrants in order to reject or further scrutinize suspicious individuals. Among numerous mental "handicaps" (such as psychopathic personality, mood distur-

*Army recruits being screened at Camp Blanding, Florida, in 1941 (J. Baylor Roberts / National Geographic Society).*

bance, psychoneurosis, psychosis, and drug addiction), physicians were instructed to be vigilant for "homosexual proclivities" in potential recruits. The May 19, 1941, revision of this document included "homosexual proclivities" as the final item in a list of miscellaneous "deviations" requiring a psychiatric referral (Selective Service 1941, 2061). In other military medical documents, homosexuality was classified among the "psychoneuroses," along with exhibitionism and fetishism (Knight 1941, 165).

As the *Index Medicus* suggests, homosexuality was classified at the time as one of the "overt sexual perversions." These were viewed as manifestations of personality or character disorders in "psychoneurotics." In a seminar on Practical Psychiatric Diagnosis for Selective Service Registrants, Dr. Robert Knight warned that "such cases [of sexual perversion] should probably be rejected on the likelihood that their activities will bring about social ostracism, being 'picked on' and other complications in the armed forces." Knight noted, however, that "some otherwise well adjusted cases of perversion may become useful members of the army" (1941, 165). Despite this modicum of sympathy initially extended to "sexual perverts," the military categorically declared homosexual behavior and "proclivities" as incompatible with military service. Historian Allan Bérubé (1990) has documented the

*Harry Stack Sullivan, about 1935 (Washington School of Medicine)*

ill effects of this military ban on those who managed to stay in the service and those given dishonorable discharges simply for being homosexual. The psychiatric profession that dedicated itself to screening out homosexuals also promised to treat the "problem of homosexuality" as it was perceived to affect the individuals discharged and the society that would receive them.

Dr. Harry Stack Sullivan, himself a homosexual, noted the far broader duties the psychiatric profession should assume besides screening (see Sidebar 4.1). These included the rehabilitation of servicemen suffering from combat fatigue, the assistance of those soldiers having difficulties reintegrating into civilian life, the protection of those recruits—such as the homosexuals—who were rejected, and most broadly, the maintenance of

## Sidebar 4.1 Harry Stack Sullivan

Harry Stack Sullivan (1892–1949) has been described as the "psychiatrist of America" and as the only American to found a major school of psychiatric thought: interpersonal or social psychiatry (Perry 1982). He was born in the small upstate New York town of Norwich to Irish-American, Catholic parents. A shy, awkward boy, Sullivan remained introverted throughout his life. Perhaps for this reason, he was particularly effective with withdrawn, schizophrenic patients. After medical studies at the Chicago College of Medicine, he served on the medical examining board during World War I and then as a medical officer in the Division of Rehabilitation. Under the mentorship of William Alanson White at St. Elizabeth's Hospital in 1922, Sullivan was drawn to psychiatry. He worked at the Sheppard and Enoch Pratt Hospital in Baltimore and lectured at the University of Maryland Medical School during the remainder of the 1920s. During the 1930s, he served as associate editor of *The American Journal of Psychiatry* and prospered in private practice.

In developing interpersonal or social psychiatry, Sullivan stressed the personal connection between psychiatrist and patient and the effect of the social field on psychiatric symptoms. Furthermore, he argued that psychiatric concepts could be applied to social problems, and he dedicated the final years of his life to addressing economic and social injustices. He was a strong advocate of racial equality.

Sullivan was not open about his homosexuality and had trouble accepting his sexuality. He argued that male homosexuality was not congenital but the product of "inordinate attachment" on the part of mothers (particularly those in unhappy marriages.) However, he wrote that group homosexual behavior was normal in preadolescence. Boys too sexually inhibited to participate in this homosexual play were at risk of stalling in their heterosexual development, particularly if they had strong attachments to older boys. Sullivan theorized that the failure to enjoy this preadolescent homosexual phase or the repression of adult homoerotic impulses could also lead to psychotic breaks (1965). He seemed to be struggling to make sense of his own experiences: his psychotic episodes and a childhood intimacy with an older boy (who also became a psychiatrist and never married). Since Sullivan believed most people were bisexual, he felt a "heterosexual adjustment" was possible through psychoanalytic treatment, but only in young men who had a strong desire to change. He regretted his inability to have a heterosexual relationship; instead, he was devoted to James Inscoe, whom Sullivan referred to as his "beloved foster son." Inscoe was fifteen years old when Sullivan first met him as a patient. The youngster moved in with Sullivan in 1927 and remained his lifelong companion and secretary.

civilian morale in the face of the German strategy of terror (1941, 211). This last role—ministering to society at large and not just the severely mentally ill—became increasingly important to the psychiatric profession in the 1940s. Although prior to the war, most psychiatrists had been based in public mental asylums, the profession would largely shift to private outpatient and community mental health care by the 1950s. It was thanks to the prominence of and demand for psychiatrists in military screening and treatment that the profession was also able to stake new claims for treating the psychoneuroses, particularly homosexuality, which continued to be represented as a threat to national security even after the war concluded.

Initially, detection of homosexuals depended on inductees' confessions, but this approach did not prove very successful. Many gay men and lesbians did not admit their homosexual orientation. Some felt it was their duty to serve. Others sought new career opportunities in the services and a means of gaining an education. Particularly for those of low socioeconomic backgrounds, military service was one way of getting away from small, rural towns that afforded few opportunities for lesbian and gay contacts. Many inductees were just young adults, fresh out of high school, who had not yet discovered their homosexual interests when they enlisted. All of these categories of homosexuals confounded psychiatrists. Dr. Manfred Guttmacher complained that "there was that pathetic group of homosexuals who had denied their abnormality to induction examiners and who had blindly hoped to adjust by living a robust life among thousands of normal military men. . . . Others with strong latent tendencies developed psychosomatic disorders and acute anxiety states" (1966, 367).

Improved, objective detection of homosexuals, independent of their confessions, seemed essential. As one psychologist, Dr. Arthur Burton warned, "Failure of recognition and clinical placement of such individuals makes their adjustment more difficult, creates administrative and disciplinary problems, and makes possible the indoctrination and contamination of individuals with normal drives" (1947, 161). Therefore, psychiatric researchers applied a variety of existing and specially developed psychological tests (such as the Rorschach, Goodenough [draw-a-man], Minnesota Multiphasic Personality Inventory [MMPI], Cornell Selectee Index, vocabulary, and Terman-Miles Masculinity-Femininity tests) to the objective detection of homosexuality and even specific types of "perverse" sexual behaviors (such as active or passive sodomy and active and passive fellatio) (Due and Wright 1945; Bergmann 1945; Darke and Geil 1948; Barnette 1942; Burton 1947). The following decade, psychologist Evelyn Hooker would show that these efforts were largely futile (see Chapter 5). But at the time, such psychological tests for homosexuality promised to be useful even beyond the Selective Service: they could be used as screening tools in penitentiaries, asylums, employment offices, or other situations where authorities found it important to isolate or exclude the sexually "perverse."

Soldiers suspected of homosexual activity, or "sodomy," had traditionally been court-martialed, but under the stress of wartime and humanitarian pressure from psychiatrists, homosexuals were increasingly given "undesirable discharges" or "blue" discharges, which had been used to handle alcoholics, drug addicts, and people with other "undesirable habits or traits of character." In order to preserve valuable personnel, certain homosexual "offenders" were deemed "reclaimable" and returned to duty. These included soldiers "guilty of first offenses, those who acted as a result of intoxication or curiosity," and those coerced by a superior (Brill 1966, 236–237). The number of those "salvaged" for further duty has been estimated at less than 1,000. Psychiatrists were increasingly involved in the evaluation and treatment of these cases as well.

Lt. Col. Lewis H. Loeser studied 270 homosexual patients in the 36th Station Hospital, where he was commanding officer. He noted that 37 percent of them entered the hospital of their own accord and voluntarily revealed their homosexuality. The majority of them were struggling to control their sexual drive and suffered from the mounting anxiety of detection. Reviewing military records, Loeser claimed that few soldiers feigned homosexuality simply to escape military duty. Loeser approached the topic and his patients with tremendous openness: "Considered coldly, without emotion or prejudice, the homosexual act is the natural sexual outlet for a numerically small group of otherwise normal people. Alone and by itself it is probably less dangerous to society than sexual promiscuity, adultery, or prostitution" (1945, 93). He reported some interesting demographic facts about his patient population. The homosexual cohort showed a preponderance of skilled trained personnel and had an above-average intelligence quotient (IQ) and education compared to army recruits as a whole. As noted in other studies, the homosexual group had a higher rate of excess alcohol use; however, he explained homosexual alcohol abuse as a means of coping with anxiety and sexual inhibition. Loeser dismissed medical attempts to change sexual orientation and instead advocated treating the neurosis that resulted from the homosexual's internal conflict with his or her sexuality. "The homosexual without conflict," he concluded, "who has accepted his status without reactions of guilt or inferiority, is a well adjusted individual who does not require nor benefit from psychotherapy. I would estimate that 50 percent belong to this category" (99). His final recommendations were equally startling for the time: sodomy should not in itself be a punishable offense in the military or a reason for discharge; homosexuals were generally law abiding and possessed significant talents and moral restraint; and there should be individual examination of any cases of infractions and not a blanket ban on homosexuals. Until the present time, the U.S. military continues to grapple with its exclusionary policy on homosexuals.

The same year as Loeser's study, the military took its most liberal position with WD Circular No. 85 (published March 23, 1946), which permitted honorable discharges for enlisted personnel who admitted "homosexual tendencies" but had not engaged in homosexual acts (Brill 1966, 238). After the war, however, new directives made it more difficult to reclaim homosexuals or give them honorable discharges.

Dr. Harry Benjamin (later a pioneer in the treatment of transsexuals) reviewed homosexuality more broadly in "Sex Problems in the Armed Forces." It was not easy to screen out homosexuals, he claimed, because "many of them, for various—including patriotic—reasons, conceal their abnormality." He guessed that the number of conscripts who pretended to be homosexual to evade service was probably small. He mainly worried about young men who turned to homosexual practices because the "normal heterosexual outlet for their libido" was blocked (1944, 241). He worried that some of these men, particularly those with a bisexual psychosexual constitution, might never revert to heterosexuality. He concluded by recommending sex education and the provision of supervised prostitutes because the suppression of prostitution only "undermines the soldier's morale by promoting auto-eroticism, sexual neuroses, and homosexuality" (243).

## Homosexuality and Paranoia

The detection of denied or repressed homosexuality was also viewed as useful for diagnostic purposes in cases of suspected sex offenses, paranoia, and schizophrenia. As noted earlier, Sigmund Freud (1911) had first suggested that paranoia might be a manifestation of repressed homosexuality: paranoiacs defend themselves against their own despised homoerotic yearnings by imagining that the object of their passion hates them. Edward Kempf (1921) had later coined a specific term, "homosexual panic," to describe the acute crisis supposedly provoked by repressed homosexual desire. Psychiatrists in the 1940s generalized the association between paranoia and homosexuality in two ways: all paranoia was suspected of having a repressed homoerotic foundation, and all homosexuals were suspected of being more or less paranoid. Even psychoanalyst Abraham A. Brill, who had earlier expressed sympathy toward homosexuals, adopted a hostile position by the 1940s:

> Having encountered hundreds of homosexuals, some of whom were prominent in artistic, philanthropic and other fields, I have

never found one who, on closer observation, did not show para- noid traits. They are all oversuspicious, "shadowy," and mistrust- ful. Most of them are unreliable, intriguing, picayune, and im- petuous. In brief, all of them show anal-sadistic character traits to lesser or greater degree. I have felt for years that this behavior was engendered by our civilization, where homosexuals are treated as outcasts. However I am convinced that this is only partially true. Most of these traits are due to anal-sadistic fixa- tions and regressions. (Brill 1940, 13)

The suspected link between homosexuality and paranoia led Dr. John R. Ernst to goad his paranoid patients into recognizing their un- conscious homosexuality in order to resolve their delusions of perse- cution (1943). He suggested, more generally, that patients' resistance to acknowledging their homosexual wishes in itself induced psy- chopathology. Self-acknowledged or repressed homosexuals were stigmatized as a threat to the military because of their supposed para- noia and "unreliableness." Selective Service psychiatrists bluntly de- clared in seminars around the country that "psychopaths are those vo- cationally unfit for service and include the eccentric, the leader in subversive activities, the emotionally unstable, the sexually perverse, those with inadequate personalities that do not adapt readily, and those who are resentful of discipline. All are not assimilable in ser- vice" (Berlien and Waggoner 1966, 162). Already during World War II, psychiatrists were linking supposed homosexual paranoia with what would later be considered the most "subversive activity": partic- ipation in the Communist Party (Bartemeier 1943).

Psychoanalysts' engagement with broader social and political is- sues had earlier been suggested by Freud's applications of psycho- analysis beyond the individual clinical setting in works such as *Civi- lization and Its Discontents* (1930) and *The Future of an Illusion* (1927). In the United States, World War II gave psychiatrists, particularly ana- lysts, higher professional status and a broader agenda: to care for the mental health of the civilian population at risk because of war fatigue and Nazi propaganda. One of the ways of doing so was to psychoana- lyze the German character in general and reveal Nazism itself as a profound, perverse form of psychopathology. A recurrent element in this psychiatric counterpropaganda was the association of fascism with homosexuality (Hewitt 1996). Ernst Röhm, chief of staff of the National Socialist Sturmabteilung (SA), was the one high-ranking Nazi leader widely known to be homosexual. Although the Nazi Party was hostile to homosexuality and sent homosexuals to concentration camps (marked with pink triangle badges), Adolf Hitler had tolerated

Röhm's homosexuality until 1934. However in June 1934, Hitler decided to order Röhm's execution and crush the SA, which had grown too powerful (Hancock 1998). Although there was no evidence to support it, American propagandists accused Hitler himself of being a paranoid sex pervert and labeled his circle of ministers a "pederasty ring" (Testis 1934; Wittels 1943). (A recent historical work argues that Hitler was indeed a homosexual [Machtan 2001].) Turning back to the history of the Roman Empire, one analyst spun a cautionary tale in explaining the fall of the empire to the "Germans" as a product of a corrupt political structure that stimulated the proliferation of sexual perversity, especially homosexuality. The menace of homosexuality was thus portrayed as a serious national threat on all fronts. In the course of the decade, the psychiatric profession effectively erected itself as a critical defender of the nation through psychiatry's expanding practice beyond the asylum in the detection and treatment of all varieties of psychoneuroses.

## Reconciling Diverse Treatment Options

A major battle within the U.S. psychiatric profession in the 1940s led to huge shifts in the institutional base and dominant therapeutic approaches of psychiatry. Historian Gerald Grob (1991) notes that the APA (originally founded in 1844 as the Association of Medical Superintendents of American Institutions of the Insane) had always represented the interests of public asylum psychiatrists. These doctors cared for the profoundly mentally ill through neurologically inspired methods of somatic therapy (such as hydrotherapy, shock therapy, and lobotomy). After the war, the APA was gradually taken over by a young generation of psychoanalytically oriented psychiatrists who had honed their skills on the battlefield. They were convinced that environmental stressors were the major cause of mental illness and that local psychotherapy, rather than institutionalization, was the best means of treating psychoneuroses and of preventing more serious psychiatric diseases.

During World War II, some 5,500 members of the U.S. military were admitted to hospitals with a diagnosis of "pathological sexuality" (in most cases homosexuality). In the hospital they were seen by psychiatrists who determined if these suspected homosexuals were "reclaimable." Those potentially in this category included first-time offenders, those who had acted under the influence of intoxicants or curiosity, and those who had been coerced by a superior (Brill 1966, 237). The hope was that with proper psychotherapy, the subjects could be restored to heterosexuality and returned to duty. "Incorrigible" homosexuals faced discharge from the military, although until 1947 they might have been entitled to an honorable discharge if they had not previously engaged in homosexual behavior and had a good service record.

As noted earlier, orthodox Freudian analysts did not believe that homosexuality could be "cured" since it was considered more of an unfortunate deviation than a pathology. Homosexuality was seen as a fixation at a universal stage of infantile bisexuality and, in most cases, it was far too deeply ingrained in the psyche to be altered. However, psychoanalyst Sandor Rado—promptly after Freud's death in 1939—posed a serious challenge to this Freudian orthodoxy by claiming that infantile bisexuality did not normally exist (Rado 1940). Therefore, *all* homosexuality was distinctly pathological and potentially curable. Alongside this radical change in the psychoanalytic theory of homosexuality, nonpsychological theories of the biological foundations and treatment of homosexuality continued to thrive in the 1940s. In many cases, psychoanalysts who claimed they could treat homosexuality promoted the use of these somatic therapies as an adjunct to psychoanalysis in recalcitrant patients who supposedly posed too much resistance to treatment.

*Somatic "Cures"*

Throughout the decade, researchers continued to pursue the existing avenues for explaining homosexual "psychopathology": genetics, endocrinology, and neurobiology. The endocrinological approach was particularly boosted by advances in the chemical analysis of the major human sex hormones in the 1920s and 1930s and by improvements in the methods for assaying hormone levels in urine (Kenen 1997). Endocrinological researchers hypothesized that female homosexuals had lower levels of estrogens and higher levels of testosterone than "normal" women (and the reverse for male homosexuals). Results from different studies were ambiguous and contradictory: some researchers suggested that any degree of abnormality was an index of homosexuality; others concluded that the mere fact that all individuals possessed both "female hormones" (estrogens) and "male hormones" (androgens) supported the Freudian thesis of universal bisexuality. Despite any convincing evidence that hormones either produced or influenced homosexuality, doctors attempted hormonal therapy for "sexual perverts." Male homosexuals, in particular, were treated with testosterone in an attempt to restore "normal" virility and heterosexuality.

Some of these small clinical trials reported marginal success. Drs. Samuel J. Glass and Roswell Johnson noted a benefit to three out of eight men treated with testosterone: one had achieved a "satisfactory adjustment"; a bisexual subject reported "predominantly heterosexual behavior"; the third, although not overtly homosexual, was relieved of his homosexual fantasies. The researchers did not dwell on the fact that the remaining subjects experienced an "intensification of the homosexual drive" (1944, 542). Another researcher, Hyman Barahal, who discovered the same phenomenon, concluded that "the amount of gonadal hormone present in the blood merely determines the force of the libido, not its direction," which suggested to him "the correctness of the psychoanalytic view" (1940, 329).

## Radical Cures: Lobotomy and Shock Therapy

The "shock therapies" (using insulin, metrazol, or electroshock to induce seizures) were developed in Europe in the 1930s for the treatment of schizophrenia. They were used frequently in the United States in the early 1940s, but electroconvulsive therapy quickly eclipsed the others in popularity. It is still used predominantly in the treatment of drug-resistant major depression. "Frontal lobotomy" or leucotomy (the surgical disconnection of sections of the frontal lobe) was first developed in Portugal in 1935 by Egas Moniz (who was awarded a Nobel Prize for this work). It was introduced the following year in the United States. Psychiatrists increasingly employed lobotomy in the 1940s, and by 1951 almost 20,000 lobotomies had been performed in the United States, particularly on women (Braslow 1997, 127). Although it might have diminished agitation and aggressive behavior in some patients, lobotomy was associated with high mortality (5 percent) and varying degrees of intellectual, behavioral, and emotional impairment. Its use declined rapidly after the introduction of antipsychotic drugs in the mid-1950s.

Psychiatrists resorted to these radical therapies for severely mentally ill patients who were likely to be institutionalized chronically, such as schizophrenics. It does not appear that they were commonly used to treat homosexuality alone. In the documented cases in which they were used on homosexuals, other factors were the primary target: the subjects were psychotic, sexually molested minors or displayed marked cross-gendered behavior.

Neurobiological theories and therapies were also made to fit within the paradigm of psychoanalysis. In the 1940s, Dr. Newdigate Owensby of Atlanta, Georgia, was a strong advocate for the "correction of homosexuality" through metrazol shock therapy (the drug metrazol induces seizures). His medical writings are filled with contradictions that reveal the theoretical eclecticism and moral ambivalence of doctors of the time. Owensby worried that the prevalence of homosexuality was "increasing with unparalleled rapidity" and augured the "disintegration of our present code of morality." However, he also declared that "the vast majority [of homosexuals] are self supporting and, except for their sexual practices, law abiding citizens of their community. Many of them will be conscripted into the army and will doubtless become creditable soldiers" (1941, 495). He denied that they all display cross-gendered behavior, and he believed that the only reason a few wanted to change their sexual habits was to "escape the penalty exacted by society for homosexual practices" (495).

Although he employed pharmacological shock therapy, he also believed in the Freudian model that homosexuality resulted from an infantile fixation of the libido during psychosexual development. He therefore reasoned that a regimen of twenty to thirty induced seizures would free the arrested psychosexual energy and permit easier psychotherapy (1941). He reported a 100 percent success rate in curing homosexuality (see also Wile 1941–1942).

Owensby published the case of a twenty-nine-year-old lesbian who recalled being a tomboy at the earliest age. She recounted her passionate love affair with an older woman. After her beloved was killed in a car accident, the patient was grief stricken and feared she would never fit into society as a lesbian. She turned to Dr. Owensby as a last resort. Following a course of metrazol shock treatment, the patient declared herself free of any lesbian desires and, for the first time, found men attractive. "At long last I have a chance to have a complete and happy life," she concluded, "the kind of life I have always wanted but heretofore failed to have" (1941, 496). Owensby surmised that the shock therapy had liberated her libido, permitting it to "flow through normal physiological channels" (496). This patient, like others who voluntarily underwent these traumatic therapies, desperately sought a "normal," conventional life (Owensby 1940). Their "cure" (if indeed there was one) probably resulted from their strong self-motivation. We know little of their long-term "readjustment."

Opposition to such dramatic and dangerous somatic therapies arose by the second half of the decade and was a central point of contention between the older generation of asylum-based psychiatrists and the younger psychoanalysts. Many of the latter dismissed all somatic and congenitalist theories of homosexuality and insisted that homosexuality was a product of early family dynamics (as Freud had

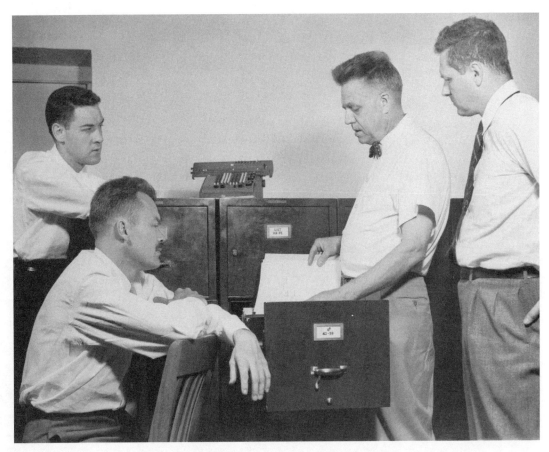

originally hypothesized). Unlike Freud, however, they advocated the "conversion" of homosexuality through psychoanalysis. Edmund Bergler (1899–1962), who had trained with Freud in Vienna, was one of the most strident voices insisting that all homosexuals were mental defectives who could be cured with intensive psychotherapy (1944, 1948). He and other advocates of homosexual conversion therapy were therefore incensed at the publication of Alfred Kinsey, Wardell Pomeroy, and Clyde Martin's study, *Sexual Behavior in the Human Male* (1948). The "Kinsey Report" (as it was widely known) concluded that "*37 percent* of the total male population has *at least some overt homosexual experience* to the point of orgasm between adolescence and old age . . . [and] *10 percent* of the males are *more or less exclusively homosexual* . . . for at least three years between the ages of 16 and 55" (650–651). In 1941 Kinsey had already forcefully criticized the hormonal theory of homosexuality; now his voluminous data served to confirm his earlier point that homosexuality was a common, widespread form of *behavior* and not a distinct clinical type of *human being*. The Kinsey Reports on men (1948) and women (1953) fueled international homosexual rights campaigns for the subsequent two decades. They would also fuel a bitter debate within the psychiatric community on the validity of the homosexuality diagnosis.

## References

Babington, Anthony. 1997. *Shell-Shock: A History of the Changing Attitudes to War Neurosis.* London: Leo Cooper.

Barahal, Hyman S. 1940. "Testosterone in Psychotic, Male Homosexuals." *Psychoanalytic Quarterly* 14: 315–330.

Barnette, Leslie W. 1942. "Study of an Adult Male Homosexual and Terman-Miles M-F Scores." *American Journal of Orthopsychiatry* 12: 346–351.

Bartemeier, Leo H. 1943. "Introduction to Psychiatry." *Psychoanalytic Review* 30: 386–398.

Benjamin, Harry. 1944. "The Sex Problem in the Armed Forces." *Urologic and Cutaneous Review* 48: 231–244.

Bergler, Edmund. 1944. "Eight Prerequisites for the Psychoanalytic Treatment of Homosexuality." *Psychoanalytic Review* 31: 253–286.

————. 1948. "The Myth of a New National Disease. Homosexuality and the Kinsey Report." *Psychiatric Quarterly* 22: 67–88.

Bergmann, Martin S. 1945. "Homosexuality on the Rorschach Test." *Bulletin of the Menninger Clinic* 9: 78–83.

Berlien, Ivan, and Raymond W. Waggoner. 1966. "Selection and Induction." Pp. 153–191 in *Neuropsychiatry in World War II,* vol. 1. Edited by John B. Coates and Arnold L. Ahnfeldt. Washington, DC: Office of the Surgeon General.

Bérubé, Allan. 1990. *Coming Out under Fire: The History of Gay Men and Women in World War II.* New York: Free Press.

Braslow, Joel. 1997. *Mental Ills and Bodily Cures: Psychiatric Treatment in the First Half of the Twentieth Century.* Berkeley: University of California Press.

Brill, Abraham Arden. 1940. "Sexual Manifestations in Neurotic and Psychotic Symptoms." *Psychiatric Quarterly* 14: 9–16.

Brill, Norman Q. 1966. "Hospitalization and Disposition." Pp. 195–253 in *Neuropsychiatry in World War II,* vol. 1. Edited by John B. Coates and Arnold L. Ahnfeldt. Washington, DC: Office of the Surgeon General.

Burton, Arthur. 1947. "The Use of the Masculinity-Femininity Scale of the Minnesota Multiphasic Personality Inventory as an Aid in the Diagnosis of Sexual Inversion." *Journal of Psychology* 24: 161–164.

Chauncey, George. 1994. *Gay New York: Gender, Urban Culture, and the Making of the Gay Male World, 1890–1940.* New York: Basic Books.

Darke, Roy A., and George A. Geil. 1948. "Homosexual Activity: Relation of Degree and Role to the Goodenough Test and to the Cornell Selectee Index." *Journal of Nervous and Mental Disease* 108: 217–240.

Due, Floyd O., and M. Erick Wright. 1945. "The Use of Content Analysis in Rorschach Interpretation: I. Differential Characteristics of Male Homosexuals." *Rorschach Research Exchange* 9: 169–174.

Ernst, John R. 1943. "Dementia Praecox Complexes." *Medical Annals of the District of Columbia* 12: 343–347.

Freud, Sigmund. [1911] 1955. "Psychoanalytic Notes upon an Autobiographical Account of a Case of Paranoia (*Dementia Paranoides*)." In *Standard Edition* 12: 1–84.

————. [1927] 1955. *The Future of an Illusion.* In *Standard Edition* 21: 3–56.

————. [1930] 1955. *Civilization and Its Discontents.* In *Standard Edition* 21: 59–145.

Geil, George A. 1944. "The Use of the Goodenough Test for Revealing Male Homosexuality." *Journal of Criminal Psychopathology* 6: 307–321.

Glass, S. J., and Roswell Johnson. 1944. "Limitations and Complications of Organotherapy in Male Homosexuality." *Journal of Clinical Endocrinology* 4: 540–544.

Grob, Gerald. 1991. *From Asylum to Community: Mental Health Policy in Modern America.* Princeton, NJ: Princeton University Press.

Guttmacher, Manfred S. 1966. "The Mental Hygiene Consultation Services." Pp. 349–371 in *Neuropsychiatry in World War II,* vol. 1. Edited by John B. Coates and Arnold L. Ahnfeldt. Washington, DC: Office of the Surgeon General.

Hancock, Eleanor. 1998. "'Only the Real, the True, the Masculine Held Its Value': Ernst Röhm, Masculinity, and Male Homosexuality." *Journal of the History of Sexuality* 8: 616–641.

Henry, George W. 1937. "Psychogenic Factors in Overt Homosexuality." *American Journal of Psychiatry* 93: 889–908.

Hewitt, Andrew. 1996. *Political Inversions: Homosexuality, Fascism, and the Modernist Imaginary.* Stanford, CA: Stanford University Press.

Kempf, Edward John. 1921. *Psychopathology.* St. Louis, MO: C. V. Mosby.

Kenen, Stephanie H. 1997. "Who Counts When You're Counting Homosexuals? Hormones and Homosexuality in Mid-twentieth-century America." Pp. 197–218 in *Science and Homosexualities.* Edited by V. Rosario. New York: Routledge.

Kinsey, Alfred C., Wardell B. Pomeroy, and Clyde E. Martin. 1948. *Sexual Behavior in the Human Male.* Philadelphia: W. B. Saunders.

Kinsey, Alfred C., Wardell B. Pomeroy, Clyde E. Martin, and Paul H. Gebhard. 1953. *Sexual Behavior in the Human Female.* Philadelphia: W. B. Saunders.

Knight, Robert P. 1941. "Recognizing the Psychoneurotic Registrant." *Bulletin of the Menninger Clinic* 5: 161–166.

Loeser, Lewis. 1945. "The Sexual Psychopath in the Military Service." *American Journal of Psychiatry* 102: 92–101.

Machtan, Lothar. 2001. *The Hidden Hitler.* New York: Basic Books.

Owensby, Newdigate. 1940. "Homosexuality and Lesbianism Treated with Metrazol." *Journal of Nervous and Mental Disease* 92: 65–66.

————. 1941. "The Correction of Homosexuality." *Urologic and Cutaneous Review* 45: 494–496.

Perry, Helen Swick. 1982. *Psychiatrist of America: The Life of Harry Stack Sullivan.* Cambridge: Harvard University Press.

Rado, Sandor. 1940. "A Critical Examination of the Concept of Bisexuality." *Psychosomatic Medicine* 2: 459–467.

Selective Service System. 1941. "Minimum Psychiatric Inspection. Medical Circular No. 1—Revised." *Journal of the American Medical Association* 116, no. 18: 2059–2061.

Sullivan, Harry Stack. 1941. "Psychiatry and the National Defense." *Psychiatry* 4: 201–212.

————. 1965. *Collected Works.* New York: Norton.

Testis, Ernst. 1934. "The Revenge of the Pederasty Ring: Brown Leaders and the Brown Boys of Bolivia." Translated by Miles Wright from *Das dritte Reich stellt sich vor* (1933). *Medical Review of Reviews* 40: 197–205.

Wile, Ira S. 1941–1942. "Sex Offenders and Sex Offenses Classification and Treatment." *Journal of Criminal Psychopathology* 3: 11–31.

Wittels, Fritz. 1943. "Struggles of a Homosexual in Pre-Hitler Germany." *Journal of Criminal Psychopathology* 4: 408–423.

## Further Reading

Thanks to a number of interviews with gays and lesbians who served in the military service, Allan Bérubé constructs a poignant narrative in *Coming Out under Fire: The History of Gay Men and Women in World War II* (New York: Free Press, 1990). It was recently made into a gripping feature documentary film by Arthur Dong, *Coming Out under Fire* (New York: Zeitgeist Films, 1994).

Nathan Hale, Jr.'s, *The Rise and Crisis of Psychoanalysis in the United States: Freud and the Americans, 1917–1985* (New York: Oxford University Press, 1995) traces the vicissitudes of psychoanalysis since World War I. In *Great and Desperate Cures: The Rise and Decline of Psychosurgery and Other Radical Treatments for Mental Illness* (New York: Basic Books, 1986), Elliot S. Valenstein examines why lobotomies and electroshock therapy quickly became popular in the early half of the century. They were particularly used in public asylums such as those in California. Focusing on this context, Joel Braslow's *Mental Ills and Bodily Cures: Psychiatric Treatment in the First Half of the Twentieth Century* (Berkeley: University of California Press, 1997) tries to understand how they were seen as effective interventions.

# 5

## *The Cold War and the Sexual Revolution*

In a 1948 lecture to the Midwestern Association of College Psychiatrists and Clinical Psychologists, Dr. Benjamin Glover observed that "since the war there has been a noticeable increase in cases of homosexuality as well as other socially offending sex cases" at the University of Wisconsin at Madison, where he practiced (1951, 377). The majority of these were veterans, he noted. Many of them were culturally and politically suspect as well: they consorted with Negroes, and they liked music, "especially impressionistic and classical," or else Negro jazz. Although there was only one "radical politico with much publicity," Glover concluded that "there is a narcissistic selfishness in their disregard for people as a whole, no nationalistic or patriotic feeling, a general disdain of inheritance and social values of law, religion and the betterment of mankind" (382). New patients tended to crop up in the emergency room in a panic each time that newspapers exposed secret homosexual groups in Madison.

As Glover's lecture suggests, the 1950s was a decade of conflicting trends in the social and medical presence of homosexuals. The same year that Glover delivered his lecture, Alfred C. Kinsey, Wardell Pomeroy, and Clyde Martin published *Sexual Behavior in the Human Male* (see Sidebar 5.1). It instantly made homosexuality a hot topic of debate because of its evidence that homosexual behavior was far more prevalent than ever before imagined. Postwar social transformations and homosexual relationships forged among military service people also stimulated new, urban gay and lesbian communities and organizations in the 1950s. The Servicemen's Readjustment Act, better know as the GI Bill (of Rights), passed in 1944, subsidized home and business loans, job training, and higher education, which probably brought many of the homosexual veterans to Glover's campus as well as the big cities. Yet this increasing gay presence prompted legal and political crackdowns during a time of profound social conservatism.

Alfred C. Kinsey in 1953 (center) surrounded by his colleagues at the Indiana University Institute for Sex Research, now named the Kinsey Institute. Left to right, front row, seated: Cornelia Christenson, Hedwig O. Lester, Claude C. Martin. Behind them: Jean M. Brown, Paul Gebhard, William Dellenbeck, Wardell Pomeroy, Ritchie Davis, Eleanor Roehr, Dorothy Collins (William Dellenbeck/Bettmann/Corbis)

The medical interest in homosexuality also betrayed opposing tendencies. The Kinsey Report prompted further research on "normal" homosexuals that contradicted a century of pathologizing theories. But it also provoked vehement denunciations by some health professionals dedicated to "curing" society of homosexuals.

## The Kinsey Reports

The two Kinsey Reports on sexual behavior in men and women, published in 1948 and 1953, respectively, were immediate international bestsellers. The first one especially prompted abundant medical commentary, both laudatory and vitriolic. The Kinsey Report on men also served as a direct spur to the "homophile" rights movement that emerged publicly in the 1950s. Kinsey's studies presented massive amounts of data from detailed interviews of almost 11,000 white American men and women. In a paperback book titled *About the Kinsey Report* (published only months after Kinsey's volume), Donald P. Geddes (1948) zeroed in on why the rather numbing mass of Kinsey data had produced such a shock: Americans' *actual* sexual behavior bore little resemblance to their popular *ideals* of sexuality.

Kinsey's data on masturbation alone shattered long-standing popular and professional opinions. After more than two centuries of medical writings condemning masturbation as an injurious activity,

## Sidebar 5.1 Alfred C. Kinsey

Alfred C. Kinsey (1894–1956) received his Sc.D. in zoology from Harvard University in 1919. He then began research and teaching at Indiana University, where he would remain his entire career. In the 1920s and 1930s, he did extensive research on gall wasps, publishing four books on the subject. He also wrote several biology textbooks. A radical shift in his research began in 1938, when he became the coordinator of a new course on marriage and discovered the poverty of scientific information on human sexuality. He started informally interviewing colleagues and students to gather information about their sexual lives. In the process, he began perfecting the detailed sexual history interview and statistical methods that would be the cornerstone of his future research. He applied to the National Research Council for a grant to expand his work and was supported by the Committee for Research in the Problems of Sex with funds from the Rockefeller Foundation. Kinsey and his team ultimately interviewed 5,460 white men and 5,385 white women. Data on 177 black college-educated men and 223 women were not used in the original reports but were published later by Paul Gebhard and Alan Johnson (1979).

The first report, *Sexual Behavior in the Human Male,* was published in January 1948, with two Indiana colleagues: Wardell B. Pomeroy, a psychologist, and Clyde Martin, a statistician. It promptly became a bestseller in the United States and around the world through numerous reprintings and translations. It was simultaneously praised as a groundbreaking work of science and reviled as a spur to immorality. Kinsey and his colleagues recognized that his subject group was not a representative sample of the U.S. population. Homosexuals in particular were over-represented because Kinsey sought out members of homophile groups and the homosexual communities of Chicago, Los Angeles, San Francisco, New York, and Philadelphia, encouraging them to recruit friends and associates to participate. In order to gather more detailed information from these subjects, the Kinsey team developed a special battery of questions. The inclusion criteria for this "homosexual sample" were that the individual had to have fifty or more postpubescent homosexual contacts or twenty or more homosexual partners. Over 2,066 men and 475 women met these criteria—an indication of a strong homosexual skew in the data.

Anthropologist Paul H. Gebhard joined the group in the preparation of *Sexual Behavior in the Human Female* (1953). They found that the factors of age and class, which corresponded to significant differences in the frequency and type of male sexual activity, were less important in women. However, upper-class women tended to engage in more homosexual behavior than lower-class women—the inverse finding from that of the male study. The women's movement seemed to have made an impact, since they discovered that a higher percentage of women coming of age after World War I were sexually active than earlier generations. The report on women also generated much controversy. Congressman Lewis B. Heller declared it "the insult of the century against women."

the Kinsey Report now showed that those who *did not* masturbate were the abnormal minority of 10 percent. Kinsey's keen interest in class differences led to the discovery that the professional and educated classes masturbated *more* than the lower class, which found its "sexual outlet" more frequently in premarital and extramarital intercourse, as well as homosexual activity. Kinsey had long objected to the notion of the "homosexual" as a discrete category of human being that was diametrically opposed to the "heterosexual." In an astute and biting critique of hormonal research on homosexuality, Kinsey wrote in 1941, "More basic than any error brought out in the analysis of the above data [on the hormone levels of "homosexuals" versus "normals"] is the assumption that homosexuality and heterosexuality are two mutually exclusive phenomena emanating from fundamentally and, at least in some cases, inherently different types of individuals" (1941, 425). Instead, he insisted that homosexuality was simply one form of sexual outlet—and by no means a rare or exclusive one. The Kinsey Report again criticized "the tendency to categorize sexual activity under two heads, and of a failure to recognize the endless gradations that actually exist" (1948, 650). It therefore introduced a 0 to 6 scale to classify behavior on a *continuum* from exclusively heterosexual (0) to exclusively homosexual (6).

Simply by asking about sexual *acts* rather than *identities,* Kinsey discovered that a surprisingly large number of people were not exclusively heterosexual. He found that 37 percent of his male subjects had engaged in at least one homosexual act to the point of orgasm at some time between adolescence and old age. This was one of the report's most highly publicized statistics. It inspired actor Harry Hay (whom Kinsey had interviewed in 1940) to believe there had to be enough homosexuals to form an organization of "homophiles," which gradually blossomed into the Mattachine Society in 1951 (Timmons 1990, 134).

The "10 percent" figure that continues to be widely quoted as Kinsey's measure of the prevalence of homosexuals in the population in fact has a more restricted meaning. Kinsey found that 10 percent of his male subjects are "more or less exclusively homosexual (i.e., rate 5 or 6) for at least three years between the ages of 16 and 55" (1948, 651). The corresponding estimate for unmarried women between the ages of twenty-five and thirty-five was 2–6 percent and for married women in that age range was only 1 percent (1953, 473–474). Kinsey found that only 4 percent of men were "exclusively homosexual" (i.e., rate 6) for their entire lives (1948, 651). This percentage is about the same as that found in subsequent demographic studies. It was the larger 37 percent figure that was more frequently quoted by early homophiles, many of whom had been or were married and therefore were not "exclusively homosexual" (Kinsey scale 6).

The significance of Kinsey's data was promptly criticized, even by his supporters. His interview sample overrepresented midwesterners (particularly Indianans), prison inmates, and homosexuals.

The reports also only presented data from white subjects. Neverthe-less, many physicians and sexologists declared it revolutionary and one of the most important scientific works of the twentieth century. Some psychoanalysts welcomed Kinsey's data as objective support of Sigmund Freud's claims for the power of the sexual drive. The Kinsey Reports exposed how outdated and even hypocritical current sexual mores and laws were. Geddes pointed out that 95 percent of the male population would be eligible for incarceration if the truth of their sex-ual lives was known! Writing in Geddes's anthology, Professor Ashley Montague (1948) reasoned that hypocritical and unrealistic legal and social attitudes contributed to both an excessive preoccupation with sex and mounting pathologies of sexuality.

Kinsey's findings and the response to them strongly suggested that so-called crimes and immoral acts such as homosexuality should be destigmatized, given their surprising prevalence. That was cer-tainly the report's own conclusion:

> In view of the data which we now have on the incidence and fre-quency of the homosexual, and in particular on its coexistence with the heterosexual in the lives of a considerable portion of

*The Los Angeles Mattachine Society meets for a discrete Christmas party. Harry Hay (in chair), with (left to right) Dale Jennings, Rudi Gernreich, Stan Witt, Bob Hull, Chuck Rowlands, and Paul Bernard (Jim Gruber, International Gay Information Center Archives, Manuscripts & Archives Division, New York Public Library).*

the male population, it is difficult to maintain the view that psychosexual reactions between individuals of the same sex are rare and therefore abnormal or unnatural, or that they constitute within themselves evidence of neuroses or even psychoses. (Kinsey, Pomeroy, and Martin 1948, 659)

This normalizing view was a powerful message for homosexuals at the time and directly stimulated expressions of homosexual rights, such as the formation of the Mattachine Society and the publication of Donald Webster Cory's book *The Homosexual in America* (see Sidebar 5.3). Many psychiatrists and social guardians who were committed to the pathologization of homosexuality refused to change their views. They reasoned that the mounting frequency of a

*Dr. Blanche M. Baker, M.D., Ph.D., author of the "Toward Understanding" column in ONE Magazine (ONE Institute and Archives, Los Angeles)*

**Sidebar 5.2 ONE, Inc., and Science**
The idea of a homophile magazine arose in October 1952 during a meeting of the Los Angeles Mattachine Society, an early gay organization. The result, *ONE Magazine: The Homosexual Viewpoint*, was first published in January 1953. Its parent group, ONE, Inc., was founded as "an organization that should serve as spokesman for the millions of homosexual American men and women, and, through its publications, as a public forum for discussions of the whole question." It presented original essays, news digests, book reviews, poetry, and fiction. By the mid-1950s, thousands of copies of each issue were circulating around the country.

The editors of *ONE* were particularly interested in reporting on the biomedical perspective on homosexuality, since they trusted that science could provide the most authoritative and objective demonstration that homosexuality was natural. Members of ONE, Inc., cooperated with Evelyn Hooker and Alfred Kinsey in their research. Hooker spoke at the ONE Institute, and summaries of her articles were reprinted in *ONE*. Kinsey was the first person from outside Los Angeles to subscribe to the magazine. Upon his death, *ONE* published a warm tribute to Kinsey. The editors concluded: "We shall always be grateful for the legacy that he left to us and to all who insist upon sexual freedom" (Pedersen 1956, 6).

## Sidebar 5.3 "Toward Understanding"—the Gay Advice Column

Beginning in January 1959, *ONE Magazine* started running a regular advice column entitled "Toward Understanding" by Dr. Blanche M. Baker, a former surgeon turned psychiatrist. The purpose of the column was to "create a better understanding of homosexual problems through the psychiatric viewpoint." However, "Dr. Blanche" (as she signed her replies) was no orthodox psychiatrist—she was an extraordinarily sympathetic one. According to gay activist Jim Kepner, she "electrified" the audience at the ONE Midwinter Institute in January 1955 by "calling most gays wonderful, well adjusted, often highly talented people." In her first column in 1959, she made her mission clear: "I trust that I may be able to shed some light into the gloom of fear, shame, guilt, disgust and lack of self confidence which surround the lives of all too many homophiles at the present time" (Baker 1959a, 26).

Her warm, gay-affirmative stance is evident in this one exchange:

Dear Dr. Baker,

Only in ONE Magazine can I find some expression of my own feeling. If anyone would know just how badly I need the affection of someone, and of my own gender, it would naturally be you people at ONE. We so-called "gay" people are a lonely race; our satisfactions are generally brief and are not long-lasting. . . .

I am a college student. . . . Although I am in my early twenties, it was just a week ago that I had my physical for the Army. I decided to be truthful and marked my form affirmative for "homosexual inclinations." I was rejected. But I was well satisfied with the private manner in which the matter was dealt.

I do hope to have a reply soon.

Mr. P. I. E.

Ohio

Dear P. I. E.,

Thanks for your kind comments regarding ONE. The chief purpose of the magazine is to help homosexuals to understand themselves and to help integrate them into society. If you were closer to Los Angeles you would find ample companionship with the members of ONE, Inc. . . . To overcome your loneliness, I would suggest that you move to some city where there is a chapter of the Mattachine Society, where social activities are part of the varied program.

I am happy that you were so frank about your rejection by the Army. . . . Many homosexuals suffer needlessly because they fear revealing themselves to Uncle Sam. Of course homosexuals must be discreet but when dealing with the Armed Forces it is far better to reveal the truth than to run the risk of being caught and "branded" with a dishonorable discharge.

Sincerely,

Dr. Blanche (Baker 1959b, 26)

---

crime did not justify its decriminalization. For them, the lessons to be learned from the Kinsey Report lay in the direction of better understanding sexual practices in order to more effectively promote monogamous heterosexuality. Writing in Geddes's anthology, Dr. O. Spurgeon English, head of the psychiatry department at Temple University

Medical School, expressed this view with much condescension: "To condemn homosexuality will never accomplish anything, but to accept it and work for its elimination should help everybody" (1948, 111).

Other critics were even less kind—toward homosexuals or Kinsey. The publication of *Sexual Behavior in the Human Female* (the Kinsey Report on women) in 1953 also instigated a number of medical reactions. A book reviewer for the *Psychiatric Quarterly* (Review 1954a; Review 1954b) praised Edmund Bergler and William Kroger's hostile volume, *Kinsey's Myth of Female Sexuality: The Medical Facts*, while condemning as liberal and "scientifically valueless" a laudatory anthology by psychologist Albert Ellis. The reviewer further insulted Kinsey's approach as "naïve-behavioristic," and concluded that Kinsey's "'findings,' highly publicized, have done more damage to sexology and psychiatry than their worst enemies had been capable of inflicting previously" (1954c, 152). In retrospect, it now appears that Bergler, a psychoanalyst obsessed with condemning homosexuality, was far more damaging and embarrassing to the profession.

### Edmund Bergler and the Psycho-Persecution of Homosexuals

Edmund Bergler began psychoanalytic practice in Vienna in 1927, serving on the staff of the Freud Psychoanalytic Clinic. He was its assistant director for four years until 1937, when it was closed down by the Nazis. He emigrated to New York City the following year and lectured at the Psychoanalytic Institute there. He wrote prolifically on a variety of subjects: impotence and frigidity, marital discord, sexual neuroses, and gambling. But from the mid-1940s on, he devoted most of his energies to "curing and deglamorizing" the disease of homosexuality (1943, 1944, 1947). He was an effective self-promoter. So, although his string of books on homosexuality tended to be repetitive and strident, he was a widely cited authority in the popular media for the psychiatric view that homosexuality was a neurosis that could be cured.

The cornerstone of his theorizing was the notion of the "breast complex," which he had described with Ludwig Eidelberg in 1933. They focused on the infantile psychic trauma of weaning and the oral stage rather than the oedipal drama that Freud emphasized. Weaning supposedly led to oral aggression against the mother and, in the case of male homosexuals, the substitution of the penis for the lost breast. This passive loss could be restituted by aggressive oral compulsions to incorporate the breast-penis through masturbation, fellatio, and anal sex (in which hand, mouth, and anus, respectively, serve the receptive role). Bergler also repeatedly decried homosexuals as "injustice collectors": they were "psychic masochists" unconsciously seeking to be punished for their guilty feelings. Nevertheless, they were spreading their perversion, especially to adolescents.

Bergler swiftly reacted to the Kinsey Report in an article entitled "The Myth of a New National Disease" (1948). Kinsey had directed stinging criticism at psychoanalysts whom he accused of bringing rigid, moralistic views of "normality" to their study of homosexuality and who disingenuously ignored elements of homosexuality in their own life histories. Bergler, in return, lambasted Kinsey for misrepresenting psychoanalytic views, or, more insidiously, Bergler charged Kinsey with resisting Freudian facts because of Kinsey's own unconscious conflicts. Bergler suspected that a disproportionate number of homosexuals had participated in the study in order to appease their guilt. He fundamentally differed from Kinsey on the nature and frequency of homosexual behavior: it could never be indulged in unproblematically since it betrayed deep psychic defects. Kinsey had boldly suggested that homosexual relationships were short-lived mainly because they lacked social supports and the legal restraints of heterosexual marriage. Bergler objected that homosexuals were by definition neurotic and were only capable of brief, psychopathological relationships.

Bergler insisted, unlike Kinsey, that homosexuality was a neurotic disease and was curable. Indeed, if Kinsey's figures were accurate, Bergler estimated that homosexuality was "the predominant disease" in the United States. Kinsey's results and his attempts to depathologize homosexuality, Bergler feared, would do profound social harm. Homosexuals would feel there was scientific evidence for maintaining and spreading their perversion. "Borderline cases" would more easily turn to homosexuality. Sexually unsatisfied women would all conclude that an impotent male partner was a "fairy." But perhaps most worrisome during the Cold War, Kinsey's results on homosexuality would be "politically and propagandistically used against the United States abroad, stigmatizing the nation as a whole in a whisper campaign" since there were no comparable statistics for other countries.

Bergler launched his own counterattack to "deglamorize homosexuality" through popular books and radio and television broadcasts. In *1000 Homosexuals* (1959), he claimed that a conspiracy of silence in the mass media led homosexuals to feel they were misunderstood and discriminated against. Somewhat contradictorily, he also believed that this lent homosexuality an allure of danger and difference. He fueled a broad publicity campaign to demonstrate that homosexuality was neither mysterious nor glamorous but a painful and disabling illness. From Bergler's own published transcripts of analytic sessions, it is evident that he badgered, bullied, and outright insulted patients who did not conform to his theories. Analyst and historian Kenneth Lewes concludes that many of Bergler's articles are "a disgrace to the journals in which they appear, and their editors must bear the accusation of bad judgment or pusillanimity" (1988, 154). Although Bergler was an embarrassment to the psychoanalytic profession in later life, his ideas were widely publicized in the popular and professional press and are still cited in the most virulent homophobic propaganda as authoritative evidence of the psychopathology of homosexuality.

Although Bergler may have been a zealot, he had close counterparts among more mainstream psychoanalysts. Dr. Frank Caprio's *Female Homosexuality* was the first medical monograph dedicated to lesbianism, a topic largely neglected by analysts. Caprio frequently cites Bergler and often sounds like him: "Female homosexuality is a form of cooperative or mutual masturbation at best. It represents an unconscious defense mechanism—a symptomatic expression of a neurotic personality—a disturbance in the infantile psychosexual development—a regression to narcissism—a manifestation of an emotional maladjustment" (1954, 303). Like Bergler and other analysts, Caprio was supremely confident in the powers of psychoanalysis: "Lesbians can be cured if they are earnest in their desire to be cured. Adequate self-knowledge via psychoanalysis is essential to effect a permanent cure" (307).

## Aggressive Psychoanalysis

Bergler's and Caprio's writings reflect a widespread therapeutic optimism and aggressiveness that had evolved since Sandor Rado's 1940 challenge to the Freudian theory of universal bisexuality (see Chapter 4). Adopting Rado's view of homosexuality as a pathological adaptation, Dr. John Poe (1952) reported his successful treatment of a "passive homosexual" man. Sixty-five sessions of psychotherapy over eight months supposedly resulted in the conversion of this thirty-nine-year-old "obligatory homosexual" into a happily married heterosexual.

Analysts' new sense of therapeutic potency in molding sexuality is also reflected in a paper delivered at the 1953 meeting of the American Psychoanalytic Association by Drs. Lawrence Kolb and Adelaide Johnson of the Mayo Clinic. For them, sexuality was highly volatile: homosexuality could be accidentally or unconsciously encouraged by parents or analysts. Inversely, they felt homosexuality was curable through psychoanalysis. They recommended that therapists take a stern position: threaten to terminate analysis if the patient did not discontinue all homosexual activity (1955).

Given some psychiatrists' belief in the malleability of sexuality, it is clear why they feared that Kinsey's "permissive" views would only incite further homosexuality. Dr. Hyman Barahal dismissed Kinsey's attempts to portray homosexuality as normal because it was commonplace. Neurosis was also widespread but none-the-less pathological. And homosexuality, Barahal wrote, "is only a symptom of a neurotic structure" (1953, 437). He described a patient who today might identify as transgendered. She was a twenty-two-year-old working-class lesbian who sought a medical permit to cross-dress. Since childhood she had wanted to dress as a boy. She had become self-sufficient at age fifteen and had worked in various factories during wartime, which was common since so many men were engaged in military service. Following the lead of Helene Deutsch (see Chapter 3), Barahal concluded that female transvestitism "is not a manifestation of homosexuality but of a drive for masculinity. Qualitatively, it does not differ essentially from other similarly-motivated disturbances in the sphere of feminine psychology. The supposedly happily-married woman who is eternally competing with her husband is the more subtle type of the same problem. Homosexuality has no meaning except as a multidetermined manifestation of neurosis" (438). Barahal's formulation reflects the conservative 1950s attitudes toward sexuality and gender: female independence, lesbianism, and cross-dressing all were collapsed into a diagnosis of neurosis.

## Homosexuality beyond the Couch

Although Kinsey's subject sample was not statistically representative of the U.S. population, it still presented the largest collection of *nonclinical* individuals. Most psychiatric studies, however, were skewed toward subjects who presented themselves at psychiatrists' offices presumably because of emotional problems. Besides Kinsey's work, other 1950s research on nonclinical homosexual populations further undermined the model of homosexuality as a disease in itself.

Clellan S. Ford and Frank A. Beach's *Patterns of Sexual Behavior* (1951) examined homosexuality cross-culturally and in nonhuman primates. Relying on data from the Yale Human Relations Area Files, they found that homosexual behavior was considered normal for certain members of forty-nine of seventy-six foreign cultures studied. Although some of this information was known—for example, concerning the Native American *berdache*—they presented it in a more positive light. They found that homosexual activity was sometimes an essential element in rites of passage for certain cultures. In other societies it was accepted as normal premarital activity. Cross-dressed, homosexually

*Evelyn Hooker
(courtesy of
Jonathan Marshall)*

active individuals such as the *berdache* were even revered figures in a number of American Indian tribes.

After reviewing animal observations, they concluded that homosexual behavior was present in nearly all animal species. It was not restricted to displays of dominance or an outlet of last resort. It could also be found accompanied by signs of erotic arousal and pleasure. Sexual responsiveness to both sexes, they reported, was a natural element of our "fundamental mammalian heritage" (Ford and Beach 1951, 259). Ford and Beach, like Kinsey three years earlier, concluded that homosexuality could not justifiably be deemed pathological. Furthermore, "social forces"—not biology—"condition the individual exclusively to heterosexual stimuli" (265).

The most influential research on the mental health of "normal" homosexuals was conducted by psychologist Evelyn Hooker, beginning in the 1940s (see Sidebar 5.4). Hooker had socialized with many gay men leading regular, successful lives who constituted a distinct minority group in Los Angeles (Hooker 1956). They convinced her that the psychiatric view of homosexuality was biased by samples drawn from clinical and institutionalized subjects. With a grant from the National Institute of Mental Health and volunteers selected from local homophile groups (the Mattachine Society and ONE, Inc.), Hooker compared the psychological performance of these homosexuals to heterosexual males matched for age and educational level. Judging from projective tests such as the Rorschach (inkblot), Hooker (1957) found that her homosexual and heterosexual subjects did not differ significantly in their degree of psychological adjustment. Equally important, experienced psychologists, when blinded to the sexual orientation of the matched subjects, could not accurately distinguish between the responses of homosexuals and heterosexuals beyond mere chance (Hooker 1958 and 1959). Hooker later recounted how the distinguished psychologists who had blindly rated the tests were so certain that they could differentiate the homosexuals from the heterosexuals that they asked to reevaluate the tests. They still failed to consistently distinguish the projective tests by sexual orientation (Schmiechen 1992).

## Sidebar 5.4 Evelyn Hooker

Evelyn Hooker (1907–1996) earned her Ph.D. in psychology at the Johns Hopkins University. She began her career as an experimental psychologist at the University of California at Los Angeles (UCLA) in 1939. Sam From, a student in her introductory psychology class, befriended her and later introduced her to his gay social circles. Here she encountered successful homosexuals leading stable lives and not seeking psychiatric help. They eventually began urging her to study "people like them" to counter the psychiatric literature's focus on clinical or criminal homosexuals. In 1953, she applied for a National Institute of Mental Health (NIMH) grant to conduct this work. In her "Reflections of a 40-Year Exploration," she recalls that she launched into this new area of research with much trepidation. The McCarthy witch hunts of homosexuals were raging, and the general societal and professional atmosphere toward homosexuals was also hostile. When she went to see the chairman of the Psychiatry Department at UCLA, Normal Q. Brill, to discuss her study of "normal male homosexuals," he reacted with astonishment. "He rose from his chair," she recalled, "and said, 'What do you think you are doing? There is no such person'" (Hooker 1993, 450).

She recognized that in this atmosphere she had to approach her subjects nonjudgmentally and with a guarantee of absolute confidentiality. She therefore conducted all interviews herself in the seclusion of her well-isolated home study, where her friend, gay novelist Christopher Isherwood, had lived for a while. Her informants eventually took her to gay parties, bars, and organizations. Based on her experiences, Hooker would write about the great social diversity of homosexual men and their "gay worlds" (1965). With great perspicacity, she analyzed the gay bar as a center for public socializing and a "free market" of homosexual leisure and sexuality. She detailed with an ethnographer's eye the rituals of "cruising" and the "one-night stand." Drawing on sociological and psychological studies of "minority groups," she argued that what were commonly viewed as homosexual personality defects resulted from the "strains of a hostile heterosexual society" and not individual inner dynamics or psychopathology.

In her research in the late 1950s, she used projective tests such as the Rorschach (ink blot) to compare homosexual and heterosexual male volunteers matched by age, IQ, and educational level. When experts judged the results, they could not significantly distinguish between the two groups of subjects. Furthermore, two-thirds of the homosexual men demonstrated average to superior psychological adjustment. "When I saw that," she later recalled, "I wept with joy. I knew that the psychiatrists would not accept it then. But sometime!" (1993, 452).

In 1969, she was called upon to chair an NIMH task force on homosexuality, which would set forth broad goals for research and social policy. The publication of the task force's final report was delayed for two years because of internal dissent and institutional controversy. It recommended that homosexuality no longer be viewed as a psychopathology and that it be decriminalized. It was not until 1975 that the American Psychological Association officially adopted the former view. In 1992, it honored her with its Distinguished Contribution in the Public Interest award. That year, Richard Schmiechen released a documentary about her life, *Changing Our Minds: The Story of Dr. Evelyn Hooker,* which was nominated for an Academy Award in 1993. Her research is so groundbreaking and controversial that it continues to be attacked by those insisting that homosexuality is pathological.

Hooker acknowledged that some homosexuals suffered from psychological disorders and had difficulties maintaining intimate relationships. However, she attributed this problem not to an intrinsic psychopathology of homosexuality but to social stigmatization and victimization, just like other minority groups. In her publications in professional journals and homophile magazines and in her public appearances, she cogently argued that it was not homosexuals who needed to convert but society that needed to change its attitude toward homosexuality (Hooker 1993).

## Transsexualism

The Victorian legacy of "sexual inversion" endured well into the twentieth century. Even in 1965, psychiatrist Judd Marmor would still use it as the title of an anthology on homosexuality. However, as we have seen, it collapsed a variety of issues into one. The inversion model of the lesbian was of a male soul in a female body and vice versa for the homosexual man. The invert was presumed to possess a variety of cross-sexed traits from the most superficial aspects of clothing and gesture to the deepest anatomical and physiological markers: hips, hormones, and neurons. Ultimately, the invert longed to be of the opposite sex and sought the love of "normally" sexed people, not other inverts. Many homosexuals and some psychiatrists had complained in the late nineteenth century that this model failed to describe most homosexuals, who were physically indistinguishable from heterosexuals and had no desire to alter their sex. Nevertheless, the inversion model persisted. Indeed, current research hypothesizing that gay men had been sissy boys or have feminine hypothalamuses or other brain structures remains in this vein.

In particular, the inversion model collapsed together three issues that we see as quite distinct today: homosexuality, transvestism, and transsexuality. Although Magnus Hirschfeld coined the term *transvestite* in 1910 as a type distinct from the homosexual, he felt that cross-sexed behavior and dress was a distinctive symptom of inversion. The first people to have undergone "genital transformation" surgery were diagnosed by their German surgeon as "homosexual transvestites" (Abraham 1931). However, in the 1950s, transsexualism definitively broke away from homosexuality—at least in the medical literature.

In 1952, Danish doctors Christian Hamburger, George Stürup, and E. Dahl-Iversen performed sex reassignment surgery on an American GI, George Jorgensen. The new "blonde beauty," Christine Jorgensen, received worldwide media attention (Meyerowitz 1998). Yet in the original article on the procedure, the doctors described it as the hormonal and surgical treatment for "genuine transvestitism" (1953). Through the efforts of endocrinologist Harry Benjamin, the phenomenon of transsexualism came to be classified as a distinct medical entity. The Harry Benjamin International Gender Dysphoria Association was founded as a clearinghouse for professional information on transsexualism and for the development of professional guidelines for the ethical treatment of transsexuals.

Benjamin even published an article by a heterosexual transvestite. The author, a psychologist writing under the pseudonym C. V. Prince (1956), attempted to distinguish homosexuality, transvestitism, and transsexualism for his fellow psychologists and psychoanalysts. He observed that all three forms of behavior (in men) were attributed to "feminine identification." However, he believed that this notion explained nothing. It was vague and, in fact, covered three different aspects of "femininity": anatomy and sexual behavior, the psychology of gender, and social attitudes toward women. The distinctions Prince was trying to articulate are comparable to those of "gender role" and "gender identity" being developed at the time by psychologist John Money (1955) in reference to intersexed or hermaphroditic children. In Prince's attempt to elaborate clear distinctions, he suggested a one-to-one correspondence: the "passive" homosexual sought a feminine sexuality, the transsexual felt he had a feminine psyche, and the transvestite adopted a feminine social role. He recognized that these distinctions were too simplistic but wanted to make it clear that not all transvestites were homosexual, nor did they reject their masculinity as did transsexuals.

Despite these attempts to define transsexualism as an independent diagnosis, many psychiatrists continued to associate homosexuality with the desire for change of sex. For example, Dr. Paul Miller (1958) published a study titled "The Effeminate Passive Obligatory Homosexual," in which he presented psychological data on fifty homosexuals incarcerated in a special medical unit for federal prisoners in Springfield, Missouri. He noted that they were isolated to protect them from sexual assault and because of "the tension they create among other inmates who vie for their favors" (612). Although the subjects were identified as homosexuals, 36 percent of them reportedly wanted sex reassignment surgery.

## The Decline of Somaticism

During the 1950s, somatic therapies, such as lobotomies and electroconvulsive therapy, quickly fell out of favor. This trend accelerated after the introduction of Thorazine (an antipsychotic and "major tranquilizer") and other psychoactive drugs, beginning in 1954. Somatic approaches to explaining and treating homosexuality were also on the decline. Although some sexologists continued to study homosexuality as a congenital and organic disorder—notably the twin studies of Franz Kallmann (see Sidebar 5.5)—most psychiatrists leaned toward the psychodynamic model.

Ironically, even though Kinsey was openly hostile toward psychoanalysis, the Kinsey Reports could be viewed as evidence for the psychological explanation of homosexuality. The head of the Department of Psychiatry at Temple University Medical School, O. Spurgeon English, in his "Primer on Homosexuality," praised Kinsey's research. It demonstrated, English concluded, that homosexual activity is very common, was present at all social and occupational levels, and had a broad variety of expressions—from one-timers to exclusive homosexuals. "The homosexual" could no longer be seen as a discrete and "rare phenomenon—even a clinical curiosity" (1953, 55).

English dismissed all the previous hereditary, glandular, and hormonal theories of homosexuality. He even discarded the model of homosexuality as a psychopathic defect. The cumulated cases "point to the fact that homosexuality is a personality component that is found in many people suffering from a neurosis" (57). He presented as a certainty the various psychoanalytic explanations of the genesis of homosexuality. The "readjustment" of homosexuals was a difficult matter, however, for it depended on the degree of "fixation" of homosexuality in the patient's personality. It was as difficult to remove as any severe neurosis or psychotic pattern. In any case, the only promise of cure was through "long and tedious . . . intensive psychiatric treatment, preferably Freudian psychoanalysis, carried on five times weekly" for two years or more (57). The more optimistic goal was simply the management of homosexuality as a personality disturbance. The patient could thus be directed to recreational pursuits and healthy social associations that might prevent him from engaging in criminal behavior. In other words, the patient could be coached to enjoy celibacy.

Although English did not want psychiatry to condone homosexuality, he did urge that homosexuals be treated with compassion. "There is too much tendency to judge the man or woman who confesses to homosexual behavior as a person who is obscene, perverted, wicked, lustful, and irresponsible, or one who undermines the mores of society," he complained. "These accusations can also be leveled at heterosexuals as well" (59). And indeed they were, for at the time he

## Sidebar 5.5 Homosexuals in the Family

By the 1950s, hormonal and genetic theories of the causation of homosexuality had largely fallen out of fashion in U.S. biomedicine. Nevertheless, Franz J. Kallmann (1897–1965), a human geneticist, continued to pursue this line of research. As historian Garland Allen (1997) has detailed, Kallmann did much of his training and early research in Berlin under Ernst Rüdin. A psychiatrist who advocated racial hygiene, Rüdin collaborated in the formulation of the 1933 German sterilization law—eugenics legislation aimed at preventing "defective" people from reproducing. In the 1930s, Kallmann was studying schizophrenia as a hereditary disease. He recommended the eugenic sterilization of all schizophrenics and their "eccentric" family members in order to stamp out the disease.

Ironically, Kallmann had to flee Germany in 1935 because he was half Jewish himself and therefore a likely victim of Nazi eugenic policy. In the United States, he eventually became chief of psychiatric research at the New York State Psychiatric Institute affiliated with Columbia University. He was elected president of the American Society of Human Genetics in 1951, and it was at that year's annual meeting of the Society that he presented a report entitled "Twin and Sibship Study of Overt Male Homosexuality."

Given the dominance of psychodynamic theories at the time, Kallmann was defensive about his research. He relied particularly on the Kinsey Report to reject the psychoanalytic model of homosexuality. Instead, he returned to Richard von Krafft-Ebing's hereditary hypothesis. Kallmann studied the sexuality of forty pairs of monozygotic (identical) twins and forty-five pairs of dizygotic (fraternal) twins. If homosexuality was inherited, he expected the monozygotic brother of each homosexual subject to also be homosexual since the two shared identical genes. Since heterozygotic twins had fewer genes in common, they should have a lower concordance rate for homosexuality.

Indeed, Kallmann found that the dizygotic twins' concordance rate for homosexuality was 11.5 to 42.3 percent (depending on their Kinsey heterosexual-homosexual rating). But *every* monozygotic cotwin of an "overt homosexual" was at least a Kinsey 3 or higher, that is, frequently to exclusively homosexual (Kallmann 1952). He felt his results cast considerable doubt on the psychodynamic theories and greatly bolstered the genetic theory. His study called for more research into the genetics of homosexuality, he concluded. "The urgency of such work is undeniable as long as this aberrant type of behavior continues to be an inexhaustible source of unhappiness, discontentment, and a distorted sense of human values."

As Allen points out, Kallmann's research is riddled with methodological problems, and it was heavily criticized by psychodynamically oriented psychiatrists at the time. His call for more genetic research on homosexuality went unheeded for decades. Ironically, it was only after gay liberation and the depathologization of homosexuality that scientists would seriously revive the genetic theory of homosexuality.

was writing, the McCarthy witch hunts were busy accusing hundreds of Americans of being communist sympathizers and homosexuals. In fact, more people were dismissed from government jobs for their sexual orientation than their political affiliation. The decline of the somatic model and the general acceptance of the psychological model of homosexuality directly fueled the ideology of these purges.

In February 1950, just days after Senator Joseph McCarthy accused the State Department of being riddled with communists, the under-secretary of state drew attention to the dismissal of numerous homosexuals from the State Department. In an April 1950 newsletter to Republican Party workers, Guy G. Gabrielson, Republican national chairman, lambasted the Truman administration for harboring "subversives" and "traitors." He continued: "Perhaps as dangerous as the actual Communists are the sex perverts who have infiltrated our government in recent years" ("Perverts" 1950, 25).

In a preliminary Senate study, a Washington police officer in the vice squad estimated that 3,500 perverts were employed by the government. Countering the mounting hysteria, Dr. R. H. Felix, director of the National Institute of Mental Health, assured senators that there was no reason to believe that the prevalence of "confirmed homosexuals" in the government was any greater than the 4 percent figure Kinsey had estimated for the general population. Senator Kenneth Wherry, Republican floor leader, ridiculed Dr. Felix's statement, which seemed to imply that "none should complain if the Government has its share" of criminals (White 1950, 8). In this spirit of zero tolerance, the Senate authorized an investigation on June 7, 1950, into the "employment of homosexuals and other sex perverts in the government."

The Investigations Subcommittee examined all government agencies and District of Columbia police records since January 1, 1947. It also consulted "eminent physicians and psychiatrists" in the production of the "Hoey Report," which was released December 15, 1950, and was informally named after North Carolina senator Clyde R. Hoey, chair of the Investigations Subcommittee. The committee discovered that there was considerable professional disagreement on the matter of homosexuality. Nevertheless, it found that "most authorities believe that sex deviation results from psychological rather than physical causes, and in many cases there are no outward characteristics or physical traits that are positive as identifying marks of sex perversion" (U.S. Congress 1950, 2). Therefore, not all homosexual men are effeminate, nor are all lesbians masculine.

The report betrays a particular anxiety toward those homosexuals or bisexuals who *appear* normal. "The active, aggressive, male type [of homosexual] is almost exclusively attracted to the passive type of homosexual or to young men and boys who are not necessarily homosexual. . . . Bisexual individuals are often married and have children, and except for their perverted activities they appear to lead normal lives" (3). The flamboyant queen or butch lesbian could be easily spotted and excluded from employment, but "normal"-appearing homosexuals, like communists, could evade detection and infiltrate the government. Kinsey's data only heightened anxieties that homosexuals were legion and hidden everywhere.

The Hoey Report concluded that "those who engage in acts of homosexuality and other perverted sex activities are unsuitable for employment in the Federal Government" for two reasons: they are committing illegal and immoral acts, and they constitute security risks because they are easy blackmail targets. The subcommittee relied on the medical evidence to bolster their conclusions. The psychoanalytic model explained that homosexuality was a neurotic arrest of psychosexual development at an infantile stage. The Hoey Report could therefore claim that "those who engage in overt acts of perversion lack the emotional stability of normal persons" (4), which also "makes them more susceptible to the blandishments of the foreign espionage agent" (5)—akin to children being tempted by candy. D. Milton Ladd, the assistant to the director of the Federation Bureau of Investigation (FBI) (who was then J. Edgar Hoover, now suspected of being a closeted homosexual) testified that "high Russian intelligence officials" were systematically seeking out such American government officials, "hoping to find a chink in their armor and a weakness upon which they might capitalize at the appropriate time" (quoted in U.S. Congress 1950, 6).

Since homosexuality was no longer believed to be congenital, there was also the fear that it was contagious, especially through pederastic seduction of naive youth. "These perverts will frequently attempt to entice normal individuals to engage in perverted practices," the report warned. "This is particularly true in the case of young and impressionable people. . . . One homosexual can pollute a Government office" (4). "Eminent psychiatrists" had informed the subcommittee that homosexuals sought their own kind; therefore, if they were in a position to influence hiring, homosexuals would place other perverts in government jobs.

The Hoey Report only lent further official sanction to a homosexual purge that had already begun that April. In the previous thirty-nine months (January 1, 1947, until April 1, 1950), 3,245 military personnel and 192 civilian government employees had been investigated on sex perversion charges. But in the seven subsequent months (April 1, 1950, until November 1, 1950) the rate of accusations and investigations had skyrocketed: 1,135 military personnel and 382 civilian government employees were investigated and the vast majority had resigned or were dismissed (U.S. Congress 1950, 24–25). Although the report suggested that those accused be examined by medical psychiatrists, it noted that psychological tests "are by no means conclusive." (Indeed, in a few years Evelyn Hooker would show that they were largely useless in detecting homosexuality.) The report instead promoted close collaboration between government agencies, local police, and the FBI in routing out suspected perverts. A rather bleak and terrifying decade lay ahead for homosexuals, not just in government service but throughout the United States. As historian John D'Emilio (1989) has documented, the persecution of homosexuals and the communist witch hunts were intertwined events in the Cold War politics of the 1950s. Both were campaigns to impose ideological conformity—sexually and politically.

## The Psychiatric Response

Although psychiatrists had lent "scientific" support to these "sex pervert" witch hunts and were increasingly advocating the treatment of homosexuals, some leaders of the profession objected to this persecution. In January 1955, a special committee of the Group for the Advancement of Psychiatry (GAP) released its "Report on Homosexuality with Particular Emphasis on This Problem in Governmental Agencies." Psychoanalyst William Menninger had founded GAP after the end of World War II, prompted by the need to deal with the millions of people rejected or dismissed from the military—many of whom were homosexuals. GAP consisted of 150 leaders in psychiatry concerned with reappraising old concepts in mental health and making new policy recommendations. Many had also served as psychiatrists in the war. Its president at the time was Dr. Walter E. Barton, who would later be the medical director of the American Psychiatric Association (APA) in the early 1970s when it decided to delete homosexuality from its official list of mental diseases.

The GAP Report surveyed the history of homosexuality from antiquity to the present and reviewed the various theories of the cause of homosexuality. Reflecting the psychoanalytic consensus of the time, the report dismissed the genetic, hormonal, and endocrinological theories of the previous decades. It acknowledged that there might be some biological substrate but that the actual persistence of homosexual behavior in an individual was a product of "an arrest in psychosexual development" (GAP 1955, 3). Therefore, they declared shock therapy, psychosurgery, and hormonal therapies ineffective and praised psychotherapy as the only beneficial treatment. Although these were the same theories that had informed the Hoey Report, the GAP committee was largely critical of the government's actions.

"In government settings as well as in civilian life," the GAP Report concluded, "homosexuals have functioned with distinction, and without disruption of morale or efficiency. Problems of social maladaptive behavior, such as homosexuality, therefore need to be examined on an individual basis, considering the place and circumstances, rather than from inflexible rules" (6) With 20/20 hindsight, they warned that "investigations are prone to turn into 'witch hunts'" (6). As in the late nineteenth century, the medical profession's humane desire to save homosexuals from legal persecution—while retaining them as psychiatric patients—did little to relieve gay people's suffering or to quell the homosexual roundups that continued into the 1960s.

*Moving from Reaction to Revolution*

The conservative and often reactionary atmosphere of the United States in the 1950s during the Cold War was an unlikely setting for a growing gay and lesbian political consciousness. The success of the psychoanalytic model of homosexuality, although it could be based on a sympathetic (if often condescending) approach to gays and lesbians, turned out to be generally hostile toward them. Psychiatrists, feeling empowered with a technique for analyzing and altering the psyche, believed they could "readjust" homosexuals. If a "cure" failed, it was the patient's fault: the result of excessive "resistance" to therapy. Gay patients could thus spend years of almost daily analytic sessions on the couch, struggling to overcome their perverse desires and forcing themselves to remain in unhappy heterosexual marriages (Duberman 1991; Isay 1996).

Simultaneously, researchers from outside psychiatry were gradually undermining a century's worth of pathologizing theories. Kinsey and his colleagues, Ford and Beach, as well as Hooker, also understood homosexuality as a psychological phenomenon rather than a hereditary or hormonal one. However, they viewed it in larger sociological and cultural terms. Bravely distancing themselves from centuries of moralistic condemnation of homosexuality, these researchers could begin to shatter the representation of homosexuality as a rare disease. Furthermore, they suggested that it was society's homophobia that was unnatural, pathogenic, and irrational. These changing conceptions in sociology, anthropology, and psychology would fuel the hopes of lesbians and gays well into the 1960s.

## References

Abraham, Felix. 1931. "Genitalumwandlungen an zwei männlichen Transvestiten." *Zeitschrift für Sexualwissenschaft und Sexualpolitik* 18: 223–226.

Allen, Garland E. 1997. "The Double-Edged Sword of Genetic Determinism: Social and Political Agendas in Genetic Studies of Homosexuality, 1940–1994." Pp. 242–270 in *Science and Homosexualities*. Edited by V. Rosario. New York: Routledge.

Baker, Blanche M. 1959a. "Toward Understanding." *ONE* 7, no. 1 (January): 25–27.

———. 1959b. "Toward Understanding." *ONE* 7, no. 3 (March): 25–26.

Barahal, Hyman S. 1953. "Female Transvestitism and Homosexuality." *Psychiatric Quarterly* 27: 390–438.

Bergler, Edmund. 1943. "The Respective Importance of Reality and Fantasy in the Genesis of Female Homosexuality." *Journal of Criminal Psychopathology* 5: 27–48.

———. 1944. "Eight Prerequisites for the Psychoanalytic Treatment of Homosexuality." *Psychoanalytic Review* 31: 253–286.

———. 1947. "Differential Diagnosis between Spurious Homosexuality and Perversion Homosexuality." *Psychiatric Quarterly* 21: 399–409.

———. 1948. "The Myth of a New National Disease: Homosexuality and the Kinsey Report." *Psychiatric Quarterly* 22: 67–88.

———. 1959. *1000 Homosexuals. Conspiracy of Silence, or Curing and Deglamorizing Homosexuals?* Paterson, NJ: Pageant Books.

Caprio, Frank Samuel. 1954. *Female Homosexuality: A Psychodynamic Study of Lesbianism*. Foreword by Karl M. Bowman. New York: Citadel Press.

Cory, Donald Webster (pseudonym for Edward Sagarin). 1951a. *The Homosexual in America: A Subjective Approach*. Introduction by Albert Ellis. New York: Greenberg.

D'Emilio, John. 1989. "The Homosexual Menace: The Politics of Sexuality in Cold War America." Pp. 226–240 in *Passion and Power: Sexuality in History*. Edited by Kathy Peiss and Christina Simmons. Philadelphia: Temple University Press.

Duberman, Martin. 1991. *Cures: A Gay Man's Odyssey*. New York: Dutton.

English, Oliver Spurgeon. 1948. "Sex and Human Love." Pp. 96–112 in *About the Kinsey Report*. Edited by Donald P. Geddes and E. Currie. New York: Signet.

———. 1953. "A Primer on Homosexuality." *GP* (American Academy of General Practice) 7: 55–60.

Ford, Clellan S., and Frank A. Beach. 1951. *Patterns of Sexual Behavior*. New York: Harper.

GAP (Group for the Advancement of Psychiatry). 1955. *Report on Homosexuality with Particular Emphasis on This Problem in Governmental Agencies*. Report no. 30. Topeka, KS: GAP.

Gebhard, Paul H., and Alan B. Johnson. 1979. *The Kinsey Data: Marginal Tabulations of the 1938–1963 Interviews Conducted by the Institute for Sex Research*. Philadelphia: Saunders.

Geddes, Donald P. 1948. "New Light on Sexual Knowledge." Pp. 5–25 in *About the Kinsey Report*. Edited by Donald P. Geddes and E. Currie. New York: Signet.

Glover, Benjamin H. 1951. "Observations on Homosexuality among University Students." *Journal of Nervous and Mental Disease* 113: 377–387.

Hamburger, Christian, George K. Stürup, and E. Dahl-Iversen. 1953. "Transvestism: Hormonal, Psychiatric, and Surgical Treatment." *Journal of the American Medical Association.* 152: 391–396.

Hooker, Evelyn. 1956. "A Preliminary Analysis of Group Behavior of Homosexuals." *Journal of Psychology* 42: 217–225.

———. 1957. "The Adjustment of the Male Overt Homosexual." *Journal of Projective Techniques* 21: 18–31.

———. 1958. "Male Homosexuality in the Rorschach." *Journal of Projective Techniques* 22: 33–54.

———. 1959. "What Is a Criterion?" *Journal of Projective Techniques* 23: 278–281.

———. 1965. "Male Homosexuals and Their 'Worlds.'" Pp. 83–107 in *Sexual Inversion: The Multiple Roots of Homosexuality.* Edited by Judd Marmor. New York: Basic Books.

———. 1993. "Reflections of a 40-year Exploration." *American Psychologist* 48: 450–453.

Isay, Richard. 1996. *Becoming Gay: The Journey to Self-Acceptance.* New York: Pantheon.

Kallmann, Franz J. 1952. "Twin Sibship Study of Overt Male Homosexuality." *American Journal of Human Genetics* 4: 136–146.

Kinsey, Alfred C. 1941. "Homosexuality." *Journal of Clinical Endocrinology* 1: 424–428.

Kinsey, Alfred C., Wardell B. Pomeroy, and Clyde E. Martin. 1948. *Sexual Behavior in the Human Male.* Philadelphia: W. B. Saunders.

Kinsey, Alfred C., Wardell B. Pomeroy, Clyde E. Martin, and Paul H. Gebhard. 1953. *Sexual Behavior in the Human Female.* Philadelphia: W. B. Saunders.

Kolb, Lawrence C., and Adelaide M. Johnson. 1955. "Etiology and Therapy of Overt Homosexuality." *Psychoanalytic Quarterly* 24: 506–515.

Lewes, Kenneth. 1988. *The Psychoanalytic Theory of Male Homosexuality.* New York: Simon and Schuster.

Meyerowitz, Joanne. 1998. "Sex-change and the Popular Press: Historical Notes on Transsexuality in the United States, 1930–1955." *GLQ* 4: 159–187.

Miller, Paul R. 1958. "The Effeminate Passive Obligatory Homosexual." *Archives of Neurology and Psychiatry* 80: 612–618.

Money, John. 1955. "Hermaphroditism, Gender and Precocity in Hyperadrenocorticism: Psychological Findings." *Bulletin of the Johns Hopkins Hospital* 96: 253–264.

Pedersen, Lyn. 1956. "A Tribute to Dr. Kinsey." *ONE* 4, no. 6 (August–September): 7–12.

"Perverts Called Government Peril." 1950. *New York Times,* April 19, 25.

Poe, John S. 1952. "The Successful Treatment of a 40-year-old Passive Homosexual Based on an Adaptational View of Sexual Behavior." *Psychoanalytic Review* 39: 23–32.

Prince, C. V. 1956. "Homosexuality, Transvestism, and Transsexualism: Reflections on Their Etiology and Differentiation." *American Journal of Psychotherapy* 10: 80–85.

Review of *Kinsey's Myth of Female Sexuality* by Edmund Bergler and William S. Kroger. 1954b. *Psychiatric Quarterly* 28: 152–153.

Review of *Sex Life of the American Woman and the Kinsey Report* by Albert Ellis. 1954a. *Psychiatric Quarterly* 28: 152.

Review of *Sexual Behavior in the Human Female* by Alfred Kinsey and associates. 1954c. *Psychiatric Quarterly* 28: 148–152.

Schmiechen, Richard, dir. 1992. *Changing Our Minds: The Story of Dr. Evelyn Hooker.* David Haugland and James Harrison, producers. San Francisco: Frameline.

Timmons, Stuart. 1990. *The Trouble with Harry Hay: Founder of the Modern Gay Movement.* Boston: Alyson.

U. S. Congress. Senate. 1950. *Employment of Homosexuals and Other Sex Perverts in Government.* [Hoey Report]. 81st Congress, 2nd sess. S. Doc. 241.

White, William S. 1950. "Inquiry by Senate on Perverts Asked." *New York Times,* May 20, 8.

## Further Reading

One of Alfred Kinsey's collaborators, Wardell B. Pomeroy, wrote the official biography of Kinsey and the institute that now bears his name: *Dr. Kinsey and the Institute for Sex Research* (New York: Harper and Row, 1972). James H. Jones's account, *Alfred C. Kinsey: A Public/Private Life* (New York: W. W. Norton, 1997), is far more controversial for its revelations of Kinsey's own experimental sex life and that of the members of the institute. Shortly before her death, the life and research of psychologist Evelyn Hooker was made into a poignant documentary film by Richard Schmiechen, James Harrison, and David Haugland. *Changing Our Minds: The Story of Dr. Evelyn Hooker* (San Francisco: Frameline, 1992) also offers glimpses into the lives and political organizing of gays in 1950s Los Angeles.

Harry Hay founded the Los Angeles Mattachine Society and continues to be a radical gay activist. In the process of recounting Hay's life, Stuart Timmons's *The Trouble with Harry Hay: Founder of the Modern Gay Movement* (Boston: Alyson, 1990) also tracks the history of the homophile movement to which Hay has been so devoted. John D'Emilio analyzes the development of the broader gay rights movement from a sociological perspective in *Sexual Politics, Sexual Communities: The Making of a Homosexual Minority in the United States, 1940–1970* (Chicago: University of Chicago Press, 1983).

# 6

## *The Triumph and Decline of Psychiatric Models*

The 1960s was the decade of cultural revolutions in the United States. The science of homosexuality was about to experience its own upheavals. By the 1960s, organic and constitutional models of homosexuality had largely been marginalized in favor of updated psychoanalytic and other psychological explanations. The largest and most scientific psychoanalytic study, coordinated by Dr. Irving Bieber in New York City, seemed to confirm theories of the familial causation of homosexuality. Therefore, it optimistically supported analytic conversion therapy. Meanwhile, psychiatrists and psychologists, adopting behaviorist approaches, experimented with "avoidance conditioning" to de-eroticize homosexuality in gay men (Birk, Huddleston, and Miller 1971).

Ironically, the emergence of homophile groups in the 1950s, particularly lesbian groups, facilitated the recruitment of experimental subjects. After largely neglecting lesbianism for half the century, psychiatric researchers began conducting small studies on the psychology and psychoanalysis of female homosexuals. The growing emergence of gay men and lesbians from the closet also paved the way for group therapy.

Although mental health workers were exuding an unprecedented therapeutic optimism for the conversion of homosexuals into "normal" heterosexuals, pressures were mounting for the depathologization of homosexuality. The black civil rights and women's liberation movements were inspiring gays and lesbians to condemn decades of medical stigmatization. The "sexual revolution" of the 1960s assaulted traditional sexual morals that had erected marital, coital heterosexuality as the only acceptable form of erotic behavior (D'Emilio and Freedman 1988, 300–318). Within psychiatry and psychology, a few courageous, liberal professionals were advancing the extremely unorthodox proposition that homosexuality per se was not a form of psychopathology. These forces came to a head in 1969 with the Stonewall riots in New York. At 1:20 A.M. on June 28, 1969, the police raided the Stonewall Inn, a Mafia-run gay bar in Greenwich Village. This harassment was routine, but that evening the gay men, lesbians, and drag queens (many of them people of color) fought back, leading to five days of rioting. "Nobody's gonna fuck with me!" "Ain't gonna take this shit!" "Gay power!" were the cries that exploded that evening (Duberman 1993, 196). The ensuing radicalization of the gay rights movement swiftly led to political pressure on the mental health professions and a dramatic about-face in the psychiatric stance toward homosexuality.

## Validating the Psychoanalytic Approach

Like much other nineteenth-century medical theorizing, Sigmund Freud's psychoanalytic publications were based on personally collected, anecdotal clinical experiences. Furthermore, many of Freud's central ideas were not even based on his clinical encounters but on his auto-analysis or the reinterpretation of previously published material. He had never analyzed a homosexual man when he wrote his main statement on the subject in the *Three Essays on the Theory of Sexuality* (1905) (see Chapter 2). Psychoanalytic pronouncements on lesbianism were based on just a handful of cases. By midcentury, standards in biomedical science had become much more rigorous, and such skimpy evidence seemed most unscientific. Kinsey's studies—with more than 1,000 subjects examined systematically—especially rendered the body of psychoanalytic writings highly suspect. In order to lend some scientific weight to the psychoanalytic view of homosexuality, a research committee of the Society of Medical Psychoanalysts of New York began a large-scale study in 1952 under the direction of Irving Bieber. It was primarily funded by the National Institute of Mental Health (NIMH), and the results were published in 1962 in *Homosexuality: A Psychoanalytic Study.*

Bieber and the committee distributed an extensive questionnaire to members of the society, requesting that they provide information on male homosexual clients they knew well. If they had no homosexual patients, the psychoanalysts were to provide information on heterosexual clients. These served as the comparison population rather than a proper control group since the committee made no attempts to match the two groups for socioeconomic or clinical factors or to include nonpatients. Ultimately, they examined information on 106 homosexual and 100 heterosexual men. The committee's conclusions generally supported Sandor Rado's theorization of homosexuality over Freud's: in other words, homosexuality emerged as a neurotic adaptation to unconscious fears of women and heterosexuality. They firmly rejected all previous researchers' claims that homosexuality was hereditary, normal, or free of psychopathology. "The homosexual relationship," the analysts declared, "served to fulfill a range of *irrational defensive and reparative needs*" (Bieber 1962, 252). At best, it was "*one* kind of adaptation in the face of crippling circumstances of growth and development" (254). Given the committee's psychoanalytic bent, these circumstances centered on the mother-father-child triad.

They sketched the typical dysfunctional family constellation that generates a homosexual boy—a scenario that continues to have popular currency. The classic homosexual boy's mother was "close binding," egotistical, overprotective, seductive, but also puritanical. She fundamentally inhibited her son's masculinity and interfered with his heterosexual development. The typical homosexual's father was detached, hostile, minimizing, and openly rejecting. Although some of these elements may have been true in individual cases, we cannot know if they generated homosexuality or were its consequence. Nor is it clear that these are specific to homosexuals since the committee deemed that only 8 percent of the *heterosexuals'* fathers were "reasonably 'normal' parents" (114). Apparently, 1950s fatherhood in general was riddled with psychopathology. Or at least, a troubled parental relationship was a major reason male New Yorkers, heterosexual and homosexual alike, sought psychoanalytic treatment.

The study nevertheless ended on an optimistic note concerning the treatment of homosexuals. It reported that 27 percent of the group of homosexuals and bisexuals had achieved an "exclusively heterosexual adaptation" thanks to psychoanalysis (301). The prognosis was especially good for bisexual men, those who commenced psychoanalysis before the age of thirty-five, and those who persisted with more than 350 hours of analysis. Therefore, both analyst and homosexual simply had to persevere with treatment to restore the "*biologic norm*" of heterosexuality. Bieber and his committee felt that the psychoanalytic cure of homosexuality was finally validated as a "scientific fact" (319).

## The Emergence of Lesbians

Bieber's study, like most psychoanalytic publications on homosexuality, focused on male homosexuality because, as Bieber noted, "it was considered to be a key problem in psychoanalytic theory" (Bieber 1962, vii). The profession was dominated by men and concentrated on male psychology, despite the fact that many of Freud's most important cases were women and that more women sought analysis than men. Fewer homosexual women sought treatment than homosexual men: it is not clear whether they were under fewer social, legal, and familial pressures; were more content with their sexuality; or distrusted and could not afford psychoanalysts. Beginning in the 1960s, however, psychiatrists began paying more attention to lesbianism. Ironically, this may have been because of growing lesbian visibility and political organizing in groups such as the Daughters of Bilitis (DOB).

The DOB was the first lesbian political organization in the United States. It was founded in San Francisco in 1955 by Del Martin, Phyllis Lyon, and three other lesbian couples. It began publishing its monthly magazine, *The Ladder,* in October 1956. Under the leadership of Barbara Gittings, a New York City chapter of the DOB opened in 1958. Gittings would become editor of *The Ladder* from 1963 to 1966, as well as a leading figure in homophile activism (Katz 1976). In the early 1970s she would also become a key figure in the struggle with the American Psychiatric Association to depathologize homosexuality (see Chapter 7).

The DOB conducted a survey of its members and published the results of the 157 replies in *The Ladder* (Conrad 1959, 1960) (see Sidebar 6.1). This study served as a reference point for subsequent psychiatric studies, including a study of female homosexuality sponsored by the Society of Medical Psychoanalysts. This study was modeled on Bieber's study of males, but only 50 lesbians were being treated by the 150 psychoanalysts polled. Dr. Harvey Kaye, leader of the research committee, noted that they were only able to obtain completed questionnaires on 24 subjects (Kaye et al. 1967). He was far more cautious than Bieber about whether this was a representative sample. In particular, Kaye had to acknowledge that 75 percent of the respondents to the DOB questionnaire felt they had no need for psychotherapy.

The Kaye study nevertheless echoed the previous research on male homosexuals. It concluded that "homosexuality in women, rather than being a conscious volitional preference, is a massive adaptational response to a crippling inhibition of normal heterosexual development" (633). Lesbians tended to fear men, male genitals, and pregnancy, and their feminine identification had been inhibited by their parents. Typically, they had been tomboys with fathers who were possessive, puritanical, and exploitative. Nevertheless, the researchers found that these women had an even more "fundamental

**Sidebar 6.1 Daughters of Bilitis Survey of Homosexuals**

The September 1959 issue of *The Ladder,* the journal of the Daughters of Bilitis (DOB), presented an analysis of a survey distributed to their readers. It was written by Florence Conrad, director of the DOB research committee, who believed that only scientific data would convince doctors and society that homosexuality was not a disorder. The study prompted the circulation of a similar questionnaire among members of the Mattachine Society and ONE, Inc. A total of 157 women and 100 men replied. The following September, *The Ladder* published a comparison of these questionnaires.

The DOB recognized that the studies presented a nonrepresentative sample of homosexuals, since the subjects were all self-selected and members of homosexual rights groups. The respondents to both surveys were almost entirely Caucasian Americans and tended to belong to a higher educational and professional status than the general U.S. population. Although the number of participants was relatively small, these surveys were larger than most psychiatric studies and presented data on homosexuals outside a clinical setting. Therefore, psychiatrists took note of them, particularly the lesbian data that were remarkably missing from the medical literature.

Over 90 percent of both male and female respondents identified as predominantly to exclusively homosexual (Kinsey scale ratings of 4 to 6). More men than women reported growing up in stable, two-parent families; however, slightly more of the men reported unhappy adolescences (39 percent versus 36 percent of women). About 42 percent of each group were out to their family, and a third of these families were accepting. More of the men reported having other homosexuals in the family (21 percent versus 14 percent of the women).

More of the women than men were daily or heavy drinkers. However, more men went to gay bars, presumably for socializing and sexual liaisons. More men than women had been arrested (30 percent versus 12 percent), mainly for "disorderly conduct" and charges related to overt homosexuality. The questions on sexual life brought out interesting gender differences. The men were more precocious in their awareness of their homosexuality and their first sexual encounter than the women. Conrad noted that more of the men had trouble interpreting the word "relationship" in the survey: "Where women were sometimes uncertain whether to count an emotional relation that was not specifically sexual, men had trouble deciding whether to count—and generally did not count—specifically sexual experiences that were not emotional" (1960, 18). The author reasoned that this difference might explain why so many more women (72 percent) than men (46 percent) reported being in a relationship, whereas 46 percent of men reported being simultaneously in several homosexual relations and none of the women did. Although the most sexually active man reported 5,000 short sexual relations (ten times more than the most active woman), the majority of both men and women reported one to five short relationships. The men's longest relationships tended to be shorter than women's.

Contrary to much of the medical literature, the majority of men were flexible in terms of the gender role they played in sexual relationships (57 percent). However, a large number of both men (30 percent) and women (38 percent) reported a predominantly masculine role. More men than women reported difficulty in adjusting to their homosexuality (57 percent versus 33 percent) and seeking psychotherapy (35 percent versus 29 percent). From these results, Conrad arrived at two main conclusions. First, men were more sexually active. Second, men also had more problems than women in adjusting to their homosexuality both personally

*(continues)*

and socially. Conrad reasoned that, "In a society that is male-oriented and where masculine values have a higher prestige, the lot of any male who rejects these values in any way is difficult. . . . Lesbians, on the other hand, when they reject the traditional role of women, may be harmonizing their behavior not only with their own inclinations, but also with the really dominant values of society" (1960, 25).

In 1965, Conrad engaged in an animated debate in the pages of *The Ladder* on the value of this and other scientific studies of homosexuality. Frank Kameny argued that it was time to stop gathering further data or engaging scientists in polite debate, because "research into homosexuality does not really matter!" (1965b, 26). It was time to simply insist homosexuals were equal and not sick.

heterosexual drive" than the homosexual men. Therefore, the prospects for psychotherapy were even more sanguine: Kaye reported a 50 percent improvement rate (633).

A rather different picture of lesbianism appeared just two years later. Washington University psychiatrists Marcel Saghir and Eli Robins not only referred to the DOB study in their work but recruited subjects through the DOB and three male homophile organizations. The two psychiatrists recognized that this sample was self-selected and skewed toward homosexually committed women of a higher socioeconomic status than the U.S. female population as a whole. Nevertheless, it was a nonclinical sample: 61 percent had never had psychotherapy, and none of them were in psychoanalysis. Saghir and Robins were not interested in speculating about the infantile origins of homosexuality but in collecting data on the development and sexual behavior of their fifty-five subjects. They found that these lesbians earned over twice the median income of employed civilian women and were better educated. They were not dysfunctional neurotics. On the contrary, Saghir and Robin concluded that "a homosexual woman is able to produce and achieve, despite any psychological and social handicaps that she might have to cope with" (1969, 199).

Their subjects revealed a great variety of sexual practices. Saghir and Robins found that the traditional notion that lesbians engaged in fixed, polarized roles of masculine-feminine, "butch-fem," or active-passive was largely inaccurate. Even the small minority of women who set up binary social roles of "breadwinner" versus "housewife" did so in a transient way. Unlike previous studies, this one found that homosexual women tended to form relatively stable and faithful relationships. The majority of these women, unlike Kaye's subjects, had never had heterosexual attractions. For most of them, homosexual psychological responses began in preadolescence and became more intense and exclusive with adulthood. Less than a fourth of them were bisexual. Again, this study pointed out that research participants recruited from different settings (Kaye's from psychoanalytic practices versus Saghir and Robins's from the nonclinical DOB) could have dramatically different characteristics. Saghir and Robins's most significant theoretical conclusion was that, in considering female versus male homosexuality, more attention had to be paid to psychological responses rather than focusing on overt sexual behaviors (as with the Kinsey sexual outlet scale) (201).

## Tackling Sissies and Tomboys

As studies increasingly drew attention to preadolescent sexuality and with the professional evolution of child psychology, researchers began searching for early manifestations of homosexuality. Victorian psychiatrists had declared from the start that "sexual inversion" in adults was characterized by reversed gender behavior: virile women and effeminate men. Early-twentieth-century psychoanalysts had also reported that their adult patients had manifested such behavior as children. But it was in the 1960s that psychologists began focusing on sissy and tomboy children, primarily with the aim of early detection of and prevention of homosexuality.

Pediatricians Harry Bakwin and Ruth M. Bakwin, of the New York University College of Medicine, had suggested in 1953 that parental encouragement of gender-appropriate behavior might be useful. Based on a recently published twin study (Kallmann 1952), they tended to believe that homosexuality was largely hereditary. They recommended that efforts to reorient childhood "homosexual trends" be done with care not to stigmatize the children. However, they ended on a pessimistic note, observing that other psychiatrists had failed to prevent homosexuality.

Research by John Money and his colleagues at Johns Hopkins University on gender development in hermaphroditic children was central to 1960s work on sissies and tomboys. Money developed the notion of "gender role" as "all those things that a person says or does to disclose himself or herself as having the status of a boy or man, or a girl or woman, respectively. It includes but is not restricted to sexuality in the sense of eroticism" (Money 1955, 254). Money's team argued that gender role was entirely socially malleable early in life.

Therefore, infants born with ambiguous genitalia could be surgically "corrected" and then successfully reared as either males or females so long as gender assignment was done before age three and preferably before eighteen months. In addition to their concern for developing a stable gender identity in these children, Money and his colleagues worried about surgeons accidentally creating homosexuals by not assigning the correct gender (Money and Ehrhardt 1972).

In 1961, Money and his student Richard Green reported on their experience with eleven sissy boys and provided recommendations for managing gender deviance. Green continued doing research in this area through gender identity clinics in Los Angeles and London. He published *The "Sissy Boy Syndrome" and the Development of Homosexuality* in 1987. In their 1960s articles, Green and Money insisted that childhood effeminacy and transvestitism were not just benign "phases" but warning signs of homosexuality. They were thus contradicting the Freudian dogma of universal homosexuality during the "latency" stage in preadolescent boys. These effeminate traits were to be taken as indicative of a "gender-role disorder," which was possibly the result of improper "imprinting" as described by ethologists, or animal behavior researchers (Money, Hampson, and Hampson 1957). Green and Money recommended that parents view effeminacy as a "handicap" that might be treated with early and sustained coaching in manliness. Nevertheless, they urged that the effeminate boy not be punished. Treating physicians should reassure the parents that despite their son's handicap, he might still lead a productive life. "There have been many illustrious homosexuals in the history of civilization," they concluded. "Some parents are reassured by this historical knowledge" (Green and Money 1961, 290).

*Aversion Therapy*

While some psychologists were recommending that children be subjected to behavior modification techniques to prevent homosexuality (Rekers 1972), others were developing new "aversion therapies" for reorienting *adult* homosexuals. The use of aversive stimuli or punishment as a means of curtailing unwanted behavior can be as simple and quotidian as scolding or spanking. The scientific study and formal application of aversion therapy springs from research on conditioned reflexes by Russian physiologist Ivan Pavlov (1849–1936) and in behaviorist psychology by the American psychologist B. F. Skinner (1904–1990). Pavlov described *classical conditioning*: associating a novel stimulus with a stimulus that automatically evokes the response

### Sidebar 6.2 Chemical Aversion Therapy in the 1980s

Steve was a model Mormon boy growing up in an upper-middle-class family in Provo, Utah. His parents were educated professionals. He had a brother and two sisters. He was not an aggressive, athletic child and always felt different from his peers. Although he had had some sexual experiences at age eight with a neighborhood boy, he did not see himself as gay. He dated Mormon girls, and his postponement of sexual activity was approved of by them and his family on religious grounds. During his two-year Mormon mission, he began to be troubled by his attraction to his male companions. Yet he went to college, and by all outward appearances he was a high-achieving student and dedicated church member—except for his failure to marry. Given the intense cultural pressures to marry promptly after his mission, Steve was becoming increasingly distressed by his inability to commit to a heterosexual relationship and his growing awareness of homoerotic interests.

He finally sought psychiatric assistance in 1981 and was assured that since he had not yet acted on his homosexual tendencies and was motivated to become straight, he was a good candidate for therapy. He was referred to a psychologist who began aversive conditioning. Initially he was berated for his homoerotic tendencies, in what he now deems was emotionally abusive treatment. This treatment was followed by the "next level" of aversion therapy using an emetic (a drug that causes nausea and vomiting). After being administered the drug by a psychiatrist, Steve was to listen to his own cassette-taped recording of the most homoerotic encounter he could imagine. The doctors downplayed the effects of the drug and left him alone one evening in the basement of an abandoned building. Steven soon began to experience severe nausea, vomiting, and chills—with no one to turn to for assistance with the potentially life-threatening effects of the emetic. Fortunately, he managed to drive home safely and restore his body temperature.

The psychologist nevertheless suggested simply switching to a different form of aversion therapy, in which he would self-administer electrical shocks to his penis whenever he had homoerotic feelings. At this point, Steve realized the treatment was far too dangerous to his physical and mental health. Shortly thereafter, he met a young gay man and, despite tremendous apprehension, had his first gay experience. They began dating, and Steve felt he had finally found himself: he was far happier and more secure than he had ever been. He came out to one of his sisters, who reacted terribly and asked him to have no further contact with her children. His mother learned about his homosexuality and was irate. She informed his boss and the president of the university where he worked, leading to his prompt dismissal. The university police called him in for interrogation, trying to coerce him to name other homosexuals on campus. He refused to participate in these McCarthyesque roundups.

Unemployed, destitute, and disowned by his family, he realized he had to leave Utah to begin a new life. He got a job in Los Angeles and soon started a long-term relationship with a man. It was only when trouble arose between them that he began to realize that psychotherapy might be helpful for dealing with the traumatic events of his life. He began long-term, supportive psychotherapy with a gay therapist and also participated in a gay therapy group for eight years. He has learned to acknowledge the harm that social and medical homophobia have caused him in the past and has even been able to go beyond his anger to lead a productive and happier life.

*(continues)*

(for example, inducing salivation in a dog solely by ringing a bell by repeatedly associating the ringing with food presentation). Skinner developed *operant conditioning:* a behavior is rewarded (or punished) each time it occurs in order to increase (or decrease) its frequency. Aversion therapy was probably first employed for the treatment of alcohol abuse when psychologists used electric shock in 1925 and chemical aversion therapy ten years later (Rachman 1965). The latter is still available in the form of Antabuse (disulfuram), a drug that induces nausea after alcohol consumption.

Both methods were employed in combating homosexuality. *Electrical shock* was used in 1935 in conjunction with an instruction to the subject to engage in homoerotic fantasizing (Max 1935). The method was reportedly successful after four months in 95 percent of cases. Relying on experimental models in rats, one group of researchers placed their barefoot human subject in a small room with an electrified floor. The subject was shocked in conjunction with slides of nude men. They reported that he successfully converted to bisexuality after four thousand trials (Thorpe, Schmidt, and Castell 1963).

In the late 1950s, psychiatrist Kurt Freund turned to *chemical aversion therapy* in the form of emetics (drugs that induce vomiting). Practicing first in Prague and then Toronto, Freund administered apomorphine injections to induce nausea and vomiting while the homosexual subjects were shown slides of nude and dressed men. For positive reinforcement, the same subjects were later given testosterone injections and shown films of naked and seminude women. Only slightly more than 10 percent of subjects who volunteered for the therapy still refrained from homosexual behavior after five years (Freund 1960). Freund also developed penile plethysmography: a technique using a rubber-band-like device wrapped around the penis to detect changes in penile volume or circumference, which are recorded on a polygraph machine. It was like a penile lie detector test—erotic arousal (erection) could be measured physiologically and objectively. It was used to detect erotic arousal even when the subject might be deceitful (as in cases of suspected pedophilia) (Freund 1965).

In the mid-1960s behavior therapists began recommending electrical shocks applied to the hands or feet rather than apomorphine for aversion therapy since electrical shocks could provide instantaneous and transient painful stimuli that could be utilized in a variety of more sophisticated conditioning approaches (Rachman 1965). *Contingent shock therapy* relied on Freund's penile plethysmography—electrical shocks were delivered to the finger tips in response to penile engorgement while the subject looked at homoerotic images. Some researchers tried to associate homosexual words, rather than images, with electrical shock. This *covert sensitization* technique was slightly more humane since it only involved imagined homoerotic stimuli in association with imagined aversive thoughts: nausea, vomiting, diarrhea, or syphilitic sores.

Behaviorists also employed a variety of more complex conditioning regimens. M.P. Feldman and M.K. MacCulloch (1964) used *anticipatory avoidance conditioning* with electrical shock. The subject was shown a slide of an attractive male and if he did not switch off the image within eight seconds he received a shock until he did. By making the subject an active participant in the procedure, they explained, "it is hoped that the behavior will be 'stamped in,' and that the habit of not gazing at, or thinking about, male partners, both essential preludes of homosexual activity, will be set up" (168). They followed the male picture with that of a woman, "hence associating a female image with relief of anxiety." After twenty-eight of these twenty-minute shock sessions, the patient reported a decline in homosexual fantasies and satisfactory heterosexual intercourse—with a plan to marry. However, there was no long term follow-up.

In addition to the lack of follow-up analyses, these studies suffered from numerous other methodological weaknesses, including lack of control groups or objective measures of erotic readjustment to heterosexuality. Nevertheless, aversion therapy was employed on homosexual men throughout the 1960s and 1970s; it was still being used in the 1980s (see Sidebar 6.2).

Aversion therapy increasingly came under criticism in the 1970s. John Money, in a 1972 editorial, posed the hypothetical experiment of subjecting heterosexuals to shocks each time a heterosexual stimulus was shown. It is unlikely that these individuals would become homosexual, Money reasoned. "It is rather more likely," he explained, "that they would have become sexually inhibited, anxious, or sexually apathetic" (1972, 79). After having advocated the use of behavior modification techniques on children to prevent homosexuality, Money was clearly affected by the gay pride movement that sprung up in 1969. He concluded his editorial with a warning and a strong recommendation to the profession: "Therapeutic zeal in the absence of effective therapeutic technique produces charlatanism. It is timely, therefore, for medicine to respect the arguments of the homosexual militants and not to discriminate against them by insidiously lending credence to the assumption that all homosexuals and their behavior are, if not bad and wrong, sick" (81).

By 1976, even one of the strongest advocates of homosexual aversion therapy, Australian psychiatrist Nathaniel McConaghy, was more circumspect. In an article entitled "Is a Homosexual Orientation Irreversible?" he basically answered in the positive. After comparing a number of different modes of aversion therapy and positive conditioning, he found that the former significantly reduced penile volume response to pictures of nude men. Treated men also curtailed their homosexual feelings and behavior; however, they did not develop heterosexual interests, nor had his aversion therapy interventions altered their sexual orientation. He suggested that what he had produced instead was a "focal experimental neurosis" (562).

In 1987, the American Medical Association's Council on Scientific Affairs issued a report on aversion therapy. It reviewed uses of aversive techniques in a variety of conditions, including homosexuality. Although not outright condemning of these experimental treatment procedures, it did note that by the 1980s the treatment of homosexuality was appropriate only when the patient was distressed by his or her sexual orientation. The report concluded that most of these studies were flawed in design and methodology, casting serious doubts on their claims (AMA 1988).

### Group Therapy

Another therapeutic approach promoted in the 1960s, group psychotherapy, was less punitive yet insidious in its own way. It was especially advocated by Dr. Samuel Hadden of the Neuropsychiatric Service of the University of Pennsylvania Medical Center. In a 1966 address to the American Academy of Occupational Medicine, he was keenly aware of the changing political climate. He warned his medical brethren that "while most problems about homosexuality involve dealing with the individual, you may soon find that you have to deal with his bargaining agency—the homophile organization—or with the Civil Liberties Union" (1966a, 284). Organized homosexual groups were now posing "considerable resistance" to the understanding of homosexuality as an illness. Their view of homosexuality as a normal condition was clearly trickling down to individuals since Hadden noted that even many of the patients that saw him because they were anxious and depressed did not want to alter their homosexuality but instead wanted to "live with it more comfortably" (1966a, 285).

Hadden found that groups of homosexuals were quite effective in breaking down individuals' defenses surrounding their sexuality. His descriptions of group sessions sound like confrontations between the characters in Mart Crowley's play and film *The Boys in the Band:* psychologically insightful but profoundly guilt-ridden, self-hating homosexuals (1968). Hadden described how each time a new member tried to defend his gay lifestyle or criticize social homophobia, others would come to the defense of social norms and try to shatter the newcomer's rationalizations. The group would chastise members for exhibiting gay mannerisms. Even hostile individuals who insulted others with epithets such as "cocksucker" could provoke the others to find their behaviors disgusting. Hadden concluded that "to find homosexuality attacked by fellow homosexuals is extremely anxiety-producing, but the anxiety thus activated can be utilized to help members commit themselves to treatment" (1966b, 17). Hadden had discovered that in an atmosphere of growing progay militancy, promoting self-hatred from within homosexual groups could be an effective means of deflating gay pride. Hadden was unabashed in revealing his feelings of hostility and disgust concerning his clients. He concluded his lecture by quoting a *Time* editorial: "[Homosexuality] is a pathetic little second-rate substitute for reality, a pitiable flight from life. . . . It deserves no encouragement, no glamorization, . . . no pretense that it is anything but a pernicious sickness" (1966a, 288).

Unlike earlier researchers, Hadden's work met with strong opposition from homosexuals, who had become increasingly emboldened to condemn science. In Philadelphia on April 1, 1965, Hadden lectured as usual on his work, at several points even comparing homophile groups to the Nazis and the Ku Klux Klan. Echoing prejudices from the 1950s, he claimed that Russian defectors were homosexuals. This time the homosexuals challenged him. Frank Kameny, leader of the Washington Mattachine Society, asked on what scientific basis Hadden claimed homosexuality was a pathology, aside from defining it a priori as such. "When Dr. Hadden's responses continued in terms of 'I think' and 'We feel,' Dr. Kameny declared, 'This is not science, Dr. Hadden; this is faith'" ("Faith and Fury" 1965, 21).

*Professional Unorthodoxy: The NIMH Task Force on Homosexuality*

The therapeutic zeal of Hadden and the shock therapists toward the extinction of homosexuality may have been common in medical and psychological circles of the time, but it was increasingly being met by criticism not only from homophile groups but also some medical leaders. One of the most powerful homosexual rights statements of the 1960s emerged from the National Institute of Mental Health. In September 1967, the director of the NIMH appointed fifteen scientists and legal scholars to a Task Force on Homosexuality, chaired by psychologist Evelyn Hooker. The group was charged with reviewing existing knowledge concerning mental health issues of homosexuality and making recommendations for NIMH research on the subject. The publication of their final report was delayed until October 1969 because of internal disputes. Three of the fifteen members dissented from the majority's recommendations as to social policy, which were unusually sympathetic to homosexuals. This progressive stance was, no doubt, in large part thanks to the influence of Hooker.

The report began by arguing that homosexuality itself was not a mental illness but that the social oppression and the fear of discovery were a potent source of anxiety and poor mental health for homosexuals. It endorsed the establishment of a NIMH Center for the Study of Sexual Behavior and outlined the kinds of research, prevention, and treatment issues it should pursue. The task force recommended expanded training of mental health professionals in human sexuality. Finally, it tackled the sensitive matter of social policy recommendations. It acknowledged that the NIMH was not primarily an organization for formulating social policy, but the task force recognized that scientific research, particularly concerning homosexuality, had important policy implications. Even before new knowledge became available, the report advocated social change because most researchers in the field "are strongly convinced that the extreme opprobrium that our society has attached to homosexual behavior, by way of criminal statutes and restrictive employment practices, has done more social harm than good and goes beyond what is necessary for the maintenance of public order and human decency" (Livingood 1969, 6).

Echoing the recommendations of the British Wolfenden Commission (1957), the task force called for the decriminalization of homosexuality between consenting adults. Furthermore, it criticized job discrimination against homosexuals:

> Many homosexuals are good citizens, holding regular jobs and leading productive lives. The existence of legal penalties relating to homosexual acts means that the mental health problems of homosexuals are exacerbated by the need for concealment and the emotional stresses arising from this need and from the opprobrium of being in violation of the law. . . . A number of eminent [legal] bodies . . . [have recommended the removal] of legal penalties against acts in private among consenting adults. . . . We believe that such a change would reduce the emotional stresses upon the parties involved and thereby contribute to an improvement in their mental health. . . .
>
> It is recommended that there be a reassessment of current employment practices and policy relating to employment of homosexual individuals with a view toward making needed changes. . . .
>
> To be sure, full equity in employment, full security, and full acceptance in society for homosexuals will not be achieved by changes in the law alone, but such changes may help to facilitate the recasting of public attitudes that are ultimately needed. (Livingood 1969, 6)

The task force's recommendations could have been a template for the demands of the militant gay rights movement that was emerging in the mid-1960s. Many of these suggestions have yet to be achieved: homosexual acts are still outlawed in almost half of U.S. states, and only seven states protect homosexuals from employment discrimination. Yet the report's concluding statement uncannily suggests what was to come in the 1970s: "Many people believe we are currently undergoing a revolution in sexual mores and behavior. The interest on the part of the NIMH in the study of sexual behavior is both timely and in the best tradition of its basic concern with improving the mental health of the nation" (6–7).

In a separate paper accompanying the NIMH report, psychiatrist Judd Marmor made several liberal challenges he would reformulate in 1972 during the debate in the American Psychiatric Association (APA) over the termination of the homosexuality diagnosis. Mental health itself was a relative concept, he noted: probably no one was perfectly healthy. Sexual deviance, in particular, probably should not be considered an illness since sexual behavior varied enormously and homosexuals differed from heterosexuals only in their sexual object preference. He posed a critical question: "Is it possible that certain

*Judd Marmor
(courtesy of Judd
Marmor)*

other commonly described characteristics of homosexuals—such as feelings of inadequacy, lack of masculine self-esteem, ambivalence, chronic anxieties, and various defensive attitudes of superiority, hostility, etc., are secondary consequences of derogatory attitudes towards homosexuals in our culture?" (Marmor 1972, 56).

Three members of the task force, Henry W. Rieken, president of the Social Science Research Council, and the anthropologists Clellan Ford and Anthony F. C. Wallace (of Yale University and the University of Pennsylvania, respectively), dissented from the majority's social policy recommendations. They felt that the scientific information on homosexuality was insufficient to make such sweeping recommendations. Furthermore, they felt that the NIMH, in any case, should not be proposing social policy. Wallace feared that relying on the authority of incomplete "science" to promote expressions of "liberal" social values was "in the long run destructive of the credibility of science itself" (Livingood 1969, 72). His reservations seem disingenuous at best, since the work of science is never complete, particularly in psychiatry. Furthermore, incomplete data never seem to have stopped earlier doctors from advocating *punitive* social policy toward homosexuals or, for that matter, women, people of color, immigrants, and other marginal groups.

*Antipsychiatry and the Myth of Diagnosis*

Wallace was probably alluding to a broader political attack on the credibility of science beyond the matter of homosexuality. Throughout the 1960s, many historians and sociologists of science were questioning the transcendental truth claims of science and examining the influence of social, economic, and political factors in shaping scientific knowledge. In *The Structure of Scientific Revolutions* (1962), Thomas Kuhn argued that science progressed not via a logical road to the truth but through nonrational forces and periodic conflicts. The knowledge base of psychiatry came under particular attack. French historian Michel Foucault, in *Madness and Civilization* (1961), proposed that the rise of psychiatry and mental asylums in eighteenth-century France was a means of incarcerating social and political undesirables. Foucault was part of an antipsychiatry movement that became popular in the United States thanks in part to the writings of psychiatrists such as R. D. Laing and Thomas Szasz.

In *The Myth of Mental Illness* (1961), Szasz argued that psychiatry had developed the notion of insanity as a means of assuming the moral policing functions that had once belonged to religious institutions. Deviant behavior was reconceptualized as "mental illness" in the psychiatric profession's effort to claim scientific expertise and social power. He specifically addressed the "diagnosis" of homosexuality in his essay, "Legal and Moral Aspects of Homosexuality" (1965). Szasz bluntly declared that the criminalization of homosexuality was a form of moral persecution and reflected society's antisexual ethos. Antihomosexual sentiment in general society, he ventured, results from the perception that homosexuals undermine the value of heterosexuality by rejecting it. The psychiatric treatment of homosexuality as a disease was simply the rationalization of this popular prejudice. He unflinchingly declared the psychiatric "conversion" of homosexuals as an expression of the "tyranny of the majority." Instead, he advocated a model of democracy in which minorities were not oppressed: "Coercive measures aimed at reducing diversity of opinion or action, whether in the sexual or in the intellectual sphere, are destined to constrict society and thus the human personality" (1965, 138). Szasz's radical, antipsychiatric critique coincided with the attitude of a new generation of gay activists in the late 1960s who were rebelling against the myth of homosexual psychopathology.

## The Patients Revolt

The 1960s was a decade of intense debates and struggles over the nature of U.S. democracy, both domestically and internationally. Women and black Americans began to self-consciously organize themselves as political groups to demand equal legal and social treatment. For two decades, homophile groups had been politely advocating the integration of homosexuals into mainstream society. They collaborated with scientific efforts to explain homosexuality in the hopes that objective data would prove that homosexuality was not an immoral choice but a deeply ingrained, natural imperative. However, by the mid-1960s, the more militant tone of the other civil rights movements began to stimulate a few homophile groups to confront the medical establishment head on.

Frank Kameny (1965b), himself an astrophysicist, declared the "emphasis on research has had its day!" He argued that most of the psychiatric work on homosexuality was biased and abysmally bad science. It was time to militantly assert that homosexuality was *not* a disease but a normal variant of human sexuality (1965a). Like many homosexuals, Kameny had been purged from his government job in the 1950s because of his sexual orientation. He had fought his dismissal as a discrimination case up to the Supreme Court but lost. In 1951 he founded the Washington, D.C., chapter of the Mattachine Society with the aim of developing a militant approach to homophile politics, akin to that of the new black civil rights movement. "We ARE right," he asserted, "those who oppose us are both factually and morally wrong. . . . We must DEMAND our rights, boldly, not beg cringingly for mere privileges" (1965a, 14). In a speech to the New York Mattachine Society, he made the disease model of homosexuality central to this emerging militant politics: "The entire homophile movement . . . is going to stand or fall upon the question of whether or not homosexuality is a sickness, upon taking a firm stand on it" (quoted in Bayer 1987, 82). Kameny himself would spearhead the battle to depathologize homosexuality.

*Picketing for homosexual rights in front of the White House, May 21, 1965. Franklin Kameny is the second in line (Bettmann / Corbis).*

With strong lobbying by Kameny in 1965, the Washington Mattachine Society adopted a resolution declaring that "homosexuality is not a sickness, disturbance, or other pathology in any sense, but is merely a preference, orientation, or propensity on a par with and not different in kind from heterosexuality" (Kameny 1965b, 11n.). The New York chapter soon followed suit. When Charles Socarides spoke at the 1968 convention of the American Medical Association in San Francisco and called for a "national center for sexual rehabilitation," homophile protesters demanded equal time for gay sympathizers to present the case for nonpathology. Members of the Columbia University Student Homophile League made similar demands that same year when they demonstrated at the College of Physicians and Surgeons during a panel discussion on homosexuality that represented it as a disease (Bayer 1987). After the eruption of the Stonewall riots in 1969, gay politics decisively turned away from accommodation, setting the stage for a full frontal attack on the American Psychiatric Association.

## References

AMA (American Medical Association, Council on Scientific Affairs). 1988. "Aversion Therapy." *Connecticut Medicine* 52: 42–48.

Bakwin, Harry, and Ruth M. Bakwin. 1953. "Homosexual Behavior in Children." *Journal of Pediatric* 43: 108–111.

Bayer, Ronald. 1987. *Homosexuality and American Psychiatry: The Politics of Diagnosis.* Princeton, NJ: Princeton University Press.

Bieber, Irving. 1962. *Homosexuality: A Psychoanalytical Study.* New York: Vintage.

Birk, Lee, William Huddleston, and Elizabeth Miller. 1971. "Avoidance Conditioning for Homosexuality." *Archives of General Psychiatry* 25:314–323.

Conrad, Florence. 1959. "Some Facts about Lesbians." *The Ladder* 3 (September): 4–26.

————. 1960. "Some Comparisons between Male and Female Homosexuals." *The Ladder* 4 (September): 4–25.

Crowley, Mart. 1968. *The Boys in the Band.* New York: Farrar, Straus and Giroux.

D'Emilio, John, and Estelle Freedman. 1988. *Intimate Matters: A History of Sexuality in America.* New York: Harper and Row.

Duberman, Martin. 1993. *Stonewall.* New York: Dutton.

English, Oliver Spurgeon. 1948. "Sex and Human Love." Pp. 96–112 in *About the Kinsey Report.* Edited by D. P. Geddes and E. Currie. New York: Signet.

"Faith and Fury." 1965. *The Ladder* 9 (May): 20–21.

Feldman, M. P., and M. K. MacCulloch. 1964. "A Systematic Approach to the Treatment of Homosexuality by Conditioned Aversion: Preliminary Report." *American Journal of Psychiatry* 121: 167–171.

Foucault, Michel. [1961] 1973. *Madness and Civilization: The History of Insanity in the Age of Reason.* Translated by R. Howard. New York: Vintage.

Freund, Kurt. 1960. "Some Problems in the Treatment of Homosexuality." In *Behaviour Therapy and the Neuroses.* Edited by H. J. Eysenck. London: Pergamon.

———. 1965. "Diagnosing Heterosexual Pedophilia by Means of a Test of Sexual Interest." *Behavior Research and Therapy* 3: 229–234.

Green, Richard. 1987. *The "Sissy Boy Syndrome" and the Development of Homosexuality.* New Haven, CT: Yale University Press.

Green, Richard, and John Money. 1961. "Effeminacy in Prepubertal Boys: Summary of Eleven Cases and Recommendations for Case Management." *Pediatrics* (February): 286–291.

Hadden, Samuel B. 1966a. "Newer Treatment Techniques for Homosexuality." *Archives of Environmental Health* 13: 284–288.

———. 1966b. "Treatment of Male Homosexuals in Groups." *International Journal of Group Psychotherapy* 16: 13–22.

Kallmann, Franz J. 1952. "Twin Sibship Study of Overt Male Homosexuality." *American Journal of Human Genetics* 4:136–146.

Kameny, Franklin. 1965a. "Does Research into Homosexuality Matter?" *The Ladder* 9 (May): 14–20.

———. 1965b. "Emphasis on Research Has Had Its Day." *The Ladder* 9 (October): 10–14, 23–26.

Katz, Jonathan Ned. 1976. *Gay American History: Lesbians and Gay Men in the U.S.A.* New York: Thomas Y. Crowell.

Kaye, Harvey E., Soll Berl, Jack Clare, Mary R. Eleston, Benjamin S. Gershwin, Patricia Gershwin, Leonard S. Kogan, Clara Torda, and Cornelia B Wilbur. 1967. "Homosexuality in Women." *Archives of General Psychiatry* 17: 626–634.

Kuhn, Thomas. [1962] 1970. *The Structure of Scientific Revolutions.* 2nd ed. Chicago: University of Chicago Press.

Livingood, John M., ed. [1969] 1972. *National Institute of Mental Health Task Force on Homosexuality: Final Report and Background Papers.* U.S. Department of Health, Education, and Welfare Publication no. (ADM) 76–357.

Marmor, Judd. 1972. "Notes on Some Psychodynamic Aspects of Homosexuality." Pp. 55–57 in *National Institute of Mental Health Task Force on Homosexuality: Final Report and Background Papers.* Edited by J. M. Livingood. U.S. Department of Health, Education, and Welfare Publication no. (ADM) 76–357.

Max, L. 1935. "Breaking a Homosexual Fixation by the Conditioned Reflex Technique." *Psychological Bulletins* 32: 734.

McConaghy, Nathaniel. 1976. "Is a Homosexual Orientation Irreversible?" *British Journal of Psychiatry* 129: 556–563.

Money, John. 1955. "Hermaphroditism, Gender and Precocity in Hyperadrenocorticism: Psychological Findings." *Bulletin of the Johns Hopkins Hospital* 96: 253–264.

———. 1972. "Strategy, Ethics, Behavior Modification, and Homosexuality." *Archives of Sexual Behavior* 2: 79–81.

Money, John, and Anke A. Ehrhardt. 1972. *Man and Woman, Boy and Girl: Differentiation and Dimorphism of Gender Identity from Conception to Maturity.* Baltimore: Johns Hopkins University Press.

Money, John, Joan Hampson, and John L. Hampson. 1957. "Imprinting and the Establishment of Gender Role." *Archives of Neurology and Psychiatry* 77: 333–336.

Rachman, S. 1965. "Aversion Therapy: Chemical or Electrical?" *Behavioural Research Therapy* 2: 289–299.

Rekers, George Alan. 1972. "Pathological Sex-Role Development in Boys: Behavioral Treatment and Assessment." Dissertation, Department of Psychology, University of California, Los Angeles.

Saghir, Marcel T., and Eli Robins. 1969. "Homosexuality: I. Sexual Behavior of the Female Homosexual." *Archives of General Psychiatry* 20: 192–201.

Szasz, Thomas. 1961. *The Myth of Mental Illness: Foundations of a Theory of Personal Conduct.* New York: Hoeber-Harper.

———. 1965. "Legal and Moral Aspects of Homosexuality." Pp. 124–139 in *Sexual Inversion: The Multiple Roots of Homosexuality.* Edited by Judd Marmor. New York: Basic Books.

Thorpe, J. G., E. Schmidt, and D. Castell. 1963. "A Combination of Positive and Negative (Aversive) Conditioning in the Treatment of Homosexuality." *Behavioral Research Therapy* 2: 293–296.

Wolfenden Report. 1957. *Report of the Committee on Homosexual Offenses and Prostitution.* Cmd. 247. London: Her Majesty's Stationary Office.

## Further Reading

In *The Modernization of Sex: Havelock Ellis, Alfred Kinsey, William Masters, and Virginia Johnson* (New York: Harper and Row, 1976), Paul Robinson sets Alfred Kinsey's work in its historical and political context, highlighting its huge cultural impact. Similarly, he critically reviews the sexological work of William Masters and Virginia Johnson in the setting of the sexual revolution of the 1960s—to which they significantly contributed. Robinson's earlier volume, *The Freudian Left: Wilhelm Reich, Geza Roheim, Herbert Marcuse* (New York: Harper and Row, 1969) examined the political and sexual radicalism of three very original psychoanalytic theorists. Kenneth Lewes's *The Psychoanalytic Theory of Male Homosexuality* (New York: Simon and Schuster, 1988) provides the most extensive study of psychoanalytic research on homosexuality prior to its depathologization in 1973.

$7$

# "Off the Couches, into the Streets!"

Shortly after 1 A.M. on June 28, 1969, the police raided the Stonewall Inn, a seedy gay bar in New York's Greenwich Village. These police shakedowns were a regular affair, but this time the drag queens did not go quietly into the police wagon. The enraged patrons sparked a riot that lasted five days and, by many accounts, launched a gay revolution with a new defiant spirit. The following June, the Christopher Street Liberation Day March commemorated the first anniversary of the riots and spawned a growing number of gay pride parades in the United States and internationally.

This new gay liberation movement did not go unnoticed by the medical profession. An editorial in the *New England Journal of Medicine* (a leading medical journal) reported on the gleeful 1970 parade and the marchers' slogan: "Say it clear, say it loud; gay is good, gay is proud!" The journal editors published the letter with the headline: "Gay Is *What?*" The author, however, was sympathetic to gay liberation and criticized the psychiatric model of homosexual pathology: "Most homosexuals . . . do not consider themselves potential patients, and resent being relegated to a psychiatric pigeonhole. To them, the direction of their sexual drive is no more pathologic than having long hair, red skin or an unpronounceable name" (Brass 1970). A few weeks later, a medical intern in Los Angeles responded anonymously, bringing the issue closer to home (see Sidebar 7.1). Gays were not just out there on the streets but were present in significant numbers in the medical profession itself. However, like himself, they had to remain closeted. He eagerly anticipated the day when he could openly declare his love publicly and professionally. That day was not far off, but the depathologization of homosexuality and the emergence of gays from within the medical profession would face huge resistance from those psychiatrists who were convinced that homosexuality was a psychiatric illness.

## Sidebar 7.1 Gay Doctors Emerge from the Closet

In 1970 the *New England Journal of Medicine* published the following letter from a reader under the heading "Homosexuals in Medicine":

> I read the editorial entitled "Gay is *What?*" (in the October 8 issue) with much amusement. What amazes me is the naïveté within the medical profession concerning homosexuality. As an intern, I daresay that I am overwhelmed by the large proportion of physicians and medical students who are homosexual.
>
> The editorial gave me the impression that the profession, as a whole, considers itself "uninfected" by homosexuality. The prevalence of homosexuality among physicians is much greater than most people believe. Part of this can be explained by the fact that most homosexuals who enter professions do not possess the outward characteristics that easily stigmatize them as the stereotyped homosexual. Behind this is the stringent scrutinizing process of our medical schools that weed out male applicants with traces of effeminacy.
>
> Most homosexual physicians that I have had contact with are noticeably more, almost as an unnecessary need to compensate, productive, creative, and humanistic than their heterosexual colleagues. My insight into this area is quite obvious. I am homosexual. I consider myself well adjusted to my way of life and have been living rather happily in a love relationship with another homosexual for the past four years. It is unfortunate that we must restrict our relationships both socially and professionally. However, the incessant façade that one in my situation must put on during the week is tedious to say the least.
>
> I look forward to the day when I can freely express my views, my love, and sign my name to a letter such as this.
>
> Los Angeles, Cal.

## Keeping Homosexuals on the Couch

Although a few isolated voices in the nineteenth century had argued that homosexuality was a nonpathological variation of human sexuality, the most serious scientific assaults on this view began in the mid–twentieth century with the work of Alfred Kinsey and his collaborators. By the late 1960s, some psychiatrists as well as homophile activists were further casting doubt on the disease model. Resistance to this depathologization came from psychiatrists, particularly psychoanalysts, who had been indoctrinated into the theory of homosexuality as a maladaptive behavior produced in childhood by dysfunctional family dynamics. Analysts who claimed success in "curing" homosexuals especially decried the depathologization of homosexuality and the potential loss of a large patient population. One of the most persistent and vocal of these analysts was Charles Socarides (1968a). As pressure mounted, Socarides, like Edmund Bergler before him, became more shrill and intransigent.

In a 1970 article in the *Journal of the American Medical Association* (JAMA), Socarides sensationally claimed that "homosexuality is a dread dysfunction, malignant in character, which has risen to epidemiologic [*sic*] proportions" (1199). Estimating that as many as 4 million American men "suffer from this condition," Socarides warned that it was the leading illness in the country. Citing mainly himself (1968b), he reiterated the standard psychoanalytic explanations that homosexuality was a neurosis resulting from faulty sexual identity. This error of psychosexual development was supposedly the product of a pathological family: "a domineering, crushing mother . . . and an absent, weak, or rejecting father" (1970, 1200). Paranoia was common in homosexuals, he declared. Referring to the study by Irving Bieber (1962), Socarides claimed that one third of exclusively homosexual patients could be converted to exclusive heterosexuality through psychoanalysis. (In fact, Bieber only reported a 19 percent success rate for these patients.)

Socarides endorsed the decriminalization of homosexuality but not its *destigmatization*. For him, homosexuality was intrinsically an emotional illness accompanied by abhorrence for the opposite sex and the impossibility of "any relationship except on the most superficial and brittle basis, if then." He flatly declared: "There is no obligatory homosexual who can be considered to be healthy" (1970, 1201). Nevertheless, he was aware of the changing social environment: "We practice in the atmosphere of a sweeping sexual revolution. Together with the mainstream heterosexual revolt has come the announcement that a homosexual revolution is also in progress and that homosexuality should be granted total acceptance as a valid form of sexual functioning, different from but equal to heterosexuality." Such a view, he warned, was not only ignorant but also dangerous. If homosexuality were given social approval, confused adolescents, and even adults, might be driven "into a self-despising homosexual pattern" (1202).

Ten years earlier, Socarides's article would have passed uncontested since it presented a dominant attitude in psychoanalysis. But in 1970 it drew fire from *within* the medical profession. In the August 31 issue of JAMA, Dr. Edward Dreyfus pointed out the scientific flimsiness and internal contradictions of Socarides's claims. Most important, Dreyfus argued that the "problem" of homosexuals' mental illness might be dealt with in a totally different manner: "Homosexuals could be protected from persecution and accorded full civil rights. It is conceivable that these two acts alone would significantly reduce their anxieties to the extent that they would function more effectively in society" (1970, 1495).

Dr. Martin Hoffman, author of *The Gay World: Male Homosexuality and the Social Creation of Evil,* was even more critical. He charged that many of Socarides's facts were questionable and his tone was objectionable. Hoffman urged readers not to believe that Socarides presented views shared by all psychiatrists and sexologists. He argued that Socarides's paper represented a form of medical moralizing, in which "good" and "evil" were clouded in "pious statements about 'medical science'" and discussed as matters of "health" and "illness" (1970, 1496). The politics of a diagnosis and of medical moralizing were erupting that year not only in the pages of medical journals but most decisively in the American Psychiatric Association (APA).

## Storming the APA

The 1970 annual convention of the APA took place in San Francisco, one of the hotbeds of gay activism. Two panels—"Transsexualism vs. Homosexuality: Distinct Entities?" and "Issues on Sexuality"—were targeted for "zaps" by gays and their feminist allies. Gary Alinder (1972) was one of the gay liberation activists who participated in the pandemonium of these interventions. Feminists demanded changes in the psychiatric approach to women and the phallocentrism of the profession—at that time almost exclusively male and white. Gays attacked the medicalizing and treatment of homosexuality. At the first panel, Irving Bieber was called a "motherfucker," and Alinder denounced Bieber's research:

> You are the pigs who make it possible for the cops to beat homosexuals: they call us queer; you—so politely—call us sick. But it's the same thing. You make possible the beatings and rapes in prisons, you are implicated in the torturous cures perpetrated on desperate homosexuals. I've read your book, Dr. Bieber, and if that book talked about black people the way it talks about homosexuals, you'd be drawn and quartered and you'd deserve it. (Alinder 1972, 144)

Bieber's defense, that he was not trying to oppress homosexuals but to liberate them "from that which is paining them—their homosexuality," was met with scornful derision. The "torturous cures" were attacked during a paper read by Dr. Nathaniel McConaghy, a promoter of aversion therapy for homosexuality (see Chapter 6). With hundreds of psychiatrists in attendance at the Veterans Memorial Auditorium, activists shouted "vicious," "torture," and "Where did you take your residency, Auschwitz?" They demanded time to present the gay perspective on homosexuality. Psychiatrists, in turn, insulted the activists and even called for the police to shoot them. The panel's chairman adjourned the meeting before the other two papers were read, but a few psychiatrists remained to hear out the statements by gays and feminists.

Later that year, the Chicago Gay Liberation Front demonstrated at the annual convention of the American Medical Association. They distributed leaflets denouncing the myth of homosexual pathology and more broadly the psychiatrization of social oppression (see Sidebar 7.2).

*A Gay Liberation Front poster makes it clear that coming out is the route to gay happiness (courtesy of Peter Hujar).*

## Sidebar 7.2 Gays Revolt against the AMA

*The radical gay liberation movement that developed in the 1960s, unlike the earlier homophile movement, could not sanction any collaboration with medicine or psychiatry in the improvement of the social status of homosexuals. On the contrary, the medical establishment and psychiatry in particular were accused of perpetuating the broader system of sexist, racist, "antihomosexualist," capitalist oppression. In a leaflet distributed at the 1970 convention of the American Medical Association, the Chicago Gay Liberation Front made it clear that a sweeping political and professional reform was necessary:*

The establishment school of psychiatry is based on the premise that people who are hurting should solve their problems by "adjusting" to the situation. For the homosexual, this means becoming adept at straight-fronting, learning how to survive in a hostile world, how to settle for housing in the gay ghetto, how to be satisfied with a profession in which homosexuals are tolerated, and how to live with low self-esteem.

The adjustment school places the burden on each individual homosexual to learn to bear his torment. But the "problem" of homosexuality is never solved under this scheme; the antihomosexualist attitude of society, which is the cause of the homosexual's trouble, goes unchallenged. And there's always another paying patient on the psychiatrist's couch.

Dr. Socarides claims, "A human being is sick when he fails to function in his appropriate gender identity, which is appropriate to his anatomy." Who determines "appropriateness"? The psychiatrist as moralist? Certainly there is no scientific basis for defining "appropriate" sexual behavior. . . . Other than invoking moral standards, Dr. Socarides claims that homosexuality is an emotional illness because of the guilt and anxieties in homosexual life. Would he also consider Judaism an emotional illness because of the paranoia which Jews experienced in Nazi Germany?

We homosexuals of gay liberation believe that the adjustment school of therapy is not a valid approach to society.

We refuse to adjust to our oppression, and believe that the key to our mental health, and to the mental health of all oppressed peoples in a racist, sexist, capitalist society, is a radical change in the structure and accompanying attitudes of the entire social system.

Mental health for women does not mean therapy for women—it means the elimination of male supremacy. Not therapy for blacks, but an end to racism. The poor don't need psychiatrists (what a joke at 25 bucks a throw!)—they need democratic distribution of wealth. OFF THE COUCHES, INTO THE STREETS!

We see political organizing and collective action as the strategy for effecting this social change. We declare that we are healthy homosexuals in a sexist society, and that homosexuality is at least on a par with heterosexuality as a way for people to relate to each other (know any men that don't dominate women?).

Since the prevalent notion in society is that homosexuality is wrong, all those who recognize that this attitude is damaging to people, and that it must be corrected, have to raise their voices in opposition to antihomosexualism. Not to do so is to permit the myth of homosexual pathology to continue and to comply in the homosexual's continued suffering from senseless stigmatization. . . . We furthermore urge psychiatrists to refer their homosexual patients to gay

*(continues)*

Much "mental illness," they declared, was the result of the injustices of a racist, sexist, capitalist society. It was not homosexuals and women who had to change, but society. They echoed the sentiment of many gay libbers of the time: that one hour at a gay pride march could do more for one's mental health than years on the couch.

Historian Ronald Bayer (1987) documented how these activist interventions sparked the battle to expunge homosexuality from the *Diagnostic and Statistical Manual of Psychiatric Disorders* (2nd ed.) (DSM-II). The following year's APA meeting included for the first time a panel of gay and lesbian activists discussing "Lifestyles of Non-Patient Homosexuals." Members of the Washington Gay Liberation Front also staged demonstrations and pushed for the removal of a booth marketing aversive conditioning techniques for homosexuality. Activists began formally demanding that homosexuality be removed from the DSM. In November 1971, the APA's Task Force on Social Issues recommended a revision of the DSM's characterization of homosexuality in general as pathological. At the 1972 APA meeting in Dallas, Texas, gay activists were again included in the program and given a booth in the exhibition area from which to distribute leaflets arguing against the "sickness theory" of homosexuality.

This 1972 panel on homosexuality for the first time brought together activists (Frank Kameny and Barbara Gittings) and sympathetic doctors (Robert Seidenberg, Judd Marmor, and Dr. Anonymous—a masked, homosexual psychiatrist). All the speakers were highly critical of the profession's hostility toward homosexuals and the ill effects it had on clients and closeted psychiatrists, such as Dr. Anonymous. The meeting was a dramatic turning point. Increasing numbers of doctors were willing to be critical of the profession's attitudes toward homosexuals. Furthermore, new research was supporting the activists' claims.

### A Tidal Change in Professional Opinion

Psychiatrists and psychologists who had been influenced by Evelyn Hooker's work on nonpatient homosexuals began publishing their research after Stonewall. Like Kinsey, these studies recruited subjects from homophile groups rather than psychiatrists' offices and thereby came up with a rather different picture of homosexuality from that of Bieber or Socarides. Marcel Saghir, Eli Robins (head of the department of psychiatry at the Washington University School of Medicine), and two colleagues explicitly set aside presumptions of illness: "In studying the clinical aspects of homosexuality, it is not assumed that homosexuality itself is necessarily a psychiatric illness" (1970, 1079).

The four researchers compared a group of eighty-nine homosexual men recruited from Chicago and San Francisco homophile organizations to a group of thirty-five unmarried men approximately matched for age and socioeconomic status. They found little difference in the prevalence of psychopathology between the two groups. However, the homosexual men did seek psychotherapy for depression more frequently than the heterosexual men and also had somewhat higher levels of drinking problems and suicide attempts. The homosexual men dropped out of college at a higher rate than heterosexuals, which the researchers suggested might be related to struggles with sexuality at that age. Unlike previous researchers, Saghir and Robins and their colleagues did not see these problems as intrinsic to homosexuality but as secondary to coping with it. They concluded on a sympathetic note: "Despite these differences the homosexual subjects were able to achieve an educational, occupational, and economic status similar to that of the controls and significantly higher than that of single employed males" (1086). A year later, their study of lesbians came up with similar results: "The majority of [lesbians] functioned adequately and were productive with no significant disabilities" (Saghir and Robins 1971, 510).

Dr. David Rosen, a professor in the University of California at San Francisco Department of Psychiatry, reached similar conclusions based on a group of Daughters of Bilitis members studied in the late 1960s. His book, *Lesbianism: A Study of Female Homosexuality* (1974), had an enthusiastic foreword by Evelyn Hooker. It reviewed the psychiatric literature on the subject, which he noted was far less abundant than that on men and generally based on anecdotal observations. However, as was the case with male homosexuality, lesbianism had been attributed to infantile fixations and phobias and viewed as intrinsically psychopathological. Only recently had researchers begun to study nonpatient lesbians and compare them to similar heterosexual women to find no significant differences.

Rosen concluded that the only significant difference between lesbians and nonlesbians was their choice of sexual partners. Adopting the language of lesbian feminists Phyllis Lyon and Del Martin in *Lesbian/Woman* (1972), Rosen declared that lesbianism was a way of life, not a sickness. It was social ostracism and pressure to lead a dual life that produced lesbians' anxiety and tension. What should psychiatrists do about lesbianism? Rosen encouraged an activist role: "The psychiatric profession needs to help change the attitudes of society through public and medical education campaigns" (Rosen 1974, 72). In the meantime, doctors had to offer supportive psychotherapy to help lesbians deal with their sexuality, their love relationships, and the stress of social hostility. Jumping into the debate then raging in the APA, Rosen called for the deletion of homosexuality from the DSM.

## The Battle in the APA

In February 1973, Dr. Robert Spitzer of the New York State Department of Mental Hygiene arranged for the critics of the psychiatric model of homosexuality to argue their case before the APA's Committee on Nomenclature and Statistics, which governs the contents of the DSM. Spitzer was a member of the committee. Dr. Charles Silverstein of the Institute of Sexual Identity (a gay counseling center) and future coauthor of *The Joy of Gay Sex* (1977), represented gay activists. Silverstein recruited several prominent scientists and psychiatrists to buttress his arguments: Dr. Seymour Halleck (a critic of abuses of psychiatric authority), Wardell Pomeroy (one of Kinsey's colleagues), and Alan Bell (a psychologist at Kinsey's Institute for Sex Research and coauthor of a forthcoming study on homosexuality, discussed below). They reviewed the psychiatric literature on homosexuality to point out the scientific errors and poor methodology that went into constructing homosexuality as a mental disorder. Furthermore, they highlighted the oppressive social effects of the diagnosis: the job discrimination and cultural opprobrium legitimized by the stigma of disease. All this added up to untold mental anguish for homosexuals, who were thus harmed far more than they were helped by psychiatry. The nomenclature committee members were moved by these arguments and agreed to present their recommendations on the status of the homosexuality diagnosis in time for the APA convention that May.

Sensing that the Committee on Nomenclature and Statistics would decide against them, the supporters of the diagnosis (predominantly psychoanalysts) quickly organized a counteroffensive under the direction of Irving Bieber and Charles Socarides. Many of the psychoanalytic societies swiftly passed resolutions opposing any change in the DSM classification of homosexuality. Not only would such a change impinge on the livelihood of many psychoanalysts and strike at the firmly entrenched homophobia of American psychoanalysis, but it would seriously undermine the psychodynamic principles of the entire discipline. If Freudian theories of infantile traumas and psychosexual arrested development did not constitute legitimate scientific evidence of the psychopathology of homosexuality, could they be taken seriously for any other psychiatric disorders?

Psychiatrists in favor of the reform were also mobilizing. Dr. Richard Pillard, the first publicly identified gay psychiatrist and cofounder of the Homophile Community Health Center in Boston, presented the case for change to the Social Issues Committee of the Northern New England Branch of the APA (see Sidebar 7.3). His formal resolution, presented in December 1972, recommended the elimination of the homosexuality diagnosis and the inclusion of a "sexual dysfunction" class of diagnoses (including frigidity, impotence, and homosexuality) that caused psychic distress. Echoing the conclusions of Hooker's National Institute of Mental Health (NIMH) 1969 task force, Pillard recommended the decriminalization of homosexuality as well as the broadening of sex education in order to help homosexual youngsters adjust to their orientation. In March 1973, the Northern New England Branch endorsed all of Pillard's recommendations except the last one concerning adolescents.

With pressure mounting from within the profession and without, Spitzer pushed the Committee on Nomenclature and Statistics to arrive at its conclusions

*Richard Pillard, MD (Tracy Russo / courtesy of Richard Pillard)*

speedily. As he had promised Ronald Gold of the Gay Activist Alliance of New York, Spitzer organized a panel on homosexuality at the 1973 APA meeting in Honolulu, Hawaii. Included on the panel, for the first time, were representatives from both sides of the argument: Gold, Robert Stoller, Judd Marmor, and Richard Green, who favored DSM reform, and Bieber and Socarides, who argued the case for the pathology of homosexuality. The session was heavily attended, and there was strong sentiment favoring the depathologization of homosexuality—a huge reversal from just three years earlier.

Gold, hoping to secure Spitzer's support for gays, brought Spitzer along to an unpublicized meeting of gay psychiatrists at the convention. Some were incensed by this violation of confidentiality and feared for their careers. Others took advantage of the opportunity to further influence Spitzer and make him more aware of the existence of normally functioning homosexuals—even within the profession. Spitzer's position paper, circulated the following month, firmly recommended the deletion of homosexuality from the DSM. He argued that for a condition to be considered a "psychiatric disorder" and therefore warrant inclusion in the DSM, it must regularly cause distress or dysfunction. Although he did not view homosexuality as "normal" behavior, neither could he see any scientific justification in considering it a psychiatric disease given the number of homosexuals who were satisfied with their sexuality and functioned well in society. Spitzer argued that the homosexuality diagnosis should be replaced by one of "sexual orientation disturbance" to be applied to those "who are bothered by, in conflict with, or wish to change their sexual orientation" (Spitzer 1973, 1215).

In October of that year, the Council on Research and Development of the APA voted to accept Spitzer's proposal and delete homosexuality from the DSM-II. Finally, on December 15, 1973, the Board of Trustees of the APA approved the deletion and substituted a diagnosis of "sexual orientation disturbance." In theory, this diagnosis could be applied to either homosexuals or heterosexuals significantly distressed by their sexual orientation. The committee went further to condemn the criminal and social persecution of homosexuals. After over a century of circulating as a medical diagnosis and stigma, the disease of "homosexuality" was now on its way out. Newspapers around the world reported on the decision, with one journalist wryly noting it was the single greatest cure in the history of psychiatry.

The battle was not over yet. Some psychiatrists accused the APA leadership of cowardice in buckling in to gay activists. Others groused that the board's decision turned psychiatric nosology into a political rather than a scientific matter. The most conservative analysts feared that the APA's decision augured a homosexually instigated disintegration of the family and society in general. Socarides spearheaded a revolt by psychoanalysts, and the American Psychoanalytic Association in New York pressed for a general referendum on the issue. After intense lobbying in favor of the replacement of "homosexuality" with "sexual orientation disturbance," a majority of APA members voted in 1974 to approve the DSM change.

Thirty seven percent of members, however, had voted against the nomenclature change. Ronald Bayer (1987, 150) has argued that this faction mainly represented the older, conservative psychoanalysts who saw the change as an attack on their professional knowledge and independence by younger, more liberal psychiatrists committed to the social change inspired by the 1960s. Ironically, similar professional and generational conflicts had taken place in the postwar United States when young analysts had originally erected homosexuality and

## Sidebar 7.4 Recollections of the DSM Struggle

*Dr. Richard Pillard recounts the political context and theoretical stakes of the battle within the American Psychiatric Association (APA) to eliminate the diagnosis of homosexuality.*

Recall that pre-Stonewall was the decade of the 60s. The spirit of that era is difficult to portray for anyone who did not live then, and difficult to describe in a few words. The hypocrisy of the Vietnam war alienated many, particularly younger, people from the political process. This in turn led to a recognition of the relative exclusion of women and racial minorities from decision making in many venues and at many levels. The war was just one (but a major) icon of the disastrous consequences of top-down decision making. The demonstrations, sit-ins, and teach-ins of that time brought about what I think was a permanent (albeit limited) revision in how leaders thought about the distribution and exercise of power.

Psychiatry at that time was under attack from critics such as D. L. Rosenhan (1973)* and of course Thomas Szasz (1979) on the grounds that mental disorders were not real illnesses like cancer but simply labels for behavior that happened to challenge the power elite. Among the arguments were the medicalization of homosexuality (without any particular evidence) and the "hospitalization" of political dissidents in Soviet Russia by reason of a "diagnosis" of "sluggish schizophrenia." A team of American psychiatrists (led by Alan Stone, later APA President) went to Russia to examine the World War II hero, General Grigorenko, who was then committed to a mental hospital for his dissident views. The American team thought him quite sane. One is surprised that American psychiatrists were permitted the visit, but I took that as a sign that the Russian psychiatrists did not have any doubt that Grigorenko was insane; in other words, they were not being hypocritical, they just did not have a clear notion about what ought to constitute a mental disorder, which was of course the American critics' point. Thus the importance of defining mental illness.

Recognizing that any definition is arbitrary does not lessen the need to have definitions and to make them clear. Robert Spitzer undertook the task of constructing DSM-III on very concrete, operational lines and of rebutting Rosenhan, which he did in a brilliant riposte (1975). There was also some cross-cultural work by Jane Murphy and Alexander H. Leighton (1965), medical anthropologists who showed that people in other cultures have about the same frame of reference for who is insane that we do.

The conclusion of this argument was that official psychiatry was able to defend the idea that there are mental disorders and they have the same status as physical disorders (indeed, we now think they are physical disorders)—only homosexuality simply is not one of them (Pillard, e-mail letter to the author, May 16, 1997).

*\* Rosenhan's "study" consisted of introducing twelve sane pseudopatients into psychiatric wards with fake complaints of auditory hallucinations. After admission they promptly denied further hallucinations, yet they were all discharged with an official diagnosis (of either schizophrenia or manic-depressive psychosis) "in remission." Rosenhan's conclusions were that psychiatrists cannot really tell who is insane, and they overapply "global diagnoses" (such as schizophrenia).*

other neuroses as treatable diseases in their campaign to elevate the role of psychiatry in social hygiene. A new generational shift had begun to sweep these analysts to the margins of the profession, and another generation of psychiatrists started serving the needs of homosexual clients rather than trying to convert them.

### The Varieties of Homosexual Lifestyles

The DSM battle occurred alongside a revolution in the way psychologists and psychiatrists were portraying homosexuality. Reflecting the language of gay and lesbian activists, researchers were examining homosexuality not as a singular, homogeneous psychopathology but as a complex, multifaceted lifestyle, behavior, and identity.

Del Martin and Phyllis Lyon's *Lesbian/Woman* (1972) was a groundbreaking text in this vein. The authors were a lesbian couple who were founding members of the Daughters of Bilitis in San Francisco in 1955. Writing from years of experience in the secret lesbian world, the feminist movement, and the new gay rights movement, they wrote in avowedly personal, nonscientific fashion about lesbians' experiences. It was the first book-length study of lesbianism to break away from the medical model. They declared that "the Lesbian is every woman"—she took on every type of occupation, including motherhood. Martin and Lyon dispelled myths about lesbians' bodily and psychological masculinity and about their sexual activities. They repudiated the butch-femme "role playing" in which they themselves had once engaged as derivative of the oppressive model of heterosexual marriage. They documented the struggle to include lesbian issues forthrightly in the organized feminist movement and described lesbianism as a political and lifestyle decision akin to the feminist issue of reproductive choice. As noted earlier, Dr. David Rosen's monograph, *Lesbianism* (1974) hewed closely to Martin and Lyon's perspective.

The most extensive study of female and male homosexuals was produced by Kinsey's Institute for Sex Research. Written by Alan P. Bell and Martin S. Weinberg, *Homosexualities: A Study of Diversity among Men and Women* (1978) presented data on almost 1,000 homosexual men and women of the San Francisco Bay area, who were interviewed beginning in 1970. The research was funded by the NIMH and set out to address some of the questions posed by Hooker's NIMH Task Force of 1967. The study thus spanned the gay revolution, and the authors noted the new hostility among some gay activists about collaborating with scientists given their legacy of prejudiced research.

The final report, like the original Kinsey studies, set out to shatter the model of homosexuality as a diagnostic entity. As the title suggests, Bell and Weinberg emphasized the diversity of homosexual lifestyles and behaviors. On many points, their findings echoed those of the earlier Daughters of Bilitis studies of the 1960s: men were far more sexually active, whatever their dominant relationship. Women were more spread out over the Kinsey heterosexual-homosexual scale and were much more likely to have had heterosexual relations in the past year than the men. Bell and Weinberg distinguished five relationship types: close-coupleds, open-coupleds (nonmonogamous), functionals ("swinging singles"), dysfunctionals ("tormented homosexuals"), and asexuals. Among lesbians, close-coupleds were the largest group (38.4 percent), whereas the largest number of gay men were in open-coupleds (24.7 percent).

According to their results, the mental health of most homosexuals was comparable to that of heterosexuals. Bell and Weinberg found that the most unhappy and dysfunctional homosexuals were those with the most distress concerning their homosexuality. These were also the most likely to have sought mental health services and conversion therapy to heterosexuality. This was the very population that previous psychiatrists had relied on for generalizations about *all* homosexuals. The dysfunctional and asexual homosexuals differed from heterosexuals in terms of mental health almost as much as they did from other homosexuals. The researchers found that the most healthy and happy homosexuals were those in closed-coupleds, whose lifestyles most resembled those of married heterosexuals. The functional homosexuals were, however, a close second; these were energetic, cheerful people who were successful and satisfied with their sexuality and enjoyed an active sex life.

The stereotypical tortured, self-hating homosexual—trumpeted as the norm by psychoanalysts such as Edmund Bergler—did exist, but only as a minority of the post-Stonewall gay population of San Francisco. Bell and Weinberg's data suggested that the great majority of gays in the 1970s were happily coming to terms with their sexuality and leading productive lives—often quite similar to those of married couples. "Clearly," they concluded, "a deviation from the sexual norms of our society does not inevitably entail a course of life with disastrous consequences. . . . Perhaps the least ambiguous finding of our investigation is that homosexuality is not necessarily related to pathology. Thus, decisions about homosexual men and women, whether they have to do with employment or child custody or counseling, should never be made on the basis of sexual orientation alone"

(231). Bell and Weinberg thus finally lent factual, scientific support to the controversial, liberal policy recommendations of Hooker's Task Force on Homosexuality. In the space of a decade, a century of biomedical pathologization of homosexuality had been set on its head. Unfortunately, this dissociation of homosexuality from pathology would be short-lived as the 1980s witnessed the rapid escalation of a new "gay plague."

## References

Alinder, Gary. 1972. "Gay Liberation Meets the Shrinks." Pp. 141–145 in *Out of the Closets: Voices of Gay Liberation*. Edited by Karla Jay and Allen Young. New York: Douglas Books.

Bayer, Ronald. 1987. *Homosexuality and American Psychiatry: The Politics of Diagnosis*. Princeton, NJ: Princeton University Press.

Bell, Alan P., and Martin S. Weinberger. 1978. *Homosexualities: A Study of Diversity among Men and Women*. New York: Simon and Schuster.

Bieber, Irving. 1962. *Homosexuality: A Psychoanalytical Study*. New York: Vintage.

Brass, Alister. 1970. "Gay Is What?" [Letter] *New England Journal of Medicine* 283: 817.

Chicago Gay Liberation Front. [1970] 1973. A leaflet for the American Medical Association. Pp. 145–147 in *Out of the Closets: Voices of Gay Liberation*. Edited by Karla Jay and Allen Young. New York: Douglas Books.

Dreyfus, Edward G. 1970. "Homosexuality and Medicine: A Reply." *Journal of the American Medical Association* 213: 1494–1495.

Hoffman, Martin. 1970. "Homosexuality and Medicine: A Reply." *Journal of the American Medical Association* 213: 1495–1496.

Lyon, Phyllis, and Del Martin. 1972. *Lesbian/Woman*. San Francisco: Glide Urban Center.

Murphy, Jane M., and Alexander H. Leighton, eds. 1965. *Approaches to Cross-Cultural Psychiatry*. Ithaca, NY: Cornell University Press.

Pillard, Richard. 1997. E-mail letter to author, May 16.

Rosen, David H. 1974. *Lesbianism: A Study of Female Homosexuality*. Springfield, IL: Charles C. Thomas.

Rosenhan, D. L. 1973. "On Being Sane in Insane Places." *Science* 179: 250–258.

Saghir, Marcel T., and Eli Robins. 1971. "Male and Female Homosexuality: Natural History." *Comprehensive Psychiatry* 12: 503–510.

Saghir, Marcel T., Eli Robins, Bonnie Walbran, and Kathye A. Gentry. 1970. "Homosexuality: III. Psychiatric Disorders and Disability in the Male Homosexual." *American Journal of Psychiatry* 126: 1079–1086.

Silverstein, Charles, and Edmund White. 1977. *The Joy of Gay Sex: An Intimate Guide for Gay Men to the Pleasures of a Gay Lifestyle*. New York: Crown.

Socarides, Charles W. 1968a. *The Overt Homosexual*. New York: Grune and Stratton.

———. 1968b. "A Provisional Theory of Aetiology in Male Homosexuality." *International Journal of Psychoanalysis* 49: 27–37.

———. 1970. "Homosexuality in Medicine." *Journal of the American Medical Association* 212: 1199–1202.

Spitzer, Robert L. 1973. "A Proposal about Homosexuality and the APA Nomenclature: Homosexuality as an Irregular Form of Sexual Behavior and Sexual Orientation Disturbance as a Psychiatric Disorder." *American Journal of Psychiatry* 130: 1214–1216.

——. 1975. "On Pseudoscience in Science, Logic in Remission, and Psychiatric Diagnosis: A Critique of Rosenhan's 'On Being Sane in Insane Places.'" *Journal of Abnormal Psychology* 84: 442–452.

Szasz, Thomas. 1979. "The Dan White Case: Psychiatrists vs. Gays." *Inquiry* (August 6 and 20).

## Further Reading

Karla Jay and Allen Young's anthology, *Out of the Closets: Voices of Gay Liberation* (New York: Douglas Books, 1972), is a wonderful collection of essays, manifestos, and interviews from the "gay lib" activists of the heady days of radicalism right after the Stonewall riots of 1969. Martin B. Duberman's *Stonewall* (New York: Dutton, 1993), dramatically tells the story of the Stonewall Inn riots and the gay political revolution they sparked through the eyes of participants and other gay and lesbian New Yorkers of the time.

*Homosexuality and American Psychiatry: The Politics of Diagnosis* (Princeton, NJ: Princeton University Press, 1987) by Ronald Bayer is a fast-moving account of the external and internal politics that led the American Psychiatric Association to depathologize homosexuality in the early 1970s.

# 8
## From Gay Pride to the Gay Plague

The 1970s was a decade of gay liberation and euphoria incited by the Stonewall riots of 1969. There was increased public visibility of gays thanks to the proliferation of gay pride parades and gay businesses, discotheques, and publications. Along with other young Americans, lesbians and gays reveled in the sexual revolution of the era. Urban gay men, in particular, had a growing number of venues that informally or explicitly facilitated sexual encounters. The perceived promiscuity of the decade quickly instigated a social backlash by cultural conservatives. In part, it was prompted by the rising incidence of gonorrhea, syphilis, and other sexually transmitted diseases (STDs) among homosexuals and heterosexuals alike. As Allan Brandt points out in *No Magic Bullet: A Social History of Venereal Disease in the United States since 1880,* the concern over STDs was nevertheless accompanied by poor funding for sex education, prophylaxis, and the treatment of venereal diseases. This legacy of 1950s public health only exacerbated the problem. To fill in this deficit, homophile and women's health clinics sprung up in major cities to serve the needs of gay and lesbian clients. Their services included the treatment of STDs as well as psychological, gynecological, substance abuse, and other medical treatment better provided by homosexual physicians and those sympathetic to gays and lesbians.

In the early 1980s, there was a surge in fear over genital herpes, particularly in the heterosexual "general population." *Time* magazine declared herpes the "new sexual leprosy" ("Herpes" 1980). Journalists and moralists widely described it as the price of the sexual revolution of the 1980s. It was in this context of cultural anxiety over sex and disease that there appeared the first signs of deadly trouble. In 1981 doctors first reported a mysterious new immunodeficiency syndrome that would dominate subsequent medical research on homosexuals (see Sidebar 8.1). By the end of 1981, ninety-eight people had been diagnosed with what

### Rare Cancer Seen in 41 Homosexuals
### Outbreak Occurs among Men in New York
### and California—8 Died Inside 2 Years

Doctors in New York and California have diagnosed among homosexual men 41 cases of a rare and often rapidly fatal form of cancer. Eight of the victims died less than 24 months after the diagnosis was made.

The cause of the outbreak is unknown, and there is as yet no evidence of contagion. But the doctors who have made the diagnoses, mostly in New York City and the San Francisco Bay area, are alerting other physicians who treat large numbers of homosexual men to the problem in an effort to help identify more cases and to reduce the delay in offering chemotherapy treatment. The sudden appearance of the cancer, called Kaposi's Sarcoma, has prompted a medical investigation that experts say could have as much scientific as public health importance because of what it may teach about determining the causes of the more common types of cancer. . . .

In a letter alerting other physicians to the problem, Dr. Alvin E. Friedman-Kien of the New York University Medical Center, one of the investigators, described the appearance of the outbreak as "rather devastating." . . .

According to Dr. Friedman-Kien, the reporting doctors said that most cases had involved homosexual men who have had multiple and frequent sexual encounters with different partners, as many as 10 sexual encounters each night up to four times a week.

Many of the patients have also been treated for viral infections such as herpes, cytomegalovirus, and hepatitis B as well as parasitic infections such as amebiasis and giardiasis. Many patients also reported that they had used drugs such as amyl nitrate and LSD to heighten sexual pleasure. . . .

The medical investigators say some indirect evidence actually points away from contagion as a cause. None of the patients knew each other, although the theoretical possibility that some many have had sexual contact with a person with Kaposi's Sarcoma at some point in the past could not be excluded, Dr. Friedman-Kien said.

Dr. Curran [of the Centers for Disease Control and Prevention] said there was no apparent danger to nonhomosexuals from contagion. "The best evidence against contagion," he said, "is that no cases have been reported to date outside the homosexual community or in women."

Dr. Friedman-Kien said he had tested nine of the victims and found severe defects in their immunological systems. The patients had serious malfunctions of two types of cells called T and B cell lymphocytes, which have important roles in fighting infections and cancer.

would later be called acquired immune deficiency syndrome (AIDS). By the end of the decade, over 147,000 adults and adolescents had been diagnosed with AIDS—of these over 80 percent had died. Although AIDS has instigated major research efforts worldwide and led to important advances in immunology and virology, no cure or vaccine for it has been developed to date. Thanks to public health campaigns and improved treatment of associated diseases, the new infection rate and the AIDS mortality rate seem to be leveling off, but it remains a catastrophic and escalating epidemic in numerous developing nations. Its toll on the United States has been tremendous (see Sidebar 8.2).

Although AIDS has heavily afflicted intravenous drug users, hemophiliacs, and young, inner-city African Americans and Hispanics, the disease has been especially associated with gays (Treichler 1987). In the 1980s, the media regularly portrayed AIDS as the "gay plague," and it has sorely affected gay and lesbian communities. However, it has also prompted them to invent new tactics in health care advocacy and activism. AIDS has also commanded the energies of many medical and social science researchers; nevertheless, the post-Stonewall openness of lesbian and gay scientists has also fomented much other work of importance to sexually marginalized populations.

### The Emergence of Gay-Related Immunodeficiency

Randy Shilts's book *And the Band Played On* (1987) grippingly dramatized the insidious appearance of AIDS. Beginning in 1979, doctors in Los Angeles, San Francisco, and New York began seeing a handful of previously healthy young gay men with Kaposi's sarcoma (KS) and *Pneumocystis carinii* pneumonia (PCP). Both diseases were highly unusual for this population. Kaposi's sarcoma (usually a slow-growing tumor of the blood vessels that produces violet-colored skin lesions) usually occurred in young central African and elderly Mediterranean and Ashkenazi Jewish men. *Pneumocystis carinii* pneumonia is considered an "opportunistic infection"; in other words, it primarily occurs in people with debilitated immune systems (for example, organ transplant recipients on immunosuppressive drugs). As Ronald Bayer recounts in *Private Acts, Social Consequences: AIDS and the Politics of Public Health* (1989), the Centers for Disease Control (CDC) reported in June 1981 the PCP outcroppings in Los Angeles and suggested that these unusual cases might be associated with some aspect of homosexual lifestyle or sexual contact. A month later, the CDC documented clusters of severe and fatal KS in young gay men. The new phenomenon was variously referred to as gay-related immunodeficiency (GRID) or acquired immunodeficiency (AID). One of the characteristic laboratory test markers for the disorder was the decline in one type of immune system white blood cell: the helper T cells (or T4 cells).

A year later, the CDC had collected 355 reports of KS and opportunistic infections (mainly PCP) in previously healthy men. Seventy-nine percent of these were gay or bisexual men, and the majority of the others were intravenous (IV) drug users. At this point the CDC officially adopted the term *acquired immunodeficiency syndrome*. As a "syndrome," AIDS does not refer a distinct disease but a constellation of symptoms and pathologies (such as a diminished helper T-cell count, KS, PCP, and a number of other opportunistic infections). Over time, the CDC has revised the criteria for an official diagnosis of AIDS or AIDS-related complex (a now obsolete term for a less severe stage of HIV illness)—specifically, AIDS was redefined in 1987 and again in 1993.

Theories abounded as to the causation of AIDS. As the CDC had originally hypothesized, some researchers, journalists, and moralists suggested AIDS was caused by elements of the gay lifestyle: amyl nitrate ("poppers" used to heighten sexual arousal), the combination of drugs and alcohol, a complex of STD microbes, or promiscuity and presumed immune "exhaustion." Members of the religious right touted it as a divine pestilence on sodomites, calling it the wrath of God syndrome (WOGS). One psychiatrist, speaking to the graduating class of Valley Christian University, declared: "It is the oral-anal sex acts of the homosexual that are responsible for a major disease that has hit our nation. . . . Originally, the disease was called 'Gay Related Infectious Disease—GRID.' . . . The problem is acute. Either our society accepts the tenets of perverts and becomes a bastion for perversion, or we protect mature sexuality dependent upon family and social conscience" (Anchell 1985). As sociologist Steven Epstein (1996) points out, even some gay activists and at least one notable scientist, Peter Duesberg, continue to insist that these lifestyle elements are the primary cause of AIDS.

However, in 1982, virology labs in France and the United States competed to isolate and culture the suspected pathogen. The French were the first to isolate what they called lymphadenopathy-associated virus (LAV). A U.S. team identified the causative virus under the name human T-cell lymphotropic virus type III (HTLV-III) because they believed it belonged to the already known HTLV family. The two principle investigators, Luc Montagnier and Robert Gallo, still dispute who first identified the virus. Nevertheless, the name human immunodeficiency virus (HIV) was adopted by consensus in 1986. The French LAV is probably the agent associated with AIDS, and it appears that Gallo's viral cultures had become contaminated with LAV. An enzyme-linked immunosorbent assay (ELISA) for the identification of antibodies to HIV was put on the market in 1985. The ELISA does not identify the virus itself but the human antibodies produced in response to exposure to the virus. For this reason, there may be a delay of several months between actual HIV infection and a positive ELISA test result once the body has produced HIV antibodies. Newer testing methods now allow for earlier detection as well as direct estimates of the amount of virus present in a sample (the "viral load"). Nevertheless, the ELISA test in 1985 finally permitted routine screening of blood for transfusions and blood products, as well as HIV testing of individuals. (Positive ELISA tests were confirmed by a "Western blot" test, a more costly and complicated method of virus detection.)

Until the identification of a causative agent and a screening test for it, doctors and blood banks relied on the notion of "risk groups" to identify populations in danger of developing or having AIDS. These were initially identified as the "Four-H" groups: homosexuals, Haitians, hemophiliacs, and heroine addicts (as well as other IV drug users). Although it helped target certain populations for health education, medical attention, and screening from the blood donor pool, the notion of risk groups stigmatized these populations—basically equating all their members with AIDS. Meanwhile, even after HIV was identified, the U.S. Public Health Service and then U.S. president Ronald Reagan failed to mount a nationwide campaign to educate people concerning high risk *practices,* including unprotected penetrative sex, IV needle sharing, and the exchange of other bodily fluids. These were not practices the conservative administration wanted to discuss, in case it appeared to condone them.

Despite the subsequent diversification of AIDS public health messages, the disease continues to be most closely identified with gay men because of the early association and the heavy toll among homosexual men: in the first two years of the epidemic, over three-fourths of adult male AIDS cases were attributed to homosexual contact. As of December 31, 2000, 774,467 people have been reported with AIDS in the United States: 58 percent of these died and 41 percent of AIDS cases were attributed to infection through male-to-male sex. Unfortunately, after decades of battling representations of homosexuality as a perversity and a mental illness, the official psychiatric depathologization of homosexuality in the 1970s was eclipsed by the new association of gays with AIDS. Faced with a vacuum in national leadership to stem the epidemic, the gay and lesbian community organized in an unprecedented manner to press for the destigmatization, prevention, study, and treatment of AIDS.

*The Politics of Sex*

From the very start of the epidemic, members of the gay community— Larry Kramer, Michael Callen (1955–1993), Richard Berkowitz, and

ACT UP "Seize Control of the FDA" demonstration at the Food and Drug Administration (FDA) headquarters, Rockville, Maryland, October 11, 1988. ACT UP made a number of demands including a speedier drug testing and approval process, an end to double-blind placebo trials, enlarging the pools of experimental subjects, the inclusion of people with AIDS on Institutional Review Boards, and Medicaid and private insurance coverage of experimental drugs (Joan E. Biren).

numerous essayists for the *New York Native* in particular—blamed promiscuity and argued for sexual moderation among urban gay men. Others viewed this position as an abdication to internalized homophobia and an abandonment of the hard-earned sexual freedoms won in the 1960s (Crimp 1987). Battles ensued not only with departments of public health but within gay communities over the closure of bathhouses, sex clubs, and other sites for gay sexual encounters.

During the first few years of the emerging epidemic, there was much confusion, fear, and conflicting recommendations. New York's Gay Men's Health Crisis (GMHC) and the Kaposi's Sarcoma Research and Education Foundation (later renamed the San Francisco AIDS Foundation) were created in early 1982 to provide information and services to people with AIDS (PWAs). They gradually expanded their activities over the decade to serve as important political groups pressing for increased federal research funding, greater media attention, improved doctor-patient communication, more local government support for social services, and increased gay community activism. Similar groups sprang up in other major metropolitan areas where AIDS cases were concentrated. With no concrete knowledge about a pathogen, gay health associations generally advised restrict-

*Lesbians in front of the Food and Drug Administration (FDA) headquarters, Rockville, Maryland, October 11, 1988, at the ACT UP "Seize Control of the FDA" demonstration. The FDA eventually agreed to many of their demands (Joan E. Biren).*

ing the number of anonymous sex partners and avoiding sexual acts that involved the exchange of bodily fluids. Condom use was suggested in 1983 as a barrier to possible seminal transmission.

Even as information on HIV accumulated, AIDS prevention campaigns continued to be embroiled in controversy. The populations most heavily affected—gay men, injecting-drug users, and inner-city people of color—were not a constituency of great concern to the conservative Reagan administration nor to much of the general public. The risky activities involved—gay sex, illicit drug use, sex with prostitutes—were also not acts that many people wanted discussed publicly or tacitly condoned by making them safe. Therefore, erotically explicit "safe sex" educational materials—funded partly with government monies—were met with restrictive congressional guidelines imposed on the CDC in 1986. Federally funded educational materials could not contain "offensive" language or images or portray the "anogenital area" or sex acts. It therefore came as a great surprise to conservatives and liberals alike when U.S. surgeon general C. Everett Koop's *Report on Acquired Immune Deficiency Syndrome* (1986)—mailed to every household in the United States—forthrightly described risky sex practices, both homosexual and heterosexual, avoided antisex moralizing, and even recommended sex education for children. Koop, a fundamentalist Christian and an opponent of abortion, continued to be a sensible advocate for AIDS education and prevention, earning him enemies among his former right-wing allies but the kudos of gay radicals such as writer Larry Kramer.

Poster by Gran Fury, a design collective of New York ACT UP members, used as part of the "9 Days of Protest" against homophobia April 29–May 7, 1988, in New York City, Albany, and Newark (Jim Gruber, International Gay Information Center Archives, Manuscripts & Archives Division, New York Public Library).

As AIDS service agencies such as GMHC became more institutionalized and bureaucratized thanks to their own success and collaboration with state and federal agencies, some gay activists began to feel that they were not agitating enough for an all-out assault on AIDS (Patton 1990). As a result, in 1987 Larry Kramer helped found the AIDS Coalition to Unleash Power (ACT UP), a direct action group to push government agencies, pharmaceutical companies, and the public to make AIDS research and treatment a top priority. ACT UP chapters rapidly sprang up and grew throughout the United States and the world, focusing the energy and ire of many younger gay men and lesbians on the continuing AIDS epidemic and government inaction.

**READ MY LIPS**

**KISS IN**

Friday, April 29:
9:00 pm  March from Christopher & West Sts.
10:00 pm  Rally at Sheridan Square
10:30 pm  Kiss In at 6th Avenue & 8th St.
11:30 pm  Tracks—ACT UP/ACT NOW Fundraiser

**FIGHT HOMOPHOBIA: FIGHT AIDS**

SPRING AIDS ACTION '88: Nine days of nationwide AIDS related actions & protests.

Gran Fury

Thanks to colorful and emotional demonstrations choreographed for maximum media coverage, ACT UP became a model health advocacy group. It managed to accelerate drug research and testing, influence drug pricing, increase funding for AIDS research and care, and resist alarmist calls for universal HIV testing. Its Treatment and Data Committee served as a clearinghouse for the most up-to-date medical information. By the early 1990s, many of the leaders of ACT UP went on to occupy positions in public and private AIDS service organizations and the gay media. Pressure from ACT UP and other AIDS activist groups has been instrumental in maintaining public and governmental attention to AIDS (Epstein 1996). With rapid advances in the understanding of HIV and more effective treatment of opportunistic infections, the care of PWAs gradually improved. Nevertheless, the huge death toll from AIDS has been an enormous burden on the gay and lesbian community.

## Coping with AIDS

Some people infected with HIV never developed full-blown AIDS; the reason for this continues to be the object of biomedical study. The majority of HIV-positive people, however, did progress to AIDS and in the early 1980s experienced a mortality rate as high as 94 percent. The initial excitement over antiviral therapies such as zidovudine (AZT) repeatedly turned to disappointment as long-term studies of these drugs showed they did not significantly prolong survival in patients with AIDS. However, thanks to HIV testing, early diagnosis, and efficacious prophylaxis and treatment of opportunistic infections, the survival rate of people infected with HIV did improve as the decade wore on.

READ MY LIPS

**KISS IN**
Friday, April 29:
9:00 pm  March from Christopher & West Sts.
10:00 pm  Rally at Sheridan Square
10:30 pm  Kiss In at 6th Avenue & 8th St.
11:30 pm  Tracks—ACT UP/ACT NOW Fundraiser
**FIGHT HOMOPHOBIA: FIGHT AIDS**
SPRING AIDS ACTION '88: Nine days of nationwide AIDS related actions & protests.

*Poster by Gran Fury, a design collective of New York ACT UP members, used as part of the "9 Days of Protest" against homophobia April 29– May 7, 1988, in New York City, Albany, and Newark (Jim Gruber, International Gay Information Center Archives, Manuscripts & Archives Division, New York Public Library).*

With longer survival, unfortunately, the neuropsychiatric manifestations of AIDS also became more significant. As discussed by J. Hamilton Atkinson and Igor Grant (1994), these include a variety of neurological diseases (caused by HIV, opportunistic infections, and cancers), HIV-associated dementia and mild neurocognitive disorder, and psychological reactions to HIV as a chronic illness. Doctors have especially noted the role of HIV disease in triggering new or preexisting psychiatric disorders such as depression, anxiety, and alcohol and other substance abuse. HIV has also been associated with delirium, pain syndromes, and psychotic disorders, particularly in late stages of illness. Experienced doctors can often treat these fairly well with existing psychiatric medications.

The psychiatric manifestations of AIDS further complicate PWA's care as well as their own psychological distress and that of their caregivers. These people include both gay male lovers and friends, as well as a significant number of lesbians who contribute to the care of PWAs. Certain critical transition points make huge demands on individuals' coping abilities, including initial discovery of HIV serostatus, adjustment to asymptomatic HIV positivity, reactions to the first AIDS manifestations, and responses to late-stage illness. Mental health researchers have increasingly paid attention to these diverse coping issues and their effects on illness and mortality (Cournos and Forstein 2000).

In addition to its devastating effect on those infected with HIV, AIDS has had a broad impact on gay and lesbian communities. The availability of the ELISA test produced what could be seen as a new category of person—the HIV-seropositive (HIV+)—and created new pressures for "coming out" as HIV+ to family, friends, lovers, sex partners, coworkers, and, in some cases, the general public. The visible manifestations of AIDS also involuntarily outed many individuals (such as Rock Hudson, Roy Cohn, Catholic priests, and married men) as both PWAs and closeted homosexuals. Beyond the matter of seropositivity disclosure, fracture lines between HIV-positive and -negative individuals has had profound effects on gay relationships, socializing, and sex. It has widened a generational gap between gay men who had enjoyed the sexual freedom of the 1970s and newly emerging gays who mistakenly felt they could protect themselves from the disease by avoiding older men.

Although AIDS has predominantly been a disease of gay men rather than lesbians, both men and women in the 1980s suffered enormous losses of relatives, friends, and lovers. AIDS has thus improved ties between lesbians and gay men thanks to the dedication of lesbians involved in PWA care and AIDS service and fund-raising organizations. This psychological impact of AIDS has been examined in growing research on bereavement, support systems, survivor guilt, and anxieties over being and remaining HIV-negative (Springer and Lease 2000; Goldblum and Erickson 1999; Nord 1997; Leblanc, London, and Aneshensel 1997).

Foes of homosexuality, particularly conservative political and religious groups, have exploited AIDS to intensify and justify negative public perceptions of gays (as well as IV drug users and people of color) (Treichler 1999). Nevertheless, AIDS service and charity asso-

*The Names Project AIDS Memorial Quilt, displayed on the Mall in Washington, D.C., in the summer of 1987, now consists of so many panels that it more than covers the entire Mall (Joan E. Biren).*

ciations have drawn the support of a broad spectrum of nongays, from Hollywood stars to middle-class matrons, thus promoting the sympathetic public awareness of lesbians and gays to new levels, as well as providing social and legal services to PWAs, their partners, and families. Broader support has also helped suppress homophobic campaigns from the far right for nonanonymous, universal testing and even extremist proposals for quarantining of the HIV-seropositive.

## On Being Gay across the Lifespan

Although AIDS has dominated medical research involving gays and lesbians, throughout the 1980s there was a growing body of scientific work on other health and lifestyle matters. Social scientists increasingly studied gay and lesbian life at all life stages.

Adolescence has been a particularly important focus of interest because of the high suicide rates of homosexual teenagers. In the *Report of the Secretary's Task Force on Youth Suicide*, social worker Paul Gibson estimated that gay and lesbian youth are two to three times more likely to attempt suicide than their heterosexual peers (1989). Justin Richardson (1995) has pointed out weaknesses in these estimates. However, more careful research still suggests significantly

**Sidebar 8.2 AIDS Demographics**

Doctors in the United States and its territories and possessions are required to report all cases of AIDS to the Centers for Disease Control and Prevention (CDC) in Atlanta. As of December 31, 2000, there were cumulatively 774,467 reported cases of AIDS in the United States. Males accounted for 79 percent; 41 percent were infected through male-to-male sex; and 58 percent of people with AIDS had died (U.S. CDC 2001a).

The following statistics come from the cumulative data from 1981 to 2000 published by the CDC in its June 2001 *HIV/AIDS Surveillance Report*. As of June 2000, the states with the highest AIDS rates in the prior year (in descending order) were Washington, D.C., New York, Florida, Delaware, Maryland, and Massachusetts.

The mode of exposure to HIV is significantly different between the sexes. Among men, 56 percent were exposed through sex with men, 22 percent through injecting-drug use (IDU), and 5 percent through heterosexual contact with an HIV-infected woman. Among women, 41 percent were infected through IDU and 40 percent through heterosexual contact (CDC 2001d, Table 5). The CDC does not separately report female homosexual exposure. As the epidemic has progressed, the exposure rate through male-male sex and IDU has been declining faster than exposure through heterosexual contact. Female exposure through heterosexual contact has been increasing as exposure through IDU has been declining.

AIDS cases are unequally distributed across ethnic and racial groups. For all AIDS cases through June 2000, the ethnic distribution broken down by gender is as follows:

| Race/Ethnicity | Men (percent) | Women (percent) |
| --- | --- | --- |
| White, not Hispanic | 48 | 22 |
| Black, not Hispanic | 33 | 58 |
| Hispanic | 18 | 20 |
| Asian/Pacific Islander | 0.78 | 0.54 |
| American Indian/Alaskan | 0.29 | 0.32 |

HIV infection among white, Asian, and American Indian men is predominantly via sex with men, whereas HIV exposure in black and Hispanic men is more equally divided between same-sex contact and IDU. Racial and ethnic differences in women's exposure category are less dramatic, except that Asian women predominantly are infected through heterosexual contact.

The CDC estimates that 438,795 people have died of AIDS in the United States through June 2000 (CDC 2001d, Table 19). Since HIV *infection* without AIDS has not been uniformly reported to the CDC, estimates of the number of HIV-positive Americans is uncertain. Through June 2000, the total number of Americans living with HIV and AIDS was estimated at 431,924 (CDC 2001d, Table 1). The CDC estimates that 320,282 people were living with AIDS in the United States in 1999 (CDC 2001d, Table 23).

The most recent CDC *HIV/AIDS Surveillance Report* can be found at http://www.cdc.gov/hiv/stats/hasrlink.htm.

## Sidebar 8.3 HIV: The Global Pandemic

The impact of HIV and AIDS worldwide is catastrophic: it is the leading cause of death in Africa and the fourth leading cause of death globally. Although male-to-male sex is the single largest mode of transmission in the United States, heterosexual transmission is more common on other continents. According to the U.S. Centers for Disease Control (2001b), sub-Saharan Africa has been most heavily affected, with an estimated 25.3 million people infected with HIV in the year 2000; that is, 8.8 percent of the population aged fifteen to forty-nine. Botswana has the highest infection rate, estimated at 36 percent of the adult population! As in many other parts of the world, prevention and treatment campaigns are limited by poor economies and health systems. The social stigma of HIV also prevents many people from seeking HIV testing and treatment.

An estimated 640,000 people are infected with HIV in East Asia, and 5.8 million are infected in South and Southeast Asia. Thailand is one promising example of a country where a high rate of infection was curbed through an aggressive education campaign directed at sex workers and the general population.

In Eastern and Central Asia, approximately 700,000 people have been infected, and injection drug use is the most common means of transmission. In Western Europe, an estimated 540,000 people are infected, and in Latin American and the Caribbean, the estimate rises to 1.4 million infected. Brazil has managed to significantly diminish its HIV-related death rate through free, universal access to HIV therapies.

Figure: Number of adults and children estimated to be infected with HIV and AIDS worldwide in 2000. (US CDC 2001b, Figure 1)

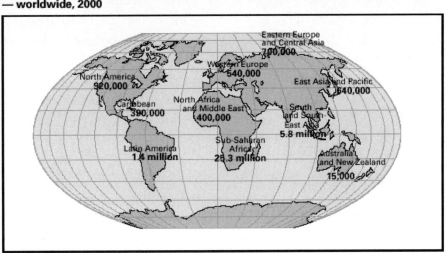

**FIGURE 1. Number\* of adults and children estimated to be infected with HIV and AIDS — worldwide, 2000**

Eastern Europe and Central Asia 700,000

Western Europe 540,000

North America 920,000

Caribbean 390,000

North Africa and Middle East 400,000

East Asia and Pacific 640,000

South and South East Asia 5.8 million

Latin America 1.4 million

Sub-Saharan Africa 25.3 million

Australia and New Zealand 15,000

\* n=36.1 million.
**Source:** Jointed United Nations Program on AIDS.

higher rates of suicidality and suicide attempts among gay compared to straight youth (Remafedi et al. 1998). Furthermore, gay adolescents' suicide attempts tend to be of a higher lethality.

Gender atypicality is one character trait that especially leads to the marginalization of youth. Such behavior has long been associated with homosexuality. In *The "Sissy Boy Syndrome" and the Development of Homosexuality* (1987), Richard Green reviewed the data on the subject and lent it much sexological and popular credence. The contributors to Gilbert Herdt's anthology *Gay and Lesbian Youth* (1989) highlight the many challenges to lesbian and gay adolescents in confronting homophobia at home, school, and society but also the many developmental lines of sexuality, particularly in different ethnic cultures.

In adulthood, lesbian and gay dating, socializing, coupling, and separation have all been the object of study. Although many homosexuals had once married and had children before coming out, in the 1970s and 1980s there were increasing numbers of lesbian and gay couples adopting, coparenting, or having children through artificial insemination. This trend has prompted research on gay parenting and the development of the children of same-sex couples or with one homosexual parent (Kirkpatrick, Smith, and Roy 1981; Bozett 1989; Patterson 1992). The studies have mostly shown that these children develop like others, demonstrating no particular skew to their gendered behavior or sexual orientation (Hoeffer 1981). If anything, lesbian and gay parents tend to be more like model parents in comparison with nongay ones (Golombok, Spencer, and Rutter 1983; Harris and Turner 1985–1986). The most recent review of this research suggests that there may well be psychological differences in the children of gay and lesbian parents. These children, especially girls, demonstrate greater gender role flexibility and they are more likely to consider same-sex relationships (Stacey and Biblarz 2001).

David P. McWhirter and Andrew Mattison of the Clinical Institute for Human Relationships in San Diego studied 156 gay couples and the changing nature of their relationships. Their results, published in *The Male Couple: How Relationships Develop* (1984), provided more detailed information than that gleaned by Bell and Weinberg in 1978. McWhirter and Mattison proposed a six-stage model of gay male relationships as they evolved from the first year of "blending," through the stages of "nesting," "maintaining," "building," and "releasing," to the third decade of relationship "renewing." Some of the factors they found that contributed to relationship longevity included complementarity of the two men; emotional fidelity more than sexual exclusivity; age difference between the two individuals; and formation of a family unit that participates jointly in civic, church, and political life. They noted that the reasons that united a couple in their first year (erotic interest and love) were very different from what kept them together in the third decade of a relationship (social, professional, and companionship concerns). The researchers pointed out, however, that each couple managed in their own way and that relationships had a life of their own.

In *Lesbian Couples* (1988), D. Merilee Clunis and G. Dorsey Green adapted McWhirter and Mattison's relationship model to the experience of women. They added a prerelationship stage, when two individuals decide whether to become involved in a relationship. They considered the role of conflict in later stages of the relationship. In long-term lesbian relationships, the issue of parenting also became salient.

Finally, social scientists have also been studying aging lesbians and gay men. This population provides historical perspective not only on the changing social conditions of homosexuality in the United States but also on the specific identity and lifestyle issues of older lesbians and gays (Kehoe 1988; Cruikshank 1990).

Much of the scientific and popular literature on gays and lesbians in the United States has focused on white Americans, but in the 1970s and 1980s, social scientists began examining homosexual behavior and identity formation in numerous foreign settings as well as among ethnic and racial minorities in the United States. This scientific work, in addition to the writings of these individuals themselves, points out similarities and contrasts in the ways of behaving and identifying sexually. It has also elucidated the psychic challenges in negotiating often conflicting identity affiliations.

Social science researchers have also examined the special health care needs of lesbian and gay men (see Sidebar 8.4). Studies such as these have promoted a more open discussion of sexuality in the health care professions. The concomitant proliferation of gay and lesbian groups in medical schools, hospitals, and professional associations has also coaxed these traditionally conservative organizations to be more sensitive to lesbian and gay colleagues as well as clients.

## The Dark Side of Gay Life

After homosexuality was depathologized in 1973, it was politically touchy to examine mental disorders in lesbian and gay populations.

However, physicians, nurses, psychologists, and other health researchers in the 1980s—many of them gay and lesbian themselves—recognized the necessity of confronting mental health problems that were especially troubling to lesbians and gays. Unlike past psychiatrists who viewed these problems as *intrinsic* to the homosexual condition and to homosexuals' supposedly inescapable self-loathing, current social scientists have highlighted social heterosexism as a major culprit of lesbian and gay mental health problems.

Since the 1940s, psychiatrists have reported a high level of alcohol abuse among male homosexuals. In a 1986 literature review, S. Israelstam and S. Lambert, noted that the volume of this work has increased since the 1960s and it has also begun to deal with lesbian alcohol consumption. In addition to the direct adverse health effects of alcoholism, researchers have been concerned with the interactions between alcohol use and other problems such as drug abuse, sexual crimes, unsafe sex, domestic violence, and mood disorders (Ziebold and Mongeon 1985). A large survey of homosexual men and women conducted by D. J. McKirnan and P. L. Peterson (1989) found significantly higher alcohol, marijuana, or cocaine use among homosexuals than the population as a whole. This was particularly true of urban homosexuals, in part because of the cultural importance of bars for this group's socializing. The authors also explained that alcohol was being used as a means of coping with the tension and cultural stresses particular to homosexuals.

Drug use by gay men has also been correlated with higher levels of unsafe sexual practices. Lesbian drug and alcohol abuse has been associated with domestic violence (Schilit, Lie, and Montagne 1990). Consciousness raising within the gay community about these problems has prompted the development of gay- and lesbian-specific drug and alcohol cessation programs. Since the late 1970s, self-help groups, Alcoholics Anonymous, treatment centers, and Gay and Lesbian Alcoholism Professionals have helped lesbians and gays remain sober and address their underlying, interrelated self-worth and sexuality issues.

Anorexia nervosa, which most commonly afflicts adolescent girls, has also emerged as a disorder in homosexual men and young men with conflicts over their sexuality. M. M. Fichter and C. Daser (1987) reviewed the growing literature on male anorexia and concluded that males with atypical gender role behavior were especially at risk for developing eating disorders. However, T. Burns and A. H. Crisp (1985) suggested that the best indicator of good outcomes in this population is the lack of repression of sexuality, with active sexual fantasy, masturbation, and sexual activity. After Stonewall and the DSM change, it has

**Sidebar 8.4 The National Lesbian Health Care Survey**

In the late 1950s, the Daughters of Bilitis conducted the first survey of lesbians in the United States (see Chapter 6). Given the small number of replies (160), its results could not be generalized to the American lesbian population as a whole, nor could it draw reliable conclusions about subpopulations of lesbians. It was nevertheless an advance over other surveys that drew on clinical populations. In 1984–1985, Judith Bradford of Virginia Commonwealth University and Caitlin Ryan of the Agency for AIDS/HIV conducted the National Lesbian Health Care Survey (NLHCS). It was published in 1987 and 1988. The study was funded in part by the National Institute for Mental Health and the National Lesbian and Gay Health Foundation, and it collected data from 1,925 lesbians from all fifty states. Given the difficulties of studying a "hidden" population, this was not a random sample, which limits the generalizability of the results. Nevertheless, the large number of replies offers a valuable and detailed glimpse into many aspects of lesbian life in the United States.

The survey was mainly distributed through lesbian health and professional organizations, as well as personal networks; therefore, the results overrepresent urban, well-educated, professional women aged twenty-five to forty-four, who were active in a variety of lesbian community organizations. The survey participants as a whole, nevertheless, resembled in many ways the overall population of American women. The NLHCS women suffered high levels of depression: over one-third reported a long period of depression some time in the past, and 11 percent were currently depressed. Eighteen percent of the lesbians reported having attempted suicide, which is comparable to the suicide rates of professional women in the United States. As with American women in general, the lesbians sampled had experienced high levels of physical and sexual abuse: 37 percent had been harshly beaten at least once, and 41 percent had been raped or sexually attacked at least once. The 45 percent of women reporting eating disorders is also in the range of women suffering these problems in the overall population (41–69 percent).

Lesbians differed from their heterosexual counterparts in several important ways. The NLHCS confirmed earlier reports that lesbians had high levels of alcohol consumption that did not decline with age (as is more common among heterosexual women). Bradford and Ryan found that 21 percent of lesbians aged fifty-five and older drank alcohol daily. They attributed this finding to the greater isolation of this group from the lesbian community and their lower level of "outness." The NLHCS found that almost three-fourths of the subjects were or had been in counseling. This agrees with other findings that lesbians used mental health services significantly more frequently than heterosexual women (77.5 percent versus 28.9 percent) (Morgan and Eliason 1992). Although many of their reasons for seeking counseling were common to all women (money, family, job, illness, lover), half of the NLHCS respondents mentioned factors particular to lesbians, especially the stress of societal oppression.

Few of the participants were openly lesbian at work (17 percent); nevertheless, the researchers found that overall outness was associated with less anxiety about exposure and better use of professional and informal counseling. For nearly half of those who did seek therapy, it lasted less than a year. Bradford and Ryan therefore concluded that, despite the stress of discrimination, many lesbians had developed strong coping skills to lead socially, politically, and professionally productive lives, particularly if they were out and maintained social supports within the lesbian community.

been important to recognize that lesbians and gay men, like heterosexuals, suffer emotional and life problems. Although these disorders do not result directly from homosexual orientation, they are still indirectly related to it because of the familial, cultural, and occupational stresses of being gay or lesbian in a predominantly heterosexual culture. Therefore, addressing the societal repression of homosexuality—rather than the "problem" of the individual's homosexuality—may often be the best route to overall improved mental and bodily health.

Social scientists and health care researchers continued to explore these basic sociological, psychological, and public health issues concerning lesbians and gay men into the 1990s. Unlike much of the research of previous decades, which was dedicated to curing homosexuality or, at best, helping homosexuals "adjust" to a heterosexual world, most recent studies are conducted from a gay-affirmative perspective dedicated to improving lesbian and gay lives in all their various manifestations.

## References

Altman, Lawrence. 1981. "Rare Cancer Seen in 41 Homosexuals." *New York Times,* July 3, A20.

Anchell, Melvin. 1985. "A Psychoanalytic Look at Homosexuality. Delivered to the Graduating Students, Valley Christian University, Fresno, CA." *Vital Speeches of the Day,* February 15, 1986, 285–288.

Atkinson, J. Hamilton, and Igor Grant. 1994. Natural History of Neuropsychiatric Manifestations of HIV Disease. *Psychiatric Clinics of North America* 17, no. 1: 17–33.

Bayer, Ronald. 1989. *Private Acts, Social Consequences: AIDS and the Politics of Public Health.* New York: Free Press.

Bozett, F. W. 1989. "Gay Fathers: A Review of the Literature." *Journal of Homosexuality* 18, nos. 1–2: 137–162.

Bradford, Judith, and Caitlin Ryan. 1988. *The National Lesbian Health Care Survey: Final Report.* Washington, DC: National Lesbian and Gay Health Foundation.

Brandt, Allan. 1987. *No Magic Bullet: A Social History of Venereal Disease in the United States since 1880.* New York: Oxford University Press.

Burns, T., and A. H. Crisp. 1985. "Factors Affecting Prognosis in Male Anorexics." *Journal of Psychiatric Research* 19: 323–328.

Clunis, D. Merilee, and G. Dorsey Green. 1988. *Lesbian Couples.* Seattle, WA: Seal Press.

Cournos, Francine, and Marshall Forstein, eds. 2000. *New Directions for Mental Health Services: What Mental Health Practitioners Need to Know About HIV and AIDS.* San Francisco: Jossey-Bass.

Crimp, Douglas. 1987. "How to Have Promiscuity in an Epidemic." Pp. 237–271 in *AIDS: Cultural Analysis, Cultural Activism.* Edited by D. Crimp. Cambridge: MIT Press.

Cruikshank, M. 1990. "Lavender and Gray: A Brief Survey of Lesbian and Gay Aging Studies." *Journal of Homosexuality* 20, nos. 3–4: 77–87.

Epstein, Steven. 1996. *Impure Science: AIDS, Activism, and the Politics of Knowledge.* Berkeley: University of California Press.

Fichter, M. M., and C. Daser. 1987. "Symptomatology, Psychosexual Development and Gender Identity in 42 Anorexic Males." *Psychological Medicine* 17: 409–418.

Gibson, Paul. 1989. "Gay Male and Lesbian Youth Suicide." In *Report of the Secretary's Task Force on Youth Suicide.* Edited by M. R. Feinleib, vol. 3. Rockville, MD: U.S. Department of Health and Human Services.

Goldblum, Peter B., and Sarah Erickson. 1999. *Working with AIDS Bereavement: A Comprehensive Approach for Mental Health Providers.* San Francisco: UCSF AIDS Health Project.

Golombok, S., A. Spencer, and M. Rutter. 1983. "Children in Lesbian and Single-parent Households: Psychosexual and Psychiatric Appraisal." *Journal of Child Psychology and Psychiatry and Allied Disciplines* 24: 551–572.

Green, Richard. 1987. *The "Sissy Boy Syndrome" and the Development of Homosexuality.* New Haven, CT: Yale University Press.

Harris, M. B., and P. H. Turner. 1985–1986. "Gay and Lesbian Parents." *Journal of Homosexuality* 12, no. 2: 101–113.

Herdt, Gilbert, ed. 1989. *Gay and Lesbian Youth.* New York: Harrington Park.

"Herpes: The New Sexual Leprosy." 1980. *Time,* July 28, 76.

Hoeffer, B. 1981. "Children's Acquisition of Sex-role Behavior in Lesbian-mother Families." *American Journal of Orthopsychiatry* 51: 536–544.

Israelstam, S., and S. Lambert. 1986. "Homosexuality and Alcohol: Observations and Research after the Psychoanalytic Era." *International Journal of the Addictions* 21: 509–537.

Kehoe, M. 1988. "Lesbians over 60 Speak for Themselves." *Journal of Homosexuality* 16, nos. 3–4: 1–111.

Kirkpatrick, Martha, Catherine Smith, and Ron Roy. 1981. "Lesbian Mothers and Their Children: A Comparative Survey." *American Journal of Orthopsychiatry* 51: 545–551.

Leblanc, A. J., A. S. London, and C. S. Aneshensel. 1997. "The Physical Costs of AIDS Caregiving." *Social Science and Medicine* 45: 915–923.

McKirnan, D. J., and P. L. Peterson. 1989. "Alcohol and Drug Use among Homosexual Men and Women: Epidemiology and Population Characteristics." *Addictive Behaviors* 14: 545–553.

McWhirter, David P., and Andrew Mattison. 1984. *The Male Couple: How Relationships Develop.* Englewood Cliffs, NJ: Prentice-Hall.

Morgan, Kris S., and Michele J. Eliason. 1992. "The Role of Psychotherapy in Caucasian Lesbians' Lives." *Women and Therapy* 13: 27–52.

Nord, David. 1997. *Multiple AIDS-related Loss: A Handbook for Understanding and Surviving a Perpetual Fall.* Philadelphia: Taylor & Francis.

Patterson, C. J. 1992. "Children of Lesbian and Gay Parents." *Child Development* 63: 1025–1042.

Patton, Cindy. 1990. *Inventing AIDS.* New York: Routledge.

Remafedi, G., S. French, M. Story, M. D. Resnick, and R. Blum. 1998. "The Relationship between Suicide Risk and Sexual Orientation: Results of a Population-Based Study." *American Journal of Public Health* 88: 57–60.

Richardson, Justin. 1995. "The Science and Politics of Gay Teen Suicide." *Harvard Review of Psychiatry* 3: 107–110.

Schilit, R., G.Y. Lie, and M. Montagne. 1990. "Substance Use as a Correlate of Violence in Intimate Lesbian Relationships." *Journal of Homosexuality* 19(3): 51–65.

Shilts, Randy. 1987. *And the Band Played On: People, Politics, and the AIDS Epidemic.* New York: St. Martin's Press.

Springer, Carrie A., and Suzanne H. Lease. 2000. "The Impact of Multiple AIDS-related Bereavement in the Gay Male Population." *Journal of Counseling and Development* 78: 297–304.

Stacey, Judith, and Timothy Biblarz. 2001. "(How) Does the Sexual Orientation of Parents Matter?" *American Sociological Review* 66:159–183.

Treichler, Paula A. 1987. "AIDS, Homophobia, and Biomedical Discourse: An Epidemic of Signification." Pp. 31–70 in *AIDS: Cultural Analysis, Cultural Activism.* Edited by D. Crimp. Cambridge: MIT Press.

———. 1999. *How to Have Theory in an Epidemic: Cultural Chronicles of AIDS.* Durham, NC: Duke University Press.

U.S. CDC (Centers for Disease Control and Prevention). 2001a. "HIV and AIDS—United States, 1981–2000." *Morbidity and Mortality Weekly Review* 50: 430–434.

———. 2001b. "The global HIV and AIDS epidemic, 2001." *Morbidity and Mortality Weekly Review* 50: 434–439.

———. 2001d. "U.S. HIV and AIDS Cases Reported through June 2000." *HIV/ AIDS Surveillance Report* 12(1). http://www.cdc.gov/hiv/stats/hasr1201. htm.

U. S. Surgeon General. 1986. *U. S. Surgeon General's Report on Acquired Immune Deficiency Syndrome.* Washington, DC: Public Health Service.

Ziebold, Thomas O., and John E. Mongeon, eds. 1985. *Gay and Sober: Directions for Counseling and Therapy.* New York: Harrington Park Press.

## Further Reading

Steven Epstein's *Impure Science: AIDS, Activism, and the Politics of Knowledge* (Berkeley: University of California Press, 1996) is the most thorough and balanced history of HIV research and activism. He examines the priority disputes between the United States and France, as well as the controversy over whether the HIV virus is the cause of AIDS. Peter Allen's *The Wages of Sin: Sex and Disease, Past and Present* (Chicago: University of Chicago Press, 2000) is a moving account of how religious moralism has tainted the treatment of AIDS as well as other venereal diseases in the past. *How to Have Theory in an Epidemic: Cultural Chronicles of AIDS* (Durham, NC: Duke University Press, 1999) collects essays by Paula A. Treichler examining the diverse and disturbing cultural reactions to AIDS since the outbreak of the epidemic. She especially examines the ways sexism, racism, and homophobia have distorted the political and social response to AIDS.

# Millennial Queers

As the visibility of lesbians and gay men grew exponentially in the last decades of the twentieth century, so did their presence in health care associations, which had enormous positive influence. By being out in their professional settings, gays and lesbians have become a sizable and powerful group in psychological and psychiatric associations. More lesbians and gay men have been able to pursue research on homosexuality and sexuality in general, which in turn has created new and rapidly evolving information on the biology and psychology of sexual orientation and the specific health care needs of gays and lesbians. The gay rights movement also stimulated the emergence of other sexual identity groups, such as bisexuals, transsexuals, and the intersexed. Although these groups are certainly not historically novel, the changing scientific and social attitude toward homosexuality has facilitated new approaches to a multiplicity of sexualities.

## The Backlash: Ex-Gay Ministries and "Reparative" Therapy

Most medical and psychological efforts throughout the first three-quarters of the twentieth century were devoted to "conversion" therapy (Haldeman 1994). This goal became problematic after the American Psychiatric Association (APA) decided in 1973 to remove the diagnosis of homosexuality from its *Diagnostic and Statistical Manual* (DSM). Many groups were not happy about this change and continued to insist that homosexuality was a treatable disorder. Some religious organizations, particularly fundamentalist Christian ministries, have continued to encourage homosexuals to change orientation. One of the largest of these "ex-gay" ministries, Exodus International (founded in 1976), preaches "Freedom from homosexuality through the power of Jesus Christ." These ministries frequently invoke the acquired immunodeficiency syndrome (AIDS) epidemic as the price of a homosexual "lifestyle." Exodus attracted particular attention in the late 1990s through an aggressive media campaign.

The ex-gay ministries have been closely associated with mental health professionals angered by the 1973 change in the DSM. A significant number of psychoanalysts in particular had opposed the change, and a few continued to argue against it. None was more vehement than Charles Socarides, who still claims that homosexuality represents a serious defect in psychosexual development and that its acceptance is damaging to society (1995). Ironically, his son is gay and served as President Bill Clinton's liaison to the gay and lesbian community.

Psychologist Paul Cameron and his colleagues (1986; 1989; 1995) have tried to associate homosexuality with incest, child molestation, and social disorder in general. He was expelled from the American Psychological Association in 1983 for ethical violations. The Nebraska Psychological Association and the American Sociological Association have condemned his misrepresentations of scientific research on homosexuality.

The National Association for Research and Therapy of Homosexuality (NARTH) includes a variety of mental health workers who believe homosexuality is treatable. Central to these groups' work is the belief that homosexuality is not primarily biological but a result of faulty parenting or homosexual seduction. NARTH's president is psychologist Joseph Nicolosi, who has advocated "reparative" therapy of homosexual men (1991). Relying on psychoanalytic principles, Nicolosi argues that homosexuality is a result of defective masculine identity resulting from poor fathering. Reparative therapy aims to redress this disorder of gender identity. These practitioners claim to be able to repair the orientation of a third or more of their homosexual clients, but it is not clear whether their clients' sexual orientation and eroticism have changed or simply their sexual behavior—if even that.

These approaches have come under criticism from professional organizations. In 1998, the APA formally opposed "reparative" or other therapy that tried to change people's sexual orientation based on the assumption that homosexuality was a mental disorder. The APA noted that the "potential risks of 'reparative therapy' are great, including depression, anxiety and self-destructive behavior, since therapist alignment with societal prejudices against homosexuality may reinforce self-hatred already experienced by the patient" (APA 2000, 1720). It reiterated this position in May 2000, adding emphatically that reparative therapists "have not produced any rigorous scientific research to substantiate their claims of cure. Until there is such research available, APA recommends that ethical practitioners refrain from attempts to change individuals' sexual orientation, keeping in mind the medical dictum to 'first, do no harm'" (APA 2000, 1719).

## Evolving Professional Attitudes

The widespread transformation in *official* professional attitudes is evident in a special review article on homosexuality by psychiatrists Richard Friedman and Jennifer Downey, published in 1994 in the *New England Journal of Medicine*—one of the world's most prestigious and widely circulating medical journals. The authors noted the complexity of the subject and the need to distinguish between different aspects of sexuality: sexual acts, erotic fantasy, social identity, and social role. They observed that much of the earlier data on the psychopathology and promiscuity of homosexuals had proven erroneous or misleading. In many ways, lesbians resembled heterosexual women, just as gay men resembled heterosexual men in their psychological and sexual profiles (aside from the gender of partners).

Homosexually active men, however, are at a higher risk than other men or lesbians of contracting various sexually transmitted diseases, most notably human immunodeficiency virus (HIV). Safe-sex campaigns in the gay community have greatly helped slow the epidemic in this group. Meanwhile, it has become increasingly prevalent among young people (both heterosexual and homosexual), intravenous drug users, and their sexual partners.

Friedman and Downey turned the spotlight on *homophobia*, which had largely been cultural and professional orthodoxy until the 1960s (see Sidebar 9.1). They identified the primary instigators as religious fundamentalism and heterosexism: "the belief in the moral superiority of institutions and practices associated with heterosexuality" (924). Studies of homophobic people paint a profile of individuals who are religious, conservative, authoritarian, ignorant of gay people, and surrounded by other homophobes. One study of college males found that those expressing the harshest homophobic attitudes also had strong penile responses to homoerotic images—suggesting homophobia functioned as a defense against forbidden desires. Friedman and Downey also noted the negative impact of homophobia within the medical community and suggested increasing the time during medical training devoted to the topic of homosexuality. An even more extensive study of professional homophobia was recently published by the Group for the Advancement of Psychiatry (GAP 2000).

Friedman and Downey (1994, 927) reported that although a larger number of women than men seem capable of experiencing bi-

## Sidebar 9.1 Heterosexism

The term *homophobia* was defined in 1971 by Kenneth T. Smith as an irrational hostility toward homosexuals. He thus turned the tables: the dominant cultural attitude toward gays and lesbians was labeled pathological, rather than homosexuality itself. In a review article on the subject, psychologist Gregory Herek (1995) argues for the use of the term *heterosexism* instead. Antigay prejudice is not necessarily irrational or based on fear, and it is not just an individual mental aberration but the product of widespread cultural values—analogous to sexism or racism. Herek thus defines heterosexism as "the ideological system that denies, denigrates, and stigmatizes any nonheterosexual form of behavior, identity, relationship, or community" (321).

In the past quarter century, psychologists have elucidated many aspects of heterosexism. As with other prejudices, a variety of negative stereotypes bolster heterosexism. Most notably, homosexuals are associated with gender-role nonconformity (what used to be called "sexual inversion" in the early part of the century): lesbians are supposedly masculine, and gay men are effeminate. Homosexuals are also perceived as threatening: molesters or seducers of youth; promiscuous vectors of contagion (especially HIV); and conspirators in the subversion of "family values," marriage, religion, and "traditional" culture. Until 1973, the psychiatric profession promulgated one of the most insidious stereotypes about homosexuals—that they were all mentally ill or, at best, developmentally stunted. These prejudices can systematically bias the observations of individuals—including scientific researchers—who may not be consciously homophobic.

Even gay people themselves are not immune to the effects of heterosexism. Alan K. Malyon (1982) examines psychotherapeutic techniques for dealing with this "internalized homophobia." Gay adolescents are especially vulnerable to these negative feelings about their same-sex desires, leading to self-doubt, self-hatred, suicide, and other self-destructive behavior. Even gay bashing can be a result. Joyce Hunter (1995) notes that lesbian teenagers may try to hide their sexual orientation by dating boys and getting pregnant. Even as adults, internalized heterosexism may compel lesbians and gays to remain in the closet and suffer depression, anxiety, relationship instability, and other psychological disorders.

Recent psychological studies of heterosexuals associate heterosexism with a number of factors: orthodox views of gender and sexuality; little experience with gay people; older age and less education; residency in rural, midwestern, or southern parts of the United States; conservative religious values; and an authoritarian or intolerant personality. Males tend to be more heterosexist than females, and gay men are reviled more than lesbians (Herek 1995, 321). These facts support a feminist analysis that antihomosexual attitudes are based on sexism and the perceived effeminacy of gay men.

Herek theorizes that heterosexism can serve a number of other functions. It may help an individual make sense of past negative experiences with gays or lesbians. Therefore, positive contact or friendship with a gay person is strongly correlated with tolerance. Heterosexism can also strengthen an individual's social identity with a particular value group (such as Christians) or sociological group (such as political conservatives or even African Americans or Hispanics). Finally, heterosexism may be an ego defense against latent homosexuality. Whatever its function, heterosexism can be manifested in antigay verbal and physical aggression. Cumulative results from studies indicate that 44 percent of gays and lesbians have been threatened with violence and 80 percent have been verbally harassed. Actual assaults are significantly underreported. Herek concludes that far more research is needed, particularly to examine why heterosexism turns to violence, how heterosexism can be eliminated, and how gays cope with it.

sexual fantasy and heterosexual activity, a subset of women seem to be as fixed and exclusive in their homosexual orientation as the majority of gay men. Adolescents questioning their sexual orientation, the authors conclude, should not be coaxed in a predetermined direction but supported through further development. Those who appear to be predominantly homosexual should be assisted in establishing a gay identity.

Friedman and Downey close with a review of recent biological work on the determination of homosexuality, which gained tremendous popular attention in the 1990s and which I will be examining in this chapter. They note that despite major gaps in our understanding about sexual orientation, particularly its psychobiology, there is sufficient evidence to dispel long-standing prejudices against homosexuals. Discrimination in many areas of the law, public policy, and the military is unwarranted. Indeed, even two military psychiatrists declared that there is no evidence to support the exclusion of homosexuals from the armed forces (Jones and Koshes 1995). Friedman's and Downey's review comes to a simple conclusion: "There are no data from scientific studies to justify the unequal treatment of homosexual people or their exclusion from any group" (928). However simple this may be, it still represents a dramatic about-face from the dominant biomedical attitude for over a century.

## Gay Twins

An important focus of the Friedman and Downey review was recent studies in the biology of sexual orientation. Ever since the nineteenth century, many "inverts" and homosexuals have argued that their erotic attraction to people of the same sex was congenital. Many scientists examining homosexuality, particularly until the 1940s, also pursued biological theories of the origins of homosexuality. In the 1990s new scientific research and heightened public interest in these hypotheses brought them back to the forefront. The first new work to gain media attention was by psychologist J. Michael Bailey and psychiatrist Richard Pillard (1991; Bailey et al. 1993). They tested the genetic hypothesis of homosexuality by examining the sexual orientation of identical (monozygotic [MZ]) twins, fraternal (dizygotic [DZ]) twins, and nontwin siblings.

If homosexuality is an inherited trait, then MZ twins—who share identical genes—should have a high concordance rate for homosexuality (that is, both twins should have the same sexual orientation). It need not be 100 percent. Bailey and Pillard and subsequent scientists have acknowledged that a complex trait such as homosexuality is probably determined by several genes and nongenetic or environmental effects (Pattatucci 1998). Also, genotypes (the genetic code) rarely give rise to complex phenotypes (manifested traits) 100 percent of the time. However, if the trait is partially heritable, then the concordance rate for DZ twins should be less than that for MZ twins but somewhat higher than that for genetically unrelated individuals.

Bailey and Pillard and their colleagues recruited homosexual or bisexual men and women with either twin or genetically unrelated siblings. Then they collected data on the sexuality of the original subjects and their siblings (if they were willing to participate). Their results generally fit the predictions. Half of the identical (MZ) twins of the male subjects were also homosexual or bisexual, and 24 percent of fraternal (DZ) twins were confirmed to also be homosexual or bisexual. Even fewer of the adopted brothers (19 percent) were homosexual or bisexual. In the female study, the concordance rates were similarly progressive: MZ twins 51 percent, DZ twins 10 percent, and adopted sisters 4 percent. Their study could not look for a "gay gene" but just suggest a hereditary influence on sexual orientation.

The authors recognized flaws in the studies' design: subjects were self-selected rather than a random sample, and identical twins tend to be reared more similarly than fraternal twins. Bailey and Pillard nevertheless concluded that there is a significant genetic influence in the development of homosexuality. This genetic impact, however, did not fully determine sexual orientation since even individuals with identical genotypes (the MZ twins) did not invariably share the same sexual orientation. Furthermore, the researchers noted significant differences between male and female sexuality and the need to be aware of gender differences in studying homosexuality: lesbians are not simply the female version of gay men.

Bailey and Pillard also questioned their subjects as to their recollections of gender nonconformity during childhood. Following the lead of some of the research mentioned in earlier chapters, they hypothesized that if homosexuality was congenital, it would be manifested in childhood as gender-atypical behavior. Such behavior used to be called "gender inversion" in the nineteenth century: lesbians were reported to be masculine, whereas homosexual men were effeminate. The two researchers found that childhood gender nonconformity was *not* associated with a higher heritability of homosexuality. However, identical twins who were both homosexual tended to report similar levels of gender nonconformity as children: that is, both lesbian twins were equally tomboyish as children or both gay male twins were equally effeminate.

## The Sexual Orientation of the Brain

There is a long history of scientific studies hypothesizing the neurobiological basis of homosexuality. Karl Heinrich Ulrichs, the nineteenth-century lawyer who lobbied for the decriminalization of sodomy in Germany, argued that male-male love was the result of a female psyche and physiology in a male body. This inversion model was further pursued by Dr. Magnus Hirschfeld in Berlin. Hirschfeld and other researchers in Germany and the United States hypothesized that homosexual people's brains developed in a way that was oppositely gendered from their apparent sex, presumably because of hereditary and hormonal factors. In the early twentieth century, Eugen Steinach, a Viennese physician, attempted to produce animal models of homosexuality through castration or transplantation of opposite-sex gonads. Hirschfeld even referred a patient to Steinach for one of these testicular implants in an attempt to "cure" homosexuality. Later experimental studies with animal models, such as rats, showed that hormonal manipulations at specific periods of development in utero could significantly alter the sexual behaviors of the adult rats as well as specific areas of their brains. Unaltered male rats aggressively mount, and females usually present their rump for mounting (lordosis). Sex hormones administered during critical periods of fetal development can invert these mounting and lordotic behaviors as well as alter focal brain regions. Thus, the manipulated female rats will attempt to mount females and males, and the manipulated male rats will assume a lordotic posture for mounting by unaltered males (Gorski 1978).

This line of thinking—connecting sex hormones, the brain, and sexual behavior—has persisted throughout the twentieth century, most notably in the work of Günther Dörner and his colleagues of the Institute for Experimental Endocrinology in Berlin (1968, 1980). Much of Dörner's research from the 1970s to the 1990s appeared in *Experimental and Clinical Endocrinology,* of which he is the editor. In a 1991 article in the journal, he reiterated his connections to the theories of Ulrichs, Hirschfeld, and Steinach: that homosexuality is determined by prenatal gendering of the brain caused by endocrinological disturbances. He hypothesizes that particular regions of the brain are responsible for gender-specific sex behavior. He relies on the rat model of sexual behavior and its experimental alteration with hormone interventions during fetal development. However, rat brains and behavior do not coincide simply with human behavior.

Same sex behavior among a variety of animals has long been observed. Often these activities were interpreted as aggressive competitions for dominance among males. However, biologist Bruce Bagemihl

(1999) argues that some of these behaviors appear to be genuine sexual acts accompanied by signs of pleasure. There are also field observations of same sex pair bonding and family units among non-human animals. Thus, current data suggest that homosexual acts are a widespread natural variant of animal sexual behavior. However, sexual *behavior* and sexual *orientation* are different phenomena that may not match: a person may claim a certain sexual orientation but behave in another fashion. Furthermore, we can never know what the sexual orientation of a rat is (let alone if it has one); we can only observe its sexual behavior. With the experimental animal model, the "feminized" male rats allow themselves to be mounted by "normal" males, but only the "bottom," mounted rats are assumed to be homosexual. Finally, it has not been shown that the affected areas in rat brains have corresponding areas in human brains.

Perhaps most controversially, Dörner has argued that homosexuality is neurologically ingrained in fetuses whose mothers experience high stress (such as war). He argues that this stress leads to intrauterine hormonal disturbances that homosexualize the fetal brain (Dörner et al. 1980). Dörner has thus persisted in trying to demonstrate that, as Ulrichs argued, homosexuality represents a form of central nervous system pseudohermaphroditism. His research has been soundly criticized by German and American scientists on both methodological and ethical grounds (Byne 1995).

Other researchers have also examined neurological differences between men and women and have searched for significant differences between homosexuals and heterosexuals. In 1990, two Dutch neuroscientists, Dick F. Swaab and Michel A. Hofman, were the first to report a neuroanatomical distinction of homosexual men: their suprachiasmatic nucleus (SCN) contained over twice as many cells as the SCN of a reference male group. However, a 1991 publication by Simon LeVay especially gained public attention. LeVay (at that time a neurobiologist at the Salk Institute) studied the interstitial nucleus of the anterior hypothalamus (INAH) in the cadaveric brains of women and men. Most of the men had died of AIDS, and their sexual orientation was retrospectively determined from their medical records. The women were presumed to be heterosexual simply because the vast majority of women are. Prior researchers had associated the INAH in humans with the sexually dimorphic nucleus (SDN) in rats. The precise function of either of these regions is still not known. LeVay reported that one particular region, the INAH3 was larger in heterosexual men than in women or homosexual men. He suggested that the region might be involved in the generation of male-typical sexual behavior. Thus, the supposedly more female conformation of the homosexual mens' INAH3 correlated with their presumably gender-atypical sexual behavior.

Other neuroscientists criticized LeVay's study for its many short-comings: small sample sizes, retrospective determination or assumption of sexual orientation, inadequate neuroanatomical measurement techniques, and the reliance on brains of men who had died of AIDS (probably with diseases or on medications having neurological and endocrinological effects) (Byne 1995). The chain of logic from rat mounting behavior to rat SDN to human INAH and human sexual orientation is also tenuous. LeVay did recognize some of these problems in an admittedly small study designed to prompt further research. He has not pursued this work any further, and his results have not been replicated.

Nevertheless, his findings continued to have enormous public appeal thanks to media attention and LeVay's own popularization of this research in his books, *The Sexual Brain* (1993) and *Queer Science* (1996). In the latter work, the frequent references to Hirschfeld and Dörner make it clear that LeVay is also advancing the neurohormonal pseudo-hermaphroditism hypothesis: critical regions of gay men's brains anatomically or functionally approach the female type. LeVay recognizes that, even if such gender-inverted neuroanatomical features exist, we cannot know if they are the cause or the result of homosexuality. His theory, however, is that these regions, like the SDN in rats, are fixed in utero or infancy (in part by genetic factors) and determine subsequent sexual orientation. How all this might happen remains a mystery.

## Maternal Transmission of Male Homosexuality

Although Bailey and Pillard offered indirect evidence for the heritability of homosexuality, more concrete and tantalizing data appeared from Dean Hamer, a molecular geneticist at the National Cancer Institute. As Hamer points out in the book he coauthored with Peter Copeland, *The Science of Desire: The Search for the Gay Gene and the Biology of Behavior* (1994), he had not previously worked on sexuality or human genetics. He was nevertheless familiar with studies pointing to the familial clustering of homosexuality and the unusually high prevalence of Kaposi's sarcoma (KS) in gay men. Therefore he obtained research funds, ostensibly to uncover genetic markers in gay men that were also associated with a heightened susceptibility to KS.

Researchers had previously suggested that gay men had more homosexual relatives on the maternal side of the family tree than on the paternal side. Almost all human males have an X and a Y sex chromosome, and the X chromosome is always inherited from the mother. By hypothesizing that homosexuality was maternally transmitted, Hamer and his team could restrict their research to the X chromosome and search there for linkages between genetic markers and male homosexuality. They studied forty families with two gay brothers and no known nonmaternal transmission of homosexuality. They found a statistically significant correlation between genetic markers on chromosomal region Xq28 and sexual orientation in this group of research subjects. Xq28 is a long stretch of DNA that could code for several hundred individual genes.

The human X chromosome is one of the most intensively studied since it has been associated with numerous severe hereditary diseases. Over twenty hereditary diseases have been linked to the Xq28 region alone, including Barth syndrome; dyskeratosis congenita; abnormal male genital development; and X-linked forms of manic-depressive illness, mental retardation, and myotubular myopathy and other muscular disorders. Hamer found no evidence to support his original grant hypothesis of a genetic link between homosexuality and Kaposi's sarcoma.

Hamer and his team were careful to note the limited scope of their findings—even if they could be replicated. They believed they had found a statistically significant association between a chromosomal region (Xq28) and male sexual orientation in a carefully selected subgroup of homosexual men: those who were "out" and had gay relatives only in the maternal line. Hamer and his colleagues had not found a single "gay gene" that determined sexual orientation. They recognized that a complex trait like homosexuality is probably influenced by several genes and has "environmental, experiential, or cultural factors" (Hamer et al. 1993, 326). Furthermore, they may have found a genetic linkage not specifically for "gayness" but some associated trait, such as self-assertiveness or "outness" in general temperament.

As with other biological research on homosexuality, the Hamer study was criticized for its small size, its simple dichotomization of sexuality onto homo- and heterosexuality, and the ethics of even pursuing a "gay gene" (Schüklenk et al. 1997). The findings were nevertheless popularized as the discovery of "the gay gene." Some gay lobbyists, many lesbians and gay men, and their families embraced this notion (Burr 1993). It helps bolster the claim that homosexuality is not a chosen lifestyle; therefore, for some people, the notion of a gay gene clears gays and their families of blame. Gay civil rights lawyers have also used the genetic claim to argue for the legal protection of homosexuality as an immutable trait (such as race, sex, or physical disability). However, the value of a "gay gene" in court is a precarious one since the legal "argument from immutability" has historically proven to be fragile in courts (Halley 1994). Furthermore, one would hope that the civil rights of gays (like those of blacks or Jews, for example) are based on broader principles of human rights rather than biological difference or abnormality.

In 1995 Stella Hu, Hamer, and their colleagues confirmed the earlier study in males but failed to find a genetic linkage between Xq28 and sexual orientation in women. The authors, echoing other biomedical researchers of female sexuality, noted that women's sexual orientation was harder than men's to classify into two categories (homo- and heterosexual) that remained fixed over the lifespan. A Canadian genetics team was *not* able to replicate Hamer's findings (Rice et al. 1999). Nonetheless, among much of the lay public—particularly gays—Hamer's results seem to have been enthusiastically accepted as conclusive evidence of the hereditary, congenital nature of male homosexuality. The major gay rights groups in the United States have also avoided criticizing gay genetics research or tackling the problematic ethical issues it evokes (Schoofs 1997).

The potential discovery of a gay gene or genes raises the possibility of prenatal screening and subsequent abortion or genetic manipulation of fetuses "at risk" of developing into homosexuals. Were it possible, should a genetic screening test for homosexuality be developed or not? And should mothers be allowed to abort fetuses that test positive for homosexuality? Hamer has argued against such measures and has vowed that he would even oppose the development of a genetic test for homosexuality (Hamer and Copeland 1994, 218). LeVay, however, has taken a more permissive, libertarian stance. He favors education of the public on homophobia rather than regulation. LeVay supports full parental genetic choice: "By allowing parents to make these choices, we will introduce a new eugenics—a democratic, 'do-it-yourself' eugenics that will circumvent the evils of the past" (1996, 271). As historian Garland Allen (1997) points out, the frightening historical lessons of scientific eugenics and state-sponsored genocide should make us far more wary.

### Lesbians and the Health Care System

Significant progress has been made in the mental health treatment of lesbians and gays men, and the AIDS crisis has drawn much attention to gay men. However, lesbian health care research has been relatively sparse. A review of this literature by the Committee on Lesbian Health Research Priorities of the Institute of Medicine nevertheless highlights several areas of study (Solarz 1999). Surveys of doctors' and nurses' attitudes toward lesbians show that they share common societal prejudices and antipathies toward lesbians. Despite the psychiatric and psychological professions' depathologization of homosexuality, many health care workers still view lesbianism as a sickness and are opposed to admitting homosexuals into the medical professions or teaching about it. Surveys of lesbians' experiences with health professionals demonstrate that lesbian clients are acutely aware of these prejudicial attitudes as well as heterosexist presumptions. These attitudes tend to instill a feeling of distrust in the clinical relationship and inhibit lesbians from revealing their sexuality to health care providers. Ultimately, these negative experiences lead lesbians to underutilize or entirely avoid the health care system.

Risa Denenberg (1995) comes to similar conclusions in her "Report on Lesbian Health." She notes that the alienation of lesbians from the health care system is accompanied by the neglect of lesbians as a demographic subgroup in most studies of women's health. Nevertheless, Denenberg identifies several distinguishing features of lesbians as a health care constituency: lesbians on average earn less than heterosexual women or men in general; they have fewer, later pregnancies and face special problems with impregnation; and they experience high levels of familial and social rejection as well as sexual abuse and harassment.

In reviewing the recent literature on lesbian health, several issues emerge (Solarz 1999). The later and lower pregnancy rate of lesbians may place them at higher risk for breast, endometrial, and ovarian cancer, but the data are inconclusive. It has long been noted that lesbians have higher levels of cigarette, alcohol, and other substance abuse than the female population as a whole (Cochran et al. 2000). This characteristic puts them at higher risk for a variety of problems associated with these drugs, including depression, accidents, and suicide. Some surveys report that lesbians have suffered childhood sexual abuse, sexual assaults, and domestic violence at a higher rate than heterosexual women, but this finding has been inconsistent. Lesbians have a higher prevalence than heterosexual women of anxiety and mood disorders and suicidal thoughts (Gilman et al. 2001).

In terms of medical care, lesbians make use of routine screening tests—such as breast exams and Papanicolau (Pap) smears—less frequently than women as a whole. Finally, lesbian-specific infectious disease risks have not been well examined. Lesbian and bisexual women have not been heavily targeted for HIV or other venereal disease prevention campaigns. Nevertheless, they do engage in risky practices since lesbians may have intravenous (IV) drug-using partners, gay or bisexual male partners, or unprotected heterosexual intercourse for the purpose of impregnation. Female-to-female transmission of venereal disease (such as trichomoniasis, bacterial vaginosis, herpes, papilloma virus, gonorrhea, and chlamydia) has also been reported. However, little research has been conducted on lesbian sexually transmitted diseases, and no standards of care have been developed. The neglect of these special risk factors in the lesbian population is leading to unknown morbidity and mortality. It can only be hoped that the poverty of lesbian health research may be partially remedied by dedicated funding such as that provided by the Lesbian Health Fund of the Gay and Lesbian Medical Association or a recent initiative of the U.S. National Institutes of Health to study lesbian, gay, bisexual, and transgendered mental health and substance abuse.

## Gay and Lesbian Health Professionals

New professional associations such as the Gay and Lesbian Medical Association (GLMA) not only provide impetus for research but also facilitate the openness of gay and lesbian health professionals and their availability to lesbian and gay patients. GLMA was founded in 1981 and includes

*Susan Love, M.D., the director of the Santa Barbara Breast Cancer Institute, is one of the most prominent lesbian physicians in the United States (Joan E. Biren).*

lesbian, gay, bisexual, and transgendered (LGBT) physicians, medical students, and their supporters. The group's central advocacy aims are to combat homophobia in the medical profession and to promote better health care for LGBT patients. It lobbied the American Medical Association (AMA) to ban discrimination on the basis of sexual orientation within its ranks. It assisted in the publication of the AMA's report on "Health Care Needs of Gay Men and Lesbians in the U.S." GLMA has been involved in the President's Advisory Council on HIV/AIDS as well as in other lobbying and advisory roles on matters concerning public health policy of concern to LGBTs. In 1997 it launched the first peer-reviewed journal on lesbian and gay health issues.

A branch of the American Medical Student Association, the Lesbian, Gay and Bisexual People in Medicine (LGBPM), serves as a support and networking group for osteopathic and allopathic medical students. It promotes the inclusion of sexual orientation and gender identity education in medical school curricula. LGBPM also has been investigating the experiences of queer physicians in residency training.

The National Lesbian and Gay Health Association (NLGHA) was founded in 1994, bringing together eleven lesbian and gay community health centers and over 20,000 lesbian and gay health care providers. The association resulted from the merger of two preexisting organizations: the National Lesbian and Gay Health Foundation and the National Alliance of Lesbian and Gay Health Clinics. The former was created in 1980 as an educational foundation and network for health educators and health care providers. It helped establish the National Association of People with AIDS and the National Association of Lesbian and Gay Alcoholism Professionals and has sponsored an annual National Lesbian and Gay Health Conference (which in 1983 became the International Forum on HIV/AIDS). The National Alliance of Lesbian and Gay Health Clinics was founded in 1992 as a network of lesbian and gay community clinics. NLGHA is dedicated to educating health professionals and policymakers regarding lesbian and gay client needs. It also provides information and referrals directly to these clients. NLGHA's National Research Institute for Lesbian and Gay Health helps identify research funding sources and facilitates the dissemination of research findings. (See the list of internet resources at the end of this chapter.)

## Gay-Affirmative Psychotherapy

Although a handful of studies on the biological basis of sexual orientation captured public attention in the 1990s, a far more substantial body of research on the psychological development and needs of gays and lesbians quickly accumulated over the last two decades of the twentieth century. As psychologist Esther Rothblum (1994) points out, the 1973 deletion of homosexuality as a diagnosis in the DSM-II prompted a general decline in psychological studies of homosexuality. Researchers were wary of studying psychopathology in gay and lesbian populations for fear of further stigmatizing them. Much work concentrated instead on gay psychosexual development, coming out, and heterosexism (see Sidebar 9.2). There has also been more work on the specific mental health needs of lesbians and gays. This is quite critical since several studies, beginning in the 1970s, have indicated that gays and lesbians seek counseling at a higher rate than heterosexuals and suffer more commonly from mood and anxieties disorders (Cochran and Mays 2000).

The services these clients receive, unfortunately, is often suboptimal. A national survey of American Psychological Association members highlighted a number of deficiencies in psychotherapeutic services to gay and lesbian clients (Garnets et al. 1991). A majority of the 2,544 respondents reported incidents in which colleagues still assumed all clients were heterosexual, viewed homosexuality as a pathology, or recommended heterosexuality as a cure. There were accounts of gross insensitivity to clients' needs because psychologists discounted gay relationships, focused on homosexuality as the root of all emotional problems, or disregarded internalized homophobia. Although many heterosexual therapists provided appropriate and sympathetic care of lesbian and gay clients, it was clear that there was a significant need for concerted education of therapists regarding homosexuality.

Psychologist Kristin Hancock (1995) focuses on several areas of concern: coming out, problems of lesbian and gay youth, antigay and other prejudice, family conflicts, relationship issues, gay and lesbian parenting, and therapist issues. In the past three decades, psychologists have examined in much detail the process of lesbian and gay male identity formation or, more narrowly, "coming out"—especially in white, middle-class youth. Given the dominant heterosexist social context and the scarcity of gay role models, adolescents going through this process are at high risk for a variety of psychological disorders, self-destructive and suicidal behaviors, and abuse by peers and family (see Sidebar 9.3). Psychologist Ritch Savin-Williams (1994) has dedicated his research to these issues. Adolescents and adults questioning their sexual orientation can greatly benefit from gay-affirmative counseling to help negotiate conflicting demands and desires during a period of identity confusion. Group therapy may be specially effective since it introduces gay youth to others like themselves in a confidential, safe context.

## Sidebar 9.2 Psychological Perspectives on Coming Out

George Chauncey points out that the term *coming out* was already being used in New York City in the 1920s to refer to one's initiation into the gay life (1994, 7). The meaning, however, shifted over time. In one of the classic sociological studies of coming out, Barry Dank simply defined it as the process of "identifying oneself as being homosexual" (1971, 180). He observed that there were two critical requirements for an individual to come out. First, the individual had to find himself or herself in a new social context with homosexuals or knowledge of homosexuality. Second, the individual had to place himself or herself in a new cognitive category—of homosexual—but first he or she had to destigmatize the old, socially stereotyped category of homosexual. Thus, the subject had to replace the homosexuality-as-mental-illness viewpoint with the homosexuality-as-way-of-life viewpoint in order to come out. Dank predicted that as the way-of-life viewpoint became increasingly prevalent, people would come out earlier in life and in greater numbers. An acceleration of outness, he believed, would transform the gay community since individuals' sex lives would be less fragmented from the rest of their social life. At this very time, of course, gay activists were demanding that the American Psychiatric Association bury the homosexuality-as-mental-illness viewpoint.

Since Dank's article was published, many social scientists have studied the process of gay and lesbian identity formation—both as self-recognition and in more public manifestations. Although this process varies enormously from one cultural context to another and for each individual, sociologist Richard Troiden offers a model with four typical stages. In *Gay and Lesbian Identity* (1988) he sketches the following evolution. During the *sensitization stage* before puberty, children who later identify as lesbian and gay feel different or marginal from their same-sex peers. Their interests, hobbies, and behaviors are often described as gender-atypical; however, few of these children see themselves as "homosexual" at this time.

With adolescence, this feeling of difference becomes focused more on matters of erotic attachment during the stage of *identity confusion*. Research indicates that boys sense and act on their same-sex attractions earlier than girls; however, in both boys and girls, the average age has been decreasing over the last few decades. These adolescents respond with denial, avoidance, or redefinition of their sexuality as bisexual or opportunistic. Some attempt to eradicate homoerotic inclinations, whereas others accept a lesbian or gay identity. During the stage of *identity assumption* (typically in or after late adolescence), individuals self-define and present themselves as homosexual: "come out." They explore the homosexual subculture, experiment sexually, and gradually accept themselves as lesbian or gay. This stage flows into one of *commitment*, when individuals consolidate their sexual, emotional, and social lives around a lesbian or gay identity and lifestyle, usually with connections to gay communities and love relationships. Being out, comfortable with one's sexuality, and well-integrated into a supportive community probably has a significant beneficial effect on mental health. Recent psychological research also suggests that the degree of outness has a positive effect on general health (including the incidence of cancer and infectious diseases) for both HIV-negative and positive men (Cole et al. 1996).

Jessica Morris and her colleagues (1995) argue against linear, progressive models of coming out that impose preconceived ideals of homosexual development or maturity. Their reading of lesbian autobiographies suggests a more complex and lifelong process of coming out that varies enormously from one woman to another and is contingent upon individuals' ethnic, community, and family backgrounds.

**Sidebar 9.3 Gay Teen Suicide and Other Adolescent Health Issues**

Are 30 percent of adolescents who commit suicide gay or lesbian? This has been a distressing and frequently quoted figure cited from a 1989 Report of the Secretary's Task Force on Youth Suicide of the U.S. Department of Health and Human Services (Gibson 1989). However, this estimate was based on a number of uncertain assumptions (Richardson 1995). The reason for a completed suicide is often unknown, and troubled gay or questioning teens who take desperate measures to end their life probably would not reveal their secret beforehand. Other studies of gay and lesbian teen suicides and suicidality are also problematic because of unrepresentative samples. However, a large 1995 survey of Massachusetts public high school students found that gay, lesbian, bisexual, or "not sure" (GBLN) youth reported a suicide attempt in the past year 3.41 times more frequently than the non-GBLN respondents (Garofalo et al. 1999). Higher rates of reported suicide attempts were especially associated with male GBLN youth, as well as girls, Hispanic ethnicity, substance use, and higher experiences of violence and victimization.

These and other studies point to the difficulties of growing up gay in the United States. Evidence suggests that the high prevalence of suicidality among GBLN teens is comparable to that of seriously distressed heterosexual adolescents; therefore, it is not simply homosexuality but its environmental impact on teenagers that may endanger them (Safren and Heimberg 1999). It is well established that lesbian, gay, bisexual, and transgender (LGBT) youth and young adults experience high levels of verbal and physical abuse: in various studies one-third to three-fourths of LGBT subjects reported having been victimized. Abused youth, runaways, and those with mental health and substance abuse problems are also more likely to engage in unprotected sex or place themselves at risk for further victimization (Ryan and Futterman 1997).

It is therefore a vital challenge to assist teens struggling with their sexuality and gender by helping them cope with socially stigmatized identities. As Caitlin Ryan and Donna Futterman point out in an extensive review of the literature on LGBT youth, "Lesbian and gay males who have integrated a positive identity show better psychological adjustment, greater satisfaction, and higher self-concept, with lower rates of depression or stress than gay people in conflict with their identity" (1997, 225). That the vast majority of LGBT people nonetheless grow up to lead productive lives points to their significant psychological resourcefulness and strength.

Clients may also need such gay-affirmative therapy in coping with social and workplace heterosexism and the insidious effects of internalized homophobia on self-esteem. The antigay prejudice of family members may be one of the most crippling emotional burdens for gay clients. A family's religious and cultural values may condemn homosexuality, delaying or preventing an individual from coming out to family members. Therapists must be sensitive to the ongoing distancing, pain, and guilt that this may cause.

Although gay and lesbian couples share many of the same problems as heterosexual couples, therapists need to be aware of specific stressors for gay and lesbian couples since they lack social approval and frequently also lack familial support. These couples may not be "out" in all contexts (particularly professional) and are more frequently interracial than heterosexual couples—and thus at greater risk for internal and external conflicts. Because of differences in gender-role socialization, lesbian couples also differ from gay male couples in many areas, such as sex, intimacy, autonomy, and communication; therefore, therapists cannot generalize about "homosexual" couples as a group. Finally, couples in which one or both members are bisexual may also have special counseling issues.

In addition to lesbian and gay couples therapy, there is a growing need for lesbian and gay family therapy. Although gays and lesbians in the past usually had children through a prior heterosexual union, they are increasingly raising children as gay couples. Adoption, alternative insemination, surrogate mothers, and coparenting are some of the approaches lesbian and gay couples are employing in order to have children. Each is often fraught with special difficulties for gays and lesbians. Therapists need to be aware of the particular needs of these families, which often face some of the most violent condemnation from culturally and religiously conservative relatives, neighbors, and politicians. Unlike those in traditional heterosexual couples, gay parental roles may require explicit negotiation. The children of these couples may also face unique challenges in school and other social settings since they have to explain to teachers and peers that they have two mommies or daddies.

The attitudes of therapists themselves have come under scrutiny. Gays and lesbians tend to prefer openly gay or lesbian therapists, precisely to avoid the ignorance or prejudice revealed by the American Psychological Association survey. Gay therapists are generally more experienced with resources and organizations in the gay community and can serve as positive role models. However, they must also contend with challenges in effectively dealing with lesbian and gay clients. Overidentification with clients can lead to a variety of problems: loss of objectivity in diagnosing serious psychopathology, boundary violations if the client is seen as a friend, or the imposition of personal norms of "outness" and appropriate gay behavior. Therapists who are insecure about their sexuality or have not analyzed their own internalized homophobia can be especially harmful to gay clients (Shelley 1998; Drescher 1998; Magee and Miller 1997).

Finally, psychologists have only recently examined the interaction between sexual orientation and other identities such as race or ethnicity, physical disability, or deafness (Cabaj and Stein 1996). Psychologist Beverly Greene (1994) has reviewed some major issues and recent research. She notes that, in the past, most of the research on homosexuality was conducted with white, middle-class subjects. Ethnic and other minority lesbians and gay men face special problems dealing with multiple marginalities and sets of biases. Their cultural group may view homosexuality as a middle-class, white deviation counter to ethnic values—particularly marriage, reproduction, religion, and the family. Meanwhile, they may simultaneously face racism and intolerance in the lesbian and gay community. Embracing one identity may feel like a betrayal of another. Therapists need to learn about the different modulations of sexual behavior and identity in their clients' cultures rather than force upon them a preset model of "coming out" or healthy homosexuality. For example, among many African American and Latino men, specific sexual acts (e.g., active versus passive) are more important in defining one's masculinity than the mere act of sex with another man (Jones and Hill 1996; Gonzáles and Espín 1996; Prieur 1998). In some Asian cultures, same-sex activity can be condoned so long as it is kept private and does not disturb a public adherence to norms of marriage and family (Chan 1995). Even the identity labels of "homosexual" or "bisexual" may not be acceptable to people from ethnic and class subgroups apart from white, urban, middle-class young men.

*Reexamining Other Nonheterosexual Identities: Bisexuality*

Although diverse expressions of sexuality have existed throughout the twentieth century and even been examined by health care professionals, medical and popular literature has been largely dominated by two opposed erotic entities: heterosexuality versus homosexuality. In the 1960s and 1970s, much of the civil rights action and lobbying of the medical associations regarding sexuality focused on gays and lesbians. Although these umbrella terms were politically expedient, they sometimes erased significant identity and lifestyle differences of the people huddled together under them. By the 1980s and especially in the 1990s, these various groups—which often felt marginalized by the increasingly mainstream gay and lesbian organizations—began to assert their autonomy. With this new visibility also came increased professional attention.

Early twentieth-century psychoanalysts and sexologists had viewed erotic attraction to both men and women (bisexuality, or "psychosexual hermaphroditism," as it was sometimes called) as a stable identity. Some theorists, such as Sigmund Freud, even believed that bisexuality was the universal, fundamental orientation humans were born with before narrowing their erotic interests. Alfred Kinsey had also argued that most people retained in fantasy or behavior some degree of bigendered eroticism—that vast region between zero and six on Kinsey's heterosexual-homosexual rating scale. Many postwar analysts, nevertheless, began to consider bisexuality as a transitional stage or a defense against fully acknowledging homosexuality. Gays and lesbians often shared this view in their hostility toward bisexuality. Some members of the gay community felt bisexuals were "sitting on the fence," were indecisive about their sexuality, or wanted to retain heterosexual social privilege while enjoying gay eroticism.

By the 1980s a number of lesbian feminists in particular began theorizing and politicizing bisexual identity (Udis-Kessler 1996). Sociologist Paula Rust (1995) theorizes bisexual identities as a landscape allowing individuals far more room to explore various gendered attractions over the life course. That flexibility was a tremendous challenge to the socially and politically established gay and lesbian identities. This was evident in the sometimes acrimonious battles to include the word *bisexual* along with *lesbian* and *gay* in the names of organizations and pride marches in the 1980s and 1990s.

In his article in *Bisexuality: The Psychology and Politics of an Invisible Minority* (1996), Ronald Fox reviews social science and mental health research on bisexuality, much of it published in the late 1980s and the 1990s. This recent work, conducted from a bisexually affirmative position, dispels notions of the psychopathology or identity instability of bisexuals. In many ways, bisexual identity development resembles that of gays and lesbians as socially marginalized groups. Mental health practitioners are increasingly recognizing the importance of validating clients' attractions to both sexes and helping them integrate bisexual eroticism into their life.

*The Transgender Phenomenon*

In the 1990s, transsexuals and intersexed people have also become increasingly visible and vocal, claiming a stable queer identity. As we saw in Chapter 1, the medical concept of homosexuality arose from a diverse collection of ideas about "gender inversion" and "psychosexual hermaphroditism." Victorian doctors and even patients described inverts having a "female soul in a male body." Cross-dressing was not uncommon for some of these inverted men and women. Dr. Magnus Hirschfeld coined the term *transvestite* in 1910 and *transsexual* in 1923; however, he believed that these phenomena were all closely tied together as various manifestations of what he viewed as "sexual intermediates" or a biological third sex between male and female. This group included homosexuals. Thus, homosexuality, transvestitism, and cross-gendered self-identification were regularly collapsed together in the medical literature until the mid–twentieth century. For example, the first two patients who underwent complete "genital transformation surgery" from male to female in 1931 were diagnosed as "homosexual transvestites," and the surgery was performed to "complete" their cross-dressing (Abraham 1931). Even Christine Jorgensen (whose sex change surgery brought transsexualism to broad public attention in 1952) was originally diagnosed with "genuine transvestitism" (Hamburger, Stürup, and Dahl-Iverson 1953; Meyerowitz 1998).

It was during the 1950s that doctors, under the leadership of endocrinologist Harry Benjamin (1966), consolidated the diagnosis of transsexualism as a phenomenon distinct from homosexuality or transvestitism. The Harry Benjamin International Gender Dysphoria Association (HBIGDA) was founded to promote the study and ethical treatment of transsexuals. HBIGDA's *Standards of Care* (1980; 2001) suggested basic principles for the treatment of transsexualism. The *Standards of Care* were designed to safeguard both patients and doctors from regretting potentially irreversible sex reassignment therapy. They include a period of counseling, "real life" experience or "passing" as the desired gender, hormone treatment, and, finally, surgical sex reassignment. Doctors were first charged with determining whether a patient was a "true" transsexual. Second, a medical team was to help transsexuals shift totally and convincingly into their new gender. Usually, this meant erasing their previous life and gender.

Many transsexual activists in the 1990s, such as Sandy Stone (1991), Kate Bornstein (1994), and Leslie Feinberg (1996), have rebelled against this gender-normalizing approach and have claimed transsexualism as a stable, healthy identity rather than a transitional mental pathology. The broader term *transgenderism,* which includes a variety of gender self-conceptions and behaviors (such as cross-dressing or gender bending), has thus become a congenial identity position for many people who feel at odds with the conventionally dichotomized gender roles and identities of male and female.

Social scientific research from a transgender-sympathetic perspective has been slowly accumulating, and it generally suggests that transgendered people can be just as psychologically well-adjusted as the overall population (Gordon 1991; Barrett 1998). Transgender affirmative therapy is also becoming more commonplace, especially in large cities. New transsexual activist groups have begun challenging the APA diagnosis of "gender identity disorder," which many transgendered people feel stigmatizes transsexualism as a mental pathology—much as "homosexuality" or "ego-dystonic homosexuality" pathologized gays and lesbians. The issue is a challenging one, however, since those individuals desiring sex reassignment require a medical diagnosis to qualify for insurance coverage of hormonal or surgical treatment. One possible option for diagnostic revision is to consider transsexualism in the same light as pregnancy: a natural, nonpathological condition that nevertheless benefits from close medical care.

## Hermaphrodites with Attitude

As we saw in Chapter 1, the medical conception of homosexuality was intimately woven with that of hermaphroditism. In Greek mythology, Hermaphroditos was a divinely beautiful being, fusing together the finest of male and female traits. Ever since antiquity, doctors have been fascinated by the possibility of hermaphroditism: possessing or appearing to possess both male and female genitals and reproductive organs (Dreger 1998). As we saw earlier, nineteenth-century embryologists discovered that the vertebrate embryo developed from a sexually undifferentiated state (often called "bisexual") before going in a definitively male or female genital direction. In a small number of cases (approximately 1 per 1,000 births) embryological development proceeds in a different direction. In so-called true hermaphroditism, both ovarian and testicular tissue are present in the gonads. In a variety of "pseudohermaphroditic" conditions, the genitals differ in size or conformation from the usual appearance of males and females: for example, a clitoris is large and looks like a phallus, a penis is small and resembles a clitoris, or the scrotal skin is unfused and looks like labia. In extremely rare cases, the genitals can appear perfectly normal but do not correspond to the chromosomal sex, that is, XX males and XY females.

Sexologists such as Magnus Hirschfeld characterized homosexuality as a variety of hermaphroditism, in which the sex of the brain and some other elements of bodily anatomy were between sexes. A long line of research, most recently that of Simon LeVay, has continued to pursue a similar hypothesis. Even the first use of the term *intersex* was by a homosexual author, writing anonymously about the history of "Similisexualism," or same-sex love (Stevenson 1908). However, as the notion of "psychosexual inversion" went into decline, doctors increasingly reserved the term *intersexual* for anatomical pseudohermaphrodites.

Since the late 1950s, sexologists and pediatric surgeons have advocated surgical interventions in infancy and childhood to try to make intersexed children's genitals appear "normal." Most often, surgery involves shortening or amputation of a large clitoris or amputation of a small penis along with female gender assignment and the subsequent creation of a surgical vagina. In male assignment, the creation of a penis that allows standing urination may involve subjecting a child to repeated genital surgeries (four or five is not uncommon, and as many as twenty-two have been reported in one case) (Kessler 1998). Psychologists such as John Money and Anke Ehrhardt (1972) argued that early, definitive gender assignment was essential to healthy parent-child bonding and infantile psychosexual development. The prevention of homosexuality was also a concern. Frequently, these intersexed individuals did not learn about their early medical history until adolescence or adulthood, when they had to cope with genital insensitivity or dysfunction.

## Sidebar 9.5 Advances in HIV Therapy

During the 1980s, HIV and AIDS rapidly grew to become a global epidemic. Although HIV became the most intensively studied virus in history, there were few advances in combating it. Safe sex and needle drug education programs helped curb the spread of the virus. Early diagnosis of HIV status and prophylaxis or treatment of opportunistic infections helped reduce mortality. The first antiretroviral agent to be tested in AIDS therapy was zidovudine (AZT), a nucleoside analogue reverse transcriptase inhibitor (NRTI). There were pitched battles to speed its approval by the U.S. Food and Drug Administration. Nevertheless, it proved to be a huge disappointment: it had many severe side effects and ultimately was found not to significantly decrease mortality rates in AIDS patients. HIV mutates so quickly that it rapidly became resistant to AZT.

During the early 1990s, however, a number of other NRTI drugs were developed and approved: didanosine (ddI), zalcitabine (ddC), stavudine (d4T), and lamivudine (3TC). All these drugs interfere with reverse transcription, the stage at which HIV RNA is converted into DNA, which can be integrated into human genetic material before being used as a template for creating new viral proteins. Used in combination, these NRTIs seemed to be more effective in slowing down the progression of disease since it took longer for the virus to develop resistance simultaneously to multiple drugs.

A major advance in HIV treatment came with the development of a new class of antiretroviral agents, the *protease inhibitors*. These drugs act later in the process of viral maturation by inhibiting the action of HIV protease, which cuts up long amino acid chains into active viral proteins. The first protease inhibitor, saquinavir, was approved in 1995. There soon followed indinavir, ritonavir, and nelfinavir. These agents, especially in double and triple combination "cocktails" with the NRTIs, proved extraordinarily effective in reducing the viral load in the blood and promoting a rise in CD4 T-cell levels (two indices of disease severity). A third class of antiretroviral agents was added to the HIV armamentarium in the mid-1990s, the non-nucleoside reverse transcriptase inhibitors (NNRTIs): nevirapine and delavirdine. These drugs directly inhibit the reverse transcriptase enzyme. The hope is that inhibiting the life cycle of HIV at multiple stages simultaneously will make it more difficult for the virus to develop drug resistance. Some people, however, develop significant short-term and long term side effects to the medications that can limit their use. The drug cocktail may also require complex dosing.

These medications have not been in use long enough (at the time of this writing) to know their long-term effectiveness; however, the results so far have been extremely heartening. The CDC notes that the introduction of the antiretroviral therapies in the mid-1990s dramatically decreased AIDS deaths and slowed the progression from HIV-positive status to AIDS. Therefore, there are more people living with HIV (U.S. CDC 2001a, 434). In 1998 there were 274,624 people living with AIDS in the United States, while in 1999 the number had increased to 322,865 (U.S. CDC 2001e). However, the annual rate of decline in new AIDS cases and AIDS mortality has been leveling off since 1997.

The greatest declines have been among white, non-Hispanic males and men who have sex with men. The benefits of antiretroviral therapy have been slower coming to blacks, Hispanics, and injecting-drug users because of their continued poor access to medical services.

The cost of these drugs is enormous (around $1,500 a month), which can drive uninsured or underinsured patients into bankruptcy and welfare status. The cost also puts these drugs out of the reach of HIV patients in developing countries that are experiencing the most severe AIDS epidemics. Other classes of antiretroviral agents are under investigation, but a vaccine—which would be the most cost-effective means of controlling the epidemic—remains elusive.

*Lesbian and gay youth have grown up in a more visible environment: many join pride parades, start support groups and clubs in high school, and identify as "queer" in order to subvert old labels (Skjold).*

In the mid-1990s, a group of intersexed adults formed the Intersex Society of North America (ISNA) to share experiences and information. Many were dissatisfied with their former treatment, which had left them emotionally scarred and genitally disfigured, with little erogenous sensation. Many ISNA members also identify themselves as lesbian or gay. As with homosexuals and transsexuals before them, some intersexed individuals are reclaiming hermaphroditism as a stable identity category, not just a pathological condition to be "cured." The activist group Hermaphrodites with Attitude has picketed medical associations, and ISNA has lobbied the U.S. Congress to extend legal prohibition of clitoridectomy (originally a law applied only to daughters of African immigrants) to American children. ISNA has urged that, except in cases of true medical emergency, these procedures be postponed until the affected individuals themselves can choose to undergo surgery (Chase 1998). In the meantime, the medical team should make its best informed decision about what gender to assign an intersexed newborn, realizing that sometimes gender assignment is incorrect even in nonintersexed children (that is, for transsexuals). The most media attention has focused on cases in which individuals were unhappy about their early sex reassignment and after much unhappiness have undergone a second sex reassignment (Colapinto 2000). Physicians have also responded to the plight of intersexed individuals and called for a more cautious approach to intervention (Diamond and Sigmundson 1997). Little intersex-affirmative scientific work or psychotherapeutic theorizing is now available. However, the Human Sexuality Committee of the Group for the Advancement of Psychiatry is currently addressing this issue, and more research will most likely be forthcoming in the next decade.

## A Queer Century?

The turn of the twenty-first century has been an exciting time for lesbians, gay men, and other people with nonheterosexual, queer sexualities. Although the AIDS epidemic remains a deadly burden on the gay community, advances in therapy have greatly lengthened and improved the life of HIV-positive individuals. AIDS education campaigns promoted by gay health organizations have proven extremely effective, although these efforts must be vigilantly maintained to inform young people and prevent "slipping" back into unsafe sex practices.

The visibility and leadership of lesbians and gay men in health care since the 1970s has prompted vast transformations in the attitudes of professional associations. As a result, U.S. psychiatric, psychological, and social work associations are some of the strongest advocates for equitable legal and social treatment of homosexuals. Although there is still need for sensitization of individual practitioners, homophobia is no longer condoned within the health care professions.

Current biological research suggests that homosexuality is a natural variant of human sexuality. New social scientific information has been dispelling negative stereotypes of homosexuality as a psychopathology and a social scourge, and affirmative psychotherapy is helping millions of lesbian, gay, bisexual, transgendered, and intersexed people lead more contented, productive lives by being able to cope with or combat persistent heterosexism and gender bias. Scientific evidence alone will not blast away millennia of homophobic values that burden society. However, professional, legal, and grassroots activism over the century, relying on scientific data, has indeed managed to accomplished a revolution in societal attitudes and permitted an unprecedented efflorescence of minority sexual communities in large and even small cities in the United States. With continued scientific and political interventions, who knows how queer the twenty-first century will be.

## Conclusion

In the past two centuries, vast transformations have occurred in the medical profession's approach to homosexuality. In the late nineteenth century, most doctors (except for medico-legal experts) would not have dealt with this subject since the "sexual perversions" belonged to the province of religion and morality. A new breed of sexologists and psychoanalysts rapidly changed that. Although some early twentieth-century psychiatric theorists were fairly liberal and tolerant, by midcentury the opposite attitude came to dominate. As the medical literature consistently presented homosexuality as a serious psychopathology, a wide range of biomedical approaches were employed to try to explain the origins of this "sexual perversion." Some researchers relied entirely on biological models, while others developed psychological and developmental models. Many physicians were eclectic and relied on multiple, interactive factors in explaining the origins of homosexuality. Those doctors who believed it was entirely hereditary tended to be pessimistic about a cure, and a few therefore promoted the chilling option of eugenics.

Of those who believed homosexuality was the result of developmental deviations, not all recommended conversion therapy—but most did. In the late 1960s, homophile and gay activism in society at large as well as within medical organizations began radically challenging the psychiatric orthodoxy on homosexual psychopathology. The most dramatic change came in 1973 with the deletion of homosexuality as a disease from the *Diagnostic and Statistical Manual* (DSM) of the American Psychiatric Association. This change continues to reverberate around the world. Only in April 2001 did the Chinese Psychiatric Association bring its own diagnostic guidelines into agreement with the DSM on the issue of homosexuality. Until then, electrical aversion therapy and other radical treatments continued to be accepted measures for "curing" homosexuality in China (Gallagher 2001).

Although these "treatments" seem barbaric, they are no doubt still being used, even in the United States. Sadly, it is often gay and lesbian individuals themselves who, in the past and in the present, seek to change their sexual orientation because they hope to conform to familial, cultural, and religious ideals of what is considered to be "normal" behavior. Although this cultural hostility toward homosexuality has been changing significantly since the 1950s, it has not been swept away by the historic medical and psychiatric declarations that homosexuality is *not* abnormal or pathological. Nor is this moral antipathy likely to be eliminated by evidence of the biological basis of sexual orientation.

Scientists have been investigating the "riddle of same-sex love" for almost two centuries, and it is yet to be solved. To date there is no convincing scientific explanation for what causes homosexuality. It is likely that multiple biological and psychological factors, as well as sociohistorical ones, shape sexual orientation and gender identity. These multiple factors probably have varying strength in molding each particular individuals' sexuality, explaining the diverse manifestations of human gender, sexuality, and sexual orientation. The scientific study of human sexuality is a fascinating yet tremendously difficult task that demands careful consideration of the subtleties of human behavior and its cultural context. The subjects of this study—lesbians, gay men, bisexuals, transgenders, intersexes, heterosexuals, and unknown identities yet to emerge—must remain vigilant in our scrutiny of this scientific research. Historical experience shows that although the biomedical sciences have the potential to benefit bodily and mental health, they may also cause great harm by giving scientific support to cultural prejudice, thus justifying it as "natural." Science is a product of human hands and minds; thus it is vulnerable to the biases and abuses of any other cultural artifact. It is the duty of everyone, not just scientists, to be an active, informed, and critical participant in the scientific enterprise.

# References

Abraham, Felix. 1931. "Genitalumwandlungen an zwei männlichen Transvestiten." *Zeitschrift für Sexualwissenschaft und Sexualpolitik* 18: 223–226.

Allen, Garland E. 1997. "The Double-Edged Sword of Genetic Determinism: Social and Political Agendas in Genetic Studies of Homosexuality, 1940–1994." Pp. 242–270 in *Science and Homosexualities*. Edited by V. Rosario. New York: Routledge.

APA (American Psychiatric Association). 2000. "Position Statement on Therapies Focused on Attempts to Change Sexual Orientation (Reparative or Conversion Therapies). Includes "Appendix 1": APA Position Statement on Psychiatric Treatment and Sexual Orientation (December 11, 1998). *American Journal of Psychiatry* 157: 1719–1721.

Bagemihl, Bruce. 1999. *Biological Exuberance: Animal Homosexuality and Natural Diversity*. New York: St. Martin's Press.

Bailey, J. Michael, and Richard C. Pillard. 1991. "A Genetic Study of Male Sexual Orientation." *Archives of General Psychiatry* 48: 1089–1096.

Bailey, J. Michael, Richard C. Pillard, M. C. Neale, and M. A. Agyei. 1993. "Heritable Factors Influence Sexual Orientation in Women." *Archives of General Psychiatry* 50: 217–223.

Barrett, J. 1998. "Psychological and Social Function Before and After Phalloplasty." *International Journal of Trasngenderism* 2, no. 1, http://www.symposion.com/ijt/ijtc0301.htm.

Benjamin, Harry. 1966. *The Transsexual Phenomenon*. New York: Julian Press.

Bornstein, Kate. 1994. *Gender Outlaw: On Men, Women and the Rest of Us*. New York: Routledge.

Burr, Chandler. 1993. "Homosexuality and Biology." *Atlantic Monthly* 271, no. 3: 47–65.

Byne, William. 1995. "Science and Belief: Psychobiological Research on Sexual Orientation." Pp. 303–344 in *Sex, Cells, and Same-Sex Desire: The Biology of Sexual Preference*. Edited by J. De Cecco and D. A. Parker. Binghamton, NY: Harrington Park.

Cabaj, R. P., and T. S. Stein, eds. 1996. *Textbook of Homosexuality and Mental Health*. Washington, DC: American Psychiatric Press.

Cameron, Paul, and Kirk Cameron. 1995. "Does Incest Cause Homosexuality?" *Psychological Reports* 76: 611–621.

Cameron, Paul, Kirk Cameron, and Kay Proctor. 1989. "Effect of Homosexuality upon Public Health and Social Order." *Psychological Reports* 64: 1167–1179.

Cameron, Paul, Kay Proctor, William Coburn, and Nels Forde. 1986. "Child Molestation and Homosexuality." *Psychological Reports* 58: 327–337.

Chan, Connie S. 1995. "Issues of Sexual Identity in an Ethnic Minority: The Case of Chinese American Lesbians, Gay Men, and Bisexual People." Pp. 87–100 in *Lesbian, Gay, and Bisexual Identities over the Lifespan*. Edited by A. R. D'Augelli and C. J. Patterson. New York: Oxford University Press.

Chase, Cheryl. 1998. "Hermaphrodites with Attitude: Mapping the Emergence of Intersex Political Activism." *GLQ* 4: 189–211.

Chauncey, George. 1994. *Gay New York: Gender, Urban Culture, and the Making of the Gay Male World, 1890–1940*. New York: Basic Books.

Cochran, Susan D., and Vickie Mays. 2000. "Relation between Psychiatric Syndromes and Behaviorally Defined Sexual Orientation in a Sample of the U.S. Population." *American Journal of Epidemiology* 151: 516–523.

Cochran, Susan D., C. Keenan, C. Schober, and V. M. Mays. 2000. "Estimates of Alcohol Use and Clinical Treatment Needs among Homosexually Active Men and Women in the U.S. Population." *Journal of Consulting and Clinical Psychology* 68: 1062–1071.

Colapinto, John. 2000. *As Nature Made Him: The Boy Who Was Raised as a Girl.* New York: HarperCollins.

Cole, Steve W., Margaret Kemeny, Shelley Taylor, and Barbara Visscher. 1996. "Elevated Physical Health Risk among Gay Men Who Conceal Their Homosexual Identity." *Health Psychology* 15: 243–251.

Dank, Barry M. 1971. "Coming Out in the Gay World." *Psychiatry* 34: 180–197.

Denenberg, Risa. 1995. "Report on Lesbian Health." *WHI* 5: 81–91.

Diamond, Milton, and Keith Sigmundson. 1997. "Sex Reassignment at Birth: Long-term Review and Clinical Implications." *Archives of Pediatric and Adolescent Medicine* 151: 298–304.

Dörner, Günther, and G. Hinz. 1968. "Induction and Prevention of Male Homosexuality by Androgen." *Journal of Endocrinology* 40: 387–388.

Dörner, Günther, T. Geier, S. L. Ahren, L. Krell, G. Munx, H. Sieler, E. Kittner, and H. Muller. 1980. "Prenatal Stress as a Possible Aetiogenetic Factor of Homosexuality in Human Males." *Endokrinologie* 75: 365–368.

Dörner, Günther, Ingrid Poppe, F. Stahl, J. Kölsch, and R. Uebelhack. 1991. "Gene- and Environment-dependent Neuroendocrine Etiogenesis of Homosexuality and Transsexualism." *Experimental and Clinical Endocrinology* 98: 141–150.

Dreger, Alice Domurat. 1998. *Hermaphrodites and the Medical Invention of Sex.* Cambridge: Harvard University Press.

Drescher, Jack. 1998. *Psychoanalytic Therapy and the Gay Man.* Hillsdale, NJ: Analytic Press.

Feinberg, Leslie. 1996. *Transgender Warriors: Making History from Joan of Arc to Dennis Rodman.* Boston: Beacon.

Fox, Ronald C. 1996. "Bisexuality in Perspective: A Review of Theory and Research." Pp. 3–50 in *Bisexuality: The Psychology and Politics of an Invisible Minority.* Edited by B. A. Firestein. Thousand Oaks, CA: Sage.

Friedman, Richard, and Jennifer Downey. 1994. "Homosexuality." *New England Journal of Medicine* 331: 923–930.

Gallagher, John. 2001. "Normal, China: The Chinese Psychiatric Association Decides That Being Gay Is No Longer a Disease." *The Advocate,* April 24, 22–24.

Garnets, Linda, Kristin Hancock, Susan Cochran, Jacqueline Goodchilds, and Letitia Anne Peplau. 1991. "Issues in Psychotherapy with Lesbians and Gay Men: A Survey of Psychologists." *American Psychologist* 46: 964–972.

Garofalo, R., R. C. Wolf, L. S. Wissow, E. R. Woods, and E. Goodman. 1999. "Sexual Orientation and Risk of Suicide Attempts among a Representative Sample of Youth." *Archives of Pediatrics and Adolescent Medicine* 153: 487–493.

Gibson, Paul. 1989. "Gay Male and Lesbian Youth Suicide." In *Report of the Secretary's Task Force on Youth Suicide.* Edited by M. R. Feinleib, vol. 3. Rockville, MD: U.S. Department of Health and Human Services.

Gilman, S. E., S. D. Cochran, V. M. Mays, M. Hughes, D. Ostrow, and R. C. Kessler. 2001. "Risk of Psychiatric Disorders among Individuals Reporting Same-Sex Sexual Partners in the National Comorbidity Survey." *American Journal of Public Health* 91: 933–939.

Gonzáles, Francisco, and Olivia M. Espín. 1996. "Latino Men, Latina Women, and Homosexuality." Pp. 583–601 in *Textbook of Homosexuality and Mental Health*. Edited by R. P. Cabaj and T. S. Stein. Washington, DC: American Psychiatric Press.

Gordon, Eric B. 1991. "Transsexual Healing: Medicaid Funding of Sex Reassignment Surgery." *Archives of Sexual Behavior* 20: 61–74.

Gorski, Roger A. 1978. "Sexual Differentiation of the Brain." *Hospital Practice* (October): 55–62.

Greene, Beverly. 1994. "Ethnic-minority Lesbians and Gay Men: Mental Health and Treatment Issues." *Journal of Consulting and Clinical Psychology* 62: 243–251.

Group for the Advancement of Psychiatry (GAP). 2000. *Homosexuality and the Mental Health Professions: The Impact of Bias.* Hillsdale, NJ: Analytic Press.

Haldeman, Douglas. 1994. "The Practice and Ethics of Sexual Orientation Conversion Therapy." *Journal of Consulting and Clinical Psychology* 62: 221–227.

Halley, Janet E. 1994. "Sexual Orientation and the Politics of Biology: A Critique of the Argument from Immutability." *Stanford Law Review* 46: 503–568.

Hamburger, Christian, Georg K. Stürup, and E. Dahl-Iversen. 1953. "Transvestism: Hormonal, Psychiatric, and Surgical Treatment." *Journal of the American Medical Association* 152: 391–396.

Hamer, Dean, and Peter Copeland. 1994. *The Science of Desire: The Search for the Gay Gene and the Biology of Behavior.* New York: Simon and Schuster.

Hamer, Dean, Stella Hu, Victoria L. Magnuson, Nan Hu, and Angela Pattatucci. 1993. "A Linkage between DNA Markers on the X Chromosome and Male Sexual Orientation." *Science* 261: 321–327.

Hancock, Kristin. 1995. "Psychotherapy with Lesbians and Gay Men." Pp. 398–432 in *Lesbian, Gay, and Bisexual Identities over the Lifespan.* Edited by A. R. D'Augelli and C. J. Patterson. New York: Oxford University Press.

HBIGDA (Harry Benjamin International Gender Dysphoria Association). 1980. *The Standards of Care: The Hormonal and Surgical Reassignment of Gender Dysphoric Persons.* Mimeographed. Distributed by HBIGDA, 1952 Union St., San Francisco, CA 94123.

———. 2001. *The Standards of Care for Gender Identity Disorders,* 6th version. *International Journal of Transgenderism* 5, no. 1. http://www.symposion.com/ijt/soc_2001/index.htm.

Herek, Gregory M. 1995. "Psychological Heterosexism in the United States." Pp. 321–346 in *Lesbian, Gay, and Bisexual Identities over the Lifespan.* Edited by A. R. D'Augelli and C. J. Patterson. New York: Oxford University Press.

Hu, Stella, Angela M. L. Pattatucci, Chavis Patterson, Lin Li, David W. Fulker, Stacey S. Cherny, Leonid Kruglyak, and Dean Hamer. 1995. "Linkage Between Sexual Orientation and Chromosome Xq28 in Males but not in Females." *Nature Genetics* 11: 248–256.

Hunter, Joyce. 1995. "At the Crossroads: Lesbian Youth." Pp. 50–60 in *Dyke Life.* Edited by Karla Jay. New York: Basic Books.

Jones, Billy E., and Marjorie J. Hill. 1996. "African American Lesbians, Gay Men, and Bisexuals." Pp. 549–561 in *Textbook of Homosexuality and Mental Health.* Edited by R. P. Cabaj and T. S. Stein. Washington, DC: American Psychiatric Press.

Jones, Franklin, and Ronald Koshes. 1995. "Homosexuality and the Military." *American Journal of Psychiatry* 152: 16–21.

Kessler, Suzanne. 1998. *Lessons from the Intersexed.* New Brunswick, NJ: Rutgers University Press.

Koopman, C., M. Rosario, and M. J. Rotheram-Borus. 1994. "Alcohol and Drug Use and Sexual Behaviors Placing Runaways at Risk for HIV Infection." *Addictive Behaviors* 19: 95–103.

LeVay, Simon. 1991. "A Difference in Hypothalamic Structure between Heterosexual and Homosexual Men." *Science* 253: 1034–1037.

———. 1993. *The Sexual Brain.* Cambridge: MIT Press.

———. 1996. *Queer Science: The Use and Abuse of Research into Homosexuality.* Cambridge: MIT Press.

Magee, Maggie, and Diana Miller. 1997. *Lesbian Lives: Psychoanalytic Narratives Old and New.* Hillsdale, NJ: Analytic Press.

Malyon, Alan K. 1982. "Psychotherapeutic Implications of Internalized Homophobia in Gay Men." Pp. 59–69 in *Homosexuality and Psychotherapy.* Edited by J. C. Gonsiorek. New York: Haworth Press.

Meyerowitz, Joanne. 1998. "Sex-change and the Popular Press: Historical Notes on Transsexuality in the United States, 1930–1955." *GLQ* 4: 159–187.

Money, John, and Anke A. Ehrhardt. 1972. *Man and Woman, Boy and Girl: Differentiation and Dimorphism of Gender Identity from Conception to Maturity.* Baltimore: Johns Hopkins University Press.

Morris, Jessica F., Amy Ojerholm, Teri Brooks, Dana Osowiecki, and Esther Rothblum. 1995. "Finding a Word for Myself: Themes in Lesbian Coming Out Stories." Pp. 36–49 in *Dyke Life.* Edited by Karla Jay. New York: Basic Books.

Nicolosi, Joseph. 1991. *Reparative Therapy of Male Homosexuality: A New Clinical Approach.* Northvale, NJ: J. Aronson.

Pattatucci, Angela. 1998. "Molecular Investigations into Complex Behavior: Lessons from Sexual Orientation Studies." *Human Biology* 70: 367–386.

Prieur, Annick. 1998. *Mema's House, Mexico City: On Transvestites, Queens, and Machos.* Chicago: University of Chicago Press.

Rice, G., C. Anderson, N. Risch, and G. Ebers. 1999. "Male Homosexuality: Absence of Linkage to Microsatellite Markers at Xq28." *Science* 284: 665–667.

Richardson, Justin. 1995. "The Science and Politics of Gay Teen Suicide." *Harvard Review of Psychiatry* 3: 107–110.

Rothblum, Esther. 1994. "Introduction to the Special Section: Mental Health of Lesbians and Gay Men." *Journal of Consulting and Clinical Psychology* 62: 211–212.

Rotheram-Borus, M. J., and C. Koopman. 1991. "Sexual Risk Behavior, AIDS Knowledge, and Beliefs about AIDS among Predominantly Minority Gay and Bisexual Male Adolescents." *AIDS Education and Prevention* 3: 305–312.

Rotheram-Borus, M. J., H. F. Meyer-Bahlburg, M. Rosario, C. Koopman, C. S. Haignere, T. M. Exner, M. Matthieu, R. Henderson, and R. S. Gruen. 1992. "Lifetime Sexual Behaviors among Predominantly Minority Male Runaways and Gay/Bisexual Adolescents in New York City." *AIDS Education and Prevention,* Supplement: 34–42.

Rotheram-Borus, M. J., H. Reid, and M. Rosario. 1994. "Factors Mediating Changes in Sexual HIV Risk Behaviors among Gay and Bisexual Male Adolescents." *American Journal of Public Health* 84: 1938–1946.

Rust, Paula C. 1995. *Bisexuality and the Challenge to Lesbian Politics: Sex, Loyalty, and Revolution.* New York: New York University Press.

Ryan, Caitlin, and Donna Futterman. 1997. "Lesbian and Gay Youth: Care and Counseling." *State of the Arts Reviews* 8, no. 2.

Safren, S. A., and R. G. Heimberg. 1999. "Depression, Hopelessness, Suicidality, and Related Factors in Sexual Minority and Heterosexual Adolescents." *Journal of Consulting and Clinical Psychology* 67: 859–866.

Savin-Williams, Ritch. 1994. "Verbal and Physical Abuse as Stressors in the Lives of Lesbian, Gay Male, and Bisexual Youths: Associations with School Problems, Running Away, Substance Abuse, Prostitution, and Suicide." *Journal of Consulting and Clinical Psychology* 62: 261–269.

Schoofs, Mark. 1997. "Geneocide: Can Scientists 'Cure' Homosexuality by Altering DNA?" *Village Voice* 42, no. 26.

Schüklenk, Udo, Edward Stein, Jacinta Kerin, and William Byne. 1997. "The Ethics of Genetic Research on Sexual Orientation." *Hastings Center Report* 27, no. 4: 6–13.

Shelley, Christopher, ed. 1998. *Contemporary Perspectives on Psychotherapy and Homosexualities.* London: Free Association Books.

Socarides, Charles W. 1995. *Homosexuality: A Freedom Too Far: A Psychoanalyst Answers 1000 Questions about Causes and Cure and the Impact of the Gay Rights Movement on American Society.* Phoenix, AZ: Adam Margrave Books.

Solarz, Andrea L. 1999. *Lesbian Health: Current Assessment and Directions for the Future.* Washington, DC: National Academy Press.

Stevenson, Edward I. P. [Xavier Mayne]. [1908] 1975. *The Intersexes: A History of Similisexualism as a Problem in Social Life.* New York: Arno.

Stone, Sandy. 1991. "The *Empire* Strikes Back: A Post-transsexual Manifesto." Pp. 280–304 in *Body Guards: The Cultural Politics of Gender Ambiguity.* Edited by Julia Epstein and Kristina Straub. New York: Routledge.

Swaab, Dick F., and Michel A. Hofman. 1990. "An Enlarged Suprachiasmatic Nucleus in Homosexual Men." *Brain Research* 537:141–148.

Troiden, Richard R. 1988. *Gay and Lesbian Identity : A Sociological Analysis.* Dix Hills, NY: General Hall.

Udis-Kessler, Amanda. 1996. "Identity/Politics: Historical Sources of the Bisexual Movement." Pp. 52–63 in *Queer Studies: A Lesbian, Gay, Bisexual, and Transgender Anthology.* Edited by Brett Beemyn and Mickey Eliason. New York: New York University Press.

U.S. CDC (Centers for Disease Control and Prevention). 2001a. "HIV and AIDS—United States, 1981–2000." *Morbidity and Mortality Weekly Review* 50: 430–434.

———. 2001c. "HIV Incidence among Young Men Who Have Sex with Men—Seven U.S. cities, 1994–2000." *Morbidity and Mortality Weekly Review* 50: 440–444.

———. 2001e. "A Glance at the HIV Epidemic." www.cdc.gov/nchstp/od/mmwr/At-a-glance%20Key%20Facts.pdf.

## Further Reading

As in other fields of science, biomedical literature on homosexuality has been growing exponentially. Readers interested in pursuing the science of sexual orientation in greater detail can turn to *Sex, Cells, and Same-Sex Desire: The Biology of Sexual Preference,* edited by J. De Cecco and D. A. Parker (Binghamton, NY: Harrington Park, 1995). For further reading on psychological issues and psychotherapy with lesbians and gay men, see *Lesbian, Gay, and Bisexual Identities over the Lifespan,* edited by A. R. D'Augelli and C. J. Patterson (New York: Oxford University Press, 1995); *Textbook of Homosexuality and Mental Health,* edited by R. P. Cabaj and T. S. Stein (Washington, DC: American Psychiatric Press, 1996); *Psychoanalytic Therapy and the Gay Man* by gay analyst Jack Drescher (Hillsdale, NJ: Analytic Press, 1998); and *Lesbian Lives: Psychoanalytic Narratives Old and New,* by lesbian analysts Maggie Magee and Diana Miller (Hillsdale, NJ: Analytic Press, 1997).

## Internet Resources

| | |
|---|---|
| www.AACAP.org | American Academy of Child and Adolescent Psychiatry |
| www.psych.org | American Psychiatric Association |
| www.APA.org | American Psychological Association |
| www.AGLP.org | Association of Gay and Lesbian Psychiatrists: information and doctor referral |
| www.cdc.gov/hiv/pubs/ brochure.htm | Centers for Disease Control: numerous AIDS informational brochures |
| www.FTM-Intl.org | FTM [Female-to-Male] International: information for FTM transgenders |
| www.gayhealth.com | Gayhealth.com: general medical information for nonprofessional audiences |
| www.GLMA.org | Gay and Lesbian Medical Association: excellent links to a variety of medical and social informational sites and support groups |
| www.HBIGDA.org | Harry Benjamin International Gender Dysphoria Association: information on transsexualism, including most recent Standards of Care |
| www.HIVnewsline.com | HIV Newsline: information on the treatment of patients with HIV infection |
| www.IFGE.org | International Foundation for Gender Education: information for transsexuals |
| www.ISNA.org | Intersex Society of North America: information on and internet support for intersexed people |

# Documents

## Gynomania (1881)

*The following is perhaps the first published case in the United States to apply the new diagnosis of "contrary sexual sensation," or what would later be called "homosexuality." Writing anonymously, the original treating doctor believed he had discovered a new form of insanity and gave it the name "gynomania." His respondent, the far more experienced Dr. Edward Spitzka, instead made a diagnosis of contrary sexual appetite. However, on close reading of the original case, did Spitzka misdiagnose the patient? It is easy for us today to accuse Spitzka of conflating "gender role," "sexual aim," and "sexual orientation." However, these terms did not exist at the turn of the twentieth century, so even a knowledgeable doctor could diagnose someone with any trace of atypical sexual behavior as being an "invert." There is also an element of erotic fetishism in the case, but this notion was only described in 1887 in the medical literature.*

### "Gynomania—A Curious Case of Masturbation"

Dr. H. sends us the following account: "Permit me to offer you for publication a brief description of a curious case of prolonged masturbation, which came before me in the course of my regular practice. The details I have gathered from the patient at various times, and give them as fully as consistent with concealment of his personality.

"The patient is a highly cultivated gentleman of high moral character, the father of three or four healthy children, the result of an unusually happy marriage. 'At an early age,' said he, 'long before puberty even, I had acquired a taste for indoor games, female pursuits, and even attire, although the latter desire was never satisfied farther than wearing girls' shoes. I was also an admirer of small waists in ladies, and at the age of fourteen tried to procure or make for myself a pair of corsets. As I grew older my fondness for female dress increased, but having no sisters I could find no opportunity to gratify it farther than reading stories of female impersonations, etc. I composed several stories entitled 'Adventures in Hoops,' and detective stories founded upon such plots. They were printed and extensively copied. To this day, said he, I seldom miss an opportunity to see men take female parts on the stage, especially the more refined ones, like Leon, Byrnes, etc.'

"At the age of twenty-one years he began the use of corsets, of which he is still very fond, and although he laced himself very tightly for several years he seems to have suffered no injury from it. He confessed that he has always derived a certain amount of sensual gratification from their use, and although at first he experienced some pain in the pubic region, and erections, he has since found that as soon as his corsets are pulled quite tightly erections cease, and that coition, as well voluntary discharges, are *impossible* when tightly laced.

"From fear of impotence or other evil that might result from masturbation before marriage, he carefully avoided voluntary discharges of semen and remained perfectly continent before marriage. He recollects, however, having had three involuntary emissions while awake. The first occurred while horseback riding, and induced him to abandon this otherwise healthful exercise. The others happened while putting on a pair of very tight shoes (ladies' boots with French heels), and buttoning them.

"After marriage he abstained from corsets and other articles of female attire (with rare exceptions), until two children had satisfied him of his potency.

"About this time our patient began to yield to the temptations which everywhere beset him, and returned to the very source whence he had first derived unlawful pleasure. But I will let him tell it. 'I purchased,' said he, 'a very stylish pair of ladies' high boots with French heels, which were at first tight enough to make me limp.' These boots he boldly wore upon the promenade in fine weather, with pants elevated to show the heel. In bad weather he was wont to put on these boots and button them in front of a long mirror, about once a week. This seldom failed to cause not only an erection but also an emission.

"When this had lost its novelty he purchased a pair of corsets, not having worn them since marriage. As often as practicable with concealment he wore these, and laced them sometimes to faintness. These two articles, buttoned boots and corsets, seemed to have a most peculiar infatuation for him. Often while riding in a street car, if a lady with a small waist or pretty foot sat opposite, he would have a sort of mental coition, he called it, with this innocent paramour, an emission. M. Roubaud mentions the only case at all similar, where a young man was impotent except with a light-haired woman wearing corsets, high boots, and a silk dress. The last three articles had a powerful influence on our patient, whether they were worn by man or woman.

"After this he advanced step by step down the ladder, purchasing various articles of female attire, until at length he bought a black silk dress, which he had made to fit him very tightly, and in which he took great pride. Curls and switches, false hair, earrings and breast pins, all aided in feeding this peculiar fire. He would even sit for hours tightly laced, while a lady hair-dresser curled and frizzed his hair like a woman. At length he went so far as to walk the city streets and even attend church, wearing his new black silk dress caught up on one side so as to expose a white fluted skirt, beneath which his high-heeled French boots were visible. With heavily padded chest, tightly squeezed waist, enormous bustle, his hair tortured into fantastic forms, his ears in screw vices, and his feet crowded into the narrowest and most uncomfortable boots, he would walk for miles, or dance for hours, with great pleasure. In fact, physical pain seemed essential to his happiness, and he thoroughly and deeply enjoyed it, if it were only the pain inflicted by female attire. He imitated their manner and habits to some extent, yet never used his disguises for improper purposes, except to excite an occasional emission.

"As before stated, he had always been an advocate of tight lacing, had read extensively upon the subject, and collected all the literature that in any way favored or defended it. He several times tried to lace himself tightly enough to faint away, but never could. He even persuaded his wife to lace, and daily tightened her corsets, until he actually reduced her waist nearly *six inches* which also gave him sensual gratification. A child born of her soon after was perfectly healthy and well formed.

"He showed me several pictures of himself in all sorts of dresses, as a ballet-girl, as Queen Elizabeth, as a Polish maiden, an old maid, the Goddess of Liberty, as Juliet, and in the plain street dress, which he wore to church a few years ago.

"Many times he swore off, but in vain. Sometimes he would remain free from his peculiar vice for weeks and months, when it would return with renewed vigor. I found him eating largely of animal food, but not of fat meat. Nitrogenous food alone suited his palate. I advised a vegetable diet, but he found it distasteful to such a degree that I was forced to withdraw it. He used no stimulants except weak tea and coffee. Gave bromides for awhile and hope at length to conquer. Have any of your readers had a similar case within their experience? I proposed the name of Gynomania for it."

## "Gynomania"

To the Editor of the *Medical Record:*

SIR—In regard to the query of a correspondent in your issue of March 19th, as to whether cases similar to the one designated by him as one of "Gynomania" have occurred to others, I would say that such cases, while not frequent, are far from being uncommon, and that they have received due consideration at the hands of eminent German and French alienists. Westphal [1869], under the head of "Conträre Sexualempfindung," and Krafft-Ebing [1877], in a very thorough paper dealing with all varieties of sexual perversion, have described cases of the same character, and shown that those states in which the patient feels himself inclined to assume the feminine dress and gestures, or goes so far as to feel himself a woman during the otherwise normally performed sexual act, are symptoms of a degenerative psychosis. There are to my knowledge about twenty cases of this perversion described in the German periodicals. Probably a much larger number occur, but are unnoticed, as they rarely fall into the hands of so careful an observer as Dr. H., and very rarely indeed are committed to asylums. They are all of them incurable. I have met with three cases of "contrary sexual appetite," and of these only one came under my notice professionally; the others were learned of through accident. Careful search should be made in cases of this kind for a hereditary history, and for anomalies in the offspring. Yours, etc.,

*E. C. Spitzka*

Dr. H—. 1881. "Gynomania—A Curious Case of Masturbation." *The Medical Record* (New York) 19: 336.

Krafft-Ebing, Richard von. 1877. "Ueber gewisse Anomalien des Geschlechtstriebs und die klinisch—forensische Verwertung derselben als eines wahrscheinlich functionellen Degenerationszeichens des zentralen Nervensystems." *Archiv für Psychiatrie und Nervenkrankheiten* 7: 291–312.

Spitzka, Edward. 1881. "Gynomania." *The Medical Record* (New York) 19: 359.

Westphal, Karl Ernest. 1869. "Die Conträre Sexualempfindung: Symptom eines neuropathischen (psychopathischen) Zustandes." *Archiv für Psychiatrie* 2: 73–108.

# In Defense of Cross-Dressing (1884)

*In 1884, the* Alienist and Neurologist, *a leading U.S. neuro-psychiatric journal, published the following letter. The author criticized a prior article by Dr. Rice for dismissing the medico-legal importance of the sexual perversions. He continued with an ambivalent defense of cross-dressing, which was closely associated with "sexual inversion." The letter suggests that cases of transvestitism were on the rise in the big cities at the end of the century.*

Mr. Editor: Will you kindly permit me to say a few words about Sexual Perversion, in reply to Dr. Rice's paper. The latter says that it has but little forensic interest in this country and I beg to differ with him. In the first place, it is quite generally admitted that lunatics and maniacs are not responsible, and irresponsible people are not to be punished for a thing that they cannot help doing.

When a man dons female attire, or vice versa, he either has an object or he has none. If he has an object, it may be good, bad or indifferent. If it is to conceal past crime, or as an aid to future crime, it is bad, and deserves punishment. If he seeks the disguise to enable him to ferret out a crime, the object is praiseworthy— detectives are allowed it. In the third case, it must be said that the sole object is pleasure or satisfaction of some sort. Crime may be a pleasure to some, but if we exclude all evil intent, is it not harmless? Another case that resembles, sometimes one and sometimes another of the above, is where it is done for a livelihood; women give this as an excuse, a plea to be allowed men's dress; men rarely.

Quite a large number of cases are occurring in all large cities, of persons arrested for dressing like the opposite sex. But few are criminals; many are highly respectable and honorable. Should they be punished as criminals? If the object is good, No! If bad, Yes! If neither, what then?

It is self-evident that no sane man will take the pains and go to the expense of obtaining a full set of female attire, and persist in the practice of wearing it until he becomes expert in its uses, initiating himself into all the mysteries of a lady's toilet, submitting voluntarily to the tortures of tight corsets and high-heeled boots and false hair, hoops, pull-backs and frizzes, unless impelled thereto by some motive stronger than mere mischief. There can be no doubt in my mind that such a miserable being deserves pity rather than punishment.

There have been several arrests in this city within five or six years for wearing female attire, and I believe nearly all the victims belonged to that innocent class, since no other object or purpose was ever proved against them.

Why should it be a *crime* to dress as you please? The dress itself inflicts punishment enough on its wearer. No one but the wearer is injured, nor need others be any the wiser for it. Certain it is that many of these poor people have suffered severe punishment at the hands of our judges, and with no one bold enough to defend them.

Is it not sad enough that they must suffer daily between two fires—love of this dress, and fear of punishment, which they have known to be swift and certain? Would the world be any the worse for allowing them this little modicum of comfort, the only pleasure they have in life, under proper restrictions? What these restrictions should be I am not prepared to say. Perhaps an asylum or retreat might be provided, where they could resort when these paroxysms came on, and there enjoy [?] in seclusion from the public eye, where the law could not reach them, such indulgences as might be deemed proper, or compelled to follow these practices until they were thoroughly cured of such desires. I know of one case, at least, that would be benefited, perhaps cured, by suitable treatment of this sort. I should be glad to hear the opinion of those of greater experience than myself.

*E. J. H.*

E. J. H. 1884. Letter to the Editor. *Alienist and Neurologist* 5: 351–352.

---

## Alice Mitchell of Memphis: A Case of Sexual Perversion or "Urning" (a Paranoiac) (1892)

*The Alice Mitchell case was a lesbian "lust murder" that received lurid media coverage in 1892 (Duggan 2000). The following medical journal article about the case presents a good example of the degeneracy theory of sexual perversion. All forms of mental or physical derangement in the family—particularly the mother—were assumed to contribute to the insane condition of psychosexual inversion. Only Alice, not her beloved Freda Ward, was viewed as the lesbian because of Alice's male physical and mental traits—especially the masculine jealousy and strength to commit murder. This construction of Alice as mentally ill is clearly stigmatizing, but it nonetheless bolstered her insanity plea in court. The psychiatric formulation of homosexuality as a mental disorder and therefore involuntary was often invoked in legal defenses. The case is also a good indicator of the growing authority that psychiatric medico-legal experts claimed for themselves in court.*

*Although the author insisted on the repulsive nature of sexual perversions, he nevertheless presented a detailed, sensationalistic account of both the Mitchell case as well as other rare, gruesome cases from Krafft-Ebing's* Psychopathia Sexualis *(1886). Same-sex "crushes" and intimate friendships between women had been considered benign or even admirable until the nineteenth century since it was unseemly for a young lady to be consorting with men. However, the Mitchell case prompted increasing suspicion of these intense same-sex relationships.*

The facts about Alice Mitchell will long be treasured in medical works on insanity, and mental and moral perversion. The medical scholar will study the case in all its lights and shades, while the public will only recall that she suddenly, in a terrible manner, with a razor, cut the throat of her dearest companion and friend, Freda Ward, a young lady of an excellent family. The natural impulse of every one was that summary justice should be dealt to avenge such an unprovoked crime. A few among the people of Memphis were so horrified that they even suggested violence. Fortunately the law took its course.

As a matter of medical jurisprudence, it is of great interest and importance that such a case should be inquired into and thoroughly analyzed by the medical profession, and I may add by the most careful and reliable medical experts. The very first impression is, that there must be something radically abnormal in the mental and physical development of such a murderess—and so it was.

The facts were that there was an unnatural affection existing between Alice Mitchell and Freda Ward. Alice Mitchell seems to have been the ardent one. The love they had for each other, to the public, seems something hard to conceive or explain, but to experts in insanity it is nothing unusual. Alice exhibited in her passion for Freda Ward all the impulses of the male sex for a female. She was to have been dressed as a man and take the bridegroom's part in the marriage ceremony. She had already even arranged with a clergyman to perform the services, but Miss Ward's friends interfered and they were separated. This disturbed Alice. When riding out with a friend, she meets Miss Ward. She suddenly stops and alights from the carriage, and overtaking Miss Ward deliberately cuts her throat with a razor which she carried for the purpose. She jumps into her buggy and drives rapidly home. She was arrested. She confessed the dreadful deed. She said she murdered her best friend because she loved her. For six months while in prison she did not exhibit any remorse or regret, but showed great devotion for the photograph of Miss Ward. And during the trial, and while the verdict was being rendered, her conduct was scarcely altered. The most reasonable conclusion of the jury, and those who have made a study of the alienated mental condition of those who commit such homicides, is that the motive must have come of mental delusion. By scientific experts it is recognized as insanity of a peculiar kind. Alice having been indicted for murder, her attorneys looked at once into the antecedents of the family for mental aberrations. They learned that the mother of Alice in her first confinement, which occurred in St. Louis, had child-bed fever and puerperal [postpartum] insanity, and was confined in an asylum, and that before the birth of Alice she was deranged, and this aberration continued until sometime after labor. I attended the mother of Alice in her first confinement in St. Louis more than thirty years ago. She became insane just after delivery and her mania was of the acute form with fever. I attended her for a month and then advised that she be sent to an asylum. She was sent to the State Asylum at Fulton, where she remained for some time—I think six months. Within a few days after her return home from the asylum, she was first informed of the death of her child, and then her mind became again unbalanced. This demented condition, however, continued only a few days, but she did not recover from the shock. She remained melancholy for a long time, suffering from hallucinations, and was infatuated with the most groundless prejudices and fears. I had occasion to see her for some three years until the family removed from St. Louis to Memphis, and I could always remark a peculiar expression about her eyes which would bring to mind her former furious delirium. I mention this matter since it is a most important factor in the case of Alice, and must not be overlooked. The fact of a real engagement of marriage with one of her own sex indicated at once that she was what is known in forensic medicine as a *sexual pervert*. On the 19th of July, 1891, a judicial inquiry was instituted before Judge Du Bose, of the criminal court of Memphis, to examine into the sanity or rather the insanity of Alice Mitchell. A commission was issued and sent from Memphis to St. Louis to take my evidence regarding the particulars of the first confinement of the mother when puerperal mania followed. Also a hypothetical case was cited describing the life of the mother, her antecedents, her family history, and mentioning the fact that other members of her family had been of unsound mind. It also described the particulars and all the peculiarities of the life of Alice, from the date of her birth to the time of the murder of Miss Ward. This was presented by a commissioner to Dr. Hammond of Washington, to Belot of Paris, as well as to myself. My affidavit stated that from the antecedents of the mother, Alice was a sexual pervert and affected with emotional monomania, without doubt hereditary, and that her condition was one of *paranoia,* resulting in homicidal mania, and consequently her condition might be regarded as intrinsic insanity. That Alice is a sexual pervert and a paranoiac is quite probable, and the jury unanimously decided that she was insane.

Of course, such a jury was not competent to go beyond the general evidence, and to give a detailed description of the evidence which revealed her mental status and the character of her insanity. But the jury was competent to decide whether she was responsible for her acts, even though she had committed murder in apparently cold blood.

Here I may say something of sexual perverts. It is a revolting subject for the laity, for they have no toleration for anything of that kind. It is strictly a scientific matter of professional interest and of great importance to the medical expert. Until recently, little has been said upon this subject in text-books of insanity. It is mentioned in the recent works of Spitzka and Shaw, but for a full elucidation we must examine the work of Krafft-Ebing [1886], Professor of Nervous Diseases in the University of Vienna.

He describes the *vita sexualis* of perverts, such as Alice Mitchell, under the classification *Urnings.* This term, used frequently by German writers upon forensic medicine, refers to those who in a sexual sense are only stimulated when consorting with their own sex. It applies to those who indulge in unnatural sexual practices. But it especially includes sensuality and sexual desire of one female for another, and a disgust for a male. The same may be said of males—mutatis mutandis. Krafft-Ebing describes the "Lesbian Love"—(tribadism), saphismus, cunnilingus, fellators, paedicatio mulierum [female pederasty], sadismus, masochismus and fetischismus. Sadismus is a fierce, wild sensuality and lust, together with cruelty before, during and after coitus. Masochismus is another form of perverted lust during the act of constupration or coitus, accompanied with cruelty and special acts to terrorize and injure the female. Fetischismus or erotic fetichism refers to the "urning" or pervert, who superstitiously adores and worships some article of clothing or some organ of the person loved; or the odor of the person loved excites the orgasm, while the desire of natural coitus is disregarded. In some cases of these unnatural perverts, under the head of "Sadismus" or "Masochismus," the subject, before he can accomplish the sexual act, must, in order to induce priapism, practice cruelty to the woman or upon some animal: e.g., he will bring along a live chicken, a duck, a rabbit, or a dog and decapitate it in her presence. And then only can he be excited to complete the sexual act. In these cases coitus is only performed when accompanied by acts of horrid cruelty, or murder after its completion. The awful murders of "Jack the Ripper," in Clerkenwell, London, can be accounted for only on this theory.

Subjects like Alice Mitchell, who come under the classification of "Urnings," are all given to cruelties to the lower animals. This seems to have been the case with her, as proved by the evidence at the trial. These facts are all unpleasant matters to deal with, but they were germane in dealing with this young woman, and they are verified by numerous cases quoted in the authoritative work of Krafft-Ebing, extending through 432 pages. It is a sad truth that the existence of sexual perverts is of frequent occurrence, especially among the upper class of society. Some months since we saw in the newspapers an account of some scandalous acts (of *pædicatio, vel cinædi,* [pederasty]) that occurred in Cavendish Square, London. They were reported in the *Pall Mall Gazette* and were of such a nature as to be unfit for publication. But what was most remarkable, the newspapers stated that princelings of royal blood and other aristocratic profligates were named as not merely participators, but the instigators and principal actors in the horrible practices. For the "good of society" and for "State reasons" legal inquiry in the Cavendish Square scandals was suspended. Sexual perverts readily recognize each other, although they may have never met before, and there exists a mysterious bond of psychological sympathy between them. Instances have been authenticated to me where such perverts when meeting another of the same sex, have at once recognized each other, and mutually become acquainted and have left in company with each other to practice together their unnatural vices. I am informed by an expert in nervous diseases, that in New York, upon the elevated railroad, these perverts travel and frequently meet others of the same sex, and leave the cars in order to be in each other's private company. Dr. Moll, in Berlin, has recently written upon the same subject as Krafft-Ebing's. Moll says he knows personally, and from authentic evidence, that there are 400 sexual perverts in Berlin, and he has reason to believe that there are half as many more. He says that they frequently consort together in localities prearranged. They meet also in certain restaurants in Berlin, and he states that the same custom exists in Paris.

The sexual function and passion are not to be trifled with. For it is nothing less than the keystone of society, and plays a rôle in forensic medicine. Horace said, "Lust, long before the time of Helen, was the dismal cause of war." The practices of sexual perverts I have alluded to, but they can not be described—they are fit to be studied only by competent medical men. These individuals are naturally objects of disgust to the laity, but in a professional man they excite the deepest sympathy. We have known many cases, sad to say, among the ministers of the Gospel—in high places—who were perverts, and one case not long since in the medical profession. Some of the most unnatural crimes that are chronicled in the newspapers result from mental aberrations that affect the sexual system. And again, the practice of a neurotic vice will intensify delusions and insanity in sexual perverts.

Among such persons, Krafft-Ebing mentions manustupration [masturbation], paedicatio mulierum, sapphism, libidinous constupration with intense violence and the killing of their victims, sadismus and masochismus are frequently practiced. Among sexual perverts, jealousy is always a prominent passion, and Alice Mitchell's separation from Freda Ward seems to have excited the most intense jealousy and the fire of this passion at the time burning in her breast was a motive for her to commit the homicide. The sexual relations of the human race are indeed mysterious, and when practiced in any unnatural manner, Nature will certainly avenge herself upon the offender. Mental disturbance and insanity will often follow.

The case of Alice Mitchell will be instanced for a long period hence as *un cas célebre,* and we feel that the verdict of the jury declaring that she was insane was just and proper. The relation of insanity to perverted sexuality is one of the most delicate matters that the physician has to treat, and it can be readily appreciated that in such cases the advice of experts and specialists in medical jurisprudence should be sought. Our mental organization and its workings are something that we can not entirely fathom, but the safety of society requires us to guard with constant care all persons who are in any way mentally irresponsible.

If the mind is derailed, self-control is lost and the
ated may not only endanger his own life, but may b
Physically, Alice Mitchell was a woman but psyc.
those of a male, and still her preferences, like ot.
sex. All this came from an abnormal neuro-psychic
lieve, was inherited. The insanity of her mother was
and that the mother was deranged before the birth, a
the delivery, is a legitimate reason for placing the daug.
not responsible for the dreadful murder which she comn
a case of sexual perversion from hereditary taint, and was
unnatural practices—primitive degenerative insanity; thoug
conjecture, as there was nothing of the kind elicited by the
such cases is more liable to be transmitted from mother to ot.
sex than to any male issue. This case of Alice Mitchell, not only t
pervert, and to the afflicted family whose daughter was so ruthl
and to society in general is indeed sad, and must cast its dark sh
wide. To the medical profession it suggests more thorough and e
mental disease. Addison once said: "Babylon in ruins is not so affecting
or so solemn as a human mind overthrown by lunacy." Publius Syrus sai
animi sananda magis quam corporis"—"Mental diseases demand of the
more attention than those of the body." So in ancient times mental maladie
considered more important to treat than somatic diseases.

> "Each thing's a feeling and a thought
> Within my soul divinely wrought;
> All this, created and combined,
> Compose my universe—my mind."

*T. Griswold Comstock, Ph.D., MD.*

Comstock, T. Griswold. 1892. "Alice Mitchell of Memphis. A Case of Sexual Perversion or 'Urning' (a Paranoiac)." *N. Y. Medical Times*, September 20, 170–173.

Duggan, Lisa. 2000. *Sapphic Slashers: Sex, Violence, and American Modernity*. Durham, NC: Duke University Press.

Krafft-Ebing, Richard von. 1886. *Psychopathia Sexualis: Eine klinische-forensische Studie*. 1st ed. Stuttgart: Ferdinand Enke.

---

## Sexual Inversion in Men (1896)

*Havelock Ellis (1859–1939) was a pioneering British sexologist. His monumental seven-volume work,* Studies in the Psychology of Sex *(1897–1927), explored the full range of human sexuality, including masturbation, cross-dressing, and female eroticism. The first volume of the series,* Sexual Inversion *(1897), was written with John Addington Symonds, a well-known man of letters and a secret homosexual. Upon its publication in Britain,* Sexual Inversion *was the object of an infamous indecency trial. Its bookseller was charged with*

*eeking to vitiate and corrupt the morals of the liege subjects of our Lady the Queen . . . and to raise and create in them lustful desires, and to bring the liege subjects into a state of wickedness, lewdness, and debauchery."* The bookseller pleaded guilty, and the book was banned in Britain. Even in the United States, its sale was restricted to doctors until the 1930s (Grosskurth 1980). Although Ellis was influenced by the theory of degeneracy and presented homosexuality as abnormal, he argued that inverts were not psychopathic and deserved greater social tolerance. His surprisingly enlightened stance for the time was undoubtedly influenced by his friendship with many talented British homosexuals and his marriage to a lesbian novelist and women's liberation activist, Edith Lees. Ellis was not given to complicated classification systems or theories of causation. But he was a keen, empathic listener and recorder of his subjects—and often included their first-person accounts in his work. His sympathy is evident in an article on sexual inversion published in the United States the year before Sexual Inversion appeared (briefly) in Great Britain.

The classification of the varieties of inversion is still a matter of some difficulty. While some authorities are inclined to regard all cases as acquired, others regard nearly every case as really congenital. . . . I regard acquired inversion as rare. . . . The determination of the congenital or acquired nature of a particular case of inversion is frequently by no means so easy as many persons who dogmatically lay down the law on one side or the other seem to believe. The case must first be presented to us in much greater fullness than we are accustomed to get it. . . . When we are able to investigate our cases with due fullness and precision I think it will be found that in many cases we may fairly call acquired there is a congenital element, and that in many cases we may fairly call congenital, some accident of environment has had an influence in developing latent tendency. . . .

I do not propose to adopt any more complex classification than the clinical distinction between simple inversion and psychosexual hermaphroditism as it is usually called; the first class including all those individuals who are sexually attracted only to their own sex, the second class those who are attracted to both sexes. . . .

### Simple Inversion

Case VI.—My parentage is very sound and healthy. Both my parents (who belong to the professional middle class) have good general health; nor can I trace any marked abnormal or diseased tendency, of mind or body, in any records of the family.

Though of a strongly nervous temperament myself, and sensitive, my health is good. I am not aware of any tendency to physical disease. In early manhood, however, owing, I believe, to the great emotional tension under which I lived, my nervous system was a good deal shattered and exhausted. Mentally and morally my nature is pretty well balanced, and I have never had any serious perturbations in these departments.

At the age of eight or nine, and long before distinct sexual feelings declared themselves, I felt a friendly attraction towards my own sex, and this developed after the age of puberty into a passionate sense of love, which, however, never found any expression for itself till I was fully 20 years of age. I was a day border at

school and heard little of school talk on sex subjects, was very reserved and modest besides; no elder person or parent ever spoke to me on such matters; and the passion for my own sex developed itself gradually, utterly uninfluenced from the outside. I never even during all this period and till a good deal later, learned the practice of masturbation. My own sexual nature was a mystery to me.

I found myself cut off from the understanding of others, felt myself an outcast, and with a highly loving and clinging temperament was intensely miserable. I thought about my male friends—sometimes boys of my own age, sometimes elder boys, and once even a master—during the day and dreamed about them at night, but was too convinced that I was a hopeless monstrosity ever to make any effectual advances. Later on it was much the same, but gradually, though slowly, I came to find that there were others like myself. I made a few special friends and at last it came to me occasionally to sleep with them and to satisfy my imperious need by mutual embraces and emissions. Before this happened, however, I was once or twice on the brink of despair and madness with repressed passion and torment.

Meanwhile, from the first, my feeling, physically, towards the female sex was one of indifference, and later on, with the more special development of sex desires, one of positive repulsion. Though having several female friends, whose society I like and to whom I am sincerely attached, the thought of marriage or cohabitation with any such has always been odious to me.

As a boy, I was attracted in general by boys rather older than myself; after leaving school I still fell in love, in a romantic vein, with comrades of my own standing. Now—at the age of 37—my ideal of love is a powerful strongly built man of my own age or rather younger—preferably of the working class. Though having solid sense and character, he need not be specially intellectual. If endowed in the latter way, he must not be too glib or refined. Anything effeminate in a man, or anything of the cheap intellectual style repels me very decisively.

I have never had to do with paederasty, so-called. My chief desire in love is bodily nearness or contact, as to sleep naked with a naked friend; the specially sexual, though urgent enough, seems a secondary matter. Paederasty, either active or passive, might seem in place to me with one I loved very devotedly and who also loved me to that degree—but I think not otherwise. I am an artist by temperament and choice, fond of all beautiful things, especially the male human form, of active slight muscular build, and sympathetic but somewhat indecisive character, though possessing self-control. I cannot regard my sexual feelings as unnatural or abnormal, since they have disclosed themselves so perfectly naturally and spontaneously within me. All that I have read in books or heard spoken about the ordinary sexual love, its intensity and passion, life-long devotion, love at first sight, etc., seems to me to be easily matched by my own experiences in the homosexual form; and with regard to the morality of this complex subject, my feeling is that it is the same as should prevail in love between man and woman—namely, that no bodily satisfaction should be sought at the cost of another person's distress or degradation. I am sure that this kind of love is, notwithstanding the physical difficulties that attend it, as deeply stirring and ennobling as the other kind, if not more so; and that I think that for a perfect relationship the actual sex gratifications (whatever they may be) probably hold a less important place in this love than in the other. . . .

## Psychosexual Hermaphroditism

This is the somewhat awkward name given to that form of inversion in which there exists a sexual attraction to both sexes. It is decidedly less common than simple inversion. We are only justified in including within this group those persons who find sexual pleasure and satisfaction both with men and with women, but in more than one of the following cases the homosexual is more powerful than the heterosexual instinct, and it is possible that these should really be regarded as cases of simple inversion. We have to remember that there is every inducement for the sexual invert to cultivate a spurious attraction to the opposite sex. In one case (XXII) the heterosexual instinct seems to have been acquired; in another, however, (XXIII) the homosexual instinct is apparently acquired.

Case XXII.—So far as is known he is hereditarily healthy on both ancestral sides.

He dates his homosexual desires from puberty. Between the ages of 16 and 20 he practised masturbation to excess. He has never felt much attraction towards women except in one case which ended (at the age of 25) in marriage. He finds marriage satisfactory on the whole but is not enthusiastic about it.

He is an artist, of good physique but highly nervous. He is sympathetic, very imaginative, regarded by his friends as a simple and beautiful nature somewhat lacking in strength.

Between the ages of 16 and 23 he had many love affairs, mostly with boys, but in one or two cases with older men. Since marriage there have been none of at all a serious character. He has in no case practised *paedicatio* [anal sex].

He regards sexual inversion as in all respects on the same level as normal sexuality.

Case XXIII.—Age 30, a brain-worker, of moderate physique and nervous temperament, not well balanced, rather passionate and jealous but thoroughly good-natured. Both parents of healthy stock, so far as is known.

He practised masturbation to a slight extent about the age of puberty. From the age of 15 or 16 he was strongly attracted to women, and had a constant succession of small love affairs culminating in a violent one which ended in disappointment. He was then twenty years of age. A few months later the homosexual instinct first showed itself, spontaneously, without any assignable cause. For about a year the normal instinct disappeared, but reappeared and still continues. His homosexual feeling is only for one person and the passion has continued, though not at the white heat of the first year or so, for ten years. His erotic dreams are about males.

He cannot afford to marry but otherwise would probably do so.

He has had no sexual relationship with his friend, although the impulse is very strong. He has been restrained, partly by fear of offence to the other person's feelings and partly by personal scruples. He used to have a horror of such threats both in his own case and that of others. He has got over this but still looks on it as doubtful, while freely confessing his own infatuation in this one case.

. . .

Case XXVI.—Englishman, independent means, aged 52, married.

His ancestry is of a complicated character. Some of his mother's forefathers in the last and earlier centuries are supposed to have been inverted.

He remembers liking the caresses of his father's footmen when he was quite a little boy. He dreams indifferently about men and women and has strong sexual feeling for women. Can copulate but does not insist on this act; there is a tendency to refined voluptuous pleasure. He has been married for many years and there are several children of the marriage.

He is not particular about the class or age of the men he loves. He feels with regard to older men as a woman does, and likes to be caressed by them. He is immensely vain of his physical beauty; he shuns *paedicatio* and does not much care for the sexual act, but likes long hours of voluptuous communion during which his lover admires him. He feels the beauty of boyhood. At the same time he is much attracted by young girls.

He is decidedly feminine in his dress, manner of walking, love of scents, ornaments and fine things. His body is excessively smooth and white, the hips and buttocks rounded. Genital organs normal. His temperament is feminine, especially in vanity, irritability and petty preoccupations. He is much preoccupied with his personal appearance and fond of admiration; on one occasion he was photographed naked as Bacchus. He is physically and morally courageous. He has a genius for poetry and speculation with a tendency to mysticism.

He feels the discord between his love for men and society, also between it and his love for his wife. He regards it as in part, at least, hereditary and inborn in him.

Herewith I conclude this series of cases. That it may not be desirable to multiply the records of such cases I most willingly admit. But inasmuch as—if we put aside my own paper on inversion in women published in this journal last year—not a single British case of inversion, outside asylums and prisons, seems yet to have been brought forward, it was clearly desirable to illustrate an unrecorded aspect of this psychic abnormality. I do not here enter into any general considerations regarding the nature of sexual inversion, since I have elsewhere done so. . . . Certain remarks concerning the treatment of sexual inversion, and also concerning the attitude of the law towards this perversion, I hope to publish on some future occasion.

*Havelock Ellis*

Ellis, Havelock. 1896. "Sexual Inversion in Men." *Alienist and Neurologist* 17: 115–150.
Grosskurth, Phyllis. 1980. *Havelock Ellis: A Biography.* New York: Knopf.

---

## Effeminate Men and Masculine Women (1900)

*Doctor William Lee Howard of Baltimore, Maryland, had written two brief medical articles on sexual perversion (1896) and psychosexual hermaphroditism (1897) before publishing the following essay. He encapsulates the fin-de-siècle anxieties concerning the rise of feminism and its anticipated impact on society and sexuality.*

Weak physiological traits, like moral traits, can be increased or decreased by education, training, and example. Environment plays a most active and powerful role in this development. The child born of parents in the prime of physiological life, each one having strong sex characteristics, is apt to show these characteristics in its development and growth, regarding its environment and education. But not so the unfortunate child born of unstable parents; of those who have assumed the responsibility of parentage when life is on the wane, or whose physical or mental activities have been in channels far removed from anticipation and thoughts of married life. Such parents belong to the physiologically degenerate class. They forget that the tendency is, in all animal life, to degenerate rather than improve. This goes on, generation after generation, unless care is exercised to introduce improved blood on one side or the other.

When a child demonstrates in its acts and tastes an indifference to the natural preference and inclination of its sex, it should be strictly confined to the companionship of that sex. Its education should be along the same lines, and every encouragement given it to develop its normal attributes. An indifferent boy who grows up an effeminate man should be allowed to share the ridicule and contempt thrust upon him with his parents, the mother being given the major part. This same mother, who shields her son from physical harm, will bring him up in the nursery with embroidery; take the poor creature, dressed up in linens and velvet, to exhibit him to female admirers; shift him off to the nursery of her hostess, where he is left to dress dolls and have his hair curled by the female attendants, and sit down to a make-believe tea party with his little girl playmates.

He grows up psychically unsexed, detested by the vigorous male, utilized as a willing servitor by the society woman, and sternly admonished by a true father if he finds him dancing attendance with all his mincing manners upon a daughter. The female with masculine ambition is always amusing and often pitiable; but the attenuated, weak-voiced neuter, the effeminate male: pity him, but blame his mother for the false training and give scorn to the father for his indifference. Even the woman, when she meets such a man, should passionately and involuntarily exclaim: "O! surgit amari aliquid."

The female possessed of masculine ideas of independence; the viragint who would sit in the public highways and lift up her pseudo-virile voice, proclaiming her sole right to decide questions of war or religion, or the value of celibacy and the curse of woman's impurity, and that disgusting antisocial being, the female pervert, are simply different degrees of the same class—degenerates. These unsightly and subnormal beings are the victims of poor mating. When a woman neglects her maternal instincts, when her sentiment and dainty feminine characteristics are boldly and ostentatiously kept submerged, we can see an antisocial creature more amusing than dangerous. When such a woman marries, which she often does for the privileges derived from attaching Mrs. to her name, the husband is certain to be one she can rule, govern, and cause to follow her in voice and action. Should this female be unfortunate enough to become a mother, she ceases to be merely amusing, and is an antisocial being. She is then a menace to civilization, a producer of nonentities, the mother of mental and physical monstrosities who exist as a class of true degenerates until disgusted Nature, no longer tolerant of the woman who would be a man, or the man who would be a woman, allows them to shrink unto death.

The female who prefers the laboratory to the nursery; the mother quick with child who spends her mornings at the club, discussing "social statics," visiting the saloons and tenements in the afternoon, distributing, with an innocence in strange contrast to her assumptions, political tracts asking the denizens to vote her ticket, is a sad form of degeneracy. Such females are true degenerates, because they are unphysiological in their physical incompleteness. The progeny of such human misfits are perverts, moral or psychical. Their prenatal life has been influenced by the very antithesis of what the real woman would surround her expected child with. The child born of the "new woman" is to be pitied. If it could be taken away from its environments, kept from the misguidance of an unwilling mother, nurtured, tutored, and directed along the sex line Nature has struggled to give it, often would the child be true to its latent normal instincts and grow to respected womanhood or manhood. Unfortunate it is that this development does not take place. The weak, plastic, developing cells of the brain are twisted, distorted, and a perverted psychic growth promoted by the false examples and teachings of a discontented mother. These are the conditions which have been prolific in producing the antisocial "new woman" and the disgusting effeminate male, both typical examples of the physiological degenerate.

It is this class that clamors for "higher education" for the woman that crowds public halls, shouting for the freedom of woman and demanding all the prerogative of the man. It is these female androids who are insulated in the dark umbrage of ignorance and delusion regarding their negative nature, who are faddist, "ism"-ites, and mental roamers. Ideally mobile, they go from the laboratory to the convent, ever restless, continuously discontented, morbidly majestic at periods, hysterically forcible at times. They form sects and societies regardless of sense or science.

They demonstrate their early perverted mental growth by their present lack of reasoning powers. They form the victims of shrewder degenerates. They claim to know more about the science of medicine without study than the men who have devoted their lives to that science. They walk broadcast, superciliously flaunting our health laws and hygienic regulations in the faces of the assumed intelligent masses, and shout their incomprehensible jargon and blasphemous voicings from the portals of their money-making mosques.

*William Lee Howard*

Howard, William Lee. 1900. "Effeminate Men and Masculine Women." *N. Y. Medical Journal* 21: 504–505.

---

## Homo Sexual Complexion Perverts in St. Louis: Note on a Feature of Sexual Psychopathy (1907)

*Charles H. Hughes was a prominent St. Louis physician and the editor of* Alienist and Neurologist *(a leading journal of psychiatry and neurology) at the time he published the following article. He betrays a widespread concern not just with the increasing visibility of homosexuality, but also with a variety of simultaneous historical preoccupations: gender confusion, miscegenation, African American migration after the Civil War, urbanization, and modernity. He expresses a commonly held belief that homosexuality was* less *common among blacks (and other races considered "primitive") than whites because perversion was supposedly a product of civilized luxury and degeneration. Other doctors asserted the opposite, that "primitive" people were* more *perverse because they lacked a civilized moral sense.*

Male negroes masquerading in woman's garb and carousing and dancing with white men is the latest St. Louis record of neurotic and psychopathic sexual perversion. Some of them drove to the levee dive and dance hall at which they were arrested in their masters' auto cars. All were gowned as women at the miscegenation dance and the negroes called each other feminine names. They were all arrested, taken before Judge Tracy and gave bond to appear for trial, at three hundred dollars each, signed by a white man.

The detectives say that the levee resort at which these black perverts were arrested is a rendezvous for scores of west end butlers, cooks and chauffeurs. Apartments in the house are handsomely furnished and white men are met there. The names of these negro perverts, their feminine aliases and addresses appear in the press notices of their arrest, but the names of the white degenerates consorting with them are not given.

Social reverse complexion homosexual affinities are rarer than non reverse color affinities, yet even white women sometimes prefer colored men to white men and vice versa. Homosexuality may be found among blacks, though this phase of sexual perversion is not so common or at least has not been so recorded, as between white males or white females. I have recorded but one male instance in my own personal observation, [specifically,] that of gentleman George, for a time a valet and later a cook who loved to masquerade in woman's attire including bonnet and shoes and could never be induced to wear any shoe but a woman's soft gaiter and who had pierced ears for rings and wore the latter at times when not laughed at too much and when they were not in pawn, for he was impecunious and easily victimized by peddlers from whom he would buy chromo pictures, mantel clocks, rings and women's combs and ornamental trinkets at fabulous unfair prices.

George's peculiar predeliction [*sic*] was for white men. He would say he "had no use for niggers" though he made his home for awhile with an aged and kindly colored woman acquaintance who trusted him for board when out of funds.

George had many foolish ways and dress propensities for a man, such as preferring a chemise for a night shirt. He had a right inguinal scrotal hernia requiring the constant wearing of a truss though he was exceedingly careless about this and suffered frequent pain because thereof, requiring my assistance. He had normal appearing masculine genitalia and could have raised a slight beard and mustache though he kept himself closely shaven, he wore his hair long though its growth was rather scant.

A Moll, Krafft-Ebing, Havelock Ellis or Kiernan [prominent sexologists] might find material in St. Louis for further contributions to their studies of reverse sexual instinct. The contraire sexual empfingdung [contrary sexual feeling] has had other illustrations here. St. Louis has duplicated the woman stabber of Berlin since she set her mark at a million inhabitants. These perverted creatures appear to be features of million peopled cities and they come into the light, if the police are vigilant. The reverse erotopath abounds among the nerve center degraded as well as the insistent and persistent erotopath of cliteromania or satyriac imperative propulsion.

Note.—These St. Louis negro perverts gave feminine names that might be-long to English or American ladies of any city. The curious may find them and the names the blacks assumed at the record office of the police courts.

*Charles H. Hughes*

Hughes, Charles H. 1907. "Homo Sexual Complexion Perverts in St. Louis." *Alienist and Neurologist* 28: 487–488.

---

## The Psychology of the Acute Homosexual Panic (1921)

*Although the connection between paranoia and homosexual desires had been suggested by Sigmund Freud in 1911, Dr. Edward Kempf formulated the specific concept of "homosexual panic" in 1921. He derived it from his experience with psychotic military personnel. In Chapter 10 of his textbook* Psychopathology, *Kempf illustrated the concept with numerous case examples. These demonstrate the characteristic psychoanalytic style of interpretation of patient symptoms, always returning to the core dynamic of repressed homosexual desire, especially "oral eroticism" (for example, fellatio). Kempf argued that recovery depended on the patient acknowledging these unconscious homosexual desires but then* not *giving in to them.*

The mechanism of the homosexual panic (panic due to the pressure of un-controllable perverse sexual cravings) is of the utmost importance in psy-chopathology, because of the frequency of its occurrence wherever men or women must be grouped alone for prolonged periods, as in army camps, aboard ships, on exploring expeditions, in prisons, monasteries, schools and asylums.

The perverse sexual craving threatens to overcome the *ego,* the individual's self-control, because the affections for winning social esteem have been pushed into an eccentric adjustment. The weakness of the *ego* is usually due to fatigue, debilitat-ing fevers, loss of a love-object, misfortunes, homesickness, the seductive pressure of some superior, or erotic companions. As the individual tends to become eccen-tric and irritable he is teased and goaded by his associates. He then loses his social influence and develops a feeling of being inferior and disrespected. . . .

A series of cases is here presented to show that the cause of the *anxiety* and *panic* is the uncontrollable, perverted segmental craving struggling with the social-ized affective cravings, the *ego,* in the same personality. The latter can only acquire gratification by doing the things that win social esteem. They constitute the ego and are spoken of as "I," "me," "myself." Naturally, when the sexual cravings can not be controlled they become disowned by the ego as a foreign influence, and the ideas and visions, or sensations they cause, are treated as being, due to a foreign in-fluence. Hence, when another individual, whose characteristics happen to coincide with the conditioned needs of the dissociated sexual cravings, thereby stimulating them, comes into the patient's environment, the patient feels he is being "hypno-tized." Often such men and women attack the innocent person or yield to the hal-lucinated assault; or even do both. When the patient says someone is "throwing voices" into his head, making him hear voices or have visions, making him have a peculiar taste in his mouth, putting poison in his food, shooting electricity into his body, hypnotizing him, going to kill, crucify, initiate him, or make him join a society or religion, or steal his manhood, etc., it has been found that *the patient is telling the physician that he has lost control of his sexual cravings which are forcing him to offer himself as a sexual object.* When the patient insists that a certain person is performing this mysterious ritual or power over him, it may be accepted that in some manner this particular person is either sexually attractive to him or is very intimately associated with someone who is sexually attractive.

The prognosis of such cases, it seems, depends largely upon *the extent of the defensive systematization of the delusions, and whether or not the patient is reacting with hatred. The presence of hatred should always be considered as dangerous under such conditions and almost sure to prevent the development of insight.*

The true significance of "poison" in the food was a riddle until the following patient showed us that it probably, usually, meant *semen.* A further careful investigation of the meaning of "poison," "filth," "dope," "drugs," "stuff," "something in the food," "cream," "powder," "saltpeter," in a series of over 200 cases, established the probability that in every instance in which a patient seriously complains that *food* has a mysterious, or hypnotic, or erotic influence upon him, it is due to the fact that the food acts as the stimulus of pernicious oral erotic cravings. This insight naturally has led us through a simple approach to the very foundations of the patient's emotional cravings and the heretofore obscure causes of this type of psychosis.

We have found that the patients who can be influenced to quit fighting the recognition of oral erotic cravings—this does not mean submission to them—fare better than the patients who struggle desperately to *eliminate* them and attack everything that arouses the craving.

In order to make it unnecessary to refer again to the facts that explain the meaning of "poison," etc., in the food, or of impulsive suicidal assaults upon the head, mouth and throat, or of swallowing extraneous material, the reader is asked to note particularly the factor of oral, homosexual eroticism and the delusions about being persecuted for having such perverse cravings in the following series of cases.

Case PD-13 was an egotistical, taciturn, rather well-built, but undersized, German, with small features, and lips which were tightly compressed into a cynical, indulgent smile. He was twenty-eight and unmarried when admitted to the hospital. He had never been able to adapt himself comfortably to any society and had attended school irregularly, had a poor education, was fond of playing truant, and frequently was arrested for vagrancy, serving two sentences of thirty days and one of six months. He worked in bicycle-repair shops and at similar odd jobs, until he was twenty-four, but was unable to submit to the dictations of an employer feeling that it referred to some inferiority. . . .

He was inclined to brood, made no friends, was very seclusive and sullen. He felt that his companions talked about him and avoided him because they thought he was "a silent worker." (He meant homosexually oral-erotic.)

At twenty-eight, his feelings of persecution due to the repressed eroticism assumed the proportions of a *pernicious repression compensation neurosis* or paranoid psychosis. He became more seclusive and would talk to no one, feeling himself to be regarded as "no good in the army." He fancied that "*broken pills*" had been put into his pudding and coffee, and complained of this as mistreatment. He said that at one time he acted as if he was asleep and heard his companions make such remarks about him as "fluter," "silent worker," "start him working," "he will be in Washington in the insane hospital soon."

He was finally confined in the Post hospital because he was suspected of taking money from a store-till. A few weeks later he was sent to St. Elizabeth's Hospital at Washington D.C.

The mental examination showed no actual impairment. He was well oriented, understood his environment, his memory was accurate, and he easily passed the special intelligence tests. The physical examination revealed no organic inferiorities.

His psychosis seemed entirely to be constituted of a struggle with intense homosexual cravings. He believed that he had been sent to this hospital as a punishment and that the men here regarded him to be a sexual pervert. His auditory hallucinations, accusing him of homosexual desires, worried him continually. He believed the accusations were made by other patients and isolated himself accordingly. He was depressed and at times wept bitterly. At other times he was quite indignant and threatening. He walked erectly, held his head up, and looked defiantly at his physicians and associates. He usually smiled in a very tolerant, superior, self-satisfied manner as if he knew something that made him superior to most men.

He complained mostly about the food, and was fed with difficulty. "They" put pills and powder in his coffee; it was "ground up so that it would dissolve." He said the milk in the coffee was "*too thick.*" "*It was not cream, it was too fat.*" His ideas about the coffee were very similar to the ideas he entertained at the army post. A few days later he cautiously revealed his true feelings about the pills in his coffee at the army post. This was told with mingled embarrassment, weeping, and affectionate smiling. The questions had to be guardedly phrased so as not to offend him or lose his confidence. He finally revealed his craving for the ingredients and that it made him "feel better," relieving his depression. He said the coffee and pudding contained something "*richer than cream, richer than milk.*" It would make him "feel hot" when he ate it and he had to open "two windows" to "cool off." He added, in his discussion of this that later he had to go to the toilet but could not pass feces because "it was too hard." (Two windows evidently referred to two orifices; in order "to cool off " to be relieved—namely, oral or anal. An erotic woman begged for cold water because she was "hot.")

He would not say definitely what this coffee contained but felt sure it made him "dream off." His smiles and tendency to become affectionate when he described the "richer than cream" were unmistakably characteristic of the homosexual advance. (Such men can not be held morally responsible for having such autonomic cravings but they are responsible for their adjustments to them.) . . .

## Summary

The acute homosexual panic may well be considered a distinct stage in the psychoses. It may be diagnosed as readily as paresis by certain cardinal symptoms (1) panic and the autonomic reactions which accompany grave fear; (2) the defensive compensation against the compulsion to seek or submit to assault; (3) the symbols used by the erotic affect and the disturbances of sensation it causes. The latter are complained of as visions, voices, electric injections, "dopey" feelings, "poison" and "filth" in the food, seductive and hypnotic influences, irresistible trance states, crucifixion, etc. It is necessary to estimate the significance of the symptoms of panic in a neutral environment and the significance of the various symbols used.

The prognosis of a homosexual panic in a soldier or sailor is usually favorable for that episode, but the future of that individual is most insecure unless he obtains insight and a fortunate sexual adjustment. In a series of several hundred cases which have been recognized in the past six years, most of the cases recovered. The recurrence of panic, later, among men who secretly reenlisted in some branch of the government's service and were returned to St. Elizabeth's Hospital, as well as the return, several years later, of men who had profoundly deteriorated after having been discharged as social recoveries, shows that the recurrence of panic results from inability to control the tendency to become perverse, i.e., biologically abnormal. This abortive tendency seems eventually to become dominant and incurable and the chapters on the causes of variations in *chronic pernicious dissociation neuroses* or dementia praecox [schizophrenia] are composed of cases that are selected to show why one type becomes paranoid (compensates), another, catatonic or submits, and another, hebephrenic [disorganized schizophrenic], or another case may show attributes that indicate a tendency to cover the whole regressive cycle and not be distinctive of any of these classical divisions.

*Edward John Kempf*

Kempf, Edward John. 1921. *Psychopathology.* St. Louis: C. V. Mosby.

---

## The Biological Sport of Fairie-ism (1934)

*"Ralph Werther" was a student in New York City (perhaps Columbia University) in the 1890s and 1900s, when he began secretly frequenting the thriving homosexual life downtown. Writing under the pseudonyms Ralph Werther, Earl Lind, and Jennie June, he published a series of medical journal articles (1918, 1920, and 1934) and two books (1918 and 1922) recounting his life and documenting the complex sexual cultures in New York City (Chauncey 1994). Calling himself an "extreme androgyne," he focused on other "fairies" like himself: cruising queens, female impersonators, and cross-dressing prostitutes. Today, we might label fairies as transgenders or drag queens, but as historian George Chauncey points out, it is hard to match past and present sexual identities. Indeed, the fairies' sexual partners were generally not other homosexuals, but self-identified "normal," virile men.*

*Although Werther rejected Freudianism, his explanation of the fairy's psychic development relied on psychoanalytic theories—particularly about narcissism and arrested psychosexual development at the infantile oral stage. Yet he primarily insisted that inversion was a congenital, biological phenomenon present around the world and throughout history. He used the biological term "sport," which refers to natural variants or mutations in plants and animals. Ultimately, he relied on a Darwinian argument, that "fairie-ism" is just a sexual variant of nature. Although he pointed out that fairie-ism was just one of many manifestations of "sexual inversion," the image of the effeminate fairie was the medical stereotype of male homosexuality at the turn of the century and is still present in popular culture today. In the following article, originally written in 1920 for Dr. Victor Robinson, Werther also details the life course of a cohort of "girl-boys" from his native Connecticut town.*

*I*

As I myself have had an extensive experience as a fairie I think it wise to state at the outset that this line of conduct was not mine because of moral depravity, but because of irrepressible instinct, and that though my open career lasted twelve years, I made a gainful occupation of my propensities for only the nine weeks during which otherwise I would have been penniless. From the age of nineteen to thirty-one, obedience to these propensities was absolutely essential for living out the scholarly life that I was regularly privileged to do. With the exception of the nine weeks, I was properly described as only an *amateur* fairie. But during the one evening per week or fortnight that I surrendered to the life, my conduct was in general the same as that of my "sister" professional fairies.

Fairies are usually of slight build, with muscular system soft and inefficient, as in a woman. They are sometimes otherwise feminesque. That is, the hair on body and limbs may be sparse and decidedly tenuous. Their skin is unusually velvety to the touch. Their breasts are often full for a male. Their legs tend to be disproportionately short, and their backs disproportionately long, as in a woman.

Fairies are probably the abnormal possessor of the biochemical force or sexual electricity peculiar to the female sex. To this may be due the mutual attraction between themselves and tremendously virile males—the latter type of man being in general alone intimate with fairies.

Instead of shaving their faces, fairies commonly eradicate the beardal hair. The hair on the body and limbs is removed with razor. The object is to render the body more beautiful, and face more womanlike. The eradication of beard must be repeated every three to four weeks. Professionals sometimes have plates substituted for their front teeth.

Psychically fairies have always felt that they belong to the female sex. They always adopt feminine names during the periods that they are under the influence of the sexual movings. Particularly they borrow the names of star actresses. With the more cultured, it has been a lifelong regret that they were not born physical females, as well as psychic.

As to the age of professional fairies, one over thirty is almost unknown. Nearly all appear to be between eighteen and twenty-five. Their career must be confined to youth. But they retain the freshness, slenderness, and litheness of youth—what might be described as "the small-boy appearance"—an abnormally long time, at least until the age of thirty. They are like women in that they have little tendency to baldness.

In addition to their feminesque anatomy and psyche, fairies are inclined to infantilism, both physical and mental. For example, the shape of the skull or face is sometimes that of an infant. The pudenda are inclined to be infantile, and not at all erectile in contact *cum femina* [with women]. On the psychic side, they are fond of being held on the lap, addressed by pet names, and otherwise babied by the ultra-virile into whose society they naturally gravitate. Their infantilism is further manifest in extreme cowardice—even being afraid in their teens to fire off a toy revolver, to play baseball for fear of getting hit, and screaming at nothing—and in their being easily moved to tears.

To sum up the natural endowment of fairies: they are not merely humans with a female soul in a male body, but they have, from the sexual point of view, never grown out of babyhood. Their craze for fellatio is only the abnormal survival through adulthood of the infant's feeding instinct.

They appear to be cousins to the morons. In some respects, they remain childlike through life, although unlike morons, some of them are able to profit by a high-school or even university education. They are nevertheless an instance of arrest of development. It is claimed that this arrest is caused in some way by the interstitial glands, and that a remedy for their effeminacy lies in an operation on these glands.

As to the frequency of fairie-ism, I estimate that the raw material—that is, the congenital girl-boys or androgynes—is, throughout the world, one to every three hundred physical males. The writer has resided in fifteen different civilized countries, and in many of these countries has explored the underworlds of the great cities. The conditions as to fairies are about the same in all civilized countries. For fairie-ism is not due to example or moral degradation, but entirely to Mother Nature.

At the dawning of adolescence, either because afflicted with congenital psychic nymphomania, or because thrown into intimate contact with a band of tremendously virile young bachelors, about one girl-boy out of every ten becomes extensively promiscuous—in other words a fairie. The degree of effeminacy varies with every girl-boy. Only in cases of extreme effeminacy do they become fairies. Some girl-boys are naturally almost devoid of the libido peculiar to girl-boys. Such may never be guilty of carnality. There are not two girl-boys exactly alike in their sexual tastes and propensities. Just as there are not two normal men or two normal women exactly alike. Variety is infinite in sex.

That is, after having myself had one of the most active careers as a fairie for twelve years in a number of different countries in numerous great cities, after having all these years been particularly observant of this phenomenon because it appeared in myself in high degree, and being myself at the same time something of a philosopher and scientist as a result of a university training and a score of years in professional life, my guess is that throughout Christendom, one out of every three thousand physical males is consigned by birth or by circumstances to a fairie career from puberty up to about the age of thirty.

Fairies may be divided into high-class and low-class. The former are for the most part recruited from the middle-class of society and have at least a grammar-school education, and rarely a high-school. As a rule, the high-class fairies are decided aesthetes. In embellishment of both their dress and their living apartments, most people would judge that they go to extremes.

The author is the only university graduate he himself has encountered in the ranks of intensive fairies. But he has been acquainted with a number of such graduates who were addicted to fellatio with one or two trusted ultra-virile friends. The combination of high intellectuality with the frivolousness of the fairie is perhaps unique in the case of the present author.

High-class fairies may again be subdivided into inmates of houses of ill fame [brothels], and the independent street-walkers. The latter always promenade the same blocks frequented by genuinely female street walkers. For about eighteen months in the last decade of the nineteenth century, the writer promenaded the Fourteenth Street bright-light district about one evening a week. Subsequently he promenaded the Bowery off and on for over two years.

On the street, fairies dress in a flashy manner, so as to be easily recognized by their prey—the tremendously virile, toward whom, I have said, they gravitate.

Particularly a red neck bow is the special badge of a fairie. Only a handful of the more rash fairies appear on the street in feminine apparel.

The low-class type were born and brought up in the slums and are much inferior in intelligence—not to say culture. While the high-class are subject to spells of acute melancholia in the realization of their condition of being misunderstood by their sexually normal fellows, and being pariahs, and from time to time even resort to suicide, the low-class fairie is perfectly contented with the niche in life which Mother Nature intended "him-her" to fill.

Low-class fairies are likely to be deeply depraved. But this depravity has supervened upon their congenital effeminacy, and is something separate and apart. While this non-sexual depravity is for the most part willful, they should receive mercy at the hands of the law because they are victims of a congenital maladjustment to Nature's plan for human reproduction, as well as victims of environment and irresponsible ignorance. Their instinctive sexual reactions do not properly lie within the realm of morality or of criminality so far as not exercised to the detriment of any other human being, or to the degree of seriously undermining their own health.

As to the charge that fairies are guilty of the dreadful crime of race suicide—that charge is a mere superstition. The numbers of the human race were never depleted by a single soul by reason of the fairies' instinctive functioning. The reason is that the adolescent roués [debauchees]—who constitute almost entirely the fairies' clientele—have not procreation as their object when they are out for a debauch. The only other alternatives for these roués are loose women or self manustupration [masturbation]. Procreation will begin only after they are through sowing their wild oats. It is too bad that such phenomena exist even in the very centers of culture. But that is the way humanity was created.

The fairies' method is generally fellatio, but often *paedicatio* [anal sex], and sometimes *inter femora* [between the thighs] or manustupration on the partner. Fairies find themselves at a great disadvantage through not being physical females. Because they wish their partners to treat them as females. With the author, fellatio was practically universal, although his partner changed over to the active role in *coitus in os* [oral sex]. As a rule, the term "sodomite" can not be applied to a fairie. Because they often abhor paedicatio.

In about one-half the instances, coitus is exceedingly painful for fairies. But their virile companion appears to them as a demigod. They are consumed with the desire to afford him keen pleasure, though it means for themselves simultaneous keen pain. They *love* their mates—in the highest sense of that word—as rarely women love men. The satisfaction that fairies—as well as androgynes in general—seek is to a very small extent physical, and almost entirely psychic. They pine to be only the slaves of the tremendously virile. But in the case of normal young men who are only mildly virile, there exists no mutual attraction with fairies.

Even in the last decade of the nineteenth century, when the writer was for years a street-walking fairie and a number of times came into conflict with the police, he found among most of them a correct understanding of fairie-ism. The stringent laws aimed at fairie-ism were even then a dead-letter to the police. Contrast with this the attitude of judges, lawyers, and a large proportion of physicians even in 1920. These intellectuals are still groping in the Dark Ages, and consider that inverts practice their perversions through choice and with deliberate disregard of public opinion! Even many of the medical profession cannot rise above their irrational horror for the union in one human body and the personality of distinctively male and female physical and psychic elements—such union as is exemplified in the bisexual fairie.

In all metropolises can be found the special resorts of fairies, which cater particularly to active pederasts—whose condition is also probably congenital. Fairies in these resorts are particularly fond of flaunting themselves entirely nude. Except for the chevelure, their forms are hairless (because depilated) and statuesque. Their faces and bodies are painted and powdered. Sometimes they are clad in loose wrappers, easily slipped off. Sometimes in full feminine attire. They feel more at home in that than in male garments. In these resorts, they now and then take their places in the center of the drinking parlor, locked in the arms of their ultra-virile wooers and perform dances such as were considered obscene a generation ago, but today grace even university receptions.

From time to time, a fairie takes "his-her" stand in the center of the room, and gives an impersonation of the cry-baby species of mademoiselle. It is a fairie's ambition and joy to mimic a budding woman. Most fairies are born actors, or "actresses," as they prefer to be called. Acting a part seems to have become second nature to them. Because from childhood, while psychically female, those brought up in the better social strata have been compelled to make-believe and act as if they were males in mind as well as body.

As already indicated, about ninety-five per cent of fairies' clientele are tremendously virile normal young men. To such of these as *coitus cum femina* [sex with women] is open, curiosity alone prompts just one experience with a fairie.

Less than two per cent are young or middle-aged *active* pederasts. These sexual intermediates are generally psychic hermaphrodites, being attracted normally toward the female sex, as well as toward male youths—either normal before the latter have outgrown the quasi-feminine physical traits of the boy or the girl-boy fairies, who tend to retain their boyishness of face and figure down to middle age.

Thirdly, less than two per cent consist of roués who are no longer potent normally, and seek in the fairie a new stimulus. The final class—likewise under two per cent—are rather young men, who, possibly from birth, have been incapable of full distention, and nevertheless are thoroughly masculine in psyche. The only method possible for them is to submit to fellatio. But their infirmity makes them bashful before female prostitutes. They therefore have recourse to a fairie.

There is no need for alarm on the part of moralists. History shows that practically identical conditions as to fairie-ism have existed since its very dawn, and nevertheless the human race has multiplied tremendously.

Since sexual intermediacy is a matter of birth, may not these intermediates be the handiwork of God? "What God hath cleansed, let no man call 'Unclean.'"


*II*


The term "androgyne" as here used is synonymous with "girl-boy" except that it includes adults as well as boy effeminants. The term has hitherto been confined to males who are physically feminesque, as well as psychically. The English language has never possessed a term other than "effeminant" to denote the girl-boy after becoming an adult. But the author prefers to stretch the meaning of "androgyne" so that it will cover all adult girl-boys. While some of them present no conspicuously feminine physical stigmata, nearly every adult girl-boy with whom the author has been acquainted—perhaps all—has decidedly lacked the full physical vigor of the virile man. It may be only an abnormally light and delicate skeletal system. For example, the author, even when in his late teens and possessing no adipose tissue, always floated on top of a stream without making the least motion. The normal slim boy has to make slight movement of the hands in order to float. Or the androgyne may possess the single feminine physical stigma of a woman's muscular system. Androgynes are as a rule less muscular than the average woman. I myself posses the female muscular system, as well as the light, delicate bony system of the female.

Going further, the only feminine physical stigma of an androgyne may be the skeletal shape (in addition to the skeletal structure). The author also possesses this; abnormally long spinal column, broad pelvis, and relatively short leg bones.

My observation has been that every adult androgyne differs from all others in respect to feminine physical stigmata. One may be naturally beardless; a second have only a spare growth of beard; a third have feminine breasts and milk glands (like the author); etc.

It is hardly necessary to explain that "androgyne" is the Greek for "man-woman." The converse term, "gynander," is the Greek for "woman-man" and is applied to the cognate biological sport—the individual possessing the female primary sexual determinants, but with the psyche masculesque, and with a tendency toward masculine conformation of parts of the body other than the genitalia.

Freud and other sexologists on the basis of inadequate data, have declared that sexual inversion is not congenital, but due to homosexual seduction by an older child in early life. I have probably made a more thorough study of male inversion than any sexologist—being myself an extreme androgyne, and having associated with androgynes more than has any one else who ever wrote for publication. I am emphatically of the opinion that the condition is practically always congenital. Only those whom birth placed on the very borderline between mild virility and homosexuality can be swung one way or the other by early sexual initiation. I am skeptical of a possible cure for pronounced inversion—even by the 1920 method of transplantation of glands. I myself exhausted in vain all the possible means of a cure thought of by alienists in the last decade of the nineteenth century.

I rejoice that the medical profession is just beginning to recognize that sexual inverts are not moral monsters meriting pariahdom, long prison terms, and even to be murdered by normally sexed prudes laboring under the delusion that they are doing society a service in ridding the world of these "monsters."

It is next to the impossible for even the medical profession to free themselves from the prejudices and superstitions inculcated in their boyhood.

A kind Providence has graciously granted the author nearly half-a-century of existence. His life experience—particularly on the sexual side—is a matter of memory rather than of present perception or of prospective enjoyment. Being thus a veteran androgyne, it has occurred to him to make a retrospect of individuals of his own type against whose canoes his own tiny shallop has happened to scrape while drifting across life's sea.

Every large city block and almost every hamlet of the world has its girl-boy. It has been my fate to pass part of my life in nearly every Christian country of the world, having over 10,000,000 inhabitants, and to mingle intimately with the inhabitants.

Because my specialty in the university happened to be modern languages, I acquired fair conversational ability in four European foreign languages. I explored the underworlds of some of the great cities of Europe as if I had been a native. I plied my instinctive avocation of fairie in them—as well as in several of the great cities of America. On the basis of these wide opportunities for observation, I estimate that throughout Christendom there exists at least one androgyne out of every three hundred possessors of the male primary sexual determinants.

Physicians possibly have not discovered them in such numbers. First, because prudery has kept the vast majority of the medical profession in absolute ignorance of the existence of this biological sport. These benighted physicians have therefore not noticed androgynes even when the latter were under their noses.

Secondly, androgynes hide their idiosyncrasies and secret practices as no other class of mankind. In order to avert suspicion, some, although never having had relations with woman, will boast to their every-day circle of excesses with that sex. At the same time they have a steady male sweetheart.

One can not rely on the average cultured androgyne's telling the truth about his own sexual nature. The reason for his deceitfulness is the irrational horror of the normally sexed for homosexuality, and the consequent acute fear of the cultured androgyne that he may be made a pariah, or even imprisoned or murdered, in case his sexual nature became known to his every-day circle.

Androgynes or passive inverts can be discovered only by careful observation, and in many cases be recognized only by those having an intimate knowledge of androgyne characteristics. Their sexual practices are nearly always unsuspected even by their parents and brothers and sisters. This is possible only because of the prevailing ignorance of the existence of sexual intermediates.

In a class of fifty boys in a school, there was one androgyne. In another class of forty, there were two. In a club of thirty young men there were two. In the best section of the village in which the writer was brought up—a section numbering 1,200 inhabitants, and with whose every child around his own age he was more or less acquainted—six girl-boys were known to him in his childhood. I was the only one on my own long block, on which about 120 people resided. One lived on each of three, neighboring blocks. The three others were schoolmates, and resided at more distant points.

The girl-boys of the community naturally drifted together. But they only walked and talked together after reaching their teens. Previously they only played girls' games with the girls.

Such is the picture of androgynism in the best section of a Connecticut village! To develop the picture further: The addiction to fellatio of these six girl-boys was common knowledge among the boys of the central school of the community. The number of boy pupils at any one time was about 150. Of only these six boys, (besides myself), during my several years attendance at this school, did I hear or perceive any indication of androgynism.

I ceased to reside in the village at the age of sixteen, but have visited it frequently down to my present age of nearly, half-a-century. Down through life, I have kept my eye closely on four of the six, who continue to reside in the village. The fifth committed suicide at the age of twelve, while the sixth moved out of my cognizance.

Three of these girl-boys, immediate on arrival at sexual maturity, became notorious among the young bloods of the village. I had a tremendously virile brother who continued to reside in the village and communicated to me the gossip among the young bloods about these androgynes. They continued to be fellators—as in early childhood.

With only one of the three was I intimately acquainted. Between the ages of fifteen and twenty, he was appointed by Mother Nature to the rôle of fairie of that cultured rural community. Tremendously virile adolescents had recourse to him regularly. After he passed the age of twenty, I have no first-hand knowledge of his sexual status. But gossip says he continues to be a fellator down to his present age of fifty.

Non-intellectual and not over-conscientious adolescent androgynes ordinarily have such relations with their tremendously virile bachelor friends. The latter are just as likely to take the initiative as is the youthful androgyne. In my own early teens, they repeatedly tried to seduce me. But I was over-conscientious, and never acquiesced between the ages of seven and eighteen, inclusive.

But positively no harm to any human being or to society as a whole arises from these conditions *imposed by Mother Nature*. On the contrary, these conditions are probably of decided benefit to society. Thus the virtue of many an adolescent virgin is preserved.

The other two of the three girl-boys who became notorious immediately after puberty adopted music as their profession. In fact, they developed into the two foremost musicians of their community. One became a widely known composer, and the other, leader of an orchestra in a nearby city. Both, enjoying a better income than the village fairie described, and being naturally high-toned and ambitious to stand well in the community, were not extensively promiscuous. They each confided in only three or four of the young bloods of the community, whom they loaded with gifts. They believed their secret practices were never even suspected by their fellows other than their few confidants. And in fact, they were never suspected by the villagers in general. They were talked about only among the liberal minded young bloods, who instinctively hid the knowledge from the common type of citizen because the latter would have bitterly persecuted the unfortunate androgynes. By exception, I learned the full facts because I knew of the sexual secrets of these androgynes as boys, and took pains to ask my young blood-brother now and then through life how these androgynes were conducting themselves. But after they passed the age of twenty-five, I could learn nothing definite—only gossip.

I still know the three when we are all close to fifty years of age. None ever married a *woman*. Moreover the "number four" androgyne, about whom I never heard a breath of scandal in his adult life, never married. All I know is that in middle life he chums with a tremendously virile bachelor young enough to be his son. A *de facto* marriage of an androgyne with a tremendously virile young bachelor is common.

The two musicians and the cultured "number four" androgyne are highly moral and highly esteemed in their community at the age of half a century. The former village fairie, however, is a notorious dipsomaniac [alcoholic], despised by everybody. At an age close to fifty years, all four enjoy fairly good health, notwithstanding all have probably indulged steadily in fellatio subsequent to puberty.

The incidence of androgynism on a physical male appears to be promotive of art in general, but particularly of music. Indeed any man choosing music as a profession incurs the risk of having homosexual stories told about himself by the fast set of his community.

Two of my university intimates were androgynes. Both were remarkably feminine psychically, and one also physically. The other was slightly feminesque physically. Both were inclined to develop adipose tissue—a common characteristic of androgynes, particularly after passing their twenties, and probably a result of their dwarfed genitalia. Both ranked well above the average university man in intellect. The one that was decidedly feminesque physically roomed year after year with the virile "X." The other students commonly referred to the pair as "X and wife." But I do not believe they were ever suspected of homosexuality, and both were highly esteemed by the college body.

The other androgyne student likewise took an ultra-virile classmate as his chum. Like the first couple, this second were practically inseparable. After graduation, they continued to be the most intimate of friends—not living in the same town, but visiting each other frequently. I never heard any question about the purely *Platonic* character of this extraordinary friendship either. Knowing my own nature, however, my own suspicion is that, in the case of both couples, relations existed in moderation—probably fellatio, the androgyne taking the more humiliating rôle. The reason the university circle suspected nothing is because they were ignorant of the existence of sexual intermediates. They of course knew that fellatio existed in the world but thought only the *scum* of mankind could be guilty of it, that it accompanied only the deepest moral depravity.

The author has to laugh whenever he uses the adjective "Platonic." Because Plato boasts in one of his dialogues that he personally has no use for a woman, and was inclined only toward the male sex. His dialogues are sickening even to me, an androgyne, because they are permeated with homosexual love. Every indication of Plato's writings is that he indulged in homosexual love frequently, being either a fellator, or the pathic [passive] in paedicatio.

*Ralph Werther* [alias Earl Lind and Jennie June]

Chauncey, George. 1994. *Gay New York: Gender, Urban Culture, and the Making of the Gay Male World, 1890–1940*. New York: Basic Books.
Werther, Ralph (alias). 1934. "The Biological Sport of Fairie-ism." [Report written in 1920 for Victor Robinson.] *Medical Review of Reviews*. (*Anthropos* 2) 40: 185–196.

---

## Why Do Homosexuals Undergo Treatment? (1934)

*Psychoanalysts from the 1930s onward have often claimed that homosexuality is a psychic illness because homosexual patients expressed terrible psychological pain and requested to change their orientation. In 1934, Dr. Ernst Bien seriously examined why homosexual patients sought his assistance. Based on his sample of twenty-two cases, he found that most of them came for anxiety symptoms. Few of them wanted to change their sexuality, despite the legal persecution of homosexuality.*

The title of this paper might just as well be: Is the fear of legal punishment the inducement to homosexuals to undergo treatment?

The stigmatization, in almost all civilized countries, of homosexuality as a "crime against nature" and the systematic punishment of homosexuals who are brought to court, often combined with economic ruin and general social disgrace, raise the question of how much the law has achieved by attempting to diminish homosexuality through criminal prosecution.

In other words: what has legislature actually contributed to the therapy and, what is still more important, to the prophylaxis of homosexuality; to what extent has it helped to check existing or developing homosexual inversion by the threat of punishment, or by the often very severe punishments actually inflicted? Taking this as a starting point, we may find here at least the general motives prompting homosexuals to undergo treatment.

I am well aware that a comprehensive answer to this complex question can only be found after thorough and unbiased medical experience with homosexuals of both sexes. On the other hand, I know how little experience neurologists generally have with homosexuals, since only a very small percentage of them come for treatment. From an examination of the literature on the subject the conclusion must be drawn that up to now this question has in general scarcely been considered, merely being touched upon now and then. I also know that it has *a priori* been taken for granted that the fear of legal consequences forms an essential motive for treatment. As an example I might mention a remark made by Stekel in regard to homosexuals ("Masturbation and Homosexuality," 1921, p. 254): "They consult the analyst only when they are in danger of coming or have actually come into conflict with the law." Therefore, I consider it well to examine my own material in this respect.

We may distinguish two groups of homosexuals who consult the physician: first, those who come for various *secondary* reasons and do not allow the subject of their inversion to be touched upon unless they are under compulsion to do so, and secondly, those who come for treatment, so to say, for *primary* reasons, that is, in order to be freed from their inversion. . . .

And now to answer the question which we raised at the beginning: Why do homosexuals undergo treatment? Most of the homosexuals whom I have observed (about 59 percent) came for treatment because of some neurotic disturbance intimately associated with the homosexuality, whereby only 5 (bisexuals) desired the removal of the homosexuality itself. The difficulty in finding a satisfactory partner was the impulse leading to treatment in a relatively large number of cases. Exceedingly few (2) gave fear of prosecution as the motive for treatment. In two cases . . . we see, a longing for a home or a family as the motive.

The surprising result of this investigation becomes apparent when we consider the question: Why do homosexuals not seek treatment? What strikes us most is that:

1. Among my patients (apart from 5 bisexuals) there was *not one* who had an instinctive longing for a change in his sexual attitude because of dissatisfaction with the homosexual activity *per se*. And that

2. There was not one who had resolved to become heterosexual because of threatening legal consequences. On the contrary, even where conviction had taken place, . . . the patient had removed to a place where he hoped to remain undisturbed by legal consequence. Finally it is striking that

3. Among my patients (with one exception . . .) there was not one case who had determined to renounce his homosexuality and to undergo treatment for fear of the social disgrace and general legal stigmatization of homosexuality as a crime.

If any general significance can be attached to the few homosexual cases dealt with in this paper, I would conclude that homosexuals submit to treatment reluctantly and only under psychic stress, while the law, which inflicts terrible punishments for homosexuality, exercises no influence whatsoever upon the willingness of homosexuals to submit to treatment.

I am well aware that such a generalization on the basis of so few cases is hardly admissible; nevertheless I should like to submit these conclusions to the medical public in the hope that they may serve as a stimulus for further research.

*Ernst Bien*

Bien, Ernst. 1934. "Why Do Homosexuals Undergo Treatment?" *Medical Review of Reviews* 40: 5–18.

Stekel, Wilhelm. 1921. *Onanie und Homosexualität: (die homosexuelle Neurose).* Berlin: Urban and Schwarzenberg.

----

## Psychogenic Factors in Overt Homosexuality (1937)

*This following study is one of the projects sponsored by the Committee for the Study of Sex Variants in the late 1930s. Historian Jennifer Terry (1999) has extensively studied the formation and work of the committee. This multidisciplinary team examined hundreds of homosexuals, gathering information on their family histories, sexual lives, and social activities (Henry 1941). They were also subjected to extensive physical examinations and medical photography and radiography. George Henry, a psychiatrist on the committee, tried to explain the cause of homosexuality by relying on a broad mix of psychological and biological theories. Although the subjects volunteered in hopes of destigmatizing homosexuality, the committee nonetheless emphasized their pathology and the prevention of homosexuality. Henry especially recommended stereotypically masculine fathers and feminine mothers as a means of preventing homosexuality. The following excerpt includes two cases and a critique by Dr. Ben Karpman that followed Henry's oral presentation at the Payne Whitney Psychiatric Clinic in New York City.*

This paper is a preliminary report of a study of 100 socially well adjusted men and women whose preferred form of libidinous gratification is homosexual and who regularly experience pleasure from homosexual relations. This study includes a detailed psychiatric investigation of the family and social background and of the personal history. In addition these individuals are being studied from a general physical, morphological and endocrine viewpoint and stereoscopic X-ray records of the head, chest and pelvis are being made.

Unfortunately the series is not yet completed and it is not possible to make comparative notations. Psychiatric investigations have already been made in more than 80 cases and the information obtained seems to justify a report of this aspect of the study.

Much of the factual data regarding the forms of homosexual expression has long been available through the excellent descriptions of many well-known students of this subject. The subsequent, theoretical generalizations of the Freudians have greatly widened the interest in homosexuality and have called attention to its intimate relation to personality disorder. Statements have been made regarding the influence of heredity, constitutional factors have been assumed and the psychogenic aspects have been stressed, but little progress has been made toward eliciting evidence of all these various factors in individual cases. It is hoped that this study will add to our knowledge of the causes of homosexuality, give indications for its treatment and call attention to adjustable factors in its prevention.

The persons who have submitted themselves for examination came voluntarily after being acquainted by a field worker with the nature of the study. They have offered themselves because of their interest in a scientific investigation of a human relationship which they believe is unjustly frowned upon by society. Most of them belong to the professional class and all have sufficient educational and social background to make a detailed psychiatric investigation profitable.

I am presenting four illustrative cases, not because they are especially unusual, but to call attention to the natural sequence of events in each case, and to the fact that each case is an individual problem, sufficiently different from others to permit of few generalizations. The names employed are of course fictitious and other precautions have been taken to conceal the identity of the persons involved.

## Case I. Lack of Masculine Ideal. Identification with Mother.

Frank Thompsen is a witty, humorous, 28-year-old son of a prominent family, received in the best homes as a popular guest and companion in spite of the fact that he has an international reputation as a homosexual. At any time after dinner he is likely to become a social liability because of excessive drinking. He has no occupation.

His family is conspicuous for its lack of effective, masculine males who might have afforded him an ideal. His father was an extremely gentle, dreamy, idealistic, effeminate person, an only son who continued to be entirely under the domination of the paternal grandmother even after his marriage. Both Frank and his father were left orphans in early childhood through the death of their respective fathers. On the maternal side the males were equally uninspiring. There were no uncles and the grandfather deserted his family. His reputation was such that he was held responsible for any delinquencies in the family. A stepfather acquired when Frank was five was helpless in dealing with the mother, who is described as being the most selfish person in the world. She has a terrific temper, and she commands by threatening or by bursting into tears.

Until Frank's father died the mother had continued under the domination of her mother and her mother-in-law. The latter not only lived with Frank's parents but was in complete control of the household. The maternal grandmother is an unyielding, capable executive who feels responsible for the entire family even to the extent of arranging for their burial. Until the mother became a widow she submitted to her own mother's domination. Then the mother rebelled and started upon a career of reckless dissipation.

As a child Frank was terrified by the attitude and manner of his maternal grandmother and he was much attached to his mother. "The family thought I was her pet." With the mother's rebellion and dissipation he gradually became disillusioned but he still feels she has tremendous charm. "I was very, very fond of her but after I was six or seven I was scared of her—frightened by her temper. She would scream herself into hysterics. We never knew when Vesuvius was going to erupt. Then I became frightfully critical. I didn't like the way she drank. I associated drinking with tantrums."

Conditions in the home proceeded from bad to worse. By the time Frank had reached puberty his stepfather had developed paresis and was confined in a mental hospital. His mother was then living with another man with whom the relationship was that of drunken brawls. "Mother would get drunk with the cook if she couldn't find anyone else. Then there would be no dinner that night. I was always terrified to bring friends home. She might be the most charming mother or she might be stinking and throw things at you. I never could tell what she was going to do."

At 16 Frank felt he had no moral obligation to remain in the home and left. He had shown a marked preference for his own sex since early childhood, including overt sexual relations. "As far back as I can remember I have been drawn to men." As soon as he left home he indulged himself without restraints. He began to drink to excess—"I took to it like a duck to water"—and he was thereafter easily seduced by either sex. In his first heterosexual experience at 17 a woman came to his room and practically forced herself upon him. He managed to avoid her thereafter. Two years later he was pursued by another young woman to the extent of becoming engaged and although she was sexually promiscuous they never had sexual relations. She left him to marry another man.

Otherwise his sexual interests and activities have been concentrated on men. He prefers the big strong man exemplified by the chauffeur to whom he was attracted at the age of five. "I haunted the garage to see him in his undershirt. I remember the blond hair on his chest. It fascinated me."

His most profound attachment was at 23 to an older man married to a virgin Lesbian. "That was the big thing in my life. It was just an emotional tempest from which I will never recover—one of those violent, incredible, intense things." This man and his wife were in turn completely dominated by another Lesbian who after a few months made it impossible for Frank to continue his relations with this man. Frank then attempted suicide by cutting his wrists and drinking bichloride of mercury. "Since then I have had constant, promiscuous homosexual encounters. None of them have meant very much. I accept sex in a very detached way."

Within the past year he has reestablished a platonic alliance with two women. One of them is his sister, five years older, whom he thoroughly disliked as a child. Her tragic marriage and his own mishaps have drawn them together. She was highly sexed and her husband was impotent. His chief interest was in pictures of beheaded women. After the husband had committed suicide in a particularly gruesome manner, she and Frank became "terribly devoted to each other—I have a tremendous respect and real love for her."

The other alliance is with a "very charming, lovely virgin," old enough to be his mother. At her suggestion he is living in her apartment. "There is no thought of physical relationship. We are just extremely good friends. We merely kiss in a casual way. She regards me as her son." She is unusually tolerant and makes no objection to his homosexual activities.

. . .

## Case IV. Disillusioned in Marriage.
## Finds a Substitute in Homosexual Liaison.

Mary Jones is a successful negro-actress who is now nearly 50 years old. She is well adjusted to her actual situation in life and has no regrets for having established homosexual relationships. She is at ease in any social group. Her soft, deep voice, friendly attitude along with an evident personal security has caused her to be sought after by both white and colored people.

Mary has little in her early life which she can look back upon with pleasure. She was an illegitimate child, the daughter of a 12-year-old colored nursemaid and of a white man in whose home her mother was employed. Her grandmother also was the illegitimate daughter of a colored woman and a white man. Mary's skin was of such a light color that she was conspicuous in a colored neighborhood where other children called her a half-white bastard.

Both the mother and the maternal grandmother were married to colored men after their respective children were born. Mary's step-father was much older than her mother of whom he was very jealous. He used to beat up the mother and this relationship added much to Mary's unhappiness as a child. Her mother really seemed more like a sister and as a matter of fact in early childhood Mary had been led to believe that her grandmother was her mother.

Mary's early training, especially her moral training, came from her grandmother. "I've always been lectured about virtue. If I were not good my grandmother said she would come back and haunt me." As a result of this training she remained a virgin until after her marriage. Precept was in marked contrast with the example set by her mother who was consistently promiscuous. "When I was six I saw mother in bed with men. I remember mother putting rouge on her cheeks. I cried and cried because I thought only bad women did that."

Even the associations with the grandmother were painful because when Mary was three her mother's step-father in a fit of jealousy killed a man who wanted to marry her mother. "That's one of the things that made my childhood so unhappy. My grandmother used to take me to prison to see him. He was in prison for life. All the children said my grandfather was a murderer."

The grandmother died when Mary was 13 and she was then turned over to a maternal aunt, Louise, with whom she had been living part of the time. The influence of Aunt Louise could hardly be considered desirable. "She was very stingy. She used to make me feel that I ate too much. She was very critical of me. She always prophesied that I was going to be a bad girl."

Three years later Mary was married to the spoiled son of a wealthy, self-made negro. She was not especially in love with him but she and her family felt that she should not neglect this opportunity for advancing her social position. The marriage proved to be a failure. Her husband never worked, drank to excess, gambled and frittered away whatever income they had. She was entirely dependent upon her father-in-law for support. She tried to be a good wife to her husband and to influence him to give up his dissipated mode of living but her efforts were of no avail. Two pregnancies were terminated by abortion because she felt she could not afford to have children.

Five years after marriage Mary had become thoroughly disillusioned but "I put up with him until after mother's death." The mother developed general paresis and Mary tried to take care of her. Even after she had to be taken to a state hospital Mary made daily visits. Her husband's dissipation gradually increased and shortly after her mother died he developed tuberculosis. She returned to him to nurse him until his death.

At 28 Mary was a widow and employed as a demonstrator. The manager of the firm was a dour, taciturn and indifferent man. She had never encountered an individual of this sort and she was fascinated by his indifference. She took the initiative in their courtship and marriage. They have been married for more than 20 years now and she has never succeeded in getting him to offer any expression of affection for her. "He would lose some of his manliness if he made such an admission." For many years after marriage she believed he was faithful to her but he was in the habit of staying out all night without explanation and she learned that he was interested in other women. This made her very unhappy. Although no contraceptive measures were used she did not become pregnant by her second husband. "I regret having no children. It's the one great unhappiness, particularly as I feel I would have made a very good mother."

Soon after Mary remarried she took part in amateur theatricals. Her unusual talents were soon recognized and her promotion was rapid. Her husband was jealous of her professional success but in recent years he has been dependent upon her for support.

Her prominence in theatrical work probably made her more attractive to women. She says, however, that all her life women had made advances to her but she would not consent "because it all seemed unnatural and abnormal." Finally at the age of 41, while dancing with a woman, "something very terrific happened to me—a very electric thing. It made me know I was homosexual." Since then she has had several alliances with both white and colored women and for the past five years she has been living with a white woman. This woman is "one of the finest women I have ever known. She has come to be very, very dear to me—not just for sex alone—it's a very great love." Mary has no regrets for having yielded to homosexual temptations. "This last relationship affords a tenderness I have never known." Nevertheless she believes she would have remained a conventional married woman if her second husband had not neglected her. "If marriage had been satisfactory I would never have had homosexual relations."

## Discussion

In the four cases which I have just cited only such details in the life history are included as are necessary in calling attention to the varied clinical picture presented by homosexuals and to the multitude of factors which contribute to a homosexual development.

The first case calls attention to the possible result of a lack of effective males in a family, especially the lack of virility in a father which the son might incorporate in his own ideals. Through the early death of his father he was not only father-less and dependent upon a feminine version of masculinity but he was completely submerged first by his maternal grandmother and then by his mother. His early attachment to his mother was a source of his later ambivalent feeling toward her when she aroused his antagonism and his critical attitude toward her dissipation. She was completely beyond his control and too mercurial to permit him to develop a sense of security with her. His experience with the women in his family instilled in him a feeling of fear or at least caution and uncertainty.

It appears that he was unable to deal with whatever his mother symbolized except through identification with her and as soon as he escaped from her immediate influence he was governed by this identification. He then began to drink to excess just as she did and he likewise became promiscuous. He was afraid of women and managed to avoid them. Being accustomed to domination and being essentially passive in his attitude he sought the companionship of older and stronger men.

As time passed he gradually reestablished an emotional relationship similar to that of his childhood. His greatest homosexual attraction was for an older man who, like himself and the other male members of his family, was incapable of maintaining a masculine relationship toward women. This man also was under the domination of two women. When the man failed him through their influence the feeling of futility in struggling against women drove him to attempt self annihilation.

His present emotional relationships seem to provide what he lacked in child-hood as well as an opportunity to give free expression to his sexual desires. He lives with and is sheltered by a devoted, indulgent mother substitute. He follows the pattern of his actual mother in drinking and in sexual promiscuity. Through the failure of another man to achieve an adult heterosexual adjustment he has found in his sister a boon companion in unconventionality. Sought after because of his social and homosexual charms he obtains adequate libidinous gratification and there is no threat to his security because of the tolerant, platonic attitude of his sister and of his mother substitute.

. . .

[In the fourth case cited, the negro] actress was exposed to a continuous series of emotional stresses which might be expected to cause gross personality distortion. All of her relatives prophesied that she would never amount to much and that she would become a bad woman. There was little in her family background to justify any other conclusion. There was no one with whom she might have identified herself and thus avoid the downward course in life which had been predicted for her. In spite of all these handicaps she now has the emotional attributes of a kindly mammy, regretful that she does not have children of her own, and in addition she has achieved success in her profession.

Even though she felt no great affection for her first husband, mutual physical charms and her sense of loyalty would have made her first marriage successful if he had not been so alcoholic and irresponsible. In her taciturn, apparently self-sufficient second husband she probably expected to find security. This proved to be another illusion. Her success as an actress made her socially and economically independent. People then began to express their appreciation of her personal charms and she was pursued by many admirers. The rigid moral code which she had followed from childhood prevented her from accepting the attentions of men.

Having the desires of a mature, healthy woman and with the fading chances of being satisfied by a jealous, unfaithful husband it is not surprising that she experienced a thrill from the embraces of a passionate woman. She was impelled by a feminine desire to serve a lover who took the initiative in expressing affection for her. She was troubled by the feeling that homosexual relations were abnormal and she doubted the constancy of a woman. She was especially skeptical of her present lover because white women are reputed to be less faithful then the colored. This lover's persistence and sincerity gradually overcame her resistance and she is at last enjoying a relationship in which tenderness and devotion are of prime importance with sexual gratification as a natural accompaniment.

In view of the observations made in these four cases it is evident that the overt homosexual is like any psychiatric patient in that his condition can be understood only through detailed information regarding the personal and family background of each person under study. Personality forces and human interrelations contributing to a homosexual development cannot be traced to their ultimate sources but it appears that the more closely a relative or friend is associated, especially in childhood, the more direct and decisive is the influence exerted. This means that the parents are in most instances chiefly responsible for the homosexual developments in their children. The parents in turn may have been distorted by the grandparents. Anyone taking the place of a parent must assume responsibility for the development of homosexual tendencies just as he does for the development of other personality characteristics.

It is necessary therefore that the parents keep themselves informed regarding the interests which servants and relatives may have in children. Not uncommonly a nursemaid, a sibling, a cousin, an uncle or an aunt may be involved in the distortion of a child's psychosexual development. It appears that boarding and non-coeducational schools are more likely to favor a homosexual development. It is generally recognized that any segregation of the sexes is likely to bring about overt expression of latent homosexual desires.

Whatever these external influences may be the majority of persons do not succumb to them and the minority who do succumb, appear to be fundamentally predisposed. Some of this predisposition may be inherited through the germ plasm but in the cases studied thus far it is rare to find overt homosexuals in more than one generation. The tendency may nevertheless be inherited because the difference between latent and overt homosexuality is often very slight. Undoubtedly there are many instances of overt homosexuality in the family of which the informants are unaware.

In a large majority of the cases the tendencies to homosexuality as shown by attitude and behavior can be observed in early childhood. Much of this may be constitutional but there are many other determinants. For instance the attitude of parents toward the sex of an expected child may be an indication of the influence which they will exert on that child. If a girl is wanted and a boy arrives the child may be treated as though he were a girl. The child senses the wishes of the parents even though nothing is said. His habitual conduct is likely to be that which elicits greatest praise or distinction. To the extent that his interests, attitude and behavior are out of harmony with his actual sex he is likely to meet with circumstances which will accentuate his deviation.

Boys appear to be somewhat more vulnerable than girls and if they show undue feminine tendencies special care should be exercised to give them opportunity to develop masculine characteristics. A boy should not be repeatedly exposed to situations in which he will be defeated and he should not be applauded for his ability to display himself in female attire.

Under ideal circumstances the father should be an understanding, tolerant but virile and decisive male. The mother should have the gentleness, patience and passivity usually associated with womanhood. Any mixture such as an effeminate father and an aggressive, masculine, mother is likely to be disconcerting to the child and accentuate homosexual tendencies.

Much of the friction between the parents of homosexuals seems to be due to the inability to make an adjustment of aggression and passivity, of masculinity and femininity. Friction between parents is so common that it is difficult to associate it with homosexuality in a child but in the cases which I have studied gross maladjustment was almost universal.

Most of the overt homosexuals have engaged for several years in some form of sex play with their own sex before they recognized their own homosexual tendencies. It is very difficult for them to get any accurate information because the subject is officially tabooed and the veiled or jesting references to it do little more than stimulate curiosity. Often misinformation is given. One young man was assured by a physician that be could not be a homosexual because he had a masculine distribution of pubic hair. He now holds this physician responsible for the further development of his homosexual tendencies.

In addition to the predisposition which a person may have in a homosexual direction his tendencies are likely to become overt in proportion to the obstacles which he encounters in attempting a heterosexual adjustment. If the first heterosexual experience is especially unpleasant, painful or unsuccessful there may be great reluctance to repeat it. If there is much discrepancy between the desires and capacities of the man and the woman either one or both may be driven to other means of gratification. One man had been satisfactorily married for several years and then became impotent when his wife began to take the initiative and particularly when she demanded that he impregnate her. They were divorced a year later and he then engaged in overt homosexual practices.

As homosexuals grow older they tend to seek younger companions. A middle aged man may employ a young adult to live with him to satisfy his vanity. It gives the impression that he is still so attractive that he can hold the affections of a young man. The age discrepancy is also a factor in the seduction of the young and inexperienced. This is especially true with women because intimacies between them are tolerated and the significance of the subtle approach of an experienced woman usually is not comprehended.

The attitude of society toward homosexuality is of course an important factor in its development. Few persons escape an overt homosexual experience at some period in life and desires are universal. The rôle which such experiences and desires play in the further development of the normal, the homosexual, the neurotic and the psychotic is not clear but it appears to be dependent upon the kind and amount of repression and the associated conflict. The so-called well adjusted homosexual is not without conflict which he may learn to conceal by bravado or express in his defiance or his contempt for conventionality. Many sincerely believe that a homosexual adjustment is normal for one so inclined provided it is kept a personal matter and doesn't involve others who are not homosexual.

Homosexuality is wide spread and involves all classes of society. As our western civilization grows older, homosexuality appears to be increasing. A century ago in this country children afforded the greatest security to the parents. With our present mode of living children are among the greatest liabilities to the parents. As a result young people are driven more and more to find substitutes for adult heterosexual relationships. Homosexuality is merely one of those substitutes. An intelligent attitude toward this problem is not possible unless it is studied and understood. Psychiatrists are best qualified to make this study. Such a study is worth while not only on its own merits but also for the additional knowledge which it will give of psychoneurotic and psychotic distortions.

## Conclusions

1. The psychogenic factors in overt homosexuality vary so widely that they should be studied in each case.
2. This study should include a detailed investigation of the emotional relationship within the family as far back as the generation of the grandparents.
3. This study should include also a detailed personal history with special attention directed to attachments and aversions along with their environmental setting.
4. Well adjusted overt homosexuals are rare.
5. A large proportion of the cases appear to be so predisposed by constitution and environment that a homosexual adjustment seems inevitable.
6. A large proportion of cases drift into a homosexual adjustment because the obstacles to heterosexual adjustment have been overwhelming.
7. The value of therapeutic assistance can be determined only after a careful study has been made of each case.
8. A large proportion of the cases could have been prevented.
9. Prevention involves eugenics as well as the mental hygiene of the predisposed individual and his family.
10. Overt homosexuality deserves the serious attention of psychiatrists both on its own merits and for the additional insight which it gives into the understanding of recognized personality disorders.

## Discussion

Dr. Ben Karpman (Washington, D.C.)—I agree with Dr. Henry with reference to the importance of homosexuality. Allowing for certain exaggeration, it might be said that the problems of psychiatry will not be solved until we solve the problem of homosexuality. Allowing fully for the constitutional basis there is no doubt about the significance of psychogenic factors in homosexuality. I have, however, a few suspicions as to some of the statements made by Dr. Henry. He points out, apparently as throwing some light on the development of homosexuality, those instances of boys brought up in families of 4 or 5 women and draws the conclusion that under such circumstances it seems quite natural for such boys to develop into homosexuals. Unfortunately, Dr. Henry does not provide us with controls from the normal population, or he might have come across cases where there was one boy in the family brought up by a number of women, who nevertheless has developed normally. I recently had under care a woman who had a definite neurosis; history showed that two of her sisters were also neurotic. There were also in the family another sister and a brother who appeared to have escaped any psychic injury. Besides them, there were a mother and a couple of aunts in the family. Yet the only boy in the family escaped the neurosis and is making a good adjustment. I know the case of another man who was the eighth child in a family of seven girls. The father made up his mind he must have a boy, no matter how many children there were in the family. This boy, the eighth child, is now a physician, a psychiatrist. There is nothing homosexual about him. How did he escape the influence of eight women in the family?

Another proof of need of control is the instance cited by Dr. Henry of parents wishing to have a boy or a girl, influencing the subsequent development of the child. I think there is some truth in that for I have seen cases of this kind. Yet I also know instances where the parents would want to train the boy as a girl and the boy would balk and refuse, developing normally. There comes to my mind the case of Pearl Berger, the notorious strikebreaker, whose parents so strongly wished to have a girl that anticipatorily they named the child to come Pearl. So far as I know he is considered one of the biggest roughnecks in the United States and if there is anything homosexual about him, it is certainly well concealed.

I should like to take issue with Dr. Henry in his treatment of homosexuality as a group. This is I believe a mistake. There is such a wide diversity of types that seemingly they have nothing in common except that of homosexual behavior. There are among them a great many individuals who never had heterosexual experiences. Again, at the other extreme end of the group, there are individuals entirely heterosexual but who have had on one or two occasions a homosexual experience. To group all these people together merely on the basis of homosexuality is, for the present at least, fictitious. We need a finer differentiation and sub-grouping.

I should like to ask Dr. Henry whether from his observation and study there is such a thing as a normal homosexual? If one accepts the psychogenetic concept that we are all bisexual and that we become heterosexual because we repress the homosexual component, then equally, one cannot become homosexual unless he represses the heterosexual side, which means neurosis.

I should like to ask Dr. Henry how he obtained his material. I do not feel that he used the straight psychoanalytic approach because I do not get in his cases the type of material and interpretation that one associates with psychoanalysis. If he has obtained that by the ordinary anamnestic approach and asking questions, I feel that this carries a certain danger because unwittingly he is going to ask leading questions and get answers which color the material.

Dr. George Henry (New York City). I am afraid I did not make myself very clear. What I wanted to emphasize was that homosexuals had to be studied as individuals. If there is any grouping, it only comes through the word "homosexual." . . .

I do not know what a normal homosexual is. I think I might answer the question by saying that some individuals seem to develop naturally into a homosexual adjustment without evident conflict, without desire to be anything else, and quite contented to be what they are. Such persons are rare, at least in my experience. . . .

I never ask questions unless it is absolutely necessary. I begin with the father, saying, "Tell me something about your father." . . .

After the pattern of the father is established, they talk pretty freely about the other members of the family. I take down in shorthand, verbatim, what they say, no matter what it is. . . . It is a record of what they say spontaneously about themselves, with a little guidance. They are all responsible individuals, and I believe they are telling me the truth.

*George W. Henry*

Henry, George W. 1937. "Psychogenic Factors in Overt Homosexuality." *American Journal of Psychiatry* 93: 889–908.

————. 1941. *Sex Variants. A Study of Homosexual Patterns.* New York: Hoeber.

Terry, Jennifer. 1999. *An American Obsession: Science, Medicine, and Homosexuality in Modern Society.* Chicago: University of Chicago Press.

---

## Can Homosexuality Be Cured? (1951)

*Aside from the "Kinsey Report" on* Sexual Behavior in the Human Male *(1948), the next greatest stimulus to homosexual organizing in the 1950s was a small book,* The Homosexual in America: A Subjective Approach *(1951a), published under the pseudonym Donald Webster Cory. Its author was a young Jewish New Yorker named Edward Sagarin. As an adolescent, Sagarin had recognized his attraction to men but had struggled against it and married. Doing so did not quell his homosexual leanings. So he sought psychoanalysis, which instead reconciled him to his sexuality. He was moved by the "Negro" rights movement starting in the late 1940s. The publication of the Kinsey Report convinced him that homosexuals were numerous and constituted an unrecognized minority group oppressed by society (Marotta 1981, 4–7).* The Homosexual in America *was an eclectic, sweeping, and inspiring book, combining sociological analysis, medical reviews, and novel psychological insights.*

*Sagarin criticized psychiatrists for generalizing about all homosexuals based on the unhappy, maladjusted individuals who sought treatment or were arrested for sex crimes. Instead, he argued that there were well-adjusted homosexuals. Psychiatric disorders arose, to the degree they did, because of social marginalization, fear of persecution, and resultant low self-esteem. In discussing the causes of homosexuality, he discarded the congenitalist views. Although he was critical of psychoanalysis, he largely favored early Freudian models: strong attachment to and identification with the mother, a need to replace the father, and faulty sexual education. Sagarin was the first to suggest in print that homosexual support groups could help people adjust to the "gay life." He called on homosexuals to go public and form a defense campaign. His was perhaps the first public call for massive "coming out."*

*Sagarin supported the new homophile groups that took up his challenge and lectured often at them. In 1964, he was a speaker at the third national convention of the Daughters of Bilitis (the first lesbian rights group) (Katz 1976, 428). He earned his Ph.D. in sociol-*

ogy and anthropology from New York University with a dissertation on the Veterans Benevolent Association, the first association of homosexual veterans in New York, which existed from 1945 to 1954 (Sagarin 1966). He went on to become a successful and prolific professor of sociology, often focusing on "deviance" (1975). Later in life, he identified himself as heterosexual and supported the psychiatric model of homosexuality as a disease (Duberman 1993, 286 n. 3).

It has frequently been stated that the homosexual can be cured, if only he wants to be, but that most homosexuals have no desire to be cured and therefore cannot be. This statement, repeated in slightly varying form, contains several partial truths that require clarification. Let us first see exactly what is being said about therapy. The *Journal of the American Medical Association* has made a statement which is typical:

> Help is available and can be effective for the homosexual person who desires it. The treatment, however, is entirely psychiatric and is nearly always a prolonged undertaking, lasting, even with intensive treatment, many months or even years. For those persons who do not want to change their makeup and even those who are not highly motivated in seeking help, treatment is practically useless.

Many types of cures have been suggested for homosexuality, and several of them I shall dismiss as having definitely not been verified. These include shock treatments (as, for instance, the use of *metrazol*) and hormone treatment by an endocrinologist. It has not been shown that homosexuals are lacking in male or female sex hormones; and to my knowledge based upon conversations with many physicians—particularly specialists—as well as with patients, no hormone treatment has ever achieved the desired results. It is entirely possible, of course, that in so widespread a condition there may be a coincidence of hormone deficiency and homosexuality; in other words, if one out of every twenty males is sexually inverted, then one out of every twenty men deficient in male hormones will likewise be of this temperament. The percentage might even increase, because a predisposition to hormone deficiency can produce a somewhat effeminate child who may therefore take refuge in the homosexual life.

It is generally recognized today, as stated by the American Medical Association and quoted above, that there is only one type of "treatment" for the homosexual, and that is at the hands of a psychiatrist or psychologist. And, it is said, there must be a genuine desire to be cured before any results can be obtained.

## "Desire to Be Cured" Questionable

It is my contention that, by the very nature of homosexuality, to speak of a "desire to be cured" is a superficial paradox. Where exclusive homosexuality is an important part of a person's temperament, it plays a role of defending the individual against a way of life which holds more terror for him than the one he is leading, and the unconscious psychological alternative to his homosexuality is, not what heterosexuality would mean to others, *but what it means to him!* He has turned away from that path because he cannot and does not want to face it, so that it is inherently a contradiction, and by definition an impossibility, to expect him to desire it.

Many people, including numerous homosexuals who are maladjusted and unhappy, will protest. They *do* want to be cured. They seek to change themselves and never cease to struggle against their own temperaments. The life they lead is hateful and repugnant to them and is counter to their will and better judgment. Their shame is a deep abyss, a bottomless pit.

Others, however, will attest to their pride and happiness and insist that they would not relinquish their sexual leanings for anything. The difficulties are compensated for by the satisfactions obtained, and they cannot conceive of life without these.

Actually, as many psychiatrists point out, the attitudes of both groups are likely to be defense mechanisms. The former, as I learned not only from my own experience but from that of many others, are only struggling to maintain self-respect. Self-condemnation relieves them of the burden of responsibility for what they are doing and therefore makes it possible for them to continue doing it. The proud and happy ones may likewise be suffering from shame and remorse, and using their boastfulness to withstand the impact of the world's harsh judgment. . . .

## "Group Therapy" Promising

From both practical considerations and the nature of the homosexual problem, I suggest that some modification of group therapy might be instituted to help people who are in the gay life. Group therapy consists of a gathering of a number of people in a sort of a meeting, under a guide or leader, to discuss their personal and psychological problems, their fears and their phobias, their frustrations and humiliations, in an effort to relieve themselves of the burden of secrecy and shame and to guide themselves by means of an interchange of intelligent opinion. Homosexual group therapy (which I am here suggesting as a possibility, although I know of no such group in existence) would have to be restricted to gay people, because the presence of anyone not sharing their impulses would inhibit the conduct of such meetings. Some ten, fifteen, or twenty people might constitute a group that would gather weekly, led perhaps by a psychiatrist or a lay therapist who should likewise be gay, and group and individual problems would come under discussion. Activities on the job, the burden of the mask, the relationships at home, the meaning of a promiscuous impulse, the effort to adjust to greater satisfaction of the physical aspects of sex, the meaning of a new novel—these and countless other problems would be analyzed.

Some will object that it is absurd to suggest that the psychiatrist be a homosexual. "Must every doctor (or psychiatrist) have an illness in order to be able to treat it?" they will ask. My proposal that the leader or analyst should be homosexual stems from the social nature of this problem. Homosexuals are, for quite obvious reasons, reluctant to discuss their problems outside their own group. In short, this is a dilemma of a socio-psychological nature, and the social aspect cannot be ignored in favor of the psychological.

The popular fallacy of cure, for which the psychiatrists are partially responsible because of their failure to speak without equivocation, is extremely harmful. Whether or not a cure for homosexuality would be socially desirable if it could be effectuated is, however, another matter.

*Donald Webster Cory* (pseudonym for Edward Sagarin)

Cory, Donald Webster (pseudonym for Edward Sagarin). 1951a. *The Homosexual in America: A Subjective Approach*. Introduction by Albert Ellis. New York: Greenberg.

———. 1951b. "Can Homosexuality Be Cured?" *Sexology* (October): 146–156.

———. 1993. *Stonewall*. New York: Dutton.

Katz, Jonathan Ned. 1976. *Gay American History: Lesbians and Gay Men in the U.S.A.* New York: Thomas Y. Crowell.

Kinsey, Alfred C., Wardell B. Pomeroy, and Clyde E. Martin. 1948. *Sexual Behavior in the Human Male*. Philadelphia: W.B. Saunders.

Marotta, Toby. 1981. *The Politics of Homosexuality*. Boston: Houghton Mifflin.

Sagarin, Edward. [1966] 1975. *Structure and Ideology in an Association of Deviants*. New York: Arno.

———. 1975. *Deviants and Deviance: An Introduction to the Study of Disvalued People and Behavior*. New York: Praeger.

---

## It Is Natural After All (1958)

ONE *magazine, a 1950s homophile periodical, was dedicated to publishing essays dealing with the biology and sociology of homosexuality. It tended to be quite deferential to scientific authorities. In the following essay, Christopher Wicks ardently claims homosexuality is genetic and therefore natural. His argument is a good example of the tremendous, long-standing appeal to gays of the genetic explanation of homosexuality.*

It has always been a paradox that Society should be most stupid about its most natural and fundamental urge: sex. Heterosexuals take it for granted; homosexuals distrust it.

More misinformation has been put on paper about homosexuality than any other subject. Every conceivable excuse has been contrived to explain or justify. Even the more recent popular books have been filled with half truths and wishful speculations, from Gide's *Corydon* to Cory's *The Homosexual in America*. Both volumes share the common fault: they are almost totally unscientific, lacking in fact and reason.

The nature of this brief article makes it impossible for me to be detailed. The substance of what follows fills volumes and will continue to do so. Nor is the essence of this article new, only unknown to the public and unsung by the scientists.

It has been four years since I completed a year's intense study on the subject of homosexuality. The work was carried on in the company of a psychiatrist, a doctor of endocrinology and a priest who was both a bio-chemist and authority on natural and moral law. Our purpose was to determine in so far as was possible the actual cause of homosexuality. In the course of this study it was necessary to take under advisement all the existing theories and to test them.

Voluminous material was sifted, writings most notable by their prejudice and lack of fact. Finally after months it became evident that all evidence pointed to a single conclusion: HOMOSEXUALITY IS GENETIC!

The idea itself is not new. But only recently has science given serious time and experiment to the study. Actually a perusal of the prominent sexologists, including Krafft-Ebing, Hirschfeld, H. Ellis and Kinsey, shows that these men all had at last to acknowledge the possibility of the genetic origin of sexual deviation.

That sex itself is determined by genes is common knowledge. Why is it so unreasonable to believe that sexual deviation is also a matter of genetics? Indeed it is not unreasonable. It is simply that our society does not wish to accept the fact. To do so would be to plead guilty to decades of persecution both physical and mental on a portion of the population the exact counting of which would startle even the most optimistic homophile. Still that hideous persecution continues in this country which is presumed to be the most progressive and Christian in the world.

Briefly our final proof was found in the studies of Doctors Myerson and Neustadt securely hidden away in scholarly medical publications. These men used the exact method the priest, psychiatrist and endocrinologist reasoned would serve as proof: a study of a number of sets of *identical* twins. These, both male and female, often separated at birth, raised in different environments, proved *in all cases without a single exception* that both were homosexual and to the *exact same degree*. The doctors concluded their study saying in effect: to be born a homosexual should be of no more consequence than being born left-handed in a predominantly right-handed society.

The real frustration in America is not that the homosexual has been born into a heterosexual society, but that thanks to his Puritan predecessors, he has been born into an *anti-sexual* society. Place man, a poly-sexual animal, in an anti-sexual society and the consequences become obvious. Man, the poly-sexual, is capable of being aroused and satisfied by the same sex, the opposite sex, animals and inanimate objects.

One of the most interesting revelations showed that there is not a single case on record of a psychological "cure" for homosexuals. The reason is simply because there is nothing to cure. Very few psychiatrists will admit this.

Not that psychological problems do not abound; they do. But those problems are not symptomatic with homosexuality. They are the result of being born into a society that does not want to understand or to admit that God would actually create as repulsive a creature as a homosexual. The only "cure" psychiatrists can effect is to get the patient to admit he or she is homosexual, to adjust to that fact and somehow manage to live a full life as such.

Since proof exists in favor of the genetic theory, why doesn't the New York Times print a headline to that effect? Why are the facts kept locked in learned dissertations? Here is material to revolutionize our thinking, more than that here is the means to free the damned consciences of thousands of men and women who have been led to believe they are committing sins and crimes. The suppression of these facts is the worst and deadliest of sins.

It follows in our study that since homosexuality is *de facto*, in whatever degree it may appear, genetic that it is also *natural*. It is as natural for the homosexual to desire the same sex as it is for the heterosexual to demand the opposite sex. Moreover, homosexuality may be moral when it is governed by those laws which govern all morality. Those laws do not speak in terms of gender, only of justice. Where is the dishonor in that which is genetic, natural and moral? There is none except that which the unjust majority levies out of fear and self imposed stupidity.

But justice and truth will triumph in time. Much of Europe has been far ahead of America in awareness of these problems. Most recently England has taken a stand in admitting that it is not contrary to nature to desire the same sex. We will have to follow eventually.

Given these truths and given equal status in society as the right-handed person, the homosexual would flourish as he did in every golden age in history. For every brilliant, creative period in time has been a homosexual age. If the truth were known, as it is only known amid the brotherhood itself, much of the world's valuable social, scientific, political, cultural and artistic progress today is being made, produced and fostered by homosexuals. Given these truths the facade of exhibitionism, the publicized unpleasant aspects associated with some homosexuals would vanish. Given case for case the breach in morals would be no more, if as great, as that made by heterosexuals. For these shows of anger, retaliation and distrust, of shame and helplessness are not inherent in the homosexual nature. They are the result of our cultural atmosphere.

In conclusion it is obvious that any broad statement as iconoclastic as: HOMOSEXUALITY IS GENETIC is subject to much discussion and argumentation. My purpose has been only to present the distillation of our study. Only that conclusion is vital. With it all else follows, no other excuse is necessary. With the knowledge comes a God-given confidence, a whole new lease on living. With it comes the profound sense of responsibility to prove to the right-handed majority that the left-handed men and women can do the same work, live as wholesome and profitable lives and leave behind as Christian a heritage to mankind.

*Christopher Wicks*

Wicks, Christopher. 1958. "It Is Natural after All." *ONE* 6, no. 1: 19–21.

---

## Does Research Into Homosexuality Matter? (1965)

*Franklin E. Kameny, Ph.D., an astrophysicist, was fired from his government job in the 1950s because of his homosexuality. He fought this discrimination in the courts, pursuing his cause up to the Supreme Court—but was unsuccessful. In 1951 he founded the Washington, D.C., chapter of the Mattachine Society with the goal of launching a new, militant approach to homosexual rights. He was tired of the homophile movement politely trying to convince doctors that homosexuals were not psychopaths. It was time for a more aggressive and assertive gay politics that forthrightly denied the legitimacy of science in bolstering social prejudice. In a series of articles in* The Ladder *(a periodical published by the Daughters of Bilitis, a lesbian group), Kameny closely tied an assault on the disease model of homosexuality to a new breed of gay militant politics. He also astutely criticized homosexuals, fascination with and reliance on scientific approaches to homosexuality.*

## Part I: On Some Aspects of Militancy in the Homophile Movement

As little as two years ago, "militancy" was something of a dirty word in the homophile movement. Long inculcation in attitudes of cringing meekness had taken its toll among homosexuals, combined with a feeling, still widely prevalent, that reasonable, logical, gentlemanly and ladylike persuasion and presentation of reasonable, logical argument, could not fail to win over those who would deny us our equality and our right to be homosexual and to live as homosexuals without disadvantage. There was—and is—a feeling that given any fair chance to undertake a dialogue with such opponents, we would be able to impress them with the basic rightness of our position and bring them into agreement with it.

Unfortunately, by this approach alone we will not prevail, because most people operate not rationally but emotionally on questions of sex in general, and homosexuality in particular, just as they do on racial questions.

It is thus necessary for us to adopt a *strongly* positive approach, a *militant* one. It is for us to take the initiative, the offensive—not the defensive—in matters affecting us. It is time that we began to move from endless talk (directed, in the last analysis, by us to ourselves) to firm, vigorous action.

We are right; those who oppose us are both factually and morally wrong. We are the true authorities on homosexuality, whether we are accepted as such or not. We must DEMAND our rights, boldly, not beg cringingly for mere privileges, and not be satisfied with crumbs tossed to us. I have been deeply gratified to note in the past year a growing spirit of militancy on the part of an increasing number of members of the homophile organizations. We would be foolish not to recognize what the Negro rights movement has shown us is sadly so: that mere persuasion, information and education are not going to gain for us in actual practice the rights and equality which are ours in principle.

I have been pleased to see a trend away from weak, wishy-washy compromise positions in our movement, toward ones of strong affirmation of what it is that we believe and want, followed by a drive to take whatever action is needed to obtain our rights. I do not of course favor uncontrolled, unplanned, ill-considered lashing out. Due and careful consideration must always be given to tact and tactics. Within the bounds dictated by such considerations, however, we must be prepared to take firm, positive, definite action—action initiated by us, not merely responding to the initiatives of others. The homophile movement increasingly is adopting this philosophy.

## Part II: On the Homophile Movement and Homosexuality as a Disease

Among the topics to which we are led by the preceding, is that of our approach to the question of homosexuality as a sickness. This is one of the most important issues—probably THE most important single issue—facing our movement today.

It is a question upon which, by rationalization after rationalization, members of the homophile movement have backed away from taking a position. It is a question upon which a clear, definite, unambiguous, no-nonsense stand MUST be taken, must be taken promptly, and must be taken by US, publicly.

There are some who say that WE will not be accepted as authorities regardless of what we say, or how we say it, or what evidence we present, and that therefore we must take no positions on these matters but must wait for the accepted authorities to come around to our position—if they do. This makes of us a mere passive battlefield across which conflicting "authorities" fight their intellectual battles. I, for one, am not prepared to play a passive role in such controversy, letting others dispose of me as they see fit. I intend to play an active role in the determination of my own fate.

As a scientist by training and by profession, I feel fully and formally competent to judge good and poor scientific work when I see them—and fully qualified to express my conclusions.

In looking over the literature alleging homosexuality as a sickness, one sees, first, abysmally poor sampling technique, leading to clearly biased, atypical samplings, which are then taken as representative of the entire homosexual community. Obviously all persons coming to a psychiatrist's office are going to have problems of one sort of another, are going to be disturbed or maladjusted or pathological, in some sense, or they wouldn't be there. To characterize ALL homosexuals as sick, on the basis of such a sampling—as Bieber, Bergler, and others have done—is clearly invalid, and is bad science.

Dr. Daniel Cappon, in his recent appalling book *Toward an Understanding of Homosexuality* (perhaps better named "Away from an Understanding of Homosexuality" or "Toward a Misunderstanding of Homosexuality") acknowledges at least this non-representative sampling and actually shows some faint signs of suggesting that perhaps there are two classes of homosexuals: patients and non-patients.

Notwithstanding Dr. Bieber's cavalier dismissal of it, Dr. Evelyn Hooker's work involving non-clinical homosexual subjects, with its very careful sampling technique and its conclusions of non-sickness, still remains convincing.

One sees secondly, in the literature alleging homosexuality as sickness, a violation of basic laws of logic by the drawing of "conclusions" which were inserted as assumptions. Dr. Bieber does this (and by implication, attributes it to his entire profession) in his statement: "All psychoanalytic theories ASSUME that homosexuality is psychopathological." Dr. Cappon says: " . . . homosexuality, BY DEFINITION, is not healthy. . . ." (Emphasis supplied in both quotations.) Obviously, if one assumes homosexuality as pathological or deems it as unhealthy at the outset, one will discover that homosexuals are sick. The "conclusions," however, can carry no weight outside the self-contained, rather useless logical structure erected upon the assumption or definition. The assumptions must be proven; the definitions must be validated. They have not been.

I am able to speak as a professional scientist when I say that we search in vain for any evidence, acceptable under proper scientific standards, that homosexuality is a sickness or disorder, or that homosexuals per se are disturbed.

On the basis of a disguised moralistic judgment (sometimes not at all disguised, as with Dr. Cappon), mixed both with a teleological approach to sexual matters, and with a classification as sickness of any departure from conformity to the statistical societal norms (on this basis, Dr. Cappon seems to come close to defining left-handedness as sickness), homosexuality has been DEFINED as pathological. We have been *defined* into sickness.

In logic, the entire burden of proof in this matter rests with those who would call us sick. We do not have to prove health. They have not shouldered their burden or proof of sickness; therefore we are not sick. These are things which it is our duty to point out, and, having pointed them out, to take strong public positions on them.

Then there are those who say that the label appended really doesn't matter. Let the homosexual be defined as sick, they say, but just get it granted that even if sick, he can function effectively and should therefore be judged only on his individual record and qualifications, and it is that state of being-judged-as-an-individual, regardless of labels, toward which we must work. This unfortunately is a woefully impractical, unrealistic, ivory-tower approach. Homosexuality is looked upon as a psychological question. If it is a sickness or disease or illness, it becomes then a mental illness. Properly or improperly, people ARE prejudiced against the mentally ill. Rightly or wrongly, employers will NOT hire them. Morally or immorally, the mentally ill are NOT judged as individuals, but are made pariahs. If we allow the label of sickness to stand, we will then have *two* battles to fight—that to combat prejudice against homosexuals per se, and that to combat prejudice against the mentally ill—and we will be pariahs and outcasts twice over. One such battle is quite enough!

Finally, as a matter of adopting a unified, coherent self-consistent philosophy, we MUST argue from a positive position of health. We cannot declare our equality and ask for acceptance and for judgment as whole persons, from a position of sickness. More than that, we argue for our RIGHT to be homosexuals, to remain homosexuals, and to live as homosexuals. In my view and by my moral standards, such an argument is immoral if we are not prepared, at the same time, to take a positive position that homosexuality is not pathological. If homosexuality indeed IS a sickness, then we have no right to remain homosexuals; we have the moral obligation to seek cure, and that only.

When we tell the various arms of organized society that part of our basic position is the request for acceptance *as homosexuals,* freed from constant pressure for conversion to heterosexuality, we are met with the argument of sickness. This occurred recently at a meeting between Washington Mattachine members and eleven representatives of all three major faiths, at which we asked for such acceptance of the homosexual into the religious community. Our entire position, our entire raison d'être for such meetings, falls to the ground unless we are prepared to couple our requests with an affirmative, definitive assertion of health—as we in Washington did in that instance.

I feel, therefore, that in the light of fact and logic, the question of sickness is a settled one and will remain so until and unless valid evidence can be brought forth to demonstrate pathology. Further, I feel that for purposes of strategy, we must say this and say it clearly and with no possible room for equivocation or ambiguity.

## Part III: On Research and the Homophile Movement

Movements tend to get themselves tied up with certain ideas and concepts, which in time assume the status of revealed and revered truth and cease being subjected to continuing, searching re-examination in the light of changed conditions. As an habitual skeptic, heretic, and iconoclast, I wish here to examine critically if briefly the value and importance to the homophile movement of research into homosexuality, of our commitment to it, and of the role, if any, which such research should play in the movement and in the activities of the homophile organizations.

I recognize that, with the deference granted to science in our culture, it is very respectable and self-reassuring and impressive to call one's group a research organization or to say that the group's purpose is research. However, at the outset one fact should be faced directly. For all their pledges of allegiance to the value of research, for all their designation of themselves as research organizations, for all their much vaunted support and sponsorship of research, NO American homophile organization that I know of has thus far done any effective or meaningful research, has sponsored any research, has supported or participated in any truly significant research (with the single exception of Dr. Evelyn Hooker's study, and while I grant that to be a major and important exception, the participation involved nothing more than supplying candidates for experimentation). The homophile movement's loss from its failure to contribute to research has been not from that failure, but from the diversion into talking ("maundering" might be a better term) about research—diversion of effort, time, and energy better expended elsewhere.

For purposes of this discussion, we can divide the objectives of relevant research into two loosely delineated classes: research into the origins and causes of homosexuality, and research into collateral aspects of the homosexual and his life and his community.

Almost always, when the homosexual speaks of research on homosexuality, he means the former class in one aspect or another: "What is the nature of homosexuality?" "What are its causes?" "Why am I a homosexual?" "Is homosexuality a sickness?" "Can the homosexual be changed?" Objectionably, "How can homosexuality be prevented?" etc.

A consideration of the rationale behind the homosexual's interest in such questions will quickly show that they are symptomatic of a thinly-veiled defensive feeling of inferiority, of uncertainty, of inequality, of insecurity—and most important, of lack of comfortable self-acceptance.

I have never heard of a single instance of a heterosexual, whatever problems he may have been facing, inquiring about the nature and origins of heterosexuality, or asking why he was a heterosexual, or considering these matters important. I fail to see why we should make similar inquiry in regard to homosexuality or consider the answers to these questions as being of any great moment to us. The Negro is not engrossed in questions about the origins of his skin color, nor the Jew in questions of the possibility of his conversion to Christianity.

Such questions are of academic, intellectual, scientific interest, but they are NOT—or ought not to be—burning ones for the homophile movement. Despite oft-made statements to the contrary, there is NO great need for research into homosexuality, and our movement is in no important way dependent upon such research or upon its findings.

If we start out—I do, on the basis presented in Part II above—with the premises (1) that the homosexual and his homosexuality are fully and unqualifiedly on par with, and the equal of, the heterosexual and his heterosexuality; and

(2) (since others have raised the question) that homosexuality is not an illness—then all these questions recede into unimportance.

We start off with the fact of the homosexual and his homosexuality and his right to remain as he is, and proceed to do all that is possible to make for him—as a homosexual (similarly in other contexts, as a Negro and as a Jew)—as happy a life, useful to self and to society, as is possible.

Research in these areas therefore is not, in any fundamental sense, particularly needed or particularly important. There is no driving or compelling urgency for us to concern ourselves with it. Those who do allege sickness have created THEIR need for THEIR research; let THEM do it.

In the collateral areas mentioned, well planned and executed research on carefully chosen projects can be of importance, particularly where it will serve to dispel modern folklore. Evelyn Hooker's research (referred to above) showing no difference outside their homosexuality itself, in its narrowest, denotive sense, between homosexual and heterosexuals, is one case in point. A study in the Netherlands by a Dr. Tolsma, which showed that the seduction of young boys by homosexuals had no effect upon their adult sexual orientation, is another. The study now under way by the Mattachine Society of Washington to obtain the first meaningful information on the actual susceptibility of homosexuals to blackmail, will probably be a third.

These are all useful projects. Dr. Hooker's has turned out to be one of our major bulwarks against the barrage of propaganda currently being loosed against us by the agents of organized psychiatry. (However, as I pointed out above, this is a bulwark not needed, in strict logic.) I shall in fact probably be using the results of all three of these collateral research projects from time to time in my presentations of our case. But these studies are not of the vital importance which could properly lead many of our homophile groups to characterize themselves as research organizations (only one of these projects actually involved a homophile organization to any significant degree) or to divert into research resources better expended elsewhere.

Research does not play the important role in our movement which much lip service attributes to it. It plays a very useful and occasionally valuable supporting roles but not more than that.

More important than the preceding, however, is the matter of this emphasis upon research, in terms of the evolution of our movement. In the earlier days of the modern homophile movement, allegiance to the alleged importance of research was reasonable. As the philosophy of the movement has formed, crystallized, and matured, and more important, as our society itself has changed—and it has changed enormously in the past fifteen years and even in the past two—the directions and emphases in our movement have changed too. As indicated in Part I of this article, the mainstream has shifted toward a more activist mode of operation.

Continued placing of primary or strong emphasis within our movement upon research will only result in the movement's loss of the lead which it is taking in the shaping, formation, and formulation of society's attitudes and policies toward homosexuality and the homosexual.

Thus, while as a scientist I will never derogate the value of research for its own sake in order to provide additional knowledge, as an active member of the homophile movement my position must be quite different. It is time for us to move away from the comfortingly detached respectability of research into the often less pleasant rough-and-tumble of political and social activism.

*Franklin Kameny*

Kameny, Franklin. 1965a. "Does Research into Homosexuality Matter?" *The Ladder* 9 (May): 14–20.

---

## Homosexuality and Cultural Value Systems (1973)

*Judd Marmor, M.D., a prominent psychoanalyst and professor of psychiatry at the University of California at Los Angeles, was one of the first heterosexual psychiatrists to argue against labeling homosexuality a disease. The following essay was originally delivered at a symposium entitled "Should Homosexuality Be in the APA Nomenclature?" at the 1973 Annual Meeting of the American Psychiatric Association (APA). In December of that year, the APA decided homosexuality was not a mental disorder.*

Proponents of the mental illness label for homosexuality base their arguments on three major themes: 1) that homosexuality is the consequence of "disordered sexual development," 2) that it is a deviation from the biological norm, and 3) that psychodynamic studies of homosexuals always reveal them to be deeply disturbed individuals.

The disordered sexual development theme is based on the finding that a certain type of disturbed parent-child relationship is a background factor in most cases. There seems to be an assumption in this theme that if there is a disturbed parent-child relationship in the background of someone with variant sexual behavior this proves that the disturbed relationship is causally responsible and that the individual with such variant behavior must be mentally ill.

There are a number of fallacies in this argument. First, we know that although most homosexuals show the "typical" family constellation, by no means do all of them. Secondly, not all people who do have such family constellations in their background become homosexual. Third (and most importantly) to call homosexuality the result of disturbed sexual development really says nothing other than that you disapprove of the outcome of that development. *All* personality idiosyncrasies are the result of background developmental differences, and *all* have specific historical antecedents. The concept of illness cannot be extrapolated on the basis of background but must rest on its own merits.

### Deviant Behavior not Necessarily Psychopathology

It is my conviction that we do not have the right to label behavior that is deviant from that currently favored by the majority as evidence per se of psychopathology. And, as a matter of fact, we do *not* do so except where we are reflecting our culture's bias toward a particular kind of deviance. In a democratic society we recognize the rights of individuals to hold widely divergent religious or ideational preferences, as long as their holders do not attempt to force their beliefs on others who do not share them. Our attitudes toward divergent sexual preferences, however, are quite different, obviously because moral values—couched in "medical" and "scientific" rationalizations—are involved.

There are some psychiatrists who would argue that individuals who adhere to unusual life-styles are indeed neurotic and that they suffer from various developmental fixations or arrests that account for their inability to adhere to the behavioral or ideational standards of the majority. Such labeling tends to define normality in terms of behavioral adjustment to cultural conventions rather than in terms of ego strengths and ego-adaptive capacities, and it puts psychiatry clearly in the role of an agent of cultural control rather than of a branch of the healing arts.

Moreover, the relativity of our contemporary sexual mores should not be ignored in any scientific approach to sexual behavior. In a cross-cultural study of 76 societies other than our own, Ford and Beach (1951) found that in nearly two-thirds of them homosexual activities were considered normal and socially acceptable, at least for certain members of the community. Nor were all these societies necessarily "primitive" ones. In ancient Greece—a society that we admire and feel indebted to culturally, philosophically, and scientifically—overt homosexual relations between older men and youths was not only considered acceptable but was an institutionalized practice cultivated by heterosexual, healthy, honorable, normal men.

## Bisexuality—Our Mammalian Inheritance

The second major argument for the illness viewpoint is that homosexuality, in contrast to other forms of behavioral deviance, is biologically unnatural. Dr. Frank Beach, the eminent biologist, has summarized the evidence on this by pointing out that bisexual behavior has been observed in more than a dozen mammalian species and "undoubtedly occurs in many others not yet studied." He concluded: "Human homosexuality reflects the essential bisexual character of our mammalian inheritance. The extreme modifiability of man's sex life makes possible the conversion of this essential bisexuality into a form of unisexuality with the result that a member of the same sex eventually becomes the only acceptable stimulus to arousal" (1950, 276).

Thus, from an objective biological viewpoint there is nothing "unnatural" about homosexual object choice. To illustrate how specious the argument is concerning the supposed biological unnaturalness of homosexuality let us consider some other conditions that are also outside of the presumably customary biological patterns. What about vegetarians? After all, most human beings are "naturally" meat-eaters, but we don't automatically label vegetarians as mentally ill. Or what about celibacy? Do we automatically assume that all people who choose a life of sexual abstinence are mentally ill simply because they do not follow the "natural" biological mating patterns? Obviously, we do not.

The third argument that is often advanced is that any careful study of the personality of homosexuals will show that they are really disturbed individuals. In contrast to Socarides, who holds the view that all homosexuals are practically borderline psychotics, Bieber concedes that many homosexuals can be well-adjusted individuals, but he argues that they still suffer from "pathology."

## Happy, Constructive, and Realistic Homosexuals

What *does* constitute the intrinsic "pathology" of a socially well-adjusted homosexual? I submit that in the view of Bieber, Socarides, and others who share their viewpoint, it is primarily that his sexual preference differs from that of the majority of society. I do not deny that there are homosexuals who, just like heterosexuals, suffer from a wide variety of personality disorders and serious mental illnesses, although much of the dis-ease that they suffer from is not intrinsic to their homosexuality but is a consequence of the prejudice and discrimination that they encounter in our society.

But I believe there is now an incontrovertible body of evidence that there are homosexual individuals who, except for their variant object choice, are happy with their lives and have made a constructive and realistic adaptation to being members of a minority group in our society. I consider the kind of evidence that Socarides marshals from his clinical practice as essentially meaningless in this regard. As I have often pointed out, if our judgment about the mental health of heterosexuals were based only on those whom we see in our clinical practices we would have to conclude that all heterosexuals are also mentally ill.

The final absurdity of this is the impossibility of trying to define at what point a person becomes a homosexual who is labeled as having a mental disorder. Some defendants of the illness theory try to justify it by saying that it applies only to obligatory homosexuality. Does this mean that only [Kinsey scale] type 6 homosexuals are mentally ill and all the others are not? Or that types 4, 5, and 6 are ill but not 1, 2, and 3? The whole process of such labeling is unpleasantly reminiscent of the Hitlerian process of trying to determine what fraction of black or Jewish ancestry a person might be permitted to have and still be considered an acceptable member of society with full legal rights.

Surely the time has come for psychiatry to give up the archaic practice of classifying the millions of men and women who accept or prefer homosexual object choices as being, by virtue of that fact alone, mentally ill. The fact that their alternative life-style happens to be out of favor with current cultural conventions must not be a basis in itself for a diagnosis of psychopathology. It is our task as psychiatrists to be healers of the distressed, not watchdogs of our social mores.

*Judd Marmor*

Beach, Frank A. 1950. *Sexual Behavior in Animals and Man.* Springfield, IL: Charles C. Thomas.

Ford, Clellan S., and Frank A. Beach. 1951. *Patterns of Sexual Behavior.* New York: Harper.

Marmor, Judd. 1973. "Homosexuality and Cultural Value Systems." *American Journal of Psychiatry* 130: 1208–1209.

# Chronology

| | |
|---|---|
| 4th c. BC | Hippocratic medical texts |
| 2nd c. AD | Galenic medical texts |
| 1533 | Henry VIII criminalizes "buggery," making it punishable by death and the loss of property |
| 1610 | The Virginia Colony establishes sodomy as a capital crime; other U.S. colonies follow suit |
| 1710? | Anonymous publication in England of *Onania, or the Heinous Sin of Self-Pollution* |
| 1760 | *Onanism, or a Medical Dissertation on the Diseases Produced by Masturbation* by Samuel-Auguste-André-David Tissot |
| 1789–1799 | French Revolution |
| 1791 | French Constituent Assembly (1789–1791) deletes antisodomy laws from the new French penal code. This subsequently becomes the model for the decriminalization of sodomy in other countries. |
| 1809 | *Philosophie zoologique* by Jean-Baptiste de Lamark |
| 1857 | *Treatise on the Physical, Intellectual, and Moral Degeneration of the Human Species and the Causes of these Morbid Varieties* by Bénédict A. Morel |
| 1857 | *Medico-legal Study of Crimes Against Decency* by Ambroise Tardieu |
| 1859 | *On the Origin of Species by Means of Natural Selection* by Charles Darwin |
| 1861–1865 | U. S. Civil War |
| 1864–1879 | Pamphlets by Karl Heinrich Ulrichs defending same-sex love as a biological phenomenon |
| 1866 | *General Morphology of Organisms* by Ernst Haeckel |
| 1868 | First German usage of *homosexual* and *heterosexual,* in a letter from Karl Maria Kertbeny to Karl Ulrichs |
| 1869 | *A Practical Treatise on Nervous Exhaustion (Neurasthenia)* by George Beard |
| 1869 | Karl Westphal describes "contrary sexual sensation" (*conträre Sexualempfindung*) as a neuropathic and psychopathic condition |
| 1878 | Arrigo Tamassia renders Westphal's term into Italian as *inversione dell'istinto sessuale* (inversion of the sexual instinct) |
| 1886 | *Psychopathia Sexualis* by Richard von Krafft-Ebing |
| 1892 | Alice Michel lesbian "lust murder" case |
| 1895 | Oscar Wilde trials |
| 1897 | *Sexual Inversion* by Havelock Ellis with John Addington Symonds |
| 1897 | Magnus Hirschfeld founds the Scientific Humanitarian Committee to defend the civil rights of homosexuals |
| 1898 | George Bedborough put on trial for selling Havelock Ellis's *Sexual Inversion* |
| 1901 | *The Social Problem of Sexual Inversion* by Magnus Hirschfeld |
| 1905 | *Three Essays on the Theory of Sexuality* by Sigmund Freud |

| | |
|---|---|
| 1982 | French virologist Luc Montagnier isolates LAV (lymphadenopathy-associated virus) as the causative agent of AIDS |
| 1982 | American virologist Robert Gallo isolates HTLV-III (human T-cell lymphotropic virus type III) as the causative agent of AIDS |
| 1986 | The name Human Immune Deficiency Virus (HIV) adopted by consensus |
| 1987 | AIDS Coalition to Unleash Power (ACT-UP) forms in New York City |
| 1987 | President Ronald Reagan speaks publicly about AIDS for the first time |
| 1987 | DSM-III-Revised deletes the diagnosis of homosexuality entirely, leaving the paraphilias and sexual dysfunctions as the two main classes of "sexual disorders" |
| 1990 | Dutch neuroscientists, Dick Swaab and Michel Hofman, first report on neuroanatomical differences between homosexual men and a reference group |
| 1991 | J. Michael Bailey and Richard C. Pillard publish findings on high concordance rate of homosexuality in identical twins |
| 1991 | Simon LeVay reports on a difference in hypothalamic structure between heterosexual and homosexual men |
| 1991 | "Posttranssexual Manifesto" by Sandy Stone |
| 1993 | Dean Hamer and colleagues report on a linkage between DNA markers on the X chromosome and homosexuality |
| 1993 | Cheryl Chase founds the Intersex Society of North America (ISNA) |
| 1994 | DSM-IV groups sexual dysfunction, the paraphilias, and gender identity disorder under the heading "sexual and gender identity disorders" |
| 1995 | Release of Saquinavir, the first protease inhibitor, for the treatment of HIV disease |
| 1998 | APA officially criticizes efforts to change sexual orientation |

# Glossary

**Acquired Immune Deficiency Syndrome (AIDS):** A syndrome characterized by a variety of disorders and pathological findings (such as low helper T-cell (T4) count, *Pneumocystis carinii* pneumonia, and Kaposi's sarcoma) associated with an advanced stage of HIV infection. The immune system is weakened, thus allowing for the spread of unusual microorganisms normally controlled by the immune system (opportunistic infections).

**Atavism:** Reappearance in an organism of behaviors or structures typical of ancestors more distant than the parents.

**Aversion therapy:** Any number of different behavior modification techniques, largely relying on operant conditioning, to diminish a behavior (for example, homoerotic arousal) by associating it with discomfort. This might be electrical shock, drug induced nausea, or an unpleasant thought.

**Bisexual:** A term first used in the nineteenth century to refer to the possession of both male and female anatomical or psychological traits, especially during embryological development. In the twentieth century, more commonly refers to erotic attraction to both males and females.

**Classical conditioning:** A technique for establishing a *conditioned reflex* whereby a stimulus not usually linked with a particular response is associated with a stimulus that automatically evokes the response by repeatedly presenting the two stimuli together (for example, inducing salivation in a dog solely by ringing a bell by repeatedly associating the ringing with food presentation).

**Conditioning:** *See* **Classical conditioning; Operant conditioning**

**Constructionism:** The philosophical position that a phenomenon is the result of sociological, cultural, or historical forces. In the case of homosexuality, the position that "sexual orientation" is not biologically fixed, but a historical phenomenon of the past two centuries in Europe and America.

**Covert sensitization:** A behavior modification technique of associating imagined target stimuli with imagined aversive thoughts (for example, associating homoerotic mental images with nausea).

**Darwinism** or **Darwinian evolution:** Refers to British naturalist Charles Darwin (1809–1882). The theory that species evolve over time through a process of natural selection. It is often contrasted with Lamarkism (or inheritance of acquired traits), although Darwin also believed in the hereditary transmission of acquired traits.

**Degeneration:** In nineteenth-century medicine, the theory that diseases and acquired ills could be transmitted from one generation to the next, thereby leading to a gradual decline in hereditary fitness and eventual termination of a family line.

**Dementia praecox:** A psychiatric diagnosis coined by German psychiatrist Emil Kraepelin (1865–1926). It referred to a group of illnesses beginning with disturbed behavior and cognition in adolescence and ending in dementia. *See also* Schizophrenia

**Determinism:** The philosophical position that a phenomenon or trait is not freely chosen but fixed by other forces: these may be biological (for example, genetic or hormonal), sociological, or familial (for example, psychoanalytic models of parental molding of the infantile psyche).

**Electroconvulsive therapy:** Psychotherapeutic technique whereby electric current is applied to the head to induce a generalized tonic-clonic (grand mal) seizure.

**Enzyme-Linked Immunosorbent Assay (ELISA):** A method for identifying the presence of antibodies to HIV in body fluids. It may be up to six months after exposure to HIV before antibody levels are detectable by ELISA.

**Essentialism:** The philosophical position that a phenomenon is the same throughout time and in different cultures. In the case of homosexuality, the belief that sexual orientation is a fixed and enduring feature of humans that is virtually identical throughout history.

**Gender:** A term that emerged in the 1950s to refer to the psychological and sociological traits distinguishing men from women. *Compare to* sex.

**Gender identity:** A term developed in the 1950s to refer to a person's self-identification as male or female. *Compare with* gender role.

**Gender role:** A term developed in the 1950s to refer to the behaviors and dress that distinguish a person as male or female. Originally, this also included the sex of erotic partners, assuming heterosexuality to be the norm. *Compare with* gender identity.

**Genotype:** The genetic constitution of an individual that codes for a particular trait. *Compare with* phenotype.

**Hermaphroditism:** From the Greek god Hermaphroditos, who possessed ideal male and female qualities. Refers to animals that possess both male and female gonads (so called, "true hermaphrodites") or ambiguous genitals ("pseudo-hermaphrodites"). Psychosexual hermaphroditism or sexual inversion, in the nineteenth century, referred to individuals with same-sex erotic attraction, who were presumed to have the neurological traits or hormonal physiology of the opposite sex.

**Heterosexual:** A term first used in the late nineteenth century to describe the erotic attraction to both males and females (what we currently call bisexual). It was later applied to erotic attraction to people of the opposite sex.

**Homophile:** From the Latin *homo,* man, or Greek *omos,* same, and *philos,* friend. A term used in the 1940s and 1950s to refer to same-sex attraction. It was seen as more positive and less stigmatizing than the medical term homosexual.

**Homosexual:** A term first used in print in German in 1869 and in English in 1892 to refer to sexual attraction to a person of the same sex. Originally, it was believed that the homosexual suffered from psychological gender inversion that led to erotic attraction to a "normal," nonhomosexual person.

**Human Immunodeficiency Virus (HIV):** The virus widely believed to be the causative agent of AIDS. This name was adopted in 1986 by consensus for a virus previous identified as LAV (Lymphadenopathy-Associated Virus) and HTLV III (Human T-Lymphotropic Virus Type III).

**Humors:** In classical medical teachings, these were four fluids that circulated in the body: blood, phlegm, yellow bile, and black bile (*melancholia*). These, in turn, were composed of paired combinations of the four elemental properties: heat, cold, dryness, and humidity. All tissues and organs were composed of combinations of the four humors. Illness was believed to be a result of an excess or imbalance of the humors (*dyscrasia*). Humoral therapy was aimed at correcting this imbalance by methods such as bleeding or purging, heating or chilling.

**Hysteria:** In classical Greek medicine, a disorder of a wandering womb (Gk., *hystera*) that caused suffocation and other pain symptoms. In the eighteenth and nineteenth centuries it referred to a neuropsychiatric disorder, predominantly of women, with unexplained pain complaints, emotional instability, dissociation, and dramatic behaviors. No longer in official psychiatric usage.

**Intersex:** A term used at the turn of the twentieth century in reference to psychosexual hermaphroditism or inversion. Dr. Richard Goldschmidt used it in 1917 in discussing the endocrinology of hermaphroditism. In current usage, it refers to diverse manifestations of ambiguous or atypical genitals.

**Inversion:** The nineteenth-century theory that the sex of the brain or psyche could be the opposite of that of the genitals, that is, psychosexual hermaphroditism. Thus the inverted woman had a masculine mind and the male invert was effeminate. Traits of inversion were supposedly found not only in erotic attraction, but also temperament, behavior, career choice, and even anatomic structure.

**Lamarkism** or **Lamarkian evolution:** Refers to French naturalist Jean-Baptiste de Lamark (1744–1829). The theory that acquired traits can be inherited. *Compare to* Darwinian evolution.

**Lesbian:** A woman erotically attracted to women. The term is derived from Lesbos, the Greek island that was the birthplace of the poet Sappho (7th cent. BC). *See also* Sapphism

**Masturbation:** From *manustupration* (pollution by the hand). Any variety of practices for provoking ejaculation or orgasm through manual stimulation or rubbing. It was referred to under numerous other terms in the medical literature: onanism, solitary vice, voluntary pollution, self-pollution, self-defilement, the crime of solitude, self-abuse, etc.

**Neurosis:** In the nineteenth century, referred to a disorder or irritation of the nerves. It later referred to a mental disorder where there was maladaptive behavior or thinking, but no loss of insight (as compared to psychosis). In the early twentieth century and in current popular usage, refers predominantly to an excess of anxiety symptoms.

**Nosology:** From the Greek *nosos,* disease. The naming and classification of diseases.

**Onanism:** Since the eighteenth century, a synonym for masturbation. The term refers to the biblical figure of Onan, who was struck down by God for spilling his seed. "Conjugal onanism" referred to *coitus interruptus* or the practice of terminating penile-vaginal sex before ejaculation, often used as a means of birth control.

**Ontogeny:** Refers to the history of the development of an individual from a fertilized egg to maturity.

**Operant conditioning:** A conditioning technique that relies on reinforcement: a behavior is rewarded (or punished) each time it occurs in order to increase (or decrease) its frequency. For example, giving a dog a biscuit every time it performs a trick on command.

**Paranoia:** In psychiatry, a disorder were there is the delusional belief of being persecuted or followed. It can be a symptom of schizophrenia or of a less debilitating personality disorder.

**Pederasty:** From the Greek *pais,* boy, and *erastes,* lover. Historically refers to sexual relations with adolescent boys, but sometimes used interchangeably with sodomy and homosexuality.

**Perversion:** In medicine, a term used most generally to refer to any serious deviation or abnormality of behavior or function. Sexual perversion referred to any aberrant sexual practice that was not penile-vaginal sex. The term was used from the nineteenth century until the 1970s, particularly in psychoanalytic writings. Now it is rarely used in medical writing.

**Phenotype:** An observable trait of an individual that is determined by genes and by the environment. *See also* genotype.

**Phylogeny:** The evolutionary or racial history of a species or organism.

**Positivism:** A philosophy developed by Auguste Comte (1798–1857) who believed that in the most advanced stage of human civilization all phenomena would be explained through the logical sequence of natural laws. More generally, refers to a philosophical position that values empirically derived scientific knowledge over theological or metaphysical knowledge.

**Psychosexual hermaphroditism:** *See* **Inversion**

**Psychosis:** A severe mental disorder where there is disturbed perception of reality. This may include hallucinations and delusions.

**Queer:** Literally, unconventional or eccentric. A slang term for homosexual. A term adopted in the 1990s by younger gays and lesbians and by academics who favored radical politics or a fluid conception of sexual identity.

**Sapphism:** Refers to love or sex between women. Alludes to the Greek poetess Sappho (7th cent. BC), who was born on the isle of Lesbos and wrote love poems to women.

**Schizophrenia:** A psychiatric diagnosis first coined by Swiss psychiatrist Eugen Bleuler (1857–1939) in 1911. He identified four characteristic findings: loose mental associations, disturbed affect, ambivalence, and autism. It was associated with the earlier diagnosis of dementia praecox. According to psychoanalytic theory, schizophrenia was the result of disturbed parent-child dynamics and possibly repressed homosexuality. The current psychiatric belief is that it is a brain disorder with a hereditary component.

**Sex:** The biological and anatomical attributes of male and female. *Compare with* gender.

**Sexual inversion:** *See* **inversion**

**Sexual orientation:** Whether a person's erotic interests are directed toward the same sex or the opposite sex.

**Sexual perversion:** *See* **perversion**

**Shock therapy:** A colloquial term used to refer to convulsive therapy (the use of electrical current or drugs to induce seizures), drug-induced insulin shock, or electrical aversion therapy.

**Sodomy:** An imprecise term sometimes used to refer to penile-anal penetration, also used more generally to refer to all nonpenile-vaginal penetration (for example, oral sex). It is often used interchangeably with pederasty and homosexuality.

**Transgenderism:** A term that emerged in the 1980s to refer to a broad spectrum of cross-gendered behavior and identification, including transsexualism and transvestism. It tends to be the preferred term for political activism and community organizing.

**Transsexualism:** A term coined by Dr. Magnus Hirschfeld (1868–1934) in 1923 in reference to "intersexuals." Dr. David O. Cauldwell used it in 1949 in describing a case of severe gender dysphoria (dissatisfaction with anatomical sex). Currently, it refers to the phenomenon of cross-gender identification and gender dysphoria. Since the 1950s, many chose to undergo hormonal and surgical sex reassignment.

**Transvestism** or **transvestitism:** The practice of dressing in clothes commonly worn by people of the opposite sex. The term "transvestite" was first introduced into the medical literature in 1910 by Magnus Hirschfeld (1868–1934). Sometimes it refers to transvestic fetishism for erotic stimulation. It is also used in reference to cross-dressing without erotic aims.

**Tribadism:** The practice of two women rubbing their genitals, or specifically their clitorises, together. Those who practice this were called *tribades.*

**Unisexual:** A term used in the late nineteenth century to refer to same-sex erotic attraction.

**Uranian:** Related to the Greek god Uranus. A term employed by Karl Heinrich Ulrichs (1825–1895) in reference to Plato's *Symposium,* where Pausanias praises the elder, heavenly Aphrodite, daughter of Uranus. Those who are inspired by her are attracted to men. Ulrichs would therefore refer to "man-manly love" as "Uranian love."

**Urning:** A term coined by Karl Heinrich Ulrichs in 1864 to refer to men whose sexual drive was directed to men—a phenomenon he called Uranian love. He argued this came about because of an innate feminine nature.

# Bibliography

Abraham, Felix. 1931. "Genitalumwandlungen an zwei männlichen Transvestiten." *Zeitschrift für Sexualwissenschaft und Sexualpolitik* 18: 223–226.

Acton, William. [1875] 1987. "The Functions and Disorders of the Reproductive Organs, in Childhood, Youth, Adult Age, and Advanced Life, Considered in Their Physiological, Social and Moral Relations." Extract, pp. 57–73 in *The Sexuality Debates*. Edited by Sheila Jeffreys. New York: Routledge and Kegan Paul.

Alinder, Gary. 1972. "Gay Liberation Meets the Shrinks." Pp. 141–145 in *Out of the Closets: Voices of Gay Liberation*. Edited by Karla Jay and Allen Young. New York: Douglas Books.

Allen, Garland E. 1997. "The Double-Edged Sword of Genetic Determinism: Social and Political Agendas in Genetic Studies of Homosexuality, 1940–1994." Pp. 242–270 in *Science and Homosexualities*. Edited by V. Rosario. New York: Routledge.

Allen, Peter. 2000. *The Wages of Sin: Sex and Disease, Past and Present*. Chicago: University of Chicago Press.

Altman, Lawrence. 1981. "Rare Cancer Seen in 41 Homosexuals." *New York Times,* July 3, A20.

AMA (American Medical Association), Council on Scientific Affairs. 1988. "Aversion Therapy." *Connecticut Medicine* 52: 42–48.

APA (American Psychiatric Association). 2000. "Position Statement on Therapies Focused on Attempts to Change Sexual Orientation (Reparative or Conversion Therapies)." Includes Appendix 1: "APA Position Statement on Psychiatric Treatment and Sexual Orientation (December 11, 1998)." *American Journal of Psychiatry* 157: 1719–1721.

Anchell, Melvin. 1985. "A Psychoanalytic Look at Homosexuality. Delivered to the Graduating Students, Valley Christian University, Fresno, CA." *Vital Speeches of the Day,* February 15, 1986, 285–288.

Atkinson, J. Hamilton, and Igor Grant. 1994. "Natural History of Neuropsychiatric Manifestations of HIV Disease." *Psychiatric Clinics of North America* 17, no. 1: 17–33.

Babington, Anthony. 1997. *Shell-Shock: A History of the Changing Attitudes to War Neurosis*. London: Leo Cooper.

Bagemihl, Bruce. 1999. *Biological Exuberance: Animal Homosexuality and Natural Diversity*. New York: St. Martin's Press.

Bailey, J. Michael, and Richard C. Pillard. 1991. "A Genetic Study of Male Sexual Orientation." *Archives of General Psychiatry* 48: 1089–1096.

Bailey, J. Michael, Richard C. Pillard, M. C. Neale, and M. A. Agyei. 1993. "Heritable Factors Influence Sexual Orientation in Women." *Archives of General Psychiatry* 50: 217–223.

Baker, Blanche M. 1959a. "Toward Understanding." *ONE* 7, no. 1 (January): 25–27.

———. 1959b. "Toward Understanding." *ONE* 7, no. 3 (March): 25–26.

Bakwin, Harry, and Ruth M. Bakwin. 1953. "Homosexual Behavior in Children." *Journal of Pediatric* 43: 108–111.

Barahal, Hyman S. 1940. "Testosterone in Psychotic, Male Homosexuals." *Psychoanalytic Quarterly* 14: 315–330.

———. 1953. "Female Transvestitism and Homosexuality." *Psychiatric Quarterly* 27: 390–438.

Barker, William S. 1903. "Two Cases of Sexual Contrariety." *St. Louis Courier of Medicine* 28: 269–271.

Barnette, Leslie W. 1942. "Study of an Adult Male Homosexual and Terman-Miles M-F Scores." *American Journal of Orthopsychiatry* 12: 346–351.

Barrett, J. 1998. "Psychological and Social Function Before and After Phalloplasty." *International Journal of Transgenderism* 2, no. 1, http://www.symposion.com/ijt/ijtc0301.htm.

Bartemeier, Leo H. 1943. "Introduction to Psychiatry." *Psychoanalytic Review* 30: 386–398.

Bayer, Ronald. 1987. *Homosexuality and American Psychiatry: The Politics of Diagnosis.* Princeton, NJ: Princeton University Press.

———. 1989. *Private Acts, Social Consequences: AIDS and the Politics of Public Health.* New York: Free Press.

Beach, Frank A. 1950. *Sexual Behavior in Animals and Man.* Springfield, IL: Charles C. Thomas.

Beard, George. [1869] 1880. *A Practical Treatise on Nervous Exhaustion (Neurasthenia).* 2nd ed. New York: W. Wood.

———. 1886. *Sexual Neurasthenia.* New York: E. B. Tweat.

Beery, Florence. 1924. "The Psyche of the Intermediate Sex." *The Medico-Legal Journal* (New York) 41: 4–9.

Bell, Alan P., and Martin S. Weinberger. 1978. *Homosexualities: A Study of Diversity among Men and Women.* New York: Simon and Schuster.

Bell, Luther Vose. 1840. *An Hour's Conference with Fathers and Sons in Relation to a Common and Fatal Indulgence of Youth.* Boston: Whipple and Damrell.

Benjamin, Harry. 1931a. "For the Sake of Morality." *Medical Journal and Record* 133: 380–382.

———. 1931b. "An Echo of and an Addendum to 'For the Sake of Morality.'" *Medical Journal and Record* 134: 118–120.

———. 1944. "The Sex Problem in the Armed Forces." *Urologic and Cutaneous Review* 48: 231–244.

———. 1966. *The Transsexual Phenomenon.* New York: Julian Press.

Bennett, Paula, and Vernon Rosario, eds. 1995. *Solitary Pleasures: The Historical, Literary, and Artistic Discourses of Autoeroticism.* New York: Routledge.

Bergler, Edmund. 1943. "The Respective Importance of Reality and Fantasy in the Genesis of Female Homosexuality." *Journal of Criminal Psychopathology* 5: 27–48.

———. 1944. "Eight Prerequisites for the Psychoanalytic Treatment of Homosexuality." *Psychoanalytic Review* 31: 253–286.

———. 1947. "Differential Diagnosis between Spurious Homosexuality and Perversion Homosexuality." *Psychiatric Quarterly* 21: 399–409.

———. 1948. "The Myth of a New National Disease: Homosexuality and the Kinsey Report." *Psychiatric Quarterly* 22: 67–88.

———. 1959. *1000 Homosexuals. Conspiracy of Silence, or Curing and Deglamorizing Homosexuals?* Paterson, NJ: Pageant Books.

Bergler, Edmund, and William S. Kroger. 1954. *Kinsey's Myth of Female Sexuality. The Medical Facts.* New York: Grune and Stratton.

Bergmann, Martin S. 1945. "Homosexuality on the Rorschach Test." *Bulletin of the Menninger Clinic* 9: 78–83.

Berlant, Lauren, and Elizabeth Freeman. 1993. "Queer Nationality." Pp. 193–229 in *Fear of a Queer Planet: Queer Politics and Social Theory.* Edited by M. Warner. Minneapolis: University of Minnesota Press.

Berlien, Ivan, and Raymond W. Waggoner. 1966. "Selection and Induction." Pp. 153–191 in *Neuropsychiatry in World War II,* vol. 1. Edited by John B. Coates and Arnold L. Ahnfeldt. Washington, DC: Office of the Surgeon General.

Bérubé, Allan. 1990. *Coming Out under Fire: The History of Gay Men and Women in World War II.* New York: Free Press.

Bieber, Irving. 1962. *Homosexuality: A Psychoanalytical Study.* New York: Vintage.

Bien, Ernst. 1934. "Why Do Homosexuals Undergo Treatment?" *Medical Review of Reviews* 40: 5–18.

Birk, Lee, William Huddleston, and Elizabeth Miller. 1971. "Avoidance Conditioning for Homosexuality." *Archives of General Psychiatry* 25: 314–323.

Blackwood, Evelyn. 1984. "Sexuality and Gender in Certain Native American Tribes." *Signs* 10: 27–42.

Blake, John B. 1984. "Mary Gove Nichols, Prophetess of Health." Pp. 359–375 in *Women and Health in America.* Edited by J. W. Leavitt. Madison: University of Wisconsin Press.

Bleys, Rudi C. 1995. *The Geography of Perversion: Male-to-Male Sexual Behavior Outside the West and the Ethnographic Imagination, 1750–1918.* New York: New York University Press.

Blumer, Alder. 1882. "A Case of Perverted Sexual Instinct (*Contrære Sexualempfindung*)." *American Journal of Insanity* 39: 22–35.

Boerhaave, Hermann. [1708] 1742. *Academic Lectures on the Theory of Physic.* 5 vols. London: W. Innys.

Bollmeier, L. N. 1938. "A Paranoid Mechanism in Male Overt Homosexuality." *Psychoanalytic Quarterly* 7: 357–367.

Bonnemaison, Julien. 1875. "Sur un cas d'hystérie chez l'homme." *Archives générales de médecine,* 6th ser., 25: 664–679.

Bornstein, Kate. 1994. *Gender Outlaw: On Men, Women and the Rest of Us.* New York: Routledge.

Boswell, John. 1994. *Same-Sex Unions in Premodern Europe.* New York: Villard.

Bowler, Peter. 1989. *Evolution: The History of an Idea.* Berkeley: University of California Press.

Bozett, F. W. 1989. "Gay Fathers: A Review of the Literature." *Journal of Homosexuality* 18, nos. 1–2: 137–162.

Bradford, Judith, and Caitlin Ryan. 1988. *The National Lesbian Health Care Survey: Final Report.* Washington, DC: National Lesbian and Gay Health Foundation.

Brandt, Allan. 1987. *No Magic Bullet: A Social History of Venereal Disease in the United States since 1880.* New York: Oxford University Press.

Braslow, Joel. 1997. *Mental Ills and Bodily Cures: Psychiatric Treatment in the First Half of the Twentieth Century.* Berkeley: University of California Press.

Brass, Alister. 1970. "Gay Is *What?*" [Letter] *New England Journal of Medicine* 283: 817.

Brill, Abraham Arden. 1913. "The Conception of Homosexuality." *Journal of the American Medical Association* 61: 335–340.

———. 1919. "Intermediary Stages of Sexual Development. Summary of a Meeting of the New York Neurological Society." *Journal of Nervous and Mental Disease* 50: 454–455.

———. 1934. "Homoeroticism and Paranoia." *American Journal of Psychiatry* 90: 956–974.

———. 1935. "The Psychiatric Approach to the Problem of Homosexuality." *The Journal-Lancet* 55: 249–252.

———. 1940. "Sexual Manifestations in Neurotic and Psychotic Symptoms." *Psychiatric Quarterly* 14: 9–16.

Brill, Norman Q. 1966. "Hospitalization and Disposition." Pp. 195–253 in *Neuropsychiatry in World War II,* vol. 1. Edited by John B. Coates and Arnold L. Ahnfeldt. Washington, DC: Office of the Surgeon General.

Buican, Denis. 1984. *Histoire de la génétique et de l'évolutionisme en France.* Paris: Presses Universitaires de France.

Bullough, Vern L., and Martha Voght. 1976. "Homosexuality and Its Confusion with the 'Secret Sin' in pre-Freudian America." Pp. 112–124 in *Sex, Society and History.* Edited by Vern L. Bullough. New York: Science History Publications.

Burckhardt, Richard. 1995. *The Spirit of System: Lamarck and Evolutionary Biology.* Cambridge: Cambridge University Press.

Burns, T., and A. H. Crisp. 1985. "Factors Affecting Prognosis in Male Anorexics." *Journal of Psychiatric Research* 19: 323–328.

Burr, Chandler. 1993. "Homosexuality and Biology." *Atlantic Monthly* 271, no. 3: 47–65.

Burton, Arthur. 1947. "The Use of the Masculinity-Femininity Scale of the Minnesota Multiphasic Personality Inventory as an Aid in the Diagnosis of Sexual Inversion." *Journal of Psychology* 24: 161–164.

Byne, William. 1995. "Science and Belief: Psychobiological Research on Sexual Orientation." Pp. 303–344 in *Sex, Cells, and Same-Sex Desire: The Biology of Sexual Preference.* Edited by J. De Cecco and D. A. Parker. Binghamton, NY: Harrington Park.

Cabaj, R. P., and T. S. Stein, eds. 1996. *Textbook of Homosexuality and Mental Health.* Washington, DC: American Psychiatric Press.

Cadden, Joan. 1993. *Meanings of Sex Difference in the Middle Ages: Medicine, Science, and Culture.* Cambridge: Cambridge University Press.

Cameron, Paul, and Kirk Cameron. 1995. "Does Incest Cause Homosexuality?" *Psychological Reports* 76: 611–621.

Cameron, Paul, Kirk Cameron, and Kay Proctor. 1989. "Effect of Homosexuality upon Public Health and Social Order." *Psychological Reports* 64: 1167–1179.

Cameron, Paul, Kay Proctor, William Coburn, and Nels Forde. 1986. "Child Molestation and Homosexuality." *Psychological Reports* 58: 327–337.

Caprio, Frank Samuel. 1954. *Female Homosexuality: A Psychodynamic Study of Lesbianism.* Foreword by Karl M. Bowman. New York: Citadel Press.

Carlston, Erin. 1997. " 'A Finer Differentiation': Female Homosexuality and the American Medical Community, 1926–1940." Pp. 177–196 in *Science and Homosexualities.* Edited by V. Rosario. New York: Routledge.

Chan, Connie S. 1995. "Issues of Sexual Identity in an Ethnic Minority: The Case of Chinese American Lesbians, Gay Men, and Bisexual People." Pp. 87–100 in *Lesbian, Gay, and Bisexual Identities over the Lifespan.* Edited by A. R. D'Augelli and C. J. Patterson. New York: Oxford University Press.

Chase, Cheryl. 1998. "Hermaphrodites with Attitude: Mapping the Emergence of Intersex Political Activism." *GLQ* 4: 189–211.

Chauncey, George. 1982–1983. "From Sexual Inversion to Homosexuality: Medicine and the Changing Conceptualization of Female Deviance." *Salmagundi* 58: 114–146.

———. 1994. *Gay New York: Gender, Urban Culture, and the Making of the Gay Male World, 1890–1940.* New York: Basic Books.

Chicago Gay Liberation Front. [1970] 1973. A leaflet for the American Medical Association. Pp. 145–147 in *Out of the Closets: Voices of Gay Liberation.* Edited by Karla Jay and Allen Young. New York: Douglas Books.

Clevenger, Shobal. 1881. "Hunger and Primitive Desire." *Science* 2: 14.

———. 1903. *The Evolution of Man and His Mind. A History and Discussion of the Evolution and Relations of the Mind and Body of Man and Animals.* Chicago: Evolution Publishing.

Clunis, D. Merilee, and G. Dorsey Green. 1988. *Lesbian Couples.* Seattle, WA: Seal Press.

Cochran, Susan D., C. Keenan, C. Schober, and V. M. Mays. 2000. "Estimates of Alcohol Use and Clinical Treatment Needs among Homosexually Active Men and Women in the U.S. Population." *Journal of Consulting and Clinical Psychology* 68: 1062–1071.

Cochran, Susan D., and Vickie Mays. 2000. "Relation between Psychiatric Syndromes and Behaviorally Defined Sexual Orientation in a Sample of the U.S. Population." *American Journal of Epidemiology* 151: 516–523.

Colapinto, John. 2000. *As Nature Made Him: The Boy Who Was Raised as a Girl.* New York: HarperCollins.

Cole, Steve W., Margaret Kemeny, Shelley Taylor, and Barbara Visscher. 1996. "Elevated Physical Health Risk among Gay Men Who Conceal Their Homosexual Identity." *Health Psychology* 15: 243–251.

Cole, Steve W., Margaret Kemeny, Shelley Taylor, Barbara Visscher, and J. Fahey. 1996. "Accelerated Course of Human Immunodeficiency Virus Infection in Gay Men Who Conceal Their Homosexual Identity." *Psychosomatic Medicine* 58: 219–231.

Comstock, T. Griswold. 1892. "Alice Mitchell of Memphis. A Case of Sexual Perversion or 'Urning' (a Paranoiac)." *N.Y. Medical Times,* September 20, 170–173.

Conrad, Florence. 1959. "Some Facts about Lesbians." *The Ladder* 3 (September): 4–26.

———. 1960. "Some Comparisons between Male and Female Homosexuals." *The Ladder* 4 (September): 4–25.

———. 1965. "Research Is Here to Stay." *The Ladder* 9 (July–August): 15–21.

Cory, Donald Webster (pseudonym for Edward Sagarin). 1951a. *The Homosexual in America: A Subjective Approach.* Introduction by Albert Ellis. New York: Greenberg.

———. 1951b. "Can Homosexuality Be Cured?" *Sexology* (October): 146–156.

———. 1956. *Homosexuality: A Cross Cultural Approach.* Julian Press.

———. 1964. *The Lesbian in America.* Introduction by Albert Ellis. New York: Citadel.

Cory, Donald Webster, and John LeRoy. 1963. *The Homosexual and His Society: A View from Within*. New York: Citadel.

Cournos, Francine, and Marshall Forstein, eds. 2000. *New Directions for Mental Health Services: What Mental Health Practitioners Need to Know about HIV and AIDS*. San Francisco: Jossey-Bass.

Crimp, Douglas. 1987. "How to Have Promiscuity in an Epidemic." Pp. 237–271 in *AIDS: Cultural Analysis, Cultural Activism*. Edited by D. Crimp. Cambridge: MIT Press.

Crowley, Mart. 1968. *The Boys in the Band*. New York: Farrar, Straus and Giroux.

———, writer and producer. 1970. *The Boys in the Band*. Directed by William Friedkin. Leo Productions, Ltd.

Cruikshank, M. 1990. "Lavender and Gray: A Brief Survey of Lesbian and Gay Aging Studies." *Journal of Homosexuality* 20, nos. 3–4: 77–87.

Dank, Barry M. 1971. "Coming Out in the Gay World." *Psychiatry* 34: 180–197.

Darke, Roy A., and George A. Geil. 1948. "Homosexual Activity: Relation of Degree and Role to the Goodenough Test and to the Cornell Selectee Index." *Journal of Nervous and Mental Disease* 108: 217–240.

D'Augelli, A. R., and C. J. Patterson, eds. 1995. *Lesbian, Gay, and Bisexual Identities over the Lifespan*. New York: Oxford University Press.

Davidson, Arnold I. 1987. "How to Do the History of Psychoanalysis: A Reading of Freud's *Three Essays on the Theory of Sexuality*." *Critical Inquiry* 13: 215–409.

Davis, Katharine Bement. 1929. *Factors in the Sex Life of Twenty-two Hundred Women*. New York: Harper and Bros. Publishers.

De Cecco, John, and David A. Parker, eds. 1995. *Sex, Cells, and Same-Sex Desire: The Biology of Sexual Preference*. Binghamton, NY: Harrington Park.

D'Emilio, John. 1983. *Sexual Politics, Sexual Communities: The Making of a Homosexual Minority in the United States, 1940–1970*. Chicago: University of Chicago Press.

———. 1989. "The Homosexual Menace: The Politics of Sexuality in Cold War America." Pp. 226–240 in *Passion and Power: Sexuality in History*. Edited by Kathy Peiss and Christina Simmons. Philadelphia: Temple University Press.

D'Emilio, John, and Estelle Freedman. 1988. *Intimate Matters: A History of Sexuality in America*. New York: Harper and Row.

Denenberg, Risa. 1995. "Report on Lesbian Health." *WHI* 5: 81–91.

Deutsch, Helene. 1932. "On Female Homosexuality." *Psychoanalytic Quarterly* 1: 484–510.

Diamond, Milton, and Keith Sigmundson. 1997. "Sex Reassignment at Birth: Long-term Review and Clinical Implications." *Archives of Pediatric and Adolescent Medicine* 151: 298–304.

Dickinson, Robert Latou, and Lura Beam. 1931. *A Thousand Marriages: A Medical Study of Sex Adjustment*. Baltimore: William and Wilkins.

———. 1934. *The Single Woman: A Medical Study in Sex Education*. Baltimore: William and Wilkins.

Dohousset. 1892. "Impregnation of One Sexual Pervert Female by Another." *Alienist and Neurologist* 13: 545–546.

Dörner, Günther, and G. Hinz. 1968. "Induction and Prevention of Male Homosexuality by Androgen." *Journal of Endocrinology* 40: 387–388.

Dörner, Günther, T. Geier, S. L. Ahren, L. Krell, G. Munx, H. Sieler, E. Kittner, and H. Muller. 1980. "Prenatal Stress as a Possible Aetiogenetic Factor of Homosexuality in Human Males." *Endokrinologie* 75: 365–368.

Dörner, Günther, Ingrid Poppe, F. Stahl, J. Kölsch, and R. Uebelhack. 1991. "Gene- and Environment-dependent Neuroendocrine Etiogenesis of Homosexuality and Transsexualism." *Experimental and Clinical Endocrinology* 98: 141–150.

Dreger, Alice Domurat. 1998. *Hermaphrodites and the Medical Invention of Sex.* Cambridge: Harvard University Press.

Drescher, Jack. 1998. *Psychoanalytic Therapy and the Gay Man.* Hillsdale, NJ: Analytic Press.

Dreyfus, Edward G. 1970. "Homosexuality and Medicine: A Reply." *Journal of the American Medical Association* 213: 1494–1495.

Duberman, Martin. 1991. *Cures: A Gay Man's Odyssey.* New York: Dutton.

———. 1993. *Stonewall.* New York: Dutton.

Duggan, Lisa. 1993. "The Trials of Alice Mitchell: Sensationalism, Sexology, and the Lesbian Subject in Turn-of-the-Century America." *Signs* 18: 791–814.

———. 2000. *Sapphic Slashers: Sex, Violence, and American Modernity.* Durham, NC: Duke University Press.

Dworkin, Sari H., and Fernando J. Gutiérrez. 1992. *Counseling Gay Men and Lesbians: Journey to the End of the Rainbow.* Alexandria, VA: American Association for Counseling and Development.

Eidelberg, Ludwig, and Edmund Bergler. 1933. "Der Mammakomplex des Mannes." *Internationale Zeitschrift für Psychoanalyse* 19: 547–583.

Ellis, Havelock. 1895. "Sexual Inversion in Women." *Alienist and Neurologist* 16: 141–158.

———. 1896. "Sexual Inversion in Men." *Alienist and Neurologist* 17: 115–150.

——— [with John Addington Symonds]. [1897] 1936. *Sexual Inversion.* In *Studies in the Psychology of Sex,* vol. 2. New York: Random House.

———. [1897–1927] 1936. *Studies in the Psychology of Sex.* New York: Random House.

English, Oliver Spurgeon. 1948. Pp. 91–112 in *About the Kinsey Report.* Edited by Donald P. Geddes and E. Currie. New York: Signet.

———. 1953. "A Primer on Homosexuality." *GP* (American Academy of General Practice) 7: 55–60.

Epstein, Steven. 1996. *Impure Science: AIDS, Activism, and the Politics of Knowledge.* Berkeley: University of California Press.

Ernst, John R. 1928. "Dementia Praecox Complexes." *Medical Journal and Record* 128: 381–386.

———. 1943. "Dementia Praecox Complexes." *Medical Annals of the District of Columbia* 12: 343–347.

Faderman, Lillian. 1981. *Surpassing the Love of Men: Romantic Friendship and Love between Women from the Renaissance to the Present.* New York: William Morrow.

———. 1991. *Odd Girls and Twilight Lovers: A History of Lesbian Life in Twentieth-Century America.* New York: Columbia University Press.

"Faith and Fury." 1965. *The Ladder* 9 (May): 20–21.

Feinberg, Leslie. 1996. *Transgender Warriors: Making History from Joan of Arc to Dennis Rodman.* Boston: Beacon.

Feldman, M. P., and M. K. MacCulloch. 1964. "A Systematic Approach to the Treatment of Homosexuality by Conditioned Aversion: Preliminary Report." *American Journal of Psychiatry* 121: 167–171.

Ferenczi, Sándor. [1911] 1916. "The Nosology of Male Homosexuality." Pp. 250–268 in *Contributions to Psychoanalysis*. Translated by Ernest Jones. Boston: Richard G. Badger.

——. [1912] 1916. "On the Part Played by Homosexuality in the Pathogenesis of Paranoia." Pp. 131–156 in *Contributions to Psychoanalysis*. Translated by Ernest Jones. Boston: Richard G. Badger.

Fichter, M. M., and C. Daser. 1987. "Symptomatology, Psychosexual Development and Gender Identity in 42 Anorexic Males." *Psychological Medicine* 17: 409–418.

Flint, Austin. 1911. "A Case of Sexual Inversion, Probably with Complete Sexual Anaesthesia." *New York Medical Journal* 94:1111–1112.

Ford, Clellan S., and Frank A. Beach. 1951. *Patterns of Sexual Behavior.* New York: Harper.

Foucault, Michel. [1961] 1973. *Madness and Civilization: The History of Insanity in the Age of Reason.* Translated by R. Howard. New York: Vintage.

——. [1976] 1990. *The History of Sexuality: An Introduction.* Translated by Robert Hurley. New York: Vintage.

Fox, Ronald C. 1996. "Bisexuality in Perspective: A Review of Theory and Research." Pp. 3–50 in *Bisexuality: The Psychology and Politics of an Invisible Minority.* Edited by B. A. Firestein. Thousand Oaks, CA: Sage.

Freedman, Estelle. 1989. "'Uncontrolled Desires': The Response to the Sexual Psychopath, 1920–1960." Pp. 199–225 in *Passion and Power: Sexuality in History.* Edited by Kathy Peiss and Christina Simmons, with R. Padgug. Philadelphia: Temple University Press.

Freud, Sigmund. [1905] 1955. *Three Essays on the Theory of Sexuality.* In *Standard Edition of the Complete Psychological Works of Sigmund Freud.* 24 vols. Edited by James Strachey. London: Hogarth Press.

——. [1911] 1955. "Psychoanalytic Notes upon an Autobiographical Account of a Case of Paranoia (*Dementia Paranoides*)." In *Standard Edition* 12: 1–84.

——. [1920] 1955. "The Psychogenesis of a Case of Homosexuality in a Woman." In *Standard Edition* 18: 146–172.

——. [1922] 1955. "Some Neurotic Mechanisms in Jealousy, Paranoia and Homosexuality." In *Standard Edition* 18: 222–232.

——. [1927] 1955. *The Future of an Illusion.* In *Standard Edition* 21: 3–56.

——. [1930] 1955. *Civilization and Its Discontents.* In *Standard Edition* 21: 59–145.

——. [1935] 1951. "A Letter from Freud." *American Journal of Psychiatry.* 107: 786–787.

——. 1953–1974. *Standard Edition of the Complete Psychological Works of Sigmund Freud.* 24 vols. Edited by James Strachey. London: Hogarth Press.

——. 1985. *The Complete Letters of Sigmund Freud to Wilhelm Fliess, 1887–1904.* Edited by Jeffrey Masson. Cambridge: Harvard University Press.

Freund, Kurt. 1960. "Some Problems in the Treatment of Homosexuality." In *Behaviour Therapy and the Neuroses.* Edited by H. J. Eysenck. London: Pergamon.

——. 1965. "Diagnosing Heterosexual Pedophilia by Means of a Test of Sexual Interest." *Behaviour Research and Therapy* 3: 229–234.

Friedman, Richard, and Jennifer Downey. 1994. "Homosexuality." *New England Journal of Medicine* 331: 923–930.

Frosch, Jack, and Walter Bromberg. 1939. "The Sex Offender: A Psychiatric Study." *American Journal of Orthopsychiatry* 9: 761–776.

Gallagher, John. 2001. "Normal, China: The Chinese Psychiatric Association Decides That Being Gay Is No Longer a Disease." *The Advocate,* April 24, 22–24.

Garnets, Linda D., Kristin Hancock, Susan Cochran, Jacqueline Goodchilds, and Letitia Anne Peplau. 1991. "Issues in Psychotherapy with Lesbians and Gay Men: A Survey of Psychologists." *American Psychologist* 46: 964–972.

Garnets, Linda D., and Douglas C. Kimmel, eds. 1993. *Psychological Perspectives on Lesbian and Gay Male Experiences.* New York: Columbia University Press.

Garofalo, R., R. C. Wolf, L. S. Wissow, E. R. Woods, and E. Goodman. 1999. "Sexual Orientation and Risk of Suicide Attempts among a Representative Sample of Youth." *Archives of Pediatrics and Adolescent Medicine* 153: 487–493.

Gay, Peter. 1984. *Education of the Senses,* vol. 1 of *The Bourgeois Experience: Victoria to Freud.* New York: Oxford University Press.

Gebhard, Paul H., and Alan B. Johnson. 1979. *The Kinsey Data: Marginal Tabulations of the 1938–1963 Interviews Conducted by the Institute for Sex Research.* Philadelphia: Saunders.

Geddes, Donald P. 1948. "New Light on Sexual Knowledge." Pp. 5–25 in *About the Kinsey Report.* Edited by Donald P. Geddes and E. Currie. New York: Signet.

Geil, George A. 1944. "The Use of the Goodenough Test for Revealing Male Homosexuality." *Journal of Criminal Psychopathology* 6: 307–321.

Gerber, Henry [Parisex, pseudonym]. [1932] 1975. "In Defense of Homosexuality." *The Modern Thinker* (June): 286–297. Reproduced in *A Homosexual Emancipation Miscellany, c. 1835–1952.* New York: Arno Press.

Gibson, Margaret. 1997. "Clitoral Corruption: Body Metaphors and American Doctors' Constructions of Female Homosexuality, 1870–1900." Pp. 108–132 in *Science and Homosexualities.* Edited by V. Rosario. New York: Routledge.

Gibson, Paul. 1989. "Gay Male and Lesbian Youth Suicide." In *Report of the Secretary's Task Force on Youth Suicide.* Edited by M. R. Feinleib, vol. 3. Rockville, MD: U.S. Department of Health and Human Services.

Gilbert, J. Allen. 1920. "Homo-sexuality and Its Treatment." *Journal of Nervous and Mental Disease* 52: 297–322.

Gilman, S. E., S. D. Cochran, V. M. Mays, M. Hughes, D. Ostrow, and R. C. Kessler. 2001. "Risk of Psychiatric Disorders among Individuals Reporting Same-Sex Sexual Partners in the National Comorbidity Survey." *American Journal of Public Health* 91: 933–939.

Glass, S. J., and Roswell Johnson. 1944. "Limitations and Complications of Organotherapy in Male Homosexuality." *Journal of Clinical Endocrinology* 4: 540–544.

Glover, Benjamin H. 1951. "Observations on Homosexuality among University Students." *Journal of Nervous and Mental Disease* 113: 377–387.

Gold, Ronald. 1973. "Stop It, You're Making Me Sick!" *American Journal of Psychiatry* 130: 1211–1212.

Golombok, S., A. Spencer, and M. Rutter. 1983. "Children in Lesbian and Single-parent Households: Psychosexual and Psychiatric Appraisal." *Journal of Child Psychology and Psychiatry and Allied Disciplines* 24: 551–572.

Gonzáles, Francisco, and Olivia M. Espín. 1996. "Latino Men, Latina Women, and Homosexuality." Pp. 583–601 in *Textbook of Homosexuality and Mental Health*. Edited by R. P. Cabaj and T. S. Stein. Washington, DC: American Psychiatric Press.

Goode, Erica. 2001. "Scientist Says Study Shows Gay Change Is Possible." *New York Times,* May 9.

Gordon, Eric B. 1991. "Transsexual Healing: Medicaid Funding of Sex Reassignment Surgery." *Archives of Sexual Behavior* 20: 61–74.

Gorski, Roger A. 1978. "Sexual Differentiation of the Brain." *Hospital Practice* (October): 55–62.

Gove, Mary S. (Nichols). 1839. *Solitary Vice: An Address to Parents and Those Who Have the Care of Children.* Portland, ME: Journal Office.

Graham, Sylvester. [1833] 1975. *A Lecture to Young Men.* New York: Arno Press.

Green, Richard. 1987. *The "Sissy Boy Syndrome" and the Development of Homosexuality.* New Haven, CT: Yale University Press.

Green, Richard, and John Money. 1961. "Effeminacy in Prepubertal Boys: Summary of Eleven Cases and Recommendations for Case Management." *Pediatrics* (February): 286–291.

Greenberg, David F. 1988. *The Construction of Homosexuality.* Chicago: University of Chicago Press.

Greene, Beverly. 1994. "Ethnic-minority Lesbians and Gay Men: Mental Health and Treatment Issues." *Journal of Consulting and Clinical Psychology* 62: 243–251.

Grob, Gerald. 1983. *Mental Illness and American Society, 1875–1940.* Princeton, NJ: Princeton University Press.

———. 1991. *From Asylum to Community: Mental Health Policy in Modern America.* Princeton, NJ: Princeton University Press.

Grosskurth, Phyllis. 1980. *Havelock Ellis: A Biography.* New York: Knopf.

Group for the Advancement of Psychiatry (GAP). 1955. *Report on Homosexuality with Particular Emphasis on This Problem in Governmental Agencies.* Report no. 30. Topeka, KS: GAP.

———. 2000. *Homosexuality and the Mental Health Professions: The Impact of Bias.* Hillsdale, NJ: Analytic Press.

Guttmacher, Manfred S. 1966. "The Mental Hygiene Consultation Services." Pp. 349–371 in *Neuropsychiatry in World War II,* vol. 1. Edited by John B. Coates and Arnold L. Ahnfeldt. Washington, DC: Office of the Surgeon General.

Dr. H—. 1881. "Gynomania—A Curious Case of Masturbation." *The Medical Record* (New York) 19: 336.

H., E. J. 1884. Letter to the Editor. *Alienist and Neurologist* 5: 351–352.

Hackfield, A. W. 1935. "The Ameliorative Effects of Therapeutic Castration in Habitual Sex Offenders." *Journal of Nervous and Mental Disease* 82: 15–29, 169–181.

Hadden, Samuel B. 1966a. "Newer Treatment Techniques for Homosexuality." *Archives of Environmental Health* 13: 284–288.

———. 1966b. "Treatment of Male Homosexuals in Groups." *International Journal of Group Psychotherapy* 16: 13–22.

Haeckel, Ernst. 1866. *Generelle Morphologie der Organismen.* 2 vols. Berlin: George Reimer.

————. [1874] 1891. *Anthropogenie, oder Entwickelungsgeschichte des Menschen.* Leipzig: W. Englemann.

Haggerty, George. 1999. *Men in Love: Masculinity and Sexuality in the Eighteenth Century.* New York: Columbia University Press.

Haldeman, Douglas. 1994. "The Practice and Ethics of Sexual Orientation Conversion Therapy." *Journal of Consulting and Clinical Psychology* 62: 221–227.

Hale, Nathan, Jr. [1971] 1995. *Freud in America,* 2 vols. New York: Oxford University Press.

————. 1995. *The Rise and Crisis of Psychoanalysis in the United States: Freud and the Americans, 1917–1985.* New York: Oxford University Press.

Hall, Radclyffe. [1928] 1980. *The Well of Loneliness.* New York: Avon.

Halley, Janet E. 1994. "Sexual Orientation and the Politics of Biology: A Critique of the Argument from Immutability." *Stanford Law Review* 46: 503–568.

Hamburger, Christian, Georg K. Stürup, and E. Dahl-Iversen. 1953. "Transvestism: Hormonal, Psychiatric, and Surgical Treatment." *Journal of the American Medical Association* 152: 391–396.

Hamer, Dean, and Peter Copeland. 1994. *The Science of Desire: The Search for the Gay Gene and the Biology of Behavior.* New York: Simon and Schuster.

Hamer, Dean, Stella Hu, Victoria L. Magnuson, Nan Hu, and Angela Pattatucci. 1993. "A Linkage between DNA Markers on the X Chromosome and Male Sexual Orientation." *Science* 261: 321–327.

Hamilton, Allan. 1895. "The Civil Responsibilities of Sexual Perverts." *American Journal of Insanity* 50: 501–511.

Hammond, William. 1882. "The Disease of the Scythians (*morbus feminarum*)." *American Journal of Neurology* 1: 339–355.

Hancock, Eleanor. 1998. "'Only the Real, the True, the Masculine Held Its Value': Ernst Röhm, Masculinity, and Male Homosexuality." *Journal of the History of Sexuality* 8: 616–641.

Hancock, Kristin. 1995. "Psychotherapy with Lesbians and Gay Men." Pp. 398–432 in *Lesbian, Gay, and Bisexual Identities over the Lifespan.* Edited by A. R. D'Augelli and C. J. Patterson. New York: Oxford University Press.

Harris, M. B., and P. H. Turner. 1985–1986. "Gay and Lesbian Parents." *Journal of Homosexuality* 12, no. 2: 101–113.

HBIGDA (Harry Benjamin International Gender Dysphoria Association). 1980. *The Standards of Care: The Hormonal and Surgical Reassignment of Gender Dysphoric Persons.* Mimeographed. Distributed by HBIGDA, 1952 Union St., San Francisco, CA 94123.

————. 2001. *The Standards of Care for Gender Identity Disorders,* 6th version. *International Journal of Transgenderism* 5, no. 1. http://www.symposion.com/ijt/soc_2001/index.htm.

Henry, George W. 1934. "Psychogenic and Constitutional Factors in Homosexuality: Their Relation to Personality Disorders." [Read to the New York Psychiatric Society, May 3, 1933.] *Psychiatric Quarterly* 8: 243–264.

————. 1937. "Psychogenic Factors in Overt Homosexuality." *American Journal of Psychiatry* 93: 889–908.

————. 1941. *Sex Variants. A Study of Homosexual Patterns.* New York: Hoeber.

Henry, George W., and Alfred Gross. 1938. "Social Factors in the Case Histories of One Hundred Underprivileged Homosexuals." *Mental Hygiene* 22: 591–611.

Herdt, Gilbert, ed. 1989. *Gay and Lesbian Youth.* New York: Harrington Park.

———. 1994. *Third Sex, Third Gender: Beyond Sexual Dimorphism in Culture and History.* New York: Zone Books.

Herek, Gregory M. 1995. "Psychological Heterosexism in the United States." Pp. 321–346 in *Lesbian, Gay, and Bisexual Identities over the Lifespan.* Edited by A. R. D'Augelli and C. J. Patterson. New York: Oxford University Press.

"Herpes: The New Sexual Leprosy." 1980. *Time,* July 28, 76.

Hewitt, Andrew. 1996. *Political Inversions: Homosexuality, Fascism, and the Modernist Imaginary.* Stanford, CA: Stanford University Press.

Hirschfeld, Magnus. [1898] 1962. "Questionnaire No. _____." Pp. 379–388 in *Minutes of the Vienna Psychoanalytic Society,* vol. 1: *1906–1908.* Edited by Herman Nunberg and Ernst Federn. New York: International Universities Press.

———. [1901] 1915. *The Social Problem of Sexual Inversion.* London: C. W. Beaumont. Reprinted in *A Homosexual Emancipation Miscellany, c. 1835–1952.* New York: Arno, 1975. Revised and abridged translation of *Was soll das Volk vom dritten Geschlecht wissen? Eine Aufklärungsschrift über gleichgeschlechtlich (homosexuelle) empfindende Menschen.* Leipzig: Max Spohr, 1901.

———. [1910] 1991. *Transvestites: The Erotic Drive to Cross-Dress.* Translated by Michael A. Lombardi-Nash. Buffalo: Prometheus. Appeared originally as *Die Transvestiten: Eine Untersuchung über den erotischen Verkleidungstrieb.* Leipzig: Max Spohr.

———. 1912. *Naturgesetze der Liebe: Eine gemeinsverständliche Untersuchung über den Liebes-Eindruck, Liebes-Drang und Liebes-Ausdruck.* Berlin: Alfred Pulvermacher.

———. 1923. "Die intersexuelle Konstitution." *Jahrbuch für sexuelle Zwischenstufen* 23: 3–27.

Hoeffer, B. 1981. "Children's Acquisition of Sex-role Behavior in Lesbian-mother Families." *American Journal of Orthopsychiatry* 51: 536–544.

Hoffman, Martin. 1970. "Homosexuality and Medicine: A Reply." *Journal of the American Medical Association* 213: 1495–1496.

"Homosexuals in Medicine." 1970. Anonymous letter in *New England Journal of Medicine* 283: 1295.

Hooker, Evelyn. 1956. "A Preliminary Analysis of Group Behavior of Homosexuals." *Journal of Psychology* 42: 217–225.

———. 1957. "The Adjustment of the Male Overt Homosexual." *Journal of Projective Techniques* 21: 18–31.

———. 1958. "Male Homosexuality in the Rorschach." *Journal of Projective Techniques* 22: 33–54.

———. 1959. "What Is a Criterion?" *Journal of Projective Techniques* 23: 278–281.

———. 1965. "Male Homosexuals and Their 'Worlds.'" Pp. 83–107 in *Sexual Inversion: The Multiple Roots of Homosexuality.* Edited by Judd Marmor. New York: Basic Books.

———. 1993. "Reflections of a 40-year Exploration." *American Psychologist* 48: 450–453.

Hoover, J. Edgar. 1937. "War on the Sex Criminal!" *New York Herald Tribune,* September 26.

Horney, Karen. 1926. "The Flight from Womanhood: The Masculinity Complex in Women, as Viewed by Men and Women." *International Journal of Psychoanalysis* 7: 324–339.

—. 1933. "The Denial of the Vagina, a Contribution to the Problem of Genital Anxieties Specific to Women." *International Journal of Psychoanalysis* 14: 57–70.

Howard, William Lee. 1896. "Sexual Perversion." *N. Y. Medico-Legal Journal* 14: 17–22.

—. 1897. "Psychical Hermaphroditism: A Few Notes on Sexual Perversion, with Two Clinical Cases of Sexual Inversion." *Alienist and Neurologist* 18: 111–118.

—. 1900. "Effeminate Men and Masculine Women." *N. Y. Medical Journal* 21: 686–687.

Howe, Joseph W. 1883. *Excessive Venery, Masturbation, and Continence. The Etiology, Pathogenesis, Treatment.* New York: Bermingham and Co.

Hu, Stella, Angela M. L. Pattatucci, Chavis Patterson, Lin Li, David W. Fulker, Stacey S. Cherny, Leonid Kruglyak, and Dean Hamer. 1995. "Linkage Between Sexual Orientation and Chromosome Xq28 in Males but not in Females." *Nature Genetics* 11: 248–256.

Hughes, Charles H. 1891a. "Note on the Virile Reflex." *Alienist and Neurologist* 12: 44–46.

—. 1891b. "Perversions of the Sexual Feeling." [Editorial.] *Alienist and Neurologist* 12: 423–425.

—. 1892. "The Alice Michel Case." [Editorial.] *Alienist and Neurologist* 13: 554–557.

—. 1893a. "Erotopathia—Morbid Eroticism." *Alienist and Neurologist* 14: 531–578.

—. 1893b. "Postscript to Paper on 'Erotopathia'—An Organization of Colored Erotopaths." *Alienist and Neurologist* 14: 731–732.

—. 1907. "Homo Sexual Complexion Perverts in St. Louis: Note on a Feature of Sexual Psychopathy." *Alienist and Neurologist* 28: 487–488.

Hunter, Joyce. 1995. "At the Crossroads: Lesbian Youth." Pp. 50–60 in *Dyke Life.* Edited by Karla Jay. New York: Basic Books.

*Index Medicus.* 1916–1956. Washington, DC: American Medical Association.

Isay, Richard. 1996. *Becoming Gay: The Journey to Self-Acceptance.* New York: Pantheon.

Israelstam, S., and S. Lambert. 1986. "Homosexuality and Alcohol: Observations and Research after the Psychoanalytic Era." *International Journal of the Addictions* 21: 509–537.

James, Robert E. 1947. "Precipitating Factors in Acute Homosexual Panic (Kempf's Disease) with a Case Presentation." *Quarterly Review of Psychiatry and Neurology* 2: 530–533.

Jay, Karla, and Allen Young. 1972. *Out of the Closets: Voices of Gay Liberation.* New York: Douglas Books.

Jones, Billy E., and Marjorie J. Hill. 1996. "African American Lesbians, Gay Men, and Bisexuals." Pp. 549–561 in *Textbook of Homosexuality and Mental Health.* Edited by R. P. Cabaj and T. S. Stein. Washington, DC: American Psychiatric Press.

Jones, Ernest. 1953. *The Life and Work of Sigmund Freud.* New York: Basic Books.

Jones, Franklin, and Ronald Koshes. 1995. "Homosexuality and the Military." *American Journal of Psychiatry* 152: 16–21.

Jones, James H. 1997. *Alfred C. Kinsey: A Public/Private Life.* New York: W. W. Norton.

Kallmann, Franz J. 1952. "Twin Sibship Study of Overt Male Homosexuality." *American Journal of Human Genetics* 4: 136–146.

Kameny, Franklin. 1965a. "Does Research into Homosexuality Matter?" *The Ladder* 9 (May): 14–20.

———. 1965b. "Emphasis on Research Has Had Its Day." *The Ladder* 9 (October): 10–14, 23–26.

Karpman, Benjamin. 1943. "Mediate Psychotherapy and the Acute Homosexual Panic (Kempf's Disease)." *Journal of Nervous and Mental Disease* 98: 493–506.

Katz, Jonathan Ned. 1976. *Gay American History: Lesbians and Gay Men in the U.S.A.* New York: Thomas Y. Crowell.

———. 1983. *Gay/Lesbian Almanac.* New York: Harper and Row.

Kay, Lily E. 2000. *Who Wrote the Book of Life? A History of the Genetic Code.* Stanford, CA: Stanford University Press.

Kaye, Harvey E., Soll Berl, Jack Clare, Mary R. Eleston, Benjamin S. Gershwin, Patricia Gershwin, Leonard S. Kogan, Clara Torda, and Cornelia B. Wilbur. 1967. "Homosexuality in Women." *Archives of General Psychiatry* 17: 626–634.

Kehoe, M. 1988. "Lesbians over 60 Speak for Themselves." *Journal of Homosexuality* 16, nos. 3–4: 1–111.

Kempf, Edward John. 1921. *Psychopathology.* St. Louis, MO: C. V. Mosby.

Kenen, Stephanie H. 1997. "Who Counts When You're Counting Homosexuals? Hormones and Homosexuality in Mid-twentieth-century America." Pp. 197–218 in *Science and Homosexualities.* Edited by V. Rosario. New York: Routledge.

Kennedy, Elizabeth L., and Madeline Davis. 1993. *Boots of Leather, Slippers of Gold: The History of a Lesbian Community.* New York: Routledge.

Kennedy, Hubert. 1988. *Ulrichs: The Life and Work of Karl Heinrich Ulrichs, Pioneer of the Modern Gay Movement.* Boston: Alyson Publications.

Kerchner, John. 1938. "Sex Crimes." *Illinois Medical Journal* 73: 171–172.

Kessler, Suzanne. 1998. *Lessons from the Intersexed.* New Brunswick, NJ: Rutgers University Press.

Kiernan, James. 1884a. "Sexual Perversion (Lecture XXVI)." *Detroit Lancet* 7, no. 11: 481–484.

———. 1884b. Letter to the Editor. *Detroit Lancet* 8: 121.

———. 1891. "Psychological Aspects of the Sexual Appetite." *Alienist and Neurologist* 12: 188–219.

———. 1892. "Responsibility in Sexual Perversion." *Chicago Medical Recorder* 3: 185–210.

Kinsey, Alfred C. 1941. "Homosexuality." *Journal of Clinical Endocrinology* 1: 424–428.

Kinsey, Alfred C., Wardell B. Pomeroy, and Clyde E. Martin. 1948. *Sexual Behavior in the Human Male.* Philadelphia: W. B. Saunders.

Kinsey, Alfred C., Wardell B. Pomeroy, Clyde E. Martin, and Paul H. Gebhard. 1953. *Sexual Behavior in the Human Female.* Philadelphia: W. B. Saunders.

Kirkpatrick, Martha, Catherine Smith, and Ron Roy. 1981. "Lesbian Mothers and Their Children: A Comparative Survey." *American Journal of Orthopsychiatry* 51: 545–551.

Knight, Robert P. 1941. "Recognizing the Psychoneurotic Registrant." *Bulletin of the Menninger Clinic* 5: 161–166.

Kolb, Lawrence C., and Adelaide M. Johnson. 1955. "Etiology and Therapy of Overt Homosexuality." *Psychoanalytic Quarterly* 24: 506–515.

Koopman, C., M. Rosario, and M. J. Rotheram-Borus. 1994. "Alcohol and Drug Use and Sexual Behaviors Placing Runaways at Risk for HIV Infection." *Addictive Behaviors* 19: 95–103.

Kopp, Marie E. 1937–1938. "Surgical Treatment as Sex Crime Prevention Measure." *Journal Criminal Law and Criminology* 28: 692–706.

Krafft-Ebing, Richard von. 1877. "Ueber gewisse Anomalien des Geschlechtstriebs und die klinisch–forensische Verwertung derselben als eines wahrscheinlich functionellen Degenerationszeichens des zentralen Nervensystems." *Archiv für Psychiatrie und Nervenkrankheiten* 7: 291–312.

————. 1882. "Perverted Sexual Feeling." Translated by E. W. Saunders. *Alienist and Neurologist* 3: 673–676.

————. 1886. *Psychopathia Sexualis: Eine klinische-forensische Studie.* 1st ed. Stuttgart: Ferdinand Enke.

————. 1888. "Perversion of the Sexual Instinct—Report of Cases." Translated by H. M. Jewett. *Alienist and Neurologist* 9: 565–581.

Kuhn, Thomas. [1962] 1970. *The Structure of Scientific Revolutions.* 2nd ed. Chicago: University of Chicago Press.

Lamarck, Jean-Baptiste. 1809. *Philosophie zoologique.* Paris: Dentru.

Landor, Henry. 1871. "Insanity in Relation to the Law." *American Journal of Insanity* 28: 56–77.

"Letter from an Invert, A." 1919. *American Journal of Urology and Sexology* 15: 454–455.

LeVay, Simon. 1991. "A Difference in Hypothalamic Structure between Heterosexual and Homosexual Men." *Science* 253: 1034–1037.

————. 1993. *The Sexual Brain.* Cambridge: MIT Press.

————. 1996. *Queer Science: The Use and Abuse of Research into Homosexuality.* Cambridge: MIT Press.

Levins, Hoag. 1996. *American Sex Machines: The Hidden History of Sex at the U.S. Patent Office.* Holbrook, MA: Adams Media Corporation.

Lewes, Kenneth. 1988. *The Psychoanalytic Theory of Male Homosexuality.* New York: Simon and Schuster.

Lichtenstein, Perry Maurice. 1921. "The 'Fairy' and the Lady Lover." *Medical Review of Reviews* 27: 369–374.

————. 1943. *A Handbook of Psychiatry.* New York: W. W. Norton.

Lind, Earl. See Ralph Werther.

Livingood, John M., ed. [1969] 1972. *National Institute of Mental Health Task Force on Homosexuality: Final Report and Background Papers.* U.S. Department of Health, Education, and Welfare Publication no. (ADM) 76–357.

Loeser, Lewis. 1945. "The Sexual Psychopath in the Military Service." *American Journal of Psychiatry* 102: 92–101.

Lydston, George Frank. 1889. "Sexual Perversion, Satyriasis, and Nymphomania." *Medical and Surgical Reporter* 61: 253–258, 281–285.

————. 1919. "The Biochemical Basis of Sex Aberrations." *Urologic and Cutaneous Review* 23: 384–385.

Lyon, Phyllis, and Del Martin. 1972. *Lesbian / Woman.* San Francisco: Glide Urban Center.

Maccubbin, Robert P., ed. 1987. *Tis Nature's Fault: Unauthorized Sexuality during the Enlightenment.* Cambridge: Cambridge University Press.

Machtan, Lothar. 2001. *The Hidden Hitler.* New York: Basic Books.

Magee, Maggie, and Diana Miller. 1997. *Lesbian Lives: Psychoanalytic Narratives Old and New.* Hillsdale, NJ: Analytic Press.

Magnan, Valentin. 1885. "Des anomalies, des aberrations et des perversions sexuelles." *Progrès médicale,* 2nd ser., 13: 49–50, 65–68, 84–86.

Malyon, Alan K. 1982. "Psychotherapeutic Implications of Internalized Homophobia in Gay Men." Pp. 59–69 in *Homosexuality and Psychotherapy.* Edited by J. C. Gonsiorek. New York: Haworth Press.

Marmor, Judd. 1972. "Notes on Some Psychodynamic Aspects of Homosexuality." Pp. 55–57 in *National Institute of Mental Health Task Force on Homosexuality: Final Report and Background Papers.* Edited by J. M. Livingood. U.S. Department of Health, Education, and Welfare Publication no. (ADM) 76–357.

———. 1973. "Homosexuality and Cultural Value Systems." *American Journal of Psychiatry* 130: 1208–1209.

———, ed. 1965. *Sexual Inversion: The Multiple Roots of Homosexuality.* New York: Basic Books.

Marotta, Toby. 1981. *The Politics of Homosexuality.* Boston: Houghton Mifflin.

Max, L. 1935. "Breaking a Homosexual Fixation by the Conditioned Reflex Technique." *Psychological Bulletins* 32: 734.

McConaghy, Nathaniel. 1976. "Is a Homosexual Orientation Irreversible?" *British Journal of Psychiatry* 129: 556–563.

McKirnan, D. J., and P. L. Peterson. 1989. "Alcohol and Drug Use among Homosexual Men and Women: Epidemiology and Population Characteristics." *Addictive Behaviors* 14: 545–553.

McWhirter, David P., and Andrew Mattison. 1984. *The Male Couple: How Relationships Develop.* Engelwood Cliffs, NJ: Prentice-Hall.

Meagher, John Francis Wallace. 1929. "Homosexuality: Its Psychobiological and Psychopathological Significance." *Urologic and Cutaneous Review* 33: 505–518.

Meyerowitz, Joanne. 1998. "Sex-change and the Popular Press: Historical Notes on Transsexuality in the United States, 1930–1955." *GLQ* 4: 159–187.

Micale, Mark S. 1990. "Charcot and the Idea of Hysteria in the Male: Gender and Mental Science, and Medical Diagnosis in Late Nineteenth-Century France." *Medical History* 34: 363–411.

———. 1995. *Approaching Hysteria: Disease and Its Interpretations.* Princeton, NJ: Princeton University Press.

Miller, Paul R. 1958. "The Effeminate Passive Obligatory Homosexual." *Archives of Neurology and Psychiatry* 80: 612–618.

Money, John. 1955. "Hermaphroditism, Gender and Precocity in Hyperadrenocorticism: Psychological Findings." *Bulletin of the Johns Hopkins Hospital* 96: 253–264.

———. 1972. "Strategy, Ethics, Behavior Modification, and Homosexuality." *Archives of Sexual Behavior* 2: 79–81.

———. 1994. "The Concept of Gender Identity Disorder in Childhood and Adolescence after 39 Years." *Journal of Sex and Marital Therapy* 20: 163–177.

Money, John, and Anke A. Ehrhardt. 1972. *Man and Woman, Boy and Girl: Differentiation and Dimorphism of Gender Identity from Conception to Maturity.* Baltimore: Johns Hopkins University Press.

Money, John, Joan Hampson, and John L. Hampson. 1957. "Imprinting and the Establishment of Gender Role." *Archives of Neurology and Psychiatry* 77: 333–336.

Montague, M. F. Ashley. 1948. "Understanding Our Sexual Drives." Pp. 59–69 in *About the Kinsey Report.* Edited by D. P Geddes and E. Currie. New York: Signet.

Moreau (de Tours), Paul. 1884. "On the Aberration of the Genesic Sense." *Alienist and Neurologist* 5: 367–385.

Morel, Bénédict A. 1857. *Traité des dégénérescences physiques, intellectuelles et morales de l'espèce humaine et des causes qui produisent ces variétés maladives.* Paris: Baillière.

Morgan, Kris S., and Michele J. Eliason. 1992. "The Role of Psychotherapy in Caucasian Lesbians' Lives." *Women and Therapy* 13: 27–52.

Morgan, Thomas Hunt. 1934. *Embryology and Genetics.* New York: Columbia University Press.

Morris, Jessica F., Amy Ojerholm, Teri Brooks, Dana Osowiecki, and Esther Rothblum. 1995. "Finding a Word for Myself: Themes in Lesbian Coming Out Stories." Pp. 36–49 in *Dyke Life.* Edited by Karla Jay. New York: Basic Books.

Mort, Frank. 1987. *Dangerous Sexualities. Medico-Moral Politics in England since 1830.* London: Routledge and Kegan Paul.

Mosse, George L. 1968. "Max Nordau and His Degeneration." Introduction to *Degeneration* by Max Nordau. New York: Howard Fertig.

———. 1985. *Nationalism and Sexuality: Respectability and Abnormal Sexuality in Modern Europe.* New York: Howard Fertig.

Murphy, Jane M., and Alexander H. Leighton, eds. 1965. *Approaches to Cross-Cultural Psychiatry.* Ithaca, NY: Cornell University Press.

Murphy, Timothy F. 1997. *Gay Science: The Ethics of Sexual Orientation Research.* New York: Columbia University Press.

Nicolosi, Joseph. 1991. *Reparative Therapy of Male Homosexuality: A New Clinical Approach.* Northvale, NJ: J. Aronson.

Nye, Robert A. 1989. "Sex Difference and Male Homosexuality in French Medical Discourse, 1800–1930." *Bulletin of the History of Medicine* 63: 32–51.

Oberndorf, Clarence Paul. 1919. "Homosexuality." [Lecture to the American Psychoanalytic Society, Atlantic City, June 1919.] *Medical Record* 96: 840–843.

———. 1929. "Diverse Forms of Homosexuality." *Urologic and Cutaneous Review* 33: 518–523.

———. 1953. *A History of Psychoanalysis in America.* New York: Grune and Stratton.

*Onania.* [1715] 1986. New York: Garland Press.

Oosterhuis, Harry. 2000. *Stepchildren of Nature: Krafft-Ebing and the Making of Sexual Identity.* Chicago: University of Chicago Press.

Otis, Margaret. 1913–1914. "A Perversion Not Commonly Noted." *Journal of Abnormal Psychology* 8: 113–116.

Oudshoorn, Nelly. 1994. *Beyond the Natural Body: An Archaeology of Sex Hormones.* New York: Routledge.

Owensby, Newdigate. 1940. "Homosexuality and Lesbianism Treated with Metrazol." *Journal of Nervous and Mental Disease* 92: 65–66.

————. 1941. "The Correction of Homosexuality." *Urologic and Cutaneous Review* 45: 494–496.

Pattatucci, Angela. 1998. "Molecular Investigations into Complex Behavior: Lessons from Sexual Orientation Studies." *Human Biology* 70: 367–386.

Patterson, C. J. 1992. "Children of Lesbian and Gay Parents." *Child Development* 63: 1025–1042.

Patton, Cindy. 1990. *Inventing AIDS.* New York: Routledge.

Pedersen, Lyn. 1956. "A Tribute to Dr. Kinsey." *ONE* 4, no. 6 (August–September): 7–12.

Peiss, Kathy, and Christina Simmons, eds. 1989. *Passion and Power: Sexuality in History.* Philadelphia: Temple University Press.

Pernick, Martin. 1985. "Politics, Parties and Pestilence: Epidemic Yellow Fever in Philadelphia and the Rise of the First Party System." Pp. 356–371 in *Sickness and Health in America.* Edited by J. W. Leavitt and R. L. Numbers. Madison: University of Wisconsin Press.

Perry, Helen Swick. 1982. *Psychiatrist of America: The Life of Harry Stack Sullivan.* Cambridge: Harvard University Press.

Pick, Daniel. 1989. *Faces of Degeneration, A European Disorder, c.1848–c.1918.* Cambridge: Cambridge University Press.

Pillard, Richard. 1997. E-mail letter to author, May 16.

Poe, John S. 1952. "The Successful Treatment of a 40-year-old Passive Homosexual Based on an Adaptational View of Sexual Behavior." *Psychoanalytic Review* 39: 23–32.

Pomeroy, Wardell B. 1972. *Dr. Kinsey and the Institute for Sex Research.* New York: Harper and Row.

Prieur, Annick. 1998. *Mema's House, Mexico City: On Transvestites, Queens, and Machos.* Chicago: University of Chicago Press.

Prince, C. V. 1956. "Homosexuality, Transvestism, and Transsexualism: Reflections on Their Etiology and Differentiation." *American Journal of Psychotherapy* 10: 80–85.

Rachman, S. 1965. "Aversion Therapy: Chemical or Electrical?" *Behavioural Research Therapy* 2: 289–299.

Rado, Sandor. 1940. "A Critical Examination of the Concept of Bisexuality." *Psychosomatic Medicine* 2: 459–467.

Rekers, George Alan. 1972. "Pathological Sex-Role Development in Boys: Behavioral Treatment and Assessment." Dissertation, Department of Psychology, University of California, Los Angeles.

Remafedi, G., S. French, M. Story, M. D. Resnick, and R. Blum. 1998. "The Relationship between Suicide Risk and Sexual Orientation: Results of a Population-Based Study." *American Journal of Public Health* 88: 57–60.

Review of *Psychopathia Sexualis with Special Reference to Contrary Sexual Instinct* by Richard von Krafft-Ebing. 1893. *American Journal of Insanity* 50: 91–95.

Review of *Castration of Sexual Perverts* by F. E. Daniel. 1895. *Alienist and Neurologist* 16: 109.

Review of *Sex Life of the American Woman and the Kinsey Report* by Albert Ellis. 1954a. *Psychiatric Quarterly* 28: 152.

Review of *Kinsey's Myth of Female Sexuality* by Edmund Bergler and William S. Kroger. 1954b. *Psychiatric Quarterly* 28: 152–153.

Review of *Sexual Behavior in the Human Female* by Alfred Kinsey and associates. 1954c. *Psychiatric Quarterly* 28: 148–152.

Rice, G., C. Anderson, N. Risch, and G. Ebers. 1999. "Male Homosexuality: Absence of Linkage to Microsatellite Markers at Xq28." *Science* 284: 665–667.

Richardson, Justin. 1995. "The Science and Politics of Gay Teen Suicide." *Harvard Review of Psychiatry* 3: 107–110.

Riggall, Robert M. 1923. "Homosexuality and Alcoholism." *Psychoanalytic Review* 10: 157–169.

Robie, Theodore R. 1927. "The Investigation of the Oedipus and Homosexual Complexes in Schizophrenia." *Psychiatric Quarterly* 1: 231–241.

Robinson, Paul. 1969. *The Freudian Left: Wilhelm Reich, Geza Roheim, Herbert Marcuse.* New York: Harper and Row.

———. 1976. *The Modernization of Sex: Havelock Ellis, Alfred Kinsey, William Masters, and Virginia Johnson.* New York: Harper and Row.

Robinson, William Josephus. 1914. "My Views on Homosexuality." *American Journal of Urology and Sexology* 10: 550–552.

———. 1925. "Nature's Sex Stepchildren." *Medical Critic and Guide* 25C: 475–477.

Rosanoff, Aaron Joshua. 1929. "Human Sexuality, Normal and Abnormal, from a Psychiatric Standpoint." *Urologic and Cutaneous Review* 33: 523–530.

———. 1935. "A Theory of Chaotic Sexuality." *American Journal of Psychiatry* 92: 35–41.

———. 1938. *Manual of Psychiatry and Mental Hygiene.* 7th ed. New York: J. Wiley; London: Chapman and Hall.

Rosario, Vernon. 1996. "Pointy Penises, Fashion Crimes, and Hysterical Mollies: The Pederasts' Inversions." Pp. 146–176 in *Homosexuality in Modern France.* Edited by J. W. Merrick and B. Ragan. New York: Oxford University Press.

———. 1997a. *The Erotic Imagination: French Histories of Perversity.* New York: Oxford University Press.

———, ed. 1997b. *Science and Homosexualities.* New York: Routledge.

———. 2000. "Gay Genes: Analyzing the Evidence of Experience." *Gender and Psychoanalysis* 5: 209–219.

Roscoe, Will. 1994. "How to Become a Berdache: Toward a Unified Analysis of Gender Diversity." Pp. 329–372 in *Third Sex, Third Gender: Beyond Sexual Dimorphism in Culture and History.* Edited by Gilbert Herdt. New York: Zone.

———. 1998. *Changing Ones: Third and Fourth Genders in Native North America.* New York: St. Martin's Press.

Rosen, David H. 1974. *Lesbianism: A Study of Female Homosexuality.* Springfield, IL: Charles C. Thomas.

Rosen, George. 1985. "The First Neighborhood Health Center Movement: Its Rise and Fall." Pp. 475–489 in *Sickness and Health in America.* Edited by J. W. Leavitt and R. L. Numbers. Madison: University of Wisconsin Press.

Rosenberg, Charles E. 1962. *The Cholera Years.* Chicago: University of Chicago Press.

———. 1987. *The Care of Strangers: The Rise of America's Hospital System.* New York: Basic Books.

Rosenhan, D. L. 1973. "On Being Sane in Insane Places." *Science* 179: 250–258.

Rothblum, Esther. 1994. "Introduction to the Special Section: Mental Health of Lesbians and Gay Men." *Journal of Consulting and Clinical Psychology* 62: 211–212.

Rotheram-Borus, M. J., and C. Koopman. 1991. "Sexual Risk Behavior, AIDS Knowledge, and Beliefs about AIDS among Predominantly Minority Gay and Bisexual Male Adolescents." *AIDS Education and Prevention* 3: 305–312.

Rotheram-Borus, M. J., H. F. Meyer-Bahlburg, M. Rosario, C. Koopman, C. S. Haignere, T. M. Exner, M. Matthieu, R. Henderson, and R. S. Gruen. 1992. "Lifetime Sexual Behaviors among Predominantly Minority Male Runaways and Gay/Bisexual Adolescents in New York City." *AIDS Education and Prevention,* Supplement: 34–42.

Rotheram-Borus, M. J., H. Reid, and M. Rosario. 1994. "Factors Mediating Changes in Sexual HIV Risk Behaviors among Gay and Bisexual Male Adolescents." *American Journal of Public Health* 84: 1938–1946.

Rotundo, Anthony. 1987. "Learning about Manhood: Gender Ideals and the Middle Class Family in Nineteenth-century America." Pp. 35–51 in *Manliness and Morality.* Edited by J. A. Mangan and James Walvin. New York: St. Martin's Press.

Dr. Rozier. 1830. *Des habitudes secrètes ou des maladies produites par l'onanisme chez les femmes.* 3rd ed. Paris: Audin.

Rust, Paula C. 1995. *Bisexuality and the Challenge to Lesbian Politics: Sex, Loyalty, and Revolution.* New York: New York University Press.

Ryan, Caitlin, and Donna Futterman. 1997. "Lesbian and Gay Youth: Care and Counseling." *State of the Arts Reviews* 8, no. 2.

Safren, S. A., and R. G. Heimberg. 1999. "Depression, Hopelessness, Suicidality, and Related Factors in Sexual Minority and Heterosexual Adolescents." *Journal of Consulting and Clinical Psychology* 67: 859–866.

Sagarin, Edward. [1966] 1975. *Structure and Ideology in an Association of Deviants.* New York: Arno.

———. 1975. *Deviants and Deviance: An Introduction to the Study of Disvalued People and Behavior.* New York: Praeger.

Saghir, Marcel T., and Eli Robins. 1969. "Homosexuality: I. Sexual Behavior of the Female Homosexual." *Archives of General Psychiatry* 20: 192–201.

———. 1971. "Male and Female Homosexuality: Natural History." *Comprehensive Psychiatry* 12: 503–510.

Saghir, Marcel T., Eli Robins, Bonnie Walbran, and Kathye A. Gentry. 1970. "Homosexuality: III. Psychiatric Disorders and Disability in the Male Homosexual." *American Journal of Psychiatry* 126: 1079–1086.

Savin-Williams, Ritch. 1994. "Verbal and Physical Abuse as Stressors in the Lives of Lesbian, Gay Male, and Bisexual Youths: Associations with School Problems, Running Away, Substance Abuse, Prostitution, and Suicide." *Journal of Consulting and Clinical Psychology* 62: 261–269.

Schilit, R., G. Y. Lie, and M. Montagne. 1990. "Substance Use as a Correlate of Violence in Intimate Lesbian Relationships." *Journal of Homosexuality* 19(3): 51–65.

Schmiechen, Richard, dir. 1992. *Changing Our Minds: The Story of Dr. Evelyn Hooker.* David Haugland and James Harrison, producers. San Francisco: Frameline.

Schoofs, Mark. 1997. "Geneocide: Can Scientists 'Cure' Homosexuality by Altering DNA?" *Village Voice* 42, no. 26.

Schreber, Daniel Paul. [1903] 1955. *Memoirs of My Mental Illness.* Translated and edited by Ida Macalpine and Richard A. Hunter. London: William Dawson and Sons.

Schüklenk, Udo, Edward Stein, Jacinta Kerin, and William Byne. 1997. "The Ethics of Genetic Research on Sexual Orientation." *Hastings Center Report* 27, no. 4: 6–13.

"Scientist Says Study Shows Gay Change Is Possible." 2001. *New York Times,* May 9.

Selective Service System. 1941. "Minimum Psychiatric Inspection. Medical Circular No. 1—Revised." *Journal of the American Medical Association* 116, no. 18: 2059–2061.

Seligman, C. G. 1902. "Sexual Inversion among Primitive Races." *Alienist and Neurologist* 23: 11–15.

Shaskan, Donald. 1939. "One Hundred Sex Offenders." *American Journal of Orthopsychiatry* 9: 565–569.

Shelley, Christopher, ed. 1998. *Contemporary Perspectives on Psychotherapy and Homosexualities.* London: Free Association Books.

Shilts, Randy. 1987. *And the Band Played On: People, Politics, and the AIDS Epidemic.* New York: St. Martin's Press.

Showalter, Elaine. 1985. *The Female Malady: Women, Madness, and English Culture, 1830–1980.* New York: Pantheon.

Shrady, George F. 1884. "Perverted Sexual Instinct." *The Medical Record* (New York) 26: 70–71.

Sibalis, Michael. 1996. "The Regulation of Male Homosexuality in Revolutionary and Napoleonic France, 1789–1815." Pp. 80–101 in *Homosexuality in Modern France.* Edited by J. Merrick and B. T. Ragan, Jr. New York: Oxford University Press.

Silverstein, Charles, and Edmund White. 1977. *The Joy of Gay Sex: An Intimate Guide for Gay Men to the Pleasures of a Gay Lifestyle.* New York: Crown.

Smith, Kenneth T. 1971. "Homophobia: A Tentative Personality Profile." *Psychological Reports* 29: 1091–1094.

Smith-Rosenberg, Carol. 1985. *Disorderly Conduct: Visions of Gender in Victorian America.* New York: Knopf.

Socarides, Charles W. 1968a. *The Overt Homosexual.* New York: Grune and Stratton.

———. 1968b. "A Provisional Theory of Aetiology in Male Homosexuality." *International Journal of Psychoanalysis* 49: 27–37.

———. 1970. "Homosexuality in Medicine." *Journal of the American Medical Association* 212: 1199–1202.

———. 1995. *Homosexuality: A Freedom Too Far: A Psychoanalyst Answers 1000 Questions about Causes and Cure and the Impact of the Gay Rights Movement on American Society.* Phoenix, AZ: Adam Margrave Books.

Socarides, Charles W., and Vamik D. Volkan, eds. 1990. *The Homosexualities: Reality, Fantasy, and the Arts.* Madison, CT: International Universities Press.

Solarz, Andrea L. 1999. *Lesbian Health: Current Assessment and Directions for the Future.* Washington, DC: National Academy Press.

Solomon, Samuel. 1800. *A Guide to Health; or Advice to Both Sexes.* 52nd ed. Stockport, England: J. Clarke.

Spiers, Herb, and Michael Lynch. 1977. "The Gay Rights Freud." *Body Politic* (Toronto) 33: 8–10.

Spitzer, Robert L. 1973. "A Proposal about Homosexuality and the APA Nomenclature: Homosexuality as an Irregular Form of Sexual Behavior and Sexual Orientation Disturbance as a Psychiatric Disorder." *American Journal of Psychiatry* 130: 1214–1216.

————. 1975. "On Pseudoscience in Science, Logic in Remission, and Psychiatric Diagnosis: A Critique of Rosenhan's 'On Being Sane in Insane Places.'" *Journal of Abnormal Psychology* 84: 442–452.

Spitzka, Edward. 1881. "Gynomania." *The Medical Record* (New York) 19: 359.

Springer, Carrie A., and Suzanne H. Lease. 2000. "The Impact of Multiple AIDS-related Bereavement in the Gay Male Population." *Journal of Counseling and Development* 78: 297–304.

Stacey, Judith, and Timothy Biblarz. 2001. "(How) Does the Sexual Orientation of Parents Matter?" *American Sociological Review* 66:159–183.

Starr, Paul. 1982. *The Social Transformation of American Medicine: The Rise of a Sovereign Profession and the Making of a Vast Industry.* New York: Basic Books.

Steakley, James D. 1997. "*Per scientiam ad justitiam:* Magnus Hirschfeld and the Sexual Politics of Innate Homosexuality." Pp. 133–154 in *Science and Homosexualities.* Edited by V. Rosario. New York: Routledge.

Stein, Edward. 1999. *The Mismeasure of Desire: The Science, Theory, and Ethics of Sexual Orientation.* New York: Oxford University Press.

Stekel, Wilhelm. 1921. *Onanie und Homosexualität: (die homosexuelle Neurose).* Berlin: Urban and Schwarzenberg.

————. 1930. "Is Homosexuality Curable?" *Psychoanalytic Review* 17: 443–451.

Stengers, Jean, and Anne Van Neck. 1984. *Histoire d'une grande peur: La masturbation.* Brussels: Editions de l'Université de Bruxelles.

Stevens, Patricia. 1992. "Lesbian Health Care Research: A Review of the Literature from 1970 to 1990." *Health Care for Women International* 13: 91–120.

Stevenson, Edward I. P. [Xavier Mayne]. [1908] 1975. *The Intersexes: A History of Similisexualism as a Problem in Social Life.* New York: Arno.

Stone, Sandy. 1991. "The *Empire* Strikes Back: A Post-transsexual Manifesto." Pp. 280–304 in *Body Guards: The Cultural Politics of Gender Ambiguity.* Edited by Julia Epstein and Kristina Straub. New York: Routledge.

Sullivan, Harry Stack. 1927. "Review of *The Invert and His Social Adjustment* by Anomaly." *American Journal of Psychiatry* 84: 532–537.

————. 1941. "Psychiatry and the National Defense." *Psychiatry* 4: 201–212.

————. 1965. *Collected Works.* New York: Norton.

Sulloway, Frank. 1983. *Freud, Biologist of the Mind.* New York: Basic Books.

Swaab, Dick F., and Michel A. Hofman. 1990. "An Enlarged Suprachiasmatic Nucleus in Homosexual Men." *Brain Research* 537: 141–148.

Szasz, Thomas. 1961. *The Myth of Mental Illness: Foundations of a Theory of Personal Conduct.* New York: Hoeber-Harper.

————. 1965. "Legal and Moral Aspects of Homosexuality." Pp. 124–139 in *Sexual Inversion: The Multiple Roots of Homosexuality.* Edited by Judd Marmor. New York: Basic Books.

————. 1979. "The Dan White Case: Psychiatrists vs. Gays." *Inquiry* (August 6 and 20).

Tardieu, Ambroise Auguste. [1857] 1878. *Etude médico-légale sur les attentats aux mœurs.* 7th ed. Paris: J.-B. Baillière.

Terry, Jennifer. 1999. *An American Obsession: Science, Medicine, and Homosexuality in Modern Society.* Chicago: University of Chicago Press.

Testis, Ernst. 1934. "The Revenge of the Pederasty Ring: Brown Leaders and the Brown Boys of Bolivia." Translated by Miles Wright from *Das dritte Reich stellt sich vor* (1933). *Medical Review of Reviews* 40: 197–205.

Thomasset, Claude, and Danielle Jacquart. 1985. *Sexualité et savoir médicale au Moyen Age*. Paris: Presses Universitaires de France.

Thorpe, J. G., E. Schmidt, and D. Castell. 1963. "A Combination of Positive and Negative (Aversive) Conditioning in the Treatment of Homosexuality." *Behavioral Research Therapy* 2: 293–296.

Timmons, Stuart. 1990. *The Trouble with Harry Hay: Founder of the Modern Gay Movement*. Boston: Alyson.

Tissot, Samuel-Auguste-André-David. [1760] 1991. *L'Onanisme, ou Dissertation physique sur les maladies produites par la masturbation*. 7th ed. Reprint ed., Paris: Editions de la Différence. Translated as *Onanism*. New York: Garland Press, 1985.

Treichler, Paula A. 1987. "AIDS, Homophobia, and Biomedical Discourse: An Epidemic of Signification." Pp. 31–70 in *AIDS: Cultural Analysis, Cultural Activism*. Edited by D. Crimp. Cambridge: MIT Press.

———. 1999. *How to Have Theory in an Epidemic: Cultural Chronicles of AIDS*. Durham, NC: Duke University Press.

Trexler, Richard. 1995. *Sex and Conquest: Gendered Violence, Political Order, and the European Conquest of the Americas*. Ithaca, NY: Cornell University Press.

Troiden, Richard R. 1988. *Gay and Lesbian Identity: A Sociological Analysis*. Dix Hills, NY: General Hall.

Trumbach, Randolph. 1998. *Sex and the Gender Revolution, vol. 1: Heterosexuality and the Third Gender in Enlightenment London*. Chicago: University of Chicago Press.

Udis-Kessler, Amanda. 1996. "Identity/Politics: Historical Sources of the Bisexual Movement." Pp. 52–63 in *Queer Studies: A Lesbian, Gay, Bisexual, and Transgender Anthology*. Edited by Brett Beemyn and Mickey Eliason. New York: New York University Press.

Ulrichs, Karl Heinrich. [1864–1879] 1994. *The Riddle of "Man-Manly" Love: The Pioneering Work on Male Homosexuality*. Translated by Michael A. Lombardi-Nash. Two volumes. Buffalo, NY: Prometheus.

U.S. CDC (Centers for Disease Control and Prevention). 2001a. "HIV and AIDS—United States, 1981–2000." *Morbidity and Mortality Weekly Review* 50: 430–434.

———. 2001b. "The Global HIV and AIDS Epidemic, 2001." *Morbidity and Mortality Weekly Review* 50: 434–439.

———. 2001c. "HIV Incidence among Young Men Who Have Sex with Men—Seven U.S. Cities, 1994–2000." *Morbidity and Mortality Weekly Review* 50: 440–444.

———. 2001d. "U.S. HIV and AIDS Cases Reported through June 2000." *HIV/AIDS Surveillance Report* 12, no. 1. http://www.cdc.gov/hiv/stats/hasr1201.htm.

———. 2001e. "A Glance at the HIV Epidemic." www.cdc.gov/nchstp/od/mmwr/At-a-glance%20Key%20Facts.pdf.

U.S. Congress. Senate. 1950. *Employment of Homosexuals and Other Sex Perverts in Government*. [Hoey Report]. 81st Congress, 2nd sess. S. Doc. 241.

U.S. Surgeon General. 1986. *U.S. Surgeon General's Report on Acquired Immune Defi-ciency Syndrome.* Washington, DC: Public Health Service.

Valenstein, Elliot S. 1986. *Great and Desperate Cures: The Rise and Decline of Psy-chosurgery and other Radical Treatments for Mental Illness.* New York: Basic Books.

Watson, James. 1980. *The Double Helix: A Personal Account of the Discovery of the Struc-ture of DNA.* New York: Norton.

Weeks, Jeffrey. 1981. *Sex, Politics, and Society: The Regulation of Sexuality since 1800.* London: Longman.

Weininger, Otto. 1918. "The Masculine Element in Emancipated Women." *American Journal of Urology and Sexology* 14: 240.

Werther, Ralph (alias) [also Earl Lind and Jennie June]. 1918. *Autobiography of an Androgyne.* Edited and introduced by Alfred W. Herzog. New York: Medico-Legal Journal.

——. 1918. "The Fairie Boy. An Autobiographical Sketch." *American Journal of Urology and Sexology* 14: 433–437.

——. 1920. "Studies in Androgynism." *Medical Life* (New York) 27: 235–246.

——. [1922] 1975. *The Female-Impersonators.* New York: Arno.

——. 1934. "The Biological Sport of Fairie-ism." [Report written in 1920 for Victor Robinson.] *Medical Review of Reviews (Anthropos 2)* 40: 185–196.

Westphal, Karl Ernest. 1869. "Die Conträre Sexualempfindung: Symptom eines neuropathischen (psychopathischen) Zustandes." *Archiv für Psychiatrie* 2: 73–108.

White, William S. 1950. "Inquiry by Senate on Perverts Asked." *New York Times,* May 20, 8.

Wicks, Christopher. 1958. "It Is Natural After All." *ONE* 6, no. 1: 19–21.

Wile, Ira S. 1941–1942. "Sex Offenders and Sex Offenses: Classification and Treatment." *Journal of Criminal Psychopathology* 3: 11–31.

Wittels, Fritz. 1943. "Struggles of a Homosexual in Pre-Hitler Germany." *Journal of Criminal Psychopathology* 4: 408–423.

Wolbarst, Abraham L. 1931. "Sexual Perversions: Their Medical and Social Impli-cations." *Medical Journal and Record* 134: 5–9, 62–65.

Wolfenden Report. 1957. "Report of the Committee on Homosexual Offenses and Prostitution." Cmd. 247. London: Her Majesty's Stationary Office.

Woodward, Samuel B. [1838] 1856. "Hints for the Young in Relation to the Health of Body and Mind." Boston: G. W. Light.

——. 1839. "Deslandes's Essay." *Boston Medical and Surgical Journal* 19: 348–349.

Ziebold, Thomas O., and John E. Mongeon, eds. 1985. *Gay and Sober: Directions for Counseling and Therapy.* New York: Harrington Park Press.

# About the Author

Vernon A. Rosario is currently a child psychiatry fellow at the Neuropsychiatric Institute of the University of California, Los Angeles. He was born in Karachi, Pakistan of Portuguese-Indian parents, and grew up in Canada, Argentina, Peru, Venezuela, and the United States. At Brown University, he earned a B.A. in French literature and an Sc.B. in bioengineering. He received his M.D. from the Harvard Medical School–Massachusetts Institute of Technology Program in Health Sciences and Technology. His Ph.D. is from the Harvard Department of the History of Science where he did research in modern European neuropsychiatry and sexology. At Harvard, he organized the fourth annual Lesbian, Bisexual, and Gay Studies Conference (1990). He is coeditor with Paula Bennett of *Solitary Pleasures: The Historical, Literary, and Artistic Discourses of Autoeroticism* (1995) and the editor of *Science and Homosexualities* (1997). He authored *The Erotic Imagination: French Histories of Perversity* (1997), which was also published in a French translation by the Lacanian School of Psychoanalysis in Paris.

Dr. Rosario practices child, adolescent, and adult psychiatry and psychotherapy. His clinical research is in human sexuality and gender, with a focus on transgendered teenagers and intersexed children. He is particularly interested in the ways in which sociological and cultural factors such as ethnicity, nationality, and class influence the development of sexuality in all its diversity. He has been awarded an American Psychoanalytic Association Fellowship and is a Laughlin Fellow of the American College of Psychiatry.